THE
GRUB-STREET
JOURNAL

NUMB. I.

The Grub-ſtreet Journal.

To be continued Weekly.

Thurſday, JANUARY 8. 1730.

The INTRODUCTION.

Dullneſs! whoſe good old cauſe I yet defend,
With whom my Muſe began, with whom ſhall end!
For thee I dim theſe eyes and ſtuff this head
With all ſuch reading as was never read. Dunciad. B. I.

Grub-ſtreet, Jan. 7. 1730.

THE beſt Things here below are liable to be corrupted, and the better Things are in their own Nature, the more miſchievous are they if corrupted †: Books are on all hands allowed to be of the greateſt Benefit to Mankind; whence I infer, that a bad Book muſt be one of the greateſt of Evils. Our Society has been always compoſed of ſuch learned and worthy Members, as have produced the beſt of Books themſelves, and done what in them lay to ſuppreſs the bad. This Procedure has drawn on them the Oppoſition of ſome Men, whoſe Malice infinitely ſurpaſſes their Ability : but after all the Pains they have taken, they have proved nothing, but that they themſelves have neither the rudeneſs of Id* of Swift, nor the Style of polite Men, nor the flumpry of honeſt Men, nor the humanity of Gentlemen, or Men of Letters : Theſe Men (if I may ſo call them) whenever they have been deſirous to run down any Book, as low, trivial, and contemptible, have beſtowed on it the Epithet of *Grub-ſtreet*, as if it was a ſufficient Note of Infamy to ſuppoſe it to come from this Place. But this Paper will abundantly convince the Publick of what Dignity, Excellence, and Uſe our Society is; and how mean and deſpicable our Adverſaries are. The Reaſons already laid down ſeem ſufficient to ſhew, why this Paper ought now to be publiſhed : it will perhaps be more difficult to ſatisfy the Publick why Something of this kind never came out before.

It is true indeed, that altho' this Society has ſubſiſted many Years, yet they have never before publiſhed any thing as a Society. But if this be an Objection, it muſt hold as ſtrong againſt other Societies of Men of Letters. The *Royal Academy of Sciences* at Paris never publiſhed any of their Memoirs till thirty Years ago ; and the *Royal Society* of London have not publiſhed any Hiſtory of themſelves, except what was done by Dr. *Sprat* ſoon after their Inſtitution. But that nothing be wanting, a learned Member is preparing an Account of the Antiquities of *Grub-ſtreet*, with it's Hiſtory, continued down to the preſent Time. So that our Account in this Paper may begin at this Inſtant ; and we may continue to give the Publick a weekly Hiſtory of the moſt important of their Tranſactions.

In the purſuit of this Deſign, the ſhall relate their admiſſions of new Members, which are very frequent. For no ſooner does any learned Gentleman publiſh a Work, which they approve of, but they immediately give him a Place among them. We

ſhall alſo communicate an Account of ſuch Books, as ſhall receive their Approbation. It may be objected perhaps, that this is already done. In the *New Memoirs of Literature*, I anſwer, That Author, tho' he gives an Account of the Works of ſeveral of our Members, and is indeed one of them himſelf, yet omits a great Number of excellent Books; the deſign of his Undertaking being chiefly to recommend thoſe which are publiſhed for one Bookſeller only. We ſhall alſo publiſh Diſſertations, as the Society and the Compoſers of them ſhall give leave; and ſometimes relate the learned Debates which happen among our Members on a great variety of Subjects. And as political Diſſertations have been always the peculiar Province of this Society, care will be taken that this Journal may never be deficient in this particular. This Branch is committed to Mr. *Quidnunc*, a worthy old Citizen, who has ſacrificed his own Advantage to that of the publick. This great Scholiaſt has undertaken to collect all the material Articles of News from the other Papers ; to digeſt them into a proper Method, and illuſtrate them with critical Obſervations. He has likewiſe ingaged to publiſh ſeveral occaſional Papers, relating to Murders, Apparitions, Prodigies, &c.

Mr. *Quidnunc's* conſtant Employment in the Service of the Society, obliges him to reſide in their Houſe, that he may always be in a readineſs to make the moſt proper Uſe of any Intelligence which may be communicated. He is accompany'd in his Reſidence, by Mr. *Poppy*, an excellent Poet ; who will not only frequently entertain the Town with ſome of his Poems in this Paper ; but is likewiſe ready to compoſe Panegyricks or Satyrs, Anagrams or Acroſticks, Copies of Verſes from Friends of Authors, or annual Salutations from City Bell-men to their worthy Maſters and Miſtreſſes, at reaſonable Rates.

I muſt not omit the mention of one very conſiderable Member, who bears the Title of Hiſtorian to the Society, *Giles Blunderbuſs,* Eſq;. The other Officers receive Salaries from the Society ; but Squire *Blunderbuſs* has generouſly declined the receiving of any of the publick Money ; ſomebody having left him ſomething to live on. We ſhall ſometimes oblige the Publick with the Characters drawn by him of our deceaſed Members.

As for my ſelf, the Care of publiſhing this Paper will lie on me. And tho' I ſhall have ſufficient Matter from the Journals of the Society, to continue the Publication of it weekly ; yet if any learned Perſons will favour me with their Correſpondence, their ingenious Communications ſhall be honourably taken notice of, by their Faithful Friend and Humble Servant,

BAVIUS.

† Theſe Words are borrow'd from Mr. Dennis, in his Preface to The Advancement of the Stage.

THE GRUB-STREET JOURNAL, NUMBER 1, PAGE 1

THE
GRUB-STREET JOURNAL

BY

JAMES T. HILLHOUSE, Ph.D.

BENJAMIN BLOM
New York

33288

First published Boston 1928
Reissued 1967 by
Benjamin Blom, Inc. New York 10452
Library of Congress Catalog Card #67-12466

PREFACE

The present study began merely as an attempt to discover the nature of Pope's connection with the *Grub-street Journal,* and incidentally to identify its editors, especially the mysterious —— Russel. A study of the *Journal* and other contemporary sources of information, however, has thrown very little light on the first and main point. It is impossible to say whether the idea of the *Journal* originated with Pope, or precisely what he had to do with it after it got under way. That it began as little more than an organ of Pope is clear enough; that fact had indeed been recognized by many writers. It can be said, however, that very soon the paper abandoned its original scheme of being simply a continuation of *The Dunciad,* and went its own ways, quite prosperously and quite independently of Pope, a fact which seems to have been ignored or slighted in previous discussion of it.

The second point, the matter of editors, Russel in particular, turned out to be much more important than it had seemed. It has been possible to add considerably to Mr. Lounsbury's account of Russel in *The First Editors of Shakespeare,* and to come to the conclusion that he was much more of a force in the *Journal* than had appeared before. In fact, it does not seem extravagant to say that during most of its life Russel *was* the *Grub-street Journal.*

As this became clear, and as further exploration revealed the fact that, despite the importance of the Pope material, the paper was very interesting quite apart from any concern of Pope's, it seemed worth while to try to give an account of it for its own sake; to make clear what was in it. The most obvious method, that of reprinting it, was impractical. It is extremely bulky, and much of it is not worth reprinting. The selection of interesting and significant items was also for several reasons unworkable and unsatisfactory. The best scheme finally seemed to be the description and discussion of the material, in chapter form. The *Journal* spent most of its time in combat; hence the matter of organization consisted largely of tracing out its campaigns and grouping them according to their nature. Thus there took form, after an introductory chapter describing the paper and sketching its history, chapters on Pope and the Dunces, on the campaigns against the textual criticism of Bentley and Theobald, on its quarrels with other periodicals, on the mass of literary and dramatic material in general, and finally on its treatment of legal, theological, and medical subjects.

Under one or another of these headings it seemed possible to organize most of the significant matter of the *Journal,* although there was a heterogeneous pile of shreds and patches that defied any order. Any of this that had any obvious importance was worked in somewhere; the rest had to be left in its present limbo. (Many items in this last group may be traced down in the Appendix.) Any subject to which the *Journal* gave a considerable amount of space, finally got itself recorded, I think, if only in a footnote reference. Much of the material in the *Journal* is sly and indirect; its true import is frequently very well concealed, and it is often very difficult to decide exactly what a writer's point of view is. I have tried, however, to look out for veiled irony and sarcasm, and I hope that other readers of the *Journal* will not find many instances where I have been gullible. In view of the fact that discussion of this sort in chapter form possibly failed to give a consistent view of the paper as a whole, it seemed necessary to add the appendix, a chronological summary, issue by issue, of the two main sections of the *Journal* and the *Courier.*

In presenting this material, I have continually quoted or paraphrased liberally, with the purpose of doing the next best thing to reprinting. If the method seems at times rather discursive, perhaps the fact that the *Journal* is at present a *rara avis* may be offered in justification. The Yale Library has a complete file of the *Journal* and also of its sequel, the *Literary Courier.* The British Museum has in the Burney Collection a number of incomplete files which supplement one another's gaps. In 1921 a complete file, including the sequel, came into the market for a moment, and then disappeared into an inaccessible private collection. The only other complete file that I have ever heard of was that of James Crossley, who announced his possession of the *Journal* and the *Literary Courier* in *Notes and Queries* in 1853. This may of course be the file which appeared in 1921. Thus there are at present accessible only two complete files of the *Journal,* one in England and one in America. In addition there is a file which is almost practically complete in the Aitken collection at the University of Texas; it lacks only nine numbers of the *Journal* and five of the *Courier*.

Most of the materials for the work were collected at the British Museum, the Bodleian, the Yale Library, and the Library of the University of Minnesota, in all of which various officials have most willingly gone out of their way to assist me. I am also under great obligation to the Library of the University of Texas, which lent me its file of the *Journal* for a very considerable period; to Mr. C. A. Moore, who was so good as to read the manuscript; and finally to the Duke University Press, which has published the book, and especially its editor, Mr. Paull F. Baum, who undertook the drudgery of editing the manuscript and seeing it safely through the press.

J. T. H.

February 6, 1928.

TABLE OF CONTENTS

ILLUSTRATIONS

CHAPTER I

THE HISTORY OF THE GRUB-STREET JOURNAL

On Thursday, January 8th, 1730, the reading public of London was offered the first number of the *Grub-street Journal*. The new paper consisted of a small folio of four pages. At its head was the information that it was "to be continued weekly," and beneath, four significant lines from *The Dunciad*, Book I.

> Dullness, whose good old cause I yet defend,
> With whom my Muse began, with whom shall end!
> For thee I dim these eyes, and stuff this head
> With all such reading as was never read.

At once it explained its mission. It was to rehabilitate the name Grub-street. It might be expected to give an account of the meetings of the Grub-street Society,—which had always existed and deserved to have its history published—with debates and dissertations, and an account of elections (which would be very frequent); "for no sooner does any learned Gentleman publish a work which they approve of, but they immediately give him a place among them." It would also furnish critical reviews of books and accounts of "Murders, Apparitions, Prodigies, etc.," and would place at the service of its readers a number of special writers—Mr. Quidnunc on politics, Mr. Poppy on poetry, and Giles Blunderbuss, Historian (to receive no salary, "somebody having left him something to live on"). And finally the writer of the article, Mr. Bavius, announced that the care of publishing the paper would lie on him. Following this announcement of policy, Mr. Quidnunc promised readers the current news, both domestic and foreign, with the name of the original paper from which he took it, and such comment as might be necessary. The remainder of the first number was filled with news items and the "Prices of stocks yesterday", and at the end the usual printer's advertisement: "London; Printed and sold by J.

Roberts in Warwick-Lane, and at the pamphlet-shops of London and Westminster, also at the Pegasus (vulgarly called the Flying-Horse) in Grubstreet. Price Two Pence."

As it had promised, it appeared again on the following Thursday and regularly thereafter for eight full years, or until the end of 1737. Then, having run its natural course and worn itself out, it expired. Its ghost, however, reluctant to leave its haunts, continued to drag out a sorry existence for some six months more under the name of the *Literary Courier of Grub-street,* and then vanished altogether.

The *Grub-street Journal* seems to have come upon the town quite unannounced and without puffs-preliminary or explanation as to the identity of founders or editors. The title of the paper, the introductory quotation, and the opening statement made it apparent that the *Journal* was to be humorous and ironical,[1] and that it was to be chiefly concerned with literature. For the present, this was all the information vouchsafed. It very soon became clear, however, that the new paper prized beyond all others the virtues of the gadfly, and that it revelled in personalities set down in gall. Another point that at once became perfectly obvious was that Alexander Pope had some sort of connection with the new venture. The first issue had opened with a quotation from *The Dunciad,* and succeeding ones drew frequently for headings upon the same poem and other satirical pieces from Pope's pen. It was likewise as plain as day that the paper was always, under its irony, reverent of him and favorable to his friends, and was correspondingly acid when a Dunce or one of his enemies was concerned. In its sardonic and ironical reversal of terms, however, the *Journal* usually referred to Pope, Swift, and their circle in some such phrase as "our profest enemies," while the unfortunate scribbler or poetaster under

[1] Apparently the original intention was that the paper should be consistently ironical. In the preface to *The Memoirs of Grub-street* (see *post*) the chief editor said that there was no reason why they should be always ironical, as that became monotonous and confined. He speaks of the *Prompter's* censure of them for inconsistency in making use of other methods than irony, and says that the paper, in order to attract all sorts of readers, was given as much variety as possible.

fire was "our friend" or "our colleague." All this obviously suggested that the *Journal* was to be a sequel to *The Dunciad*, and that a new campaign against the Dunces was under way, a campaign in which the victims might be subjected to the continuous assaults of a weekly newspaper.

The crowd of journals into the midst of which the new paper thrust itself and with which it entered into competition was by no means brilliant or striking. Professor Lounsbury, a most industrious reader of the newspapers of the period, describes himself forlornly as "wading through the interminable bog" of that literature. And one can sympathize with him. It is true that journalistic writing throws innumerable shafts of light upon the life of its time, and that many things about daily life, manners, and ideas may be learned better from newspapers than from more regular and respectable forms of literature. Nevertheless, even at their best, newspapers are bound to contain an enormous bulk of stuff that dies the day after it is written, and that from any ordinary point of view is quite incapable of resurrection. In the early eighteenth century, moreover, journalism was not at its best. The British public had at its service a sufficient number of newspapers, daily, semi-weekly, and weekly, most of them flimsy in content, and badly printed on poor paper. For news they offered a scanty collection of brief items, domestic and foreign. They informed their readers of the births, marriages, deaths, and other important events in the lives of the great, and they chronicled with all possible vividness sensational murders and other crimes of violence. Most of them were apparently in the pay of one of the great political parties and regaled their readers with endless diatribes on long since forgotten details of policy—mountains which are no longer even mole hills. When political interest waned, they filled space with discussions of philosophy or theology, or with milk-and-water moral essays cut from the pattern of the *Spectator*. On occasion, when the editor or "writer"—frequently a paper seems to have been the product of a single hack pen—was short of time or interest, one even finds a series of issues devoted to chapters quite frankly borrowed from some book already in print. There were, naturally, exceptions like the *Craftsman* and other strong political papers heavily subsidized from party treasuries, but the common run were thin and poverty-stricken. It is not surprising that most papers enjoyed a very short life. Having little in them, they were easily bred and just as easily killed; they were as ephemeral as mayflies, and their death notices are so frequent as to pass almost unremarked.

The *Grub-street Journal* rose high above the dead monotonous level. It may be that the very flatness and worthlessness of most of its contemporaries increase and emphasize its qualities and place it upon an eminence to which it could not have aspired in more distinguished surroundings. It must be admitted, moreover, that a journey through it means the crossing of many wide arid stretches. That is bound to be true of any newspaper read after its own day. And one reads also occasional complaints from correspondents in the *Journal* itself about its harping too long on a single string, or too great enthusiasm over subjects which could under no circumstances interest more than a very few special readers. But in reading it one is after all never out of sight of an oasis. If its editors had not shown a vigor and vitality such as are to be sought in vain in its contemporaries, it would not be worth while to try to rescue it from the limbo of obscurity where most of the early eighteenth-century periodicals languish. During its best years it was almost always active and lively; and even later, when it was perceptibly declining toward its end, it could be counted on for an occasional flash of its original vivacity.

In addition, the *Journal* was planned on lines which give it with later readers an advantage over even its most prosperous colleagues like the *Craftsman*. It eschewed politics[2]

---

[2] In the preface to *The Memoirs of Grub-street* (see *post*, pp. 23 ff.) it is said that the *Journal* touched politics only as it remarked upon the manners and methods of political squabbles in other papers. It did, however, occasionally show some interest in political questions, notably the excise, which it detested. In number 46 appears a defense of the Queen against the aspersions of the *London Journal*. What political leanings it

and wandered at large through a field which embraced literature of all sorts, including poetry, drama, criticism, medicine,
theology, and education; and it received correspondence from
innumerable sources on a thousand and one various subjects. In its handling of news items culled from the dailies
it also showed a keenness of dry wit and sardonic humor
which even after two hundred years make its news columns
entertaining. In its appearance, it was the equal of the highly
subsidized political papers, and infinitely superior to the
common run. Its chief attraction then as now, however, lay
in the zest with which it embarked upon controversies of all
sorts, and in its skill and vigor in prosecuting them. This is
especially true of its earlier career; later some of its quarrels dragged on interminably, and, one suspects, were kept
going to fill space.

In view of the *Journal's* propensity for personal attack,
and its obvious connection with Pope, it is not surprising
that its readers, and especially its victims, soon became dissatisfied with the modicum of whimsical information it had
vouchsafed them concerning its origins and motives. About
Mr. Poppy, Mr. Quidnunc, and Giles Blunderbuss they
evinced no curiosity; these characters were plainly fictitious.
But with Mr. Bavius, and the colleague, Mr. Maevius, whom
he soon took unto himself as an assistant, it was altogether

betrays are Tory, and Jacobite. In the first number a political editor is
named, but in the third appears a burlesque discussion in which it is
decided best to avoid politics. In 84 it made a general attack on political
journalism in a letter to "Ulrick D'Ypres" the "writer" of the *Daily
Courant,* who, it is hinted, was generally thought to be the brother of the
greatest subject in Great Britain. This letter, written by the editor, Richard Russel (see *post*), asserts the *Journal's* political impartiality and
records the party affiliations of the other papers. According to Russel,
the *Craftsman* and *Fog's Journal* were the only two papers in opposition,
while the *London Journal,* the *Free Briton,* the *Weekly Register,* the
Hyp Doctor and the *Daily Courant* were ministerial, but he states his
belief that the *Hyp Doctor* and *Weekly Register* were receiving no pay
as yet. While the *Journal* was never really friendly with any other
papers, it occasionally took sides with the opposition pair. Note, for
instance, an epigram in the *Daily Courant* (quoted in number 76) against
"D'Anvers [the *Craftsman*], Fog, and Grub" with an answer by the
Grub-street editor attacking the *Courant,* the *London Journal* and the
Free Briton. Note too the account of a quarrel between the *Craftsman*
and the *Free Briton* in 79, 80, and 81.

different. The victims of their sarcasms and aspersions showed no disposition to leave it at mere Bavius and Maevius, but at once undertook to ferret out their proper names, and to make as public as possible the facts of their private lives. About Pope's finger in the pie they were equally concerned, and although they were able to get little light on the activities of that very devious person, they were shrilly insistent not only on the fact that he had a finger in the pie, but that he had been its chief baker, and that Bavius and Maevius were mere henchmen, servilely dependent upon his whims.

The title of the paper and the introductory statement made the *Journal's* aims and purposes only fairly clear. Its original motive was much more specifically defined by Bavius some seven years later in his preface to *The Memoirs of Grubstreet*. He describes the great increase of low and ignorant writers which had followed upon the relaxation of licensing laws in the seventeenth century, and the consequent outpouring of "false histories, lewd or immoral treatises, novels, plays, or poems," and the growing practice among booksellers of fostering the production of such works, as well as of all sorts of journals and newspapers dealing in false news, puffs, and advertisements. To reform this state of affairs "was the end and design of some gentlemen, who, in order to carry it on with the greater propriety, formed themselves into an imaginary society, as meeting once a week at the Pegasus, which is a real house in Grub-street."

These gentlemen, it appears further, were interested in promoting the fortunes of good but unpopular books, in restoring life to those which had fallen into neglect, and in getting at the truth where authorities disagreed, as for instance, Pope and Swift, "the two finest writers of the age", had disagreed over Dryden's translation of Virgil.[3] Conversely, they were of course also interested in exposing the stupidity and viciousness of all sorts of bad books and of the newspapers—apparently all newspapers were bad. As a

[3] In substance, Swift had made Dryden a Grubean and joined him with Dennis, Rymer, Tate, and Durfey on account of his Virgil, which Pope declared "the most noble and spirited translation in any language."

matter of fact, the second half of this policy must have seemed more practical than the first, for in the *Journal's* columns exposure and censure far outweigh praise. Indeed it soon became evident that the *Journal* made exposure of faults, real or supposed, its chief business, and that satire and irony were the breath of life in its nostrils. Controversy became at once its daily food, and hence it got for itself not only many enemies but many readers, for it was sharp, pungent, and clever, and knew no limits in its boldness. The virulent fierceness and personality of some of its quarrels were enough to give it preëminence and distinction even in the period of George II. The editors had their own quarrels, which they conducted with great gusto, but their columns were gladly opened to all correspondents, with special encouragement to those who had axes to grind, and whose enemies were willing to fight back. Thus the *Journal's* history is a long series of quarrels carried on by the editors in their proper capacity or between correspondents, toward whom they were more or less impartial, but whom they were glad to see fighting.

In spite of the *Journal's* fondness for controversy and its long sucession of skirmishes and pitched battles, it would be inaccurate to assume that all the material contained in it was controversial. Bavius realized perhaps that a paper devoted entirely to quarrels more or less literary in nature would before long pall on the generality of its readers. Then too, at moments the tide of controversy was slack, and profitable quarrels hard to find. For these two probable reasons there is in the *Journal* an enormous bulk of moral essays, miscellaneous articles, and poems, which served to offer relaxation and variety, or merely to fill space agreeably. In fact such contributions, before they were finally printed, often gathered dust for some months or even years, to the great scandal and distress of their complaining authors.

One is almost tempted to say that no subject is left untouched in the *Journal's* columns. There are moral essays and type character sketches of the sort established by Steele and Addison. There are numerous expositions on manners—in

conversation, at church and the theater, and in dealing with
servants; there are satires on ladies' clubs, love, marriage,
curiosity, chastity, gossip, the association of children with
servants, the vanity of titles, oaths, dullness, happiness, and
so on; and there are the characters of the city flirt, the country bumpkin, the university prig, the endless talker, and the
"pretty fellow".[4] There is some satire on legal subjects, and
a great deal both of satire and direct discussion on religion
and medicine. And in addition there are innumerable items
which can only be classified as miscellaneous or nondescript.[5]

The paper seems to have caught on at once, and to have
flourished most prosperously for some five years, or through

[4] For a typical instance, note in 101 an essay on conversation signed
"A. H.," possibly Aaron Hill. The writer remarks that conversation is
supported for the sake of instruction and diversion and then criticizes
methods of story telling in conversation. He distinguishes the *insipid*
and *soporifick* types, the first marked by such phrases as *what d'ye think,
I'll tell you what, and so, and then, as I said before,* the type in which
no one syllable that could be included has been omitted, the *forgetful,*
with phrases like *Mr. what's his name?,* the atheistical, immoral type,
full of *damme, rot it,* and so forth. He also mentions the egotism of
autobiography, and speaks of the nudgers who enforce their stories with
digs of the elbow, and against whom he threatens to bring legal action
the next time he is assaulted.

[5] As for example articles on fisheries in 222 and 225. In 219 "Tom
Meanwell" suggested that the *Journal* take up the question of fishery as
very important to British commerce, and as the best means of reëstablish-
ing the woollen trade and getting back the balance of power. He praised
highly the effusions of a late pamphleteer on the subject, and offered to
undertake the task himself if the *Journal* showed itself receptive, as it
did. Some of the discussions to which the *Journal* allowed a considerable
amount of space in a number of issues, but which do not seem to have
enough interest or significance to warrant detailed treatment in the following pages, might be mentioned here:—On the death of Jezreel Jones,
naturalist, with a letter paraphrased in verse, 75, 76; an analysis of the
affairs of two fraudulent financial ventures, the Charitable Corporation
(a case of embezzlement), 127 ff., and the York Buildings Company,
251 ff.; a reprint of portions of John Gabriel's *The State of the Nation*
(John Gabriel is described as a crazy hack writer,—"he was a member
of our Society" and was imitating a mad "Mr. Gregory of Christ Church,
Oxford," who wrote under the pseudonym of Gabriel John. John Gabriel's
style justifies the description of him; it is most absurdly fantastic),
144, 152, 153, 161, 170, 196 (evidently this material was used as a convenient filler from time to time); an account of the Goole-Hudson case,
involving the marriage laws; (these articles are a summary of a pamphlet
The Contract Violated by the Reverend John Goole, 248, 249, 250); and a
series of letters on a projected scheme to reduce the interest on annuities,
379, 381, 385, 386.

1734. The fact that it very soon increased the size of its page[6] was of course a sign that it was making headway, and the utterances not only of its own editors but also of contemporary journalists, including some of its enemies, establish definitely the fact that it was successful. In the preface to the *Memoirs,* Bavius declares that in spite of opposition from various sources it "yielded a very considerable monthly dividend for a good while"; and in number 126, when it had been running two and a half years, he boasted that its circulation had increased five times since the first two months.[7] The *Weekly Register,* one of the *Journal's* fiercest opponents, although it was, in the *Journal's* oft-repeated phrase, "an obscure weekly paper," claimed in its ninety-third issue, late in 1731, that it was increasing its sales steadily, and that it was "not in the power of the authors of the Grubstreet, *with all their popularity,* to say the same." Again in a systematic attack in July, 1732, the *Register* speaks of the *Journal* as having "long subsisted very oddly, universally condemned and yet universally read." Eustace Budgell, in a survey of the London journals in the first number of the *Bee* (1733), says of "such papers as are designed for the amusement and diversion of the town," "among these the Grub-street Journal seems to claim the first place." The editors of the paper were continually explaining to their correspondents that letters were delayed or not printed at all because of the great number that came in, and as late as number 221, early in 1734, were suggesting the possibility of a more frequent

---

[6] The first issues were 9½ by 12 inches. With the eighth number the page was increased to 10 by 14; and the final size, 11 by 15, was established July 30, 1730. These figures refer to the size of the printed block; the margins vary greatly.

[7] This statement came in connection with verses by "Claudia Rufina," said by the writer to have been composed two months after the *Journal's* first appearance. The subject is the "unparalleled stupidity" of the paper, and the spirit may be judged by the lines—

> At first your Journal to elude the shame
> It feared by owning its true parents name
> Stole that of matchless Pope to give it fame.
> But soon the cheat appeared, for now we see
> 'Tis Grubstreet all, without an irony,
> Its future merit you yourself knew best
> So named it Grub and spoke the truth in jest.

publication the next winter to take care of the excellent contributions which were now crowded out or delayed until they
became stale. The republication of material from the *Journal*
in the magazines and in three books of selections attests still
further the interest of the public in the paper. Both the *Gentleman's* and the *London Magazine* made it, until the end of
1735, one of their chief sources of supply, drawing upon it
continuously for large amounts of its best material, and often
reprinting or summarizing the same articles. Conversely the
small amount of material borrowed, or in Bavius' words,
"stolen," from it after 1735, is also an accurate index of the
Journal's decline during its last years.

Its last three years were, indeed, much less happy. Mr.
Bavius, who had been the chief power in the paper since its
beginning, and the sole editor since the middle of 1731, resigned at the end of 1735. His enemy, the *Prompter,* declared
his retirement due to discomfiture on the field of battle, but
his own explanations in the *Journal* itself and in his preface
to *The Memoirs of Grub-street* seem more credible.[8] Apparently during 1735, if not before, the paper came under the
influence of persons with interests of their own and a desire
to dictate policies. He speaks of "having met with great opposition from some who were then [1735] partners in the
paper," and asserts, "they were highly offended, if any bad

---

[8] In 316, January 15, 1736, appears the announcement: "According to
resolution taken long before and communicated to some of you above
six months ago, I now resign the office of Secretary, which I have exe-
cuted either in conjunction with another person or solely by myself from
the time of the first apearance of our Journal."—He continues that since
the design of the *Journal* had been to expose, it could not but bring on
calumniations. Abuse and personal reflections had begun in the *Weekly
Register,* continued in the *Hyp Doctor* and the *Bee* and had been "lately
carried to a much greater height in the *Prompter.*" He goes on to defend
his policy, especially his practice of cutting down contributors' letters.
He says that he has tried to be fair to both sides in arguments between
correspondents but has found it very difficult, and despite his efforts has
been involved in great trouble. As the principal reason for his resignation
he alleges other work in hand and the impossiblity of doing justice to it
and the *Journal* at the same time. He hopes soon to bring out the two
volumes of select memoirs, which are now well advertised, and asks
that he may still continue, as a correspondent, to figure in the columns
of the *Journal*. A year and a half later in his preface to the *Memoirs,*
one gets still closer to the real reasons for his withdrawal.

book, in which they had any concern or interest was exposed."
From this and other hints one derives the impression that
the *Journal* had got into the hands of a group of booksellers
who would not leave Bavius "solely accountable for the
choice of the pieces published." At any rate, Bavius' withdrawal was fatal. It was his energetic and cutting satire—
"low" and malicious though it may have been at times—
that gave the paper its distinction, and without him it gradually sank. There were other contributing or complicating
causes of decay. Chief of these was the rise of the magazines, which abridged material from the dailies and weeklies,
and by supplying the public with tidbits from all the papers
ruined their subscription lists. Both in the *Journal* itself and
in his preface, Bavius dilates on the iniquity of the magazines. He also states, however, that the other papers refused
to advertise the *Journal,* and that it was persecuted at the
post-office, where the clerks often substituted other papers
for it, so that it was difficult to get it to its country subscribers.

Beset with all these difficulties, it fell upon the evil days
which culminated in its suspension at the end of 1737.

In spite of its policy of obscurity and secrecy it is possible
to glean some information from the *Journal* concerning the
details of its management, and incidentally to get some insight into the contemporary ethics of journalism in such
matters as the prerogatives of editors, their relations with
correspondents, and so forth.

Bavius himself contributed continuously and largely to
the paper. The leading articles are frequently his, and often
essays and letters from outsiders are introduced and followed
by his editorial comment. The collation of news items from
other papers[9] and the satirical comments thereon were of
course the work of Bavius, as were also by far the greater
part of the shorter prose notes and some of the verse which
went to make up a column called "From the Pegasus in
Grub-street," which began in the sixteenth issue. But from

[9] The *Journal* habitually collected the reports of a given occurrence
and printed them together to expose their infinite variety. See *post,* p. 110.

the beginning and more and more as the paper grew older Bavius depended upon correspondents to fill his columns. Practically always these correspondents signed their articles either with initials or pseudonyms, and the cases where their identity can be guessed are very few.[10] The ascriptions in *The Memoirs of Grub-street* show that the editors themselves wrote as correspondents, occasionally not disdaining the journalistic trick of carrying on both sides of a quarrel with one pen. On the other hand, they apparently saw no objection to inserting contributions from outside as their own; for they speak of the dissatisfaction of certain contributors who had failed to appreciate the signal honor of having their effusions presented as the work of Bavius. Of what would seem the perfectly allowable device of publishing letters with editorial comment, Bavius declared (221) that it must be resorted to, if statements were untrue or if matters were "carried too far against any particular set of men." It was also considered within the rights of the editor to adapt letters, to shorten, or even to lengthen and revise them. Bavius informs his contributors in number 21 that some of them "so far mistake the very design of this paper, that I am forced to lay their letters aside, or take the liberty of making many alterations in them." Indeed, Bavius stated quite frankly that where the correspondent was unknown, he should feel free to make whatever changes he wished.

The financial relations between editors and correspondents seem to have been complicated. The chief complaint

[10] In the controversy with the *Prompter*, Aaron Hill is spoken of as a former contributor. He may be the author of a few articles signed "A. H." It is also probable that Dramaticus, a writer in one of the theatrical quarrels, was Sir William Yonge. It is noted by Nichols (in *Literary Anecdotes*, III, 174) that the letter to Bavius on printing, in the *Journal* for March 20, 1735, was by William Bowyer, the printer. Nichols also throws light on satiric verses in 32 by Morell, vicar of Kew, on the rather presumptuous claims of a new editor of Isocrates, William Battie. Morell tells of his surprise at seeing his verses in the *Journal*. He says they were "borrowed or purloined—by one Bickerton, a bookseller, who married a distant relation of mine," and who inserted them in the *Journal,* in which he owned a share. (See Nichols, IV, 602, *Dictionary of National Biography,* and B. M. Add. Mss., 5832, 29766.) The most important of the few signed communications in the paper were from Lewis Theobald and Joshua Ward, the quack.

against the magazines was that they reprinted without paying for it, material for which the original publisher had given hard cash. It is extremely doubtful, however, whether the *Journal* paid anything for most of its contributions. Its uniformly high-handed, independent tone toward letter-writers, and its repeated assertion that far more was received than could be printed,[11] both point to the fact that the honor of seeing their work in the *Journal* was expected to be sufficient compensation to contributors. Indeed, it is clear that articles were sometimes published for a consideration. Thus Bavius says in a note on the Budgell-Piers controversy,[12] "The letters published in our 78th, 82d, and 83d Journals, taking up seven columns, were inserted *for nothing,* at the earnest request of Mr. Budgell; and on his repeated promise to our bookseller that he would send him some essays agreeable to the design of our paper; which he never performed." Bavius also explains[13] that while the editors do not object to puffs-preliminary, they do generally refuse to print puffs of books after their publication merely to increase sales, and that they have even gone so far as to refuse advantageous offers to insert such articles.[14] One may judge from this that

[11] A plenitude of material is indicated by the note in 53: "Correspondents are desired to send their letters for the future postage paid, we having received the last year a great many which were of no use to us," as also by one in 66 that so many letters had been received that the editors preferred to mention none specifically. But contributors could count on their being published if possible, and in the meantime they should be patient, and not send them, as some had done, to other papers, where they had appeared to slight advantage. Also in 134 notice is given that contributions must be sent at least one week in advance, and that no one need trouble to send in lampoons on private persons; which were always rejected—especially one which had been lately published in *The Post Boy* and *St. James Weekly Packet.* This second admonition was repeated in 201: "Our correspondents are desired to send us no more lampoons upon any particular person." It is clear that for a consideration the malicious or vindictive could pillory their enemies in many of the periodicals.

[12] See *Memoirs of Grub-street,* II, 101.

[13] Number 140, "Pegasus in Grub-street."

[14] In a satirical dialogue in number 114 two newspaper writers, discussing the attacks of the *Journal* on their papers, are made to say that, though booksellers liked to advertise in the *Journal* because of its wide sale, it was of no use to advertise books in its columns, since its "writers" would attack them just the same. (This the *Journal* actually did in the case of patent medicines.) They finally decide to get Henley to attack the *Journal* in his advertisements in the *Daily Journal.*

not all articles, and especially controversial or puffing ones, were published for nothing. As for advertisements, although Bavius stated in the pronouncement just quoted that the editors were the sole judges in the acceptance or rejection of them, it is improbable that many were turned away. Patent medicines and quack remedies which the *Journal* continually satirized and denounced advertised regularly in its columns. *Grubiana,* the pirated collection which the *Journal* attacked with its utmost vigor, is actually advertised at the same time as "beautifully printed in a neat pocket volume" and as being a complete collection of all the poems and "material letters" in the first one hundred and eleven issues of the *Journal.* Nor did the *Journal* disdain the advertisements of the magazines even while it was furiously assailing them as base plunderers. Yet on occasion it could boast of martyrdom to its high ideals in advertising, as when it notes the receipt of a letter from the London Punch House, offering, in case the editors would publish certain verses in praise of Punch, not only to pay well, but to advertise regularly.[15] This offer the editors refused since the verses gave an "account of its [Punch's] excellence in promoting drunkenness and lewdness," vices the practice of which the *Journal* had never recommended. Certainly the *Journal* was not always as virtuous as this notice would lead one to believe.

Indeed Bavius did protest too much. In the face of continual complaints of malice, obloquy, and scandal-mongering, he was continually asserting his innocence of all evil intention and his sole desire to expose and destroy the wicked and the pretentiously ignorant. Six months after its beginning an enemy begins an epigram on the *Journal,* "Vile, dark, and dirty"[16] and seven years later a correspondent in-

[15] Number 358.
[16] In the *Daily Journal,* July 17, 1730:
> "Vile, dark, and dirty! if thy name and face
> Be like thy work, humanity's disgrace,
> Well dost thou wear, adapted to thy task
> The Murd'rer's dagger, and the robber's mask.
> Proceed, abuse, and scatter filth around—"
These verses were reprinted in the *Grub-street Journal* for October 22, 1730 (42), and answered in about the same tone by L. Gilliver, who

sists "it has been and is your avowed constant principle and practice not to mind right or wrong, the reputations, callings, interests, and subsistence of men or families or neighborhoods, but it is your way and resolution to strike at the character of one who has not injured you."[17] In its direct replies to such charges the *Journal* was generally cold and sarcastic. In this case, for instance, Honestus, who has written very much at large, is told that he will receive an answer if he will become specific and write *sense* and English, and that the quality of his letter indicates that it comes from The Gentleman's Proper University at the Corner of Lincoln's Inn Fields"—the establishment conducted by Henley, the mountebank evangelist and educator.

In general defences and apologia, however, Bavius' tone was much higher. In looking back over the *Journal's* career, he remarks upon the charges of "lowness," pride, slander, envy, and malice, which had pursued it from the beginning, and denies them all. He declares that the paper guarded especially against calumny and slander, and that those who complain should see some of the communications the editors did not print! Correspondents, he says, found him "impartial and witty or partial and dull" according as he accepted or rejected their letters, and abused him for not publishing lewd and scurrilous matter and anonymous invective. He admits, rather naïvely, it would seem, that he had published some articles from known contributors "which we imagined for the benefit of the public, but which have turned to our private disadvantage," when the writers, having promised the paper indemnification in case of trouble, afterward refused it. Finally he challenges anyone "to produce an instance for the first six years of its life at least [the period when he

---

offered a reward for the discovery of the person who sent him a clipping of them tagged with the dire threat—

Mark well, what here enclosed I send
Or soon expect a fatal end.

All this may well have been a trick to lead up to a communication published two weeks later and signed "S—" (but very probably by Pope; it is marked "A" in *The Memoirs of Grub-street*) on violent threatening letters.

[17] Honestus, in 374.

was editor] of any valuable, useful and good book decried, or any ingenious, learned, and honest person abused in it; provided only, that no one shall name himself or any of his own works, as an instance." Similar statements had appeared periodically in the columns of the *Journal* itself. In number 49, in a general statement of policy, Bavius declared that the *Journal* was willing to publish statements it disagreed with and that any correspondent was at liberty to answer. (This was obviously an encouragement to the quarrelsome.) It served notice, however, that it would print nothing to promote lewdness or to undermine revealed religion; that any personal attack must be signed and that no person of established reputation could be attacked in its columns; and that while assaults on stupid authors would be acceptable, correspondents should not dwell on a few faults in a piece otherwise well written. In number 134, notice was served that no one need bother to send in lampoons on private persons,[18] and that a close examination of the paper "will clear us from the imputation of malice and detraction cast upon us by the renegado members of our society, who deal in nothing but the grossest calumny or stupidity." Similarly in number 221, Bavius explains the necessity of being fair to all parties, and of toning down too bitter attacks. He says further that "many persons have entertained a very wrong notion of our Journal and imagine it a proper vehicle of scandal," and declares that the paper attacks only pickpockets and corrupters of taste and morals.

In spite of these and numerous other declarations of probity, the readers of the *Journal* must have remained unconvinced. At the beginning Pope's hostility toward a given writer was enough to insure an attack on him. Moreover, the acrimony of its controversial manners undermines all faith in such protestations. The most that can be said is that the *Journal* probably did refuse personal attacks on obscure and absolutely unknown persons, as a mere matter of good policy; scandal against better known individuals was much

[18] Cf. n. 11, *ante*.

more marketable. One need note only the two striking instances of the *Journal's* attacks on Theobald's *Shakespeare*
and its treatment of that poor wretch, Eustace Budgell. No
one is going to believe that to a paper of such a marauding,
quarrelsome disposition justice and truth were primary considerations.

In one respect, on the other hand, the *Journal* deserves
credit. Most papers of the time were controlled by booksellers
who had them filled with false news, puffs of their own
stock-in-trade, and the manufactured articles of literary
hacks. Of this sort of thing the *Journal,* except perhaps at
the last, seems clear. Bavius probably spoke the truth when
he declared in number 221, "there is no paper less under the
influence of booksellers . . . than ours." Certainly there is
nothing to create suspicion against the *Journal's* publishers or
booksellers, Roberts, Gilliver, and Huggonson,[19] who seem
to have been little more than its distributors, although they
were legally responsible for what appeared in it. Various remarks by Bavius in his preface to the *Memoirs* also give color
to the belief that he refused to knuckle under to booksellers.
He speaks there of booksellers who considered the *Journal*
"against the trade" because it inveighed against their books,[20]

[19] The *Journal* had numerous booksellers at various times, but the
names of one or more of the chief three, Roberts, Gilliver ("Captain
Gulliver"), and Huggonson, were always to be found connected with it.
Roberts' name appears in the first issue, Gilliver's for the first time with
the fifteenth, and Huggonson's with the sixty-first. The names of all
three were associated with it continuously from 198 until its end. Other
names of less importance are Cogan, Jackson, Brotherton, Palmer, and
Sanders. Lawton Gilliver was at this time publisher for Pope, and was
elected bookseller to the Society of Grubstreet in a mock-serious article
in 15, wherein he is referred to as "Captain Gulliver", an appellation
which he kept ever after, even in the official booksellers' notice at the
end of the paper. Gilliver's name appears very rarely in the *Journal's*
controversies (he answered over his proper signature a libel reprinted in
42 from the *Daily Journal*) ; but Huggonson, who was a Quaker, became embroiled, apparently on his own account, in a controversy over
Quakers' tithes. (See Chapter vi, *post.*)

[20] Russel's argument here is whimsically ingenious. He says that although the *Journal* attacked certain books, the booksellers still remained
in undisturbed possession of their own books, their property rights un-
invaded, and the people were merely warned not to transfer their money
to booksellers. He adds that certain large "dealers in impressions of
waste paper" wished the *Journal* to be subservient to them and shut

and makes it clear that the interfering partners who forced his retirement were booksellers. His resentment toward the species is general; he maintains that bad booksellers are, after bad authors, the "most detestable members of society," and, implying that the *Journal* will soon die, hopes that its sequel, if it has one, will be kept out of the clutches of booksellers and mercenary authors.

It is unlikely that this hope was gratified, for the *Journal's* sequel, the *Literary Courier of Grub-street* continued in the path trod by the *Journal* in its latter years. The *Courier* in fact, although it pretended to be revivified and reincarnated, was neither. It represented merely an attempt to keep the *Journal* going by reducing its size—the printed sheet was much smaller[21]—and by giving it a new name. Many of the letters printed were old ones that the editors of the *Journal* had had on hand, and certainly none of the contributions that may have been new, struck out in new lines or opened new fields. The attacks on Orator Henley, which must have been, long since, old stories to readers of the *Journal,* were continued in the same form; and similar targets, which had already been stuck too full of arrows, continued to receive additional shafts. It is no wonder that the *Journal's* earlier public failed to come back to the *Courier,* and that, after managing to get through thirty issues, it expired without warning or apology on July 27, 1738.

The final number of the *Journal,* 418, prepared the way for its successor with the notice:

We beg pardon of our correspondents for postponing the publication of their letters and verses, which we do not doubt of their granting us, when they shall see them appear in The Literary Courier of Grub-street, which will begin to be published next Thursday [January 5, 1738] by Dr. Ephraim Quibus, Student in Physics and Astrology, an old member of our Society and whose name appears several times in our Memoirs. Into his hands all their papers shall be deliv-

---

against their competitors. A little earlier in the preface he says that the paper "succeeded beyond all expectation" without the help of any of the usual [booksellers'] artifices in establishing a paper, "and continued opposed and depreciated by the generality of booksellers and their hackney authors."

[21] The last eleven issues return to the size of the *Journal.*

ered, who will then give a particular account of the alterations and improvements designed in this new undertaking.

This account was forthcoming as promised. The *Courier* opened: "The Grub-street Journal, having for eight years successively acted its part, sometimes well, sometimes ill, like all other comedians; made its exit with the last year." The writer says that this was the result of deliberate consideration, and implies that he is in reality a new editor. He lists the errors of the *Journal*—its omission of politics, its too long continued controversies, its lack of consideration for correspondents, and the like. He announces that the *Courier* will accept letters on political subjects, acknowledge correspondence, and limit controversy. Moreover, "the heap of news," (which had, after all, been a successful department of the *Journal*) would be omitted.

There is little in the *Courier* to invite comment. The publication of old and out of date material is only too obvious. Conspicuous instances are a poem on the contest for the laureateship in 1730, a letter on Garland's *Dictionary* (which had been the subject of an old quarrel in the *Journal*), and a letter on mad dog bites[22] intended as part of a discussion the *Journal* had carried on during its last year. Bavius reappeared in a dispute with "R. C." over the moral status of the *Journal,* a repetition of long since hackneyed charges and denials, which finally trailed off into personalities and a squabble over false Latin; and also, if one may judge from the initials "R. R.,"[23] in an argument over an edition of Tacitus. As for the political articles which were to help bring the paper back into favor, they failed to materialize. A correspondent in number 19 complained that so far there had been none, and in later issues the only instances are two very obscure satires[24] which seem to be attacks on Walpole, and a single article on a treaty between France and Spain. A flagrant and elaborate puff of the *Courier* written in connection

[22] See *Literary Courier,* numbers 7, 9, and 15.
[23] Supposing that they represent Richard Russel; see the later discussion of Richard Russel as Bavius.
[24] In 24 and 25, and 28.

with the first attack on Walpole presaged the final dissolution of the paper. This last attempt to stir interest in it was
futile; it lasted for five more issues and then disappeared.

Of the three collections from the *Grub-street Journal,* the
two earlier are comparatively unimportant. The first of the
three, *Essays, Letters, and Other Occasional Pieces Relating
to the War of the Dunces,* is a small pamphlet of forty-one
pages, consisting of articles from the *Journal* for 1730 and
the first numbers of 1731.[25] Practically all of these relate, as
the title indicates, to the quarrels in which Pope was most
interested, those with James Moore-Smythe and Concanen,
and the one over the election of a poet laureate in 1730. Most
of this material is Pope's, but a few other pieces, notably a
highly indecent one on Hottentot ceremonials,[26] are included.

The second collection is generally referred to in the *Journal* as "Grubiana." It consists of selections, chiefly in verse,
from the first one hundred and eleven numbers, and is eked
out at the end with "Poems, etc., omitted," most probably
added to increase the bulk of the volume. This volume was a
rank piracy and imposture. But Bavius was not of a temper
to let such effrontery pass in silence. At once, in number
113, he denounced the book as a fraud:

Mr. Bavius presented to the Society a book entitled—"Grubiana,
or a complete collection of all the poems and material letters from the
Grubstreet Journal . . ." which after it had passed awhile from hand
to hand was voted *nemine contradicente* to be a scandalous, impudent, and abominable imposition upon the public, not containing half
pretended to in the title page; most injudiciously collected; and so
incorrectly printed as frequently to have several faults in a page
and sometimes two in a line. From whence it was concluded to be
the work of some hungry, stupid renegado member of our society,
printed and published by some mercenary wretches who are continually pestering the town either with pirated good copies wretchedly printed or with their own vile copies containing nothing but
nonsense, bawdry, or blasphemy.

Bavius also threatens arrangements to stop "this pick-pocket
edition."

The next number, 114, developed the attack further. The

<hr>

[25] The copy in the British Museum has no title-page and no date.
[26] From number 59. By Martyn, one of the editors.

first thirty pages of *Grubiana* were examined in detail, and
yielded a harvest of omissions and of sixty errata. Bavius
also replied contemptuously to defensive advertisements by
the proprietors and addressed them by name in doggerel
verses, which he reprinted in his own *Memoirs* with a note
that Hughs and Warner were named in the title-page as the
proprietors, but that other booksellers—Dormer, "who was
the chief projector," Hinton, and Hubbard—were implicated. Some months later, in number 144, Bavius remarked
that *Grubiana* had since been republished, its market value
having been destroyed, as *The Grub-street Miscellany Printed
for Mr. Bavius.* This, he says, was advertised in an obscure
weekly paper[27] owned by Hinton, but was a failure. It was
then published a third time, with the addition of a picture as *Faithful Memoirs of the Grub-street Society: Now
First Published by Mr. Bavius.* Bavius declares all three issues to be the same, and recalls the first, *Grubiana,* as "a
spurious, ill-printed book published about three months ago
. . . which we advertised against several times." According
to the description in numbers 113 and 114, this charge was
true. The only discoverable copy seems to be one of the third
issue preserved in the Bodleian. The title-page reads, "Faithful Memoirs of the Grub-street Society. Now first published
by Mr. Bavius. . . . Printed for the benefit of the Grub-
street Society and sold by the booksellers of London and
Westminster, 1732." Its running title, however, is *Grubiana;*
and at the end are to be found the advertisements of Dormer
and Hinton.

Bavius had at once taken other steps against this pirated
collection. In number 115 he gave notice that "Select Memoirs of the Society of Grubstreet" was actually in the press,
containing all the most interesting material published in the
Journal, with additions, alterations, and notes, as well as
"Hogarthian frontispieces representing to the life the au-

---

[27] The *Weekly Register,* which the *Journal* always spoke of as "an
obscure weekly paper." The name of Tim Birch, an editor or "writer"
of the *Register,* is mentioned in the verses in 114 in connection with
those of the pirating booksellers.

thors, printers, publishers and booksellers of Grub-street." He
also asked contributors to send in emendations and directions
as to the use of their signatures. For some unexplained reason the promise here made went unfulfilled, and the *Memoirs*
were delayed until the spring of 1737, the *Journal's* last year.
In number 381 (April 14, 1737) was published the first third
of the preface[28] and two weeks later came the characteristic
advertisement:

Next week will be published in two neat pocket volumes, price six
shillings bound, Memoirs of the Society of Grub-street, being a collection (to speak in the Grub-oratorical style) of very extraordinary
pieces in prose and verse published in the Grub-street Journal on a
great variety of subjects—theological, philosophical, physical, astronomical, astrological, mathematical, mechanical, oratorical, historical,
biographical, characteristical, critical, hypercritical, tragical, comical,
etc., etc., etc., etc.[29]

The *Memoirs* appear to be substantially as planned five
years earlier. They contain, however, material from the
first one hundred and thirty-eight issues, instead of the
first one hundred and fifteen, as in the original scheme, and
the preface and many of the notes on the history of the
Journal were written later. Of the "Hogarthian frontispieces" nothing is to be seen. The ironical dedication of
the two volumes to Humphrey Parsons and Francis Child,
the mayors of London for 1730 and 1731 respectively,
would seem to be part of an original plan gone somewhat
stale.

The *Memoirs* are much superior in form and matter to
Grubiana. They are well printed and are careful and accurate. Indeed the only variations noted are deliberate alterations such as had been advertised in 1732. A few articles
are very considerably revised, and in many more are to be
noticed occasional changes in phrasing. Such changes usually
seem to have been made for the sake of style; the substance
of the ideas and opinions expressed is generally the same.

[28] The other two-thirds were used to fill out the *Journal's* last two
numbers, 417 and 418.
[29] This advertisement was continued in all succeeding numbers except
the last four. The "Grub-oratorical style" was a sarcastic allusion to
Orator Henley.

HUMPHREY PARSONS, LORD MAYOR OF LONDON, 1730
(*From Number 48; cf. page 117*)

Bavius did not scruple, however, to alter content occasionally; a striking instance is an attack on Henley in number 65, which is not only made much briefer but is greatly changed in substance. It is noteworthy that revision is to be found chiefly in the contributions of Bavius himself, who edited the *Memoirs* and gave up about half the space in them to his own work. Some articles, as might be expected in volumes of this sort, are reprinted only in part, in order to save space,[30] and many others, which were considered of minor interest, are simply mentioned by title or very briefly summarized. In general the selections are well chosen and give a fairly accurate impression of the *Journal* during its first years. Most of the material relating to the *Journal* itself, the opening statement of policy, the choice of a bookseller, and so forth, is included, as are also the attacks on Pope's enemies, much of the material on Bentley's *Milton*, and the satires on the election of a laureate. Bavius also very wisely included a large number of those collations of news items from the other papers together with caustic comments of his own which form one of the *Journal's* chief attractions. Thus these volumes contain many of the most lively and amusing articles and the most telling epigrams and notes of the *Journal's* best and freshest years.

Yet the *Memoirs* are chiefly valuable for the light they throw on the *Journal's* history. In the long preface already quoted from several times, Bavius gives an account of the original purpose of the paper, its sufferings at the hands of the other papers, the magazines, and the postoffice, answers again charges of slander and malice, and gives considerable information about the relations with the paper of Pope and the various editors. Much of this material is a repetition of occasional statements in the *Journal* itself, but the sections on Pope and the editors offer specific detail which is nowhere else to be found, and which, in conjunction with a key to the signatures "A," "B," and "M," attached to certain of the articles reprinted, and standing for Pope and his

[30] For a more significant omission, see reference to Thomson, p. 27 *post*.

friends,[31] John Martyn, and Richard Russel, respectively, forms the chief source of information about the relations of Pope and of the editors with the *Journal*. In fact, without the *Memoirs* our conclusions as to the inner workings of the paper and the parts played in its history by Pope and the two chief editors would be exceedingly hazy and doubtful.[32]

Still, despite the explanations in the *Memoirs,* and the insistent investigations of contemporaries, the *Grub-street Journal* has always been shrouded in a good deal of mystery. As has already been said, its promoters left the public to find out as best it could practically all the details of its backing, editorship, and management. It was, of course, natural in the case of a journalistic venture dedicated to personal controversy and employing continually the weapons of abuse and scurrility, that the attackers should conceal themselves as well as possible, and that the attacked should take pains to frustrate their attempts at concealment. Consequently it is not to be wondered at that the points most widely discussed in connection with the paper were the personalities behind it—what Pope had to do with it, and who its "writers" or editors were.

As has already been said, the opening number plainly suggested that the paper was to be a sequel to *The Dunciad* and that Pope had launched a new campaign against the

[31] More specifically, the "A" indicated "the few pieces imagined to come from their hands." It probably meant for the most part Pope. Certain instances of anonymous contributions by his friends, Swift, Gay, Savage, and others, are not to be found. For instance, of a poem called "Pandora" in 56, Pope remarks in a letter (Elwin and Courthope, VI, 327) that he had seen "Pandora", which he supposed to be by Swift, in the *Grub-street Journal*. This might ordinarily be taken as pretty good evidence of Swift's authorship, but in the *Memoirs* the poem is unascribed. It seems reasonable to assume that Bavius would have marked "A" anything he could, for the sake of the obvious prestige. Moreover, the poem has never been assigned to Swift by his modern editors. See *post*, p. 33.

[32] In addition to the three volumes of extracts described, there is extant (in the Bodleian) *The Grub-street Miscellany in Prose and Verse. . . . Written by Mr. Bavius, Jun. F.G.S. . . .* 1731. This small volume has no connection with the *Grub-street Journal*. It is very poor stuff bolstered with the names Grubstreet and Bavius.

Dunces.[33] This suspicion must have strengthened into certainty with the later issues, with their frequent headings from Pope's satires, their attacks on such Dunces as James Moore-Smythe, James Ralph, Theobald, and Dennis, and allusions to the opposed camps of the Popeians or Parnassians and Theobaldians or Grubeans. Noteworthy allusions to Pope are, it is true, less numerous than one would expect, but what there are make it clear that Pope was for the *Grub-street Journal* the particular literary glory of the time, with Swift as an intimate companion—note, for example, an ironic allusion (in number 18) to "our most inveterate enemies, particularly Dr. Swift and Mr. Pope"—and an adoring circle of worthy but lesser lights, especially Savage,[34] Thomson, and Gay. This small circle was sacrosanct; there was never any word but of praise for any member of it. On the other hand, the old Dunces, and the new literary men who were not Pope courtiers could hope for nothing but sarcasms in the columns of the *Journal*.

A slight but significant episode in the early history of the *Journal* indicates perfectly which way the wind was blowing. In an ironic essay[35] in number 5 on "Miltonic" verse the charm of anticlimax is illustrated by a passage from Thomson's *Winter*. The citation of Thomson to appear in the company of the Dunces, and in close proximity with that notable member of the group, James Ralph, who also furnishes an instance of anticlimax, taken from his *Muses Address to the King,* is indeed remarkable, and one is prepared for retraction. In number 7, Bavius, having noted that some readers have thought Thomson a member of the society of Grubstreet because he was quoted in number 5, declares that he is not. The passage quoted is the only one in the poem worthy of the Society. But to belong to the

[33] The dates of earlier attacks are as follows:—*The Miscellanies,* including *The Bathos,* final volume March, 1728; *The Dunciad,* May 1728; *The Dunciad Variorum,* 1729.

[34] Carruthers, *Life of Pope,* p. 272, remarks that Johnson in his life of Savage, the first edition only, said that "Savage had been invited to undertake the management of the paper." He contributed several poems.

[35] By Martyn, ascribed to "B" in the *Memoirs.*

Society, *plura nitent in carmine.* The greater part of the poem is Parnassian. Scriblerus himself in *The Bathos* quoted several lines from an author "otherwise by no means of our rank," and drew his instance of Macrology from another whom he styled at the same time "one of our greatest adversaries." The point of all this is simply that the editor, who had written the offending article, had not yet learned who were to be accounted friends and who foes, and as a consequence had to make amends. Moreover, when the essay was reprinted in *The Memoirs of Grub-street,* the allusion to Thomson and the quotation from *Winter* were omitted, and the passage from Ralph stands alone to represent anticlimax.

The *Journal's* shifting attitude toward James Miller is even more significant and to the point. Early in 1730, in numbers 6 and 7, Russel had cut Miller's comedy, *The Humours of Oxford,* into ribbons.[36] Yet about a year later his poem *Harlequin Horace*[37] was distinguished by that ironic dispraise accorded to Pope, Swift, and their allies. In the Pegasus column of number 59 notice is given that the poem had been read before the Society and the election of its author canvassed. The poem, it is said, examined Horace's precepts and inverted them for the use of the Society.

When the reading was finished Mr. Poppy (who during the major part of the time had enjoyed a comfortable nap) raised himself very deliberately up from his chair and after a significant yawn which was continued through the company, moved that the author might be admitted a member. To which Mr. Maevius objected, alleging that though the performance might be of great use to the Society yet that the author (like most other critics) had not in the least observed the rules he prescribed to others, that his manner of writing was palpably Parnassian, and that therefore he was by no means worthy of having such an honor conferred on him. To this Mr. Poppy replied that the only judgment he could make of the writing was from the good effect it had upon himself; that the first dozen

[36] See *post,* p. 206.

[37] *Harlequin Horace, or, The Art of Modern Poetry,* 1731. Published by Lawton Gilliver. It is chiefly a satire on entertainments and is dedicated to John Rich, but it also attacks literary taste in general, and hence brings in allusions to the Dunces.

couplets had laid him into a sound and refreshing sleep which he looked on to be the peculiar mark of a Grubean production. Upon which Mr. Maevius made answer that this argument was very far from being in favor of the writer; very justly observing that as the performances of our members throw *others* asleep, so the works of a Parnassian had the same effect on *them*. He moreover said that it was his opinion if the thing was strictly examined it would be found they were not so much obliged to this writer as they imagined; that he very much feared there was a snake in the grass and could not help apprehending that he was little better than a spy in disguise and was sent by our adversaries, the mountaineers, with a design of undermining us and disturbing us if possible in the enjoyment of our lowland possessions; and therefore moved that some worthy member should be instantly employed to strip him of his mask. Upon which Mr. Bavius was accordingly appointed and was ordered to make his report in the next week's lucubration.

Accordingly, "next week's lucubration" gave up its first page to an ironical criticism of *Harlequin Horace,* wherein the poem is really praised and an opportunity seized to attack various Dunces. Among other points the writer notices that Gilliver, "the author of much evil to our Society by bringing to light the works of our most inveterate enemies, Pope and Swift," is the printer, and calls attention to the names of several Dunces in the dedication. He also examines the text, quoting from it liberally, and points out the ironical praise of the Dunces and the censure of Pope. Theobald especially comes in for a bludgeoning; it is suggested that his work on Shakespeare be published with the title "Shakespeare with Additions, Emendations and Alterations." This line of attack was pursued further after a lapse of six weeks. The author of the poem is charged with carrying on "maliciously and heathenishly the cause of Antigrubeanism which was in such an un-Christian-like manner begun by the Dunciad"; and Blackmore, "Namby-Pamby" [Phillips], "Tibbald" again, and Stephen Duck are satirized. There is also a tribute to Dr. Garth, and at the end an attack on lewd entertainments. This third installment is marked "to be continued," but does not seem to have been; apparently the editors had more copy than they could use, and decided that *Harlequin Horace* had had its due.

According to Lounsbury, these articles bear "clear internal evidence of Pope's handiwork." One may add that there is some external evidence also; although none of the articles appear in the *Memoirs*. An earlier article making some of the same points, especially of Theobald, had appeared in number 40, and is reprinted in the *Memoirs* with the signature "A." Doubtless Pope did have a hand in them, but that he actually wrote them himself may be doubted. If he did, why did not Bavius reprint them in the *Memoirs*? It does not seem unreasonable to assume that he would reprint and mark "A" all of Pope's work that he could. Still, before coming to any definite conclusion as to what Pope did or did not do at any time, one generally needs the clearest of external evidence. At any rate, it is perfectly plain that the Grubean who had perpetrated *The Humours of Oxford* a year before was now become a Parnassian.[38] He had written a satirical poem praising Pope and ridiculing the Dunces, a poem whose adulation Pope accepted complacently, for he wrote to Caryll, February 6, 1731, that it had "a great deal of humour." He might with due modesty have said of it and its author what he said in the same letter of Walter Harte and his *Essay upon Satire,* which is in the same vein of adulation, "a very valuable young man, but it compliments me too much."

Allusions to Pope's friends, however, are few; the chief business of the *Journal* was attack. Pope's epitaph on Fenton was reprinted (number 43) and occasionally one finds verses by "a Popeian"; for instance Savage's lines "To Mrs. Pritchard, on her appearance on the stage." The *Journal* occasionally took Swift's part when he was under attack. When the *Daily Journal* for May 2, 1730, published

---

[38] It may be asked why, in such a case, the earlier attacks on *The Humours of Oxford* were not excluded from the *Memoirs* as was the allusion to Thomson. The answer may be simply that Russel, their author, and the editor of the *Memoirs,* was obviously partial to his own work. It may be surmised, moreover, that his feelings toward Miller, who probably supplanted him in the seat of Bavius after 1735, were none of the most tender. The allusion to Thomson, on the other hand, was an obvious *faux pas,* and besides was Martyn's work.

"Verses in vindication of Sir R. Steele against Dean Swift,"
the *Journal* quoted the last five lines—

> Thus S—t, a Dean by O—d made
> A burlesque on his holy trade
> From highest summit of buffoonry fell
> (Loaded with the contempt he merits well)
> For ribald wit, to the profundest hell.

Mr. Maevius observed that the cadence of the last three
lines represented in a surprising manner the fall of the Dean
from the summit of buffoon'ry to the profundest hell, than
which as nothing could be more profound in place, so nothing could possibly be more profound in poetry. The editors
likewise printed (number 216) an account of a threatened
attempt on Swift's life and the rallying to his aid of the
principal residents "of the liberty of the dean and chapter,"
and published two poems by Swift himself—the list of his
favorite furniture and the lines on his own deafness, as well
as two epigrams on his leaving his fortune for a lunatic
asylum (numbers 267 and 273).

To Pope himself allusion is much more frequent. Lines
of his were used as headings twenty-one times during the
first two years. He is referred to as a "most inveterate
enemy," as in the passage already noted where his name is
coupled with Swift's, or as "our professed enemy," as in
an ironical rebuke in number 21 to a writer who attacked
Moore-Smythe as a scribbler, and praised Pope. In number
215, Bavius himself compared lines from Pope's *Odyssey*
with a translated fragment to show that Pope's rendering
was as close to the original and at the same time as poetical
as could be expected. There are several poems in praise of
Pope. "A young gentleman of St. Mary's Hall, Oxford"[39]
was honored by the printing (number 24) of part of a
poem, "An Essay on the Dunciad," whose only virtue must
have been that it was laudatory of Pope. Of these lines it
was said that they were "likely to be acceptable to all readers
of taste," and "it is not doubted but that this specimen will

---

[39] Walter Harte. His *Essay on Satire, particularly the Dunciad,* was
not published as a whole until January, 1731, some six months later.

excite the desire of the public for the whole piece, and it is hoped it may be a means to move the learned author to gratify it." In "The Modern Poets," (number 98) a poem by "a young gentleman of Cambridge," wherein the Dunces are abused, and Swift, Gay, and Young are praised, the author comes to the climax—

> But who like Pope the power of numbers knows,

and reflects that "the snarling tribe" may cry his verse down, but he is content with the praise of Swift, Pope, Arbuthnot, and Young—"should he [Pope] but smile—I'd count their censure praise."[40]

In the quarrel with the Dunces, Pope's name was occasionally dragged in; in number 57, of an anti-Pope letter in *Fog's Journal,* "Mr. Maevius declared that tho Mr. Pope was a professed enemy, yet he ought not to have anything false alleged against him, that to his certain knowledge several of our members had drawn great benefit from his books, but the taste of the town was indeed now so much corrupted that the booksellers offered very little for any copy levelled at him." In regard to a life of Mrs. Oldfield, whose author showed animosity toward the poet, commenting sarcastically on Pope's interest in the *Examiner* together with Swift, Bolingbroke, Prior, and Dr. Arbuthnot, and referring to "a passage in Mr. Pope's Familiar Letters to Henry Cromwell, Esq.," the *Journal* said in number 64, "These letters were procured by one Mrs. T. who sold them without the consent of either of those gentlemen to Curl, who printed them in 1727. The author was ashamed of them as trivial things, and only excusable from his youth and inexperience. See Dunciad, p. 96." Items of this sort, such as would lead one to suppose that Pope from time to time used the *Journal* for similar pronouncements, are now and then to be found. The *Journal* took notice of the controversy over Curll's publication of Pope's early letters, and when that shameless bookseller set up Pope's head as his sign, published the epigram—

[40] Other verses to Pope appear in 104, 169, 176, 180, 269, 334, 376, 378.

Curst Cur— besieged by duns to raise the cash
With P—s immortal Busto stamps* his trash
So squandering coiners, to retrieve a loss
Imprint their monarch's image on their dross.

It entered zealously into Pope's quarrel with Lord Hervey, it issued a denial of his presence at and delight in Fielding's *Pasquin,* and it published the poet's own notice of the death of his mother.[41] Moreover, when in 1737 Mr. Bavius brought out *The Memoirs of Grub-street,* a considerable number of epigrams and articles were, as noted earlier, marked with the signature "A," to indicate the authorship of Pope and his friends, and some of the epigrams at least have been reprinted as authentic by the poet's editors.[42]

* "Alluding to the custom of printing signs in title pages."—*Grub-street Journal,* number 292.

[41] See 181. For allusions to Curll and Hervey see Chapter ii *post,* and to Fielding, Chapter v *post.*

[42] The "A" appears in connection with twenty-one issues of the *Journal*: numbers 19, 20, 21, 23, 24, 25, 26, 28, 29 (all except 28 being items in Pope's campaign against Moore-Smythe, for which see Chapter ii, *post*); 32, 35, 38 (attacks on Concanen); 40, 44, 45, 46, 51 (all but 40 dealing with the laureateship; 65, 78, 106, 128.

In his edition (1858) of Pope's poems, Carruthers included twenty-seven items in verse from the *Grub-street Journal.* For only eight of these did he have the authority of the signature "A". For one of the eight (*Should Dennis print,* etc.) he has the additional proof that Warburton had ascribed it to Pope, and for another (*A gold watch found on cinder whore*) that "Pope uses the same illustration in the 'Author to Let,' ascribed to Savage." For another epigram (unascribed in the *Memoirs*) he has the evidence that Bowles discovered it in Pope's handwriting among the papers at Mapledurham. Thus for nine he cites objective evidence. One other item (verses on Tom Durfey) had been merely reprinted from Curll's *Miscellany* of 1726. The other seventeen are apparently ascribed to Pope on internal evidence; that is, they seem worthy of Pope, or like Pope. Two of them are signed "M", and one "B"; the other thirteen are unsigned. Thus Carruthers bore out his promise in his life of Pope (2nd [revised] edition 1857), where he says (p. 274), "The best of the epigrams in this journal we shall insert in Pope's poetical works." He declared that he could trace Pope's hand not only in items signed "A", but "occasionally under the signature 'M' and frequently in pieces to which no signature is attached."

Like Carruthers, Mr. Lounsbury, in *The First Editors of Shakespeare* sometimes speaks with a great assurance, seeing clear internal evidence of Pope's authorship in anonymous items. The position of Mr. R. H. Griffith (*Alexander Pope, A Bibliography,* item 231) is certainly much safer: ". . . even with this testimony [the "A"] it is difficult to assign any of the compositions to Pope himself with a feeling of sureness." Yet it would not seem unreasonable to assume that items marked "A," dealing directly with Pope's own quarrels (especially those concerning

In the conclusions drawn concerning all this material, there has been much confusion and error. Although it was perfectly obvious from the beginning that Pope had much to do with the paper, there was never any authoritative pronouncement either from him or from the editors to that effect. In fact Pope practically denied any connection with it, and its editors occasionally issued half-hearted and inconclusive statements tending to absolve Pope from any responsibility for what they published. The earlier editors of Pope, who do not mention the *Journal* at all, were either ignorant of its existence or were taken in by these statements and believed that Pope actually had nothing to do with the paper, while later writers have in general observed the Pope material and nothing else, and have discussed the *Journal* as purely and simply Pope's personal organ. Moreover, all of them, even Elwin and Courthope, have been singularly incomplete in their treatment of it, and have regularly handed down errors and misconceptions. The first student of Pope to betray a considerable acquaintance with the *Journal* was Carruthers, who gives a fairly accurate account of it and makes illuminating comments on several obscure details.[43] Of late years biographers of other figures

Moore-Smythe, Concanen, and perhaps the candidates for the laurel) and very like him in style, were *in general* from his hand. In the present work, such an assumption has been made. No item without an "A," however, has been spoken of as Pope's. It may also be said that though the issues of the first four months are full of Pope material, there seems to be no reason to believe that Pope became an actual contributor until the beginning of his quarrel with Moore-Smythe.

Later editors of Pope, among them Elwin and Courthope, have included nine of the epigrams selected by Carruthers. Of these, five (the second, fourth, fifth, sixth, and seventh in Elwin and Courthope) are distinguished by an "A", and may with some reason be assigned to Pope. Three (the first, eighth, and ninth) are unascribed in the *Memoirs,* and can be assigned to Pope only on internal evidence. One (the third), has been discovered by Mr. Griffith to be an epigram of Samuel Wesley, slightly adapted to satirical use against James Moore-Smythe. Mr. Griffith (p. 271) thinks it was originally written against a poem, probably of Smythe's, in Lewis's *Miscellany,* but was adapted for publication in the *Journal* against the *One Epistle.* Here then, would be a case where the "A", for this epigram is so marked, represented one of Pope's "friends". Pope is said to have secured subscribers for Wesley's volume of verse published in 1736. Cf. *Dictionary of National Biography.*

[43] Notably on the editors, the attacks on J. M. Smythe, and the quarrel with Aaron Hill. He also takes an interesting point of view on the

of the period, notably of Aaron Hill, Fielding, and Theobald, have drawn upon it more frequently, and also, it may be said, more accurately. But among later scholars the one who made himself most familiar with it and recognized most fully its value in connection with the study of Pope, was Professor Lounsbury, who used it extensively in his book on Pope and Theobald.

But even the impression derived from Professor Lounsbury, in spite of his close acquaintance with the material, is hardly accurate, probably because, after all, the Pope and Theobald material in the paper was alone pertinent to his subject. And as for general works on newspapers, or other books wherein are to be found passing allusions or brief accounts of the paper, all that can be said is that their information is scanty and not very accurate.

As a matter of fact, the subject is a somewhat obscure and complicated one. For, while it can be said without fear of contradiction that the *Journal* was intended at the outset as a Pope organ and very little else, that is very far from being the whole story. Most of the material which has just been described appears in the issues of the first year. The farther one reads, the less frequently does one find Pope material, and after the first two years items are very occasional indeed. Thus what had its inception as a sequel to the *Dunciad,* soon ceased to be so, and assumed a quite independent existence, with innumerable other interests and aims.

Just what the various phases of Pope's interest in the *Journal* were it is impossible to determine definitely. Pope's ways were often devious; he did not care to declare himself openly even in the beginning, and even then, when the *Journal* was primarily a vehicle for his attacks on the

Ward's Pill controversy, and has noted the change of date of the article on the laureateship which appeared in November, 1730, to November, 1729, when it was added in 1742 to *The Dunciad.* On this latter point see also Lounsbury, *First Editors of Shakespeare,* p. 389, who notes that the article was included in Savage's volume of pieces occasioned by the war of the Dunces and was later included among Pope's authorized works but dated back to November, 1729.

Dunces, and defences and puffs of himself and his friends, it is doubtful whether he held the reins of management in his own hands, or merely sent in his contributions and his general directions from a royal distance. That the *Journal's* sponsors had any confidence that Pope's hand in the venture would pass unnoticed is beyond belief. They must have known that it would be recognized at once. It would even seem probable that they relied on it as a perfectly open secret which would make the paper go well. Pope's name would be invaluable to it; practically an insurance of success.[44] Nevertheless the editors were apparently never in a position to take the full advantage of such a position by declaring it openly. Rather, as has been said before, they declared vaguely that he had nothing to do with it,[45] and had to endure Pope's denials and repudiations, and what looks suspiciously like his gradual desertion of them.

One may well suppose that Pope originally conceived of the *Journal* not only as a valuable instrument to carry on the war with the Dunces, but as one which would bring still more of the sort of glory he had reaped from the *Dunciad.* He had, in fact, long conceived such a scheme, for in a letter to Gay in 1713[46] he suggested a paper like the *Journal,* to be called *Works of the Unlearned,* a fact which his

[44] Bavius declared in the preface to the *Memoirs* that the paper did not depend for its success upon Pope; that in fact those issues containing contributions supposedly from him or his friends came far from attaining the best sales. Nevertheless, denial of the fact that Pope's prestige was valuable to the *Journal* is useless.

[45] For instance, the editors print in 219 a letter criticising unfavorably Pope's translation of Homer. Bavius says he does so "to take off the imputation which has been cast upon us as being too partially inclined in favor of one particular person." Nevertheless he goes on to examine the criticisms seriatim, and finds them unsustained, childish, marked by bad taste, and so forth.

[46] Carruthers (*Life of Pope,* p. 270) speaks of this letter as written "apparently in 1714." In Elwin and Courthope (*Works,* VII, 412) it is dated October 23, [1713]; "this letter appeared in the P. T. volume of 1735, but was not reprinted by Pope in the avowed editions of his letters." The relevant portion reads, " . . . Dr. Swift much approves what I proposed, even to the very title, which I design shall be, The Works of the Unlearned, published monthly, in which, whatever book appears that deserves praise shall be depreciated ironically, and in the same manner that modern critics take to undervalue works of value, and to commend the high productions of Grub-street."

enemies and victims were fond of insisting on as proving
his connection with the *Journal*. The value of such a paper
conducted skillfully, vigorously, and without a trace of
squeamishness, was obvious. Still, when it became evident
that the more delicate, at any rate, found the *Journal's*
manners digusting, and when its victims began to insist too
vociferously on Pope's responsibility for it,[47] he evidently
found it discreet to withdraw well into the background and
become as inconspicuous as might be in a venture which
was making itself only too well known. Such seems to be
the most logical explanation of his letter to Lord Oxford,
May 17, 1730, asserting that he "had just now seen the *Grub-
street Journal,* and disapproved it," and also of a note he
appended to the phrase "low Grub" in the *Epistle to Dr.
Arbuthnot,* where he says the *Journal* was "a paper wherein
he never had the least hand, direction or supervisal, nor the
least knowledge of its author."[48] It was of course not well
for a man of Pope's social pretensions and desires to be considered the moving force in a publication which descended
with such gusto into the miry cockpit of personal controversy. His statement to Lord Oxford was at best equivocal.
When this letter was written Pope was just beginning his
attacks on James Moore-Smythe in the *Journal,* and in addition was, it can hardly be doubted, suggesting and supervising much more that came from the pens of editors and
correspondents. The *Grub-street Journal* was too low only
for public recognition. It is too much then, to accept his own

[47] As they did repeatedly. Note especially the assertions made by the
other papers with which the *Journal* quarrelled. (See Chapter iv, *post.*)
The following by Curll (July 26, 1735; see Elwin and Courthope, VI,
448) is typical: "As to Mr. Pope's being concerned in the *Grub-street
Journal,* all his denials stand only for ciphers; for one of the Grub-street
proprietors assured me, that both himself, and Huggonson, the Quaker,
who prints the said Journal, could testify the contrary; nay farther, I
know from indisputable evidence, that Mr. Pope wrote a letter to a
certain gentleman in the most pressing instances of friendship, not to
divulge the secret of his being concerned in that paper with his writing
partner, Dr. Arbuthnot."
[48] He did not always speak badly of it. He remarks in a letter (see
Elwin and Courthope, VI, 327), "That paper would often divert you,
though it is very unequal."

implication that the paper was none of his doing. His editors have long since ceased to regard his utterances on that subject as *bona fide;* they have erred rather in allowing him a far greater share in the paper than he really had.

After its first year, Pope probably had, indeed, comparatively little to do with the *Journal*. His contributions fell off in frequency, and then ceased. He occasionally used it as a convenient medium for advertisement and public announcement. Possibly he maintained some sort of connection, generally passive in nature, with the editors. It is significant that James Miller, who, according to contemporaries, had charge of the paper during its old age, was one of the minor lights of Pope's circle. Moreover, on the occasions when Pope's name and interests were mentioned the editors invariably faced the east and bowed reverently. Yet these indications of a continued interest are, after all, slight and infrequent in comparison with the material of the early issues. It is true, the *Journal* conducted many campaigns against men whom Pope had pilloried, and who might be counted among his enemies—for instance, Budgell, Hill, Joshua Ward, and James Ralph; but it is perfectly conceivable that these quarrels, except minor ones with Lord Hervey and with Curll, were undertaken quite independently of Pope. Nor does the repeated statement by the *Journal's* victims that their persecution was due to Pope's malice and animosity carry much weight. They were also fond of taunting the editors on occasion with having been left in the lurch by a leader who had at first been strong in their support, but had abandoned them when he became fearful of being defiled with pitch.[49]

The truth of the matter probably was that he did abandon them, but kept sufficient control over the paper so that he could use it if he wished. Still, in spite of the fact that the Pope material is confined chiefly to the first year, it remains

[49] A note to number 126 in the *Memoirs* points out that one abusive epigram quoted charges that Pope was implicated in the *Journal*, while another abuses the paper on the ground that Pope actually had nothing to do with it.

the most interesting and significant part of the paper. It is
for one thing the most brilliant. Then, too, there is the mere
fact that it is Pope material and really belongs to the history
of the *Dunciad*. Besides, the fact that until lately almost no
attention has been paid to anything else in the paper has also
tended to emphasize its importance. In considering a given
item, one inevitably finds himself wondering first of all
whether Pope had any sort of interest in it.

The second center of interest in the *Grub-street Journal* is
by all odds the identity of the editors. On this point, as well
as with Pope, there has been any amount of confusion and
obscurity. There never was, of course, any disclosure of sponsors or editors; the very nature of the periodical, its primary
concern in personal controversy, precluded that. Of the details of personal organization and management we know
almost nothing absolutely, and can infer very little. We know
nothing about the finances of the paper—who supported it
at the beginning, or who later enjoyed the profits of it. Again,
although the editors themselves were discovered, it is impossible to say how they came by their employment, whether
they were partial instigators of the scheme or merely hired
servants. Nor can one pierce the veil of anonymity behind
which the innumerable correspondents almost invariably hid.
One frequently suspects them, along with Giles Blunderbuss
and Mr. Poppy, of being merely phases of Mr. Bavius, but
such suspicions remain vague and uncertain. Perhaps, however, such obscurities are no more than one should expect
in dealing with such a paper. It is hard enough to light up
unintentional and casual obscurities in history, but much
harder to illumine intentional and carefully guarded ones.

As for the identity of the editors, the only information the,
Journal itself vouchsafed was that Mr. Bavius had general
charge. There seemed, however, to be an almost equally important colleague in the person of Mr. Maevius. In fact, in
The Memoirs of Grub-street one is told that there actually
were two joint editors writing under these names, and that
Mr. Maevius occasionally usurped the pseudonym of Mr.

Bavius. Their victims and enemies had long since had more definite knowledge of the editors than this. The double-headed Mr. Bavius, having involved himself in bitter personal controversies with his brother editors of the *Hyp-Doctor,* the *Bee,* and the *Prompter,* was described by them in highly unpleasant terms and was declared to be John Martyn, and one Richard Russel, a non-juring clergyman.

Concerning the first of these there has never been any confusion or doubt. He was John Martyn, a young botanist, and served the *Journal* during its first and part of its second year.[50] His connection with it was remarked on frequently by fellow journalists, and is stated as a fact by his son, Thomas Martyn, who published a memoir of his father in 1770. He was eminent in his profession and is a well-established historical character.

The case of the second and far more important editor, Russel, is quite different. His identity has been the subject of many confused and erroneous statements, in spite of the fact that many of those whom he attacked knew perfectly well who he was, and spoke definitely and harshly about his history. Later investigators, however, have relied almost entirely on Thomas Martyn's statement that his father was associated for some years with "Dr. Russell," and that they wrote under the names of Bavius and Maevius respectively. Martyn, the son, also states that during the same period his father and "Dr. Russell," whom he denotes "a learned gentleman," were interested together in a plan, which proved abortive, of republishing *Roberti Stephani Thesaurus Linguae Latinae.*[51] This is the sum of T. Martyn's information concerning the editorship of the *Journal.* It served, however, as a basis for all succeeding statements on the subject. Carruthers, indeed, finds it strange that a botanist and a physi-

---

[50] Martyn's signature "B" in the *Memoirs* appears in connection with twenty-five issues, of which only four are of the second year, the latest being number 67. His medical and botanical interest is evident, but he also dealt with literary subjects, and, especially at first, wrote many satirical comments on news items.

[51] G. C. Gorham's reprint (1830), p. 38. Thomas Martyn does not, however, say Dr. Richard Russell, as Lounsbury implies, p. 394.

cian should have combined forces to produce a paper like
the *Journal,* but Courthope in his life of Pope[52] remarks
that Pope started the paper "under the management of his
friends Dr. John Martyn and Dr. Richard Russell." Occasionally there appears a strange variation from the original
source in Thomas Martyn, as in the article on John Martyn
in the *Dictionary of National Biography,* where the Russel
in question is made Dr. Alexander Russel, or as in the catalogue of the Hope collection of newspapers in the Bodleian,
where one may read, "The writers or conductors of this
popular paper were Richard Russell, D. D., a physician, and
John Martyn, M. D., the distinguished botanist." The author
of the Hope catalogue, being familiar with statements in
Eustace Budgell's *Bee* that Russel was a clergyman, simply
reconciled earlier and later opinions by the clever device of
making Russel both clergyman and physician. The confusion
on this point was cleared away to a considerable extent by
Professor Lounsbury, who undertook an investigation into
the identity of "Dr. Richard Russell, a physician." He discovered that there were two Dr. Richard Russells of this
period—one an eminent physician, a graduate of Leyden, a
Fellow of the Royal Society, remembered for writing on the
curative effects of sea water and his development of Brighton
as a resort; the other a man of much less note, a graduate
of Rheims and a practitioner of Reading. It is perhaps worth
adding that the latter also has preserved his identity in writing; he is the author of two published letters on professional
etiquette which are preserved in the British Museum. It was
apparently one of these two physicians, or a combination of
them—for, as Lounsbury notices, they have been confused
with each other in biographical dictionaries—that has done
duty with Pope scholars and others as an editor of the
Grub-street Journal. The improbability that either of these
physicians was concerned in the *Journal* was apparent to Mr.
Lounsbury. Their special interests and the fact that they
both lived outside London were against such a suppo-

[52] *Works,* vol. V (1889).

sition; and there was also the plain fact that all the contemporaries who expressed an opinion on the subject maintained confidently that Martyn's collaborator was one Parson Russel with a residence in Westminster. It is on the basis of contemporary evidence then, coupled with the fact that much of the material signed Bavius deals with theology and the classics, that Lounsbury comes to the conclusion that the editor in question was, as his contemporaries called him a "Mr.", and not a "Dr.", Russel, a non-juring clergyman.

Professor Lounsbury may then be said to have corrected the general belief, due merely to Thomas Martyn's careless use of the title "Dr.", that one of the editors of the *Journal* was a physician named Russel. Yet he leaves the second editor a very vague and tenuous shadow—a non-juring parson, one ————— Russel, who lived in Westminster. Fortunately, it is possible to penetrate considerably into the obscurity which hides him, and to discover enough additional details of his history so that he becomes, like his colleague Martyn, a fairly well fixed historical entity. The fact that his enemies frequently referred to him as Dicky indicates clearly enough that his name, like that of the two physicians, was Richard.[53] There is a Richard Russell (or Russel) in the Oxford records who fits the case—Richard Russell, son of a clergyman of Dallington, in Sussex. He matriculated at University College, July 9, 1698, at the age of twelve, received a B.A. in 1702 and an M.A. in 1705, and was appointed vicar of Alfriston and Selmeston in Sussex, in 1710.[54] In the British Museum are to be found several of his books and pamphlets. Two of these, which are anonymous but are ascribed respectively to Richard Russel, M.A., and to Richard Russel, are *A Discourse concerning the nature and the obligation of oaths* and *The Obligation of acting according*

---

[53] If one cares for an explanation of Thomas Martyn's allusion to "Dr. Russell," it may be surmised that he knew Russell's name was Richard, but that for him the name Richard Russell meant of course the well-known Dr. Richard Russell of Brighton fame. Or it may be that in courtesy he bestowed the title "Dr." on one whom he thought of as a learned divine.

[54] Foster, *Alumni Oxonienses.*

to conscience, especially as to oaths. A farewell sermon preached January 22, 1716. Both these pamphlets are dated 1716, and the second has a preface to the effect that it is intended as an apology for non-jurors. While these are mere ascriptions, circumstances clearly indicate Russel's authorship. There is also a four-volume translation of Quesnel, *The New Testament, with Moral Reflections,* 1719. This work is preceded by a dedication to the Earl of Winchelsea, signed Richard Russel, and by a long preface apologizing for delay in publication because of his hard usage by his successor in the livings of Alfriston and Selmeston in the diocese of Chichester, when he had to give them up in 1716 as a non-juror. He declares very bitterly that his successor would not allow him the tithes due him in arrears, and that he was forced to eke out a living by business, "for which both by genius and education I was very unfit." Hence the delay in the publication of the book, which had been long promised. Under the date of 1732 is an edition of Vida, printed by Gilliver and Nourse, publishers of the *Grub-street Journal,* and dedicated very significantly to "Alexandro Pope, Armigero, Poetarum inter Anglos Celeberrimo," with the verses

> Vidam sed carpunt multi—Carpere Maronem
> Nobile par fratrum, Maevius et Bavius.
> Carpunt te similes horum.

and the signature *Richardus Russel, Westmonasterii, Idibus Maiis, 1732.* This work had been advertised in the *Grub-street Journal,* number 3—"speedily will be published M. Hieronymi Vidae Opera Omnia . . . ex recensione R. Russel, M.A. . . ." A later advertisement contains the note "The edition in 8vo of S. S. Patrum Apostolicorum . . . undertaken by the same person, but which has been retarded by some obstacles, is now going forward with expedition; and as the greater part of it has been printed off for some time the remainder will be finished without interruption, so as certainly to be published next winter."[55] Seemingly, obsta-

---

[55] In 129, when the Vida finally appeared. It was also advertised by Gilliver on the back leaf of *Harlequin Horace* as by "R. Russel, A.M."

cles continued to retard the author, for this latter work was
not published until 1746; and its preface bears the date
"Londini, Die Festo S. Barnabae, 1746." In Nichols' *Literary Anecdotes,* moreover, are to be found records of two
Russels who were apparently his sons. One of these was
"W. Russel," a bookseller, described as being the son of a
"non-juring clergyman who was educated at St. John's College, Cambridge and kept a boarding house in Westminster
for young scholars whose parents were non-jurors," and who
was the editor of *Vida* and *Patrum Apostolicorum.* W. Russel, like his father, seems to have had a hard life, to have
failed in business and fallen to the state of an itinerant book
peddler. The second son, James, was by way of being an
artist, and wrote in 1748 *Letters from a Young Painter in
Italy.* He lived in Rome, where he made a living by acting
as a guide to Englishmen. He died in Italy in 1763.[56]

Richard Russel was, then, the son of a clergyman and an
alumnus of University College, Oxford. He had been vicar
of a country parish in Sussex and was an editor of books of
divinity and criticism. He had lost his living because of non-
juring principles, and when the *Grub-street Journal* appeared
had been without a cure for some fourteen years. He had
evidently been forced during this interval to eke out an existence by some uncongenial occupation, of which he complains,
most probably literary hackwork. Apparently, his life had
not been an easy one, or of a sort to improve his temper. His
bitter remarks concerning his successor in the Sussex living
are prophetic of his point of view and style a decade later in
the articles written for the *Journal.* Indeed, his non-juring
principles are frequently apparent; for instance he contributed[57] to number 22 a bitter answer to an attack in the
London Journal on "non-juring Jacobite priests." In number
129, he eulogizes the Jacobites abroad, and especially the

[56] See Nichols, II, 505. The only detail in this account which does not
fit into the career of Richard Russel of the *Journal* is the *St. John's
College, Cambridge.* Errors in assigning alumni to colleges, however,
were frequent. As for the allusion to the boarding house, compare the
sneers of writers in other newspapers (Chapter iv, *post*).

[57] It is reprinted in *The Memoirs of Grub-street* with his signature, "M."

Bishop of Rochester,[58] whom he represents as a pathetic, lonely exile, for their loyalty and magnanimity in refusing to accept any of the ill-gotten gains of a fraud and absconder. How he came to form the connection with the *Journal* it is impossible to say. Allusions to him as a friend of Pope's by the author of the Hope catalogue, for instance, are hardly convincing. For six years, that is through 1735, he directed the paper's fortunes, and thereafter appeared occasionally as a contributor. He also edited *The Memoirs of Grub-street,* which appeared in 1737, five years after it had been promised, and wrote a very guarded and discreet history of the *Journal* introducing those little volumes of selections. All else that can be said is that he was living as late as 1746, when he published another work of divinity. Perhaps it is worth noting that apologies for delayed appearance occur regularly in his prefaces. It is quite probable that he was pursued all his life by grim necessity and that business "for which both by genius and education he was very unfit" always hung like a millstone about his neck.

To Russel must go most of the credit for the success of the *Journal.* Martyn, Russel's colleague, if one is to judge from the ascriptions in the *Memoirs,* was by far the less important and prolific of the two; moreover, he retired early in the second year.[59] As for Pope, he was undoubtedly the chief factor at the beginning, but his aid soon became sporadic and slight. It should be noticed also that the paper did not sink with Pope's defection. On the other hand, its vogue seems to have increased steadily. Certainly for four or five years it continued to flourish with undiminished vigor, and Russel's should be the praise. The Vicar, as he was called, had a pen of remarkable skill in controversy.

[58] In the *One Epistle,* abusive of Pope (see Chapter ii, *post*), the Bishop of Rochester is referred to as a "plague of all churches". This is noted by Russel ("M") in number 22, where he also compliments a writer in *Fog's Journal* on vindicating the bishop.

[59] The signature "M" appears in ninety-eight, or approximately three-quarters, of the issues covered by the *Memoirs.* Pope's "A" and Martyn's "B", as has been noted earlier, appeared in twenty-one and twenty-five issues respectively.

He was certainly not a great writer nor a man of fine qualities or noble feelings, but for conducting journalistic quarrels—choosing profitable antagonists, dealing out vitriolic
sarcasm and irony and subtle innuendoes, in short for carrying on the business in hand,—he was eminently well-chosen.
One can hardly call him fair, frank, or kind, but these were
probably not qualities the originators of the paper were seek-
ing. They were certainly not qualities of Alexander Pope.
The *Grub-street Journal* has always been considered a round-
about expression of the personality of Pope, but the more
one learns of it the more one realizes that its peculiar and
individual tone was set rather by the personality of that
obscure person, Richard Russel, M.A.

Toward the end of his consulship, it must be admitted,
affairs ceased to go well. He complained of difficulties with
his colleagues and contributors, the pace flagged, and subscribers occasionally found fault. Hence, ostensibly tired of
journalistic bickerings and squabbles, he finally announced
that he had given over the *Journal* into the hands of a successor, who he hoped would allow him from time to time
to express himself in its columns. The identity of this new
editor was not disclosed, but the *Journal's* adversaries intimated that he was that minor Popeian, James Miller.[60]
Whoever he was, he did not succeed in restoring its fortunes.
Under him its light grew steadily duller and duller, until its
directors must have decided that it was beyond revival and
should be snuffed completely.

[60] Later, in the preface to the *Memoirs*, Russel said that since his retirement the paper had been run by a committee. It is impossible to say
whether this contradicts or merely qualifies his earlier statement.

CHAPTER II

POPE AND THE DUNCES

After its first year the *Grub-street Journal* soon came to lead a very vigorous existence quite independent of Pope. It had many irons other than his in the fire. It was of course always reverential toward him, friendly toward his friends, and hostile toward his enemies. On two later occasions it came fiercely to his aid in squabbles in his behalf with that object of his ancient hatred, the scandalous Edmund Curll, and with Lord "Fanny" Hervey. Yet after 1730 the amount of material in the *Journal* printed either directly or indirectly in Pope's interest is so slight as to be altogether inconsiderable. No one reading the paper after 1730 would gather that Pope had any special connection with it.

Yet, as has already been said, the *Journal* was unmistakably undertaken as an organ of Pope. Its chief purpose was clearly to proclaim his greatness and to denounce and expose his enemies, especially the latter, for its militant attitude toward the Dunces and others of their tribe is much more striking than its glorification of the poet. Its first issues are practically a sequel to *The Dunciad*. Their columns are thickly scattered with the names of Dunces, whom it invariably holds up to scorn and ridicule. Especially noticeable as being singled out for attack in this first period are James Moore-Smythe, Matthew Concanen, James Ralph, and the critics Lewis Theobald and Richard Bentley.

For instance, in verses on the Cambridge commencement in number 28, apropos of "iste tuus frater Tibbaldus", it is said

—et omnes
Popiades Phoebo sua debent carmina: nobis
Non ita. Quod facimus, nostrum est.

In an amusing bit of persiflage on the subject of anagrams and similar exercises, Mr. Poppy remarks in number 32:

In these kinds of wit did former members of our Society excel: in the same ways might our present members shine. But alas we are too apt to aim at writing after the Parnassian manner; in which we can never hope to succeed. Could we but be persuaded to leave the pursuit of those sorts of writing for which Nature has by no means formed us, and apply ourselves to those which seem fitted to our several capacities, we should appear much more illustrious than we do at present. Then might the labours of the industrious Mr. Theobald be well spent on anagrams, the quaint conceits of the inventive Mr. Smith might be properly bestowed on chronograms, and the ingenious Mr. Ralph might appear to a better advantage in the confinement of an acrostick than he does at present in the loose pindarick.

Against the five writers mentioned above the *Journal* conducted what may justly be described as consistent campaigns, running over considerable periods of time. Other Dunces, however, are mentioned in scattered or sporadic news items, epigrams or satirical essays. Among these, Daniel Defoe and John Dennis, the critic, are the subjects of the most significant allusions.

Satire on Defoe appears but twice, both instances, however, being interesting in view of the fact that the whirligig of time has finally cast the erstwhile Dunce and yellow journalist into the very front rank of eighteenth-century writers. The first remarks appear in number 69 on the event of his death.

On Monday in the evening died at his lodgings in Rope Makers Alley in Moorfields, the famous Mr. Daniel Defoe, in a very advanced age. *Daily Courant.*—It is no small comfort to me that my brother died in a [*good*] old age in a place made famous by the decease of several of our members; having kept himself out of the dangerous alleys of those high-flying rope-makers who would fain have sent him long ago to his long home, by the shortest way with the dissenters.

In the Pegasus column of the same issue the society's emotions were recorded:

The members were so much afflicted at the news of the death of that ancient ornament of our society, Mr. Daniel Defoe, that they were incapable of attending to the papers which were read to them. [The writer proceeds to quote an anti-clerical epigram] which by some was imagined to be the last work of the great author deceased, and an instance of his perseverance in his principles to the last, being very agreeable to the sentiments which he had frequently published both in prose and rime.

In number 90 the scene of his arrival in the Elysian Fields is recounted by "Farewell" in a letter from those regions.

As to poets, we are prodigiously overstocked with them . . . that universal genius, Mr. D- F-e lately arrived raises our admiration here as much as he did yours when alive. Among other things he frequently entertains us with accounts of the various ways of diverting the living world with newspapers, an amusement altogether unknown in the age of Augustus. He assures us that he himself at one and the same time wrote two celebrated papers, one on the Whig and one on the Tory side, with which each party were extremely well pleased. He likewise often makes us merry with the dexterity and management of booksellers in putting off their authors from time to time with little or no money, and their heavy copies, with new vamped title pages, advertisements, etc. . . .

To John Dennis there are a number of early allusions manifestly continuing the attacks of *The Dunciad*. The most important of all is the first, in the fifth number. In the essay on Miltonic verse, Dennis is cited as a prominent disciple of Milton:

I shall give one instance among many of Milton's very words being converted to Profundity, from your great Dennis. In the poem entitled *Il Penseroso* Milton has these words—

> Oft on a plat of rising ground
> I hear the far-off curfew sound,
> Over some wide-watered shore
> Swinging slow with sullen roar.

This has been admired by the injudicious as being natural; but you will agree with me, I dare say, that Nature is not to be imitated but mended. Mr. Dennis no doubt thought so, when he composed that fine apostrophe to the River Danube in his *Blenheim*—

> Thou like a bittern through thy doleful reeds
> Complaind'st in sullen and in moody groans,
> Expressing manly sorrow mixed with rage
> While thy brown billows sounding on thy shore
> And swinging slow with hoarse and sullen roar
> Kept murmuring consort to thy threatening moan.

It was natural indeed to speak of the swinging of a bell, as Milton did, but truly poetical to speak of the swinging of the billows of a river, and far above the imagination of one who had been used to live by a riverside and had no idea of the motion of its billows above what mere nature had conveyed to him.

The essayist speaks of the general necessity of replacing
Parnassian by Grubean ornament; while the Parnassian
would open an epic in a low, unmoving manner, the Grubean
opens in a very lofty strain, as in Dennis' *Battle of Ramillies*—

> I sing the triumph of that wondrous field
> Which raised the fame of pious Anna's reign
> Above the glory of great Henry's days.

When he comes to a discussion of the typical Grubean figures
of hyperbole and anticlimax, "For the first, let us cite the
never enough extolled Mr. John Dennis."

> Awaked he rises from his bed in haste
> And after him in haste the sun arose
> Impatient to behold his wondrous deeds.

The *Journal* shot a bolt of sarcasm at Dennis' critical
abilities in number 37. In that issue appears a laudatory
notice by Edmund Curll of a new translation by Earbery of
Bishop Burnet's *De Statu Mortuorum* with derogatory remarks on an older translation of the same work by Dennis.
The "person altogether unknown" was one "Charles Price",
who had sent in Curll's advertisements. The *Journal* reports:

The Society was very much surprised to see an advertisement of this
nature representing the most ancient of critics as incapable of translating a modern Latin author, and more to see a person altogether
unknown in the commonwealth of literature setting himself up as
an infallible judge of translation, of whose name they had never
heard before. Mr. Dennis, Mr. Earbery, and Mr. Curll are names
with which the learned world in general and our Society in particular are well acquainted—.

The only notable reference to Dennis as a candidate for
the laureateship appears in an article on the laureate ceremonials in number 46, probably by Pope (it is signed "A"
in the *Memoirs)*. The author suggests that a large amount
of cabbage (*brassica*) be used with the vine leaves as a
remedy for drunkenness. If Dennis were to be chosen, the
proportion of cabbage should be large, but if Theobald were
the choice it could be reduced, unless it could be taken as

symbolic of theft.[1] A really savage blow at the old critic came in an epigram by Pope himself ("A") in number 78—

> Should D—s print, how once you robbed your brother,
> Traduced your monarch, and debauched your mother;
> Say, what revenge on D—s can be had;
> Too dull for laughter, for reply too mad?
> Of one so poor you cannot take the law;
> On one so old your sword you scorn to draw.
> Uncaged then let the harmless monster rage,
> Secure in dulness, madness, want, and age.

In later years Dennis was left to his own devices except on the occasion of a theatrical benefit for him in December, 1733. The *Journal* expressed itself (number 208) in typically sarcastic verses sneering at "worth in want." The next week it reprinted from the *Daily Journal* verses in which Dennis expressed his gratitude to James Thomson, who had been partially responsible for the benefit. Dennis says that he finds in the author's mind all the Seasons except Winter, which was drawn from him himself—

> Leafless and whit'ning in a cold decay.

To this the *Journal* rather heartlessly joined the couplet—

> I'm glad to find my brother's grateful lay
> Like medlar fruit, delicious in decay.[2]

The discussion of the competition for the laureateship in the fall of 1730 abounds in names of aspirants already made famous in the verses of *The Dunciad*. The names of new luminaries, however, also appear. Typical of the treatment they received is that meted out to Stephen Duck, the Wiltshire thresher-poet, whom the *Journal* frequently found amusing during 1730 and 1731. Duck's rustic genius having attracted the attention of influential patrons, he had been brought to London, where he had soon come to be a pet at court, enjoying the favor of no less a person than the Queen

[1] Note allusions to Theobald later in this chapter.
[2] Note, however, "A Prologue by Mr. Pope, to a play for Mr. Dennis' benefit, in 1733, when he was old, blind, and in great distress, a little before his death." A strange contrast to the epigram in 78, although the tone of the prologue is not exactly that of friendship and reverence.

herself. This good fortune naturally enough led to his being considered a very probable successor to Eusden. He was of course always treated with contempt by the *Journal,* a contempt which usually expressed itself in condescending sarcasm. That Pope himself was interested in the paper's attacks on the various candidates for the laureateship is perfectly obvious, and there can be little doubt that at the very least he concurred in the editor's attitude toward Duck, who, along with his fellow poetasters, Cibber, Dennis, Theobald, and Concanen, was suffering from the *Journal's* mockery. Publicly, however, Pope pretended to be a friend of the Wiltshire thresher, although he never expressed enthusiasm over his verse. Pope's friends, moreover, were irritated by the foolish adulation paid Duck at court.[3] Pope's public professions and private feelings were often different things, and it is hard to make his expressed regard for the person of the rustic rhymer square with the summary treatment of him in the *Journal,* which was never hard on Pope's friends.

The *Journal's* first significant mention of Duck comes in two poems in number 40, October 8, 1730. The first of these, consisting of thirty lines of doggerel, begins—

> O Duck, preferred by bounteous Queen
> To cackle verse on Richmond Green,

In the second, "To Mr. Stephen Duck, the celebrated Wiltshire poet and thresher on his late preferment by her Majesty" the writer compares Homer's hard life as a wandering minstrel and Milton's poverty with Duck's easy rise to fame and fortune and compliments him on the Queen's favors. The final stanza runs—

> O may she still new favours grant
> And make the laurel thine.
> Then shall we see next New Year's Ode
> By far the last outshine.

[3] See *Dictionary of National Biography,* article on Duck. The thresher was capable on his side of rendering grateful homage to the poet. In *The Beautiful Works of the Rev. Mr. Stephen Duck, the Wiltshire Bard* (1753, edited by J. Spence) are "Lines on Richmond", written in 1731 and containing a flattering allusion to Pope.

This number also contains a puff of one James Drake, employed on a small boat, who had written some poetry but had failed to attract patronage or to achieve the honor of publication. Several specimens of his genius, perfectly conventional and platitudinous, but at any rate smoother than Duck's, are brought forward to prove that his claims are equal to those of the thresher. In spite of the fact that the style throughout is perfectly serious and that Mr. Drake's lines contain a compliment to Pope, a communication at this time in favor of a "Drake" must have been a hoax. According to the editors the writer was unknown to them, but their own attitude is indicated in a notice signed Bavius, and written by Russel ("M"), "Our President, who is no friend to punsters, desires our correspondents, if they write any more upon Stephen Duck, to forbear all witticisms upon his name, flail, etc., they being anticipated in one of these poems."[4]

The next dozen issues contain several epigrams and prose articles on Duck's candidacy and his place in literary fame. In number 45 appeared Pope's epigram—

> Shall royal praise be rhymed by such a ribald
> As fopling C—r, or attorney T—d?
> Let's rather wait one year for better luck;
> One year may make a singing swan of Duck.
> Great G—, such servants since thou well can'st lack
> Oh save the salary and drink the sack.[5]

To number 46 Bavius contributed the lines—

> Behold, ambitious of the British bays
> C—r and Duck contend in rival lays.
> But gentle Colley, should thy verse prevail

---

[4] The obvious puns were apparently irresistible, for the next week the editors announced that, "Notwithstanding the caution given by our President in our last Journal we have received several copies of verses which play upon the name of Stephen Duck. . . ." And in ensuing issues hardly a critic is able to refrain from such "witticisms"; in fact it is hard to see what some of the poet's critics would have had to say, had they not had his name and original calling to pun on.

[5] Ascribed to "A". The final couplet was amputated by Carruthers and for some reason inserted by itself in his list of Pope's contributions to the *Journal*.

Thou hast no fence, alas, against his flail.[6]
Wherefore thy claim resign, allow his right;
For Duck can thresh, you know, as well as fight.

Cibber having finally received the appointment, the *Journal* showed its favor to his opponent by announcing in number 49, "Mr. Stephen Duck is chosen a member of our Society, to qualify him to appear with a better grace as a candidate for the laurel, in case of a new vacancy; and to obviate the objection for the future, which was lately made against him." In the next issue, however, it was reported, that he "modestly declined the honor we conferred upon him, because it was done upon a wrong motive, the poems which go under his name having been printed without his knowledge in a very incorrect and imperfect manner; a genuine edition of which he designs to publish in a little time."

These remarks are, it would seem, a mock-serious allusion to an attempt by Duck, or more probably his friends, to escape responsibility for the natural crudity of his work by substituting in place of the original poems (which had, indeed, been pirated) a carefully revised and edited version. The same number (49) contains a letter from "Simple Simon" analyzing the beauties of Duck's poetry. The writer declares that the envious critics will not allow Duck to be the author of the poems published as his, although their quality proves his authorship, "at least they are such as none but his fellow threshers ought to pretend to." Simple Simon gives examples of Duck's choice of words, his expletives, figures of speech, and "notions," and quotes such lines as—

The hungry steed
Neighing, complains he wants his daily feed.

This jesting was reproved (as far as one can judge, though of course the editors were quite capable of concocting the

---

[6] Swift too wrote an epigram ridiculing Duck, especially as the object of the Queen's patronage, wherein appears the phrase, "No fence against a flail." See Swift, *Poems* (1910, edited by W. E. Browning), I, 192. This epigram in 46 is attributed by Carruthers to Pope, though it was reprinted in the *Memoirs* without a signature.

epistle themselves) in a letter signed "L. M.", the following week. L. M. maintained that Duck's poems had been printed without his consent and that the text, being very corrupt, was not a fit index to his talents. He also pointed out that there was no use in talking to Duck in such terms as *pleonasm,* which could mean nothing to him, and that it was easy enough to find errors even in the best writers. He even contended that the favorable public reception of Duck's poems indicated their worth. To this defense Simple Simon replied lightly and whimsically in number 52. He denied the last argument absolutely, pointing out that it was exactly the erratic quality of public taste that the *Grub-street Journal* was trying to correct. He also called attention to the fact that the "Duckisms" he had noted were not the sort of thing that could be explained away as printer's errors, and that likewise such corrections as had been made were quite worthy of Duck's genius. The editors supported this letter with a pretended reproof of Simple Simon for his hardness toward Duck, and appended a list of advertisements, in which apparently they took little stock, wherein Duck repudiated the edition under discussion, denied the authorship of some of the poems, and set forth a confession by a book-seller, who begged pardon of Duck and the public for his imposture.

A somewhat more serious criticism of Duck, at least in pretense, appears in number 55, where Bavius (in this case Martyn) takes Duck as a text for an essay on the dangers arising from the increase in the numbers of poets. The city, he declares, is full of poets, for every man is coming to be persuaded of his poetical abilities. He cites the example of a weaver who has burst into song, with the explanation—

Thy fortune, Duck, affects my kinder'd [*sic*] mind.—

and implies that royalty and the aristocracy should not encourage such people and lead them to give up their proper occupations. He culls many flowers from such poets; the brightest perhaps from a plagiarism of Sylvester's Du Bartas—

The bald-pate trees are periwigged with snow
Which nature from the hidebound clouds lets go.

In conclusion he speaks of the Royal Society's rules for
limiting its membership because of the propensity of so many
to consider themselves philosophers, and fears that the Grub-
street Society may be brought to the same pass.

An attack from still another angle was made in number
57. An "obscure weekly paper" (the *Weekly Register)* had
printed an epigram on Cibber and Duck, and *Fog's Journal*
for January 30, 1731 had also put forth a violently abusive
burlesque "Letter from Stephen Duck to Mr. C—y K—er,
poet laureate." This letter had been sent to *Fog's* by one "D.
T.", who said a reliable friend of his had seen the original
and had thought it ought to be published at once, "lest it be
suppressed forever." The *Journal's* editors report the pain of
some of the members who say that they cannot bear to see
one of the best and most illustrious of their brethren fallen
upon thus.

The public interest in Duck as candidate for the laurel
had probably died by this time; at any rate, except for a
few scattered allusions, he appeared no more in the *Journal.*
A few casual items, however, show that he was still regarded as one of the Grubean Society. In number 74, the
editor reprinted from the *Daily Post* the news that the
thresher-poet was being taught Latin by one of the royal
chaplains, and remarked, "I fear his learning Latin at this
time will hinder his poetical flights, and wish that he would
rather learn English." A year later (number 138) "Hobbinal
Lubbin", in applying to the Society for membership, describes himself as "a great overgrown boy at a country free
school" and asks whether they have yet admitted his "lucky
kinsman, Mr. Stephen Duck." Again in number 289 in a description of a new capitol of Grubstreet, he is assigned a
post outside the door of the laureate, there to stand on guard
with his flail against the approach of Parnassian enemies.
Below him are "three grand steps," the Bible, Milton, and the
Spectator, the three sources of his learning. The only other

notice accorded him consisted in printing (in number 393) ten lines of verse on the subject "Agar's Wish", with the note that he had written them *ex tempore* in a room by himself, to satisfy the doubts of a nobleman as to his poetic genius. The *Journal* did not deign to criticize the verses themselves, but did remark, "The person who sent the preceding letter and verses by way of puff is desired to send the next correcter, or money for correcting."[7]

The chief value of the *Journal* to Pope lay in the fact that he could use it to chastise those victims who had kicked against the pricks of *The Dunciad* and subsequent satires. Pope's annihilating wit, his pitiless use of real names and his key to *The Dunciad* reduced many of the Dunces to the point of thinking silence the best policy. But some of them, it goes without saying, tried to do as they had been done by, to return as good as they got. Indeed the sum of retaliatory pamphlets, epistles in verse, and the like, by various Dunces makes a very respectable showing, in bulk at any rate. There can be no doubt that in the minds of its founders the chief function of the paper was to be the prosecution of this warfare; they were simply to carry on the work of devastation from week to week, carefully crushing any refractory Dunce who was foolish enough to show his resentment.

During 1730, while Pope was still an active contributor, and in fact the *raison d'être* of the *Journal,* he himself dealt with two of his enemies who became violent against him, namely James Moore-Smythe and Leonard Welsted. His counter attacks upon them form, in fact, the most significant and interesting part of his writing in the *Journal.*

James Moore-Smythe and Pope had originally been on friendly terms, but had quarrelled over some lines by Pope which Smythe had borrowed for use in a comedy, *The Rival Modes,* and which Pope himself later inserted in his second

[7] For a detailed study of Stephen Duck, see Rose M. Davis, *Stephen Duck, the Thresher Poet,* University of Maine Studies, Series II, number 8, January, 1927. Miss Davis gives an account of the piracy of Duck's work in 1730 and later, and of Pope's attitude toward him (pp. 40-48).

Moral Essay. Thereafter Smythe had been held up to derision by Pope in *The Dunciad* and other satires. Early in
May, 1730, he and Leonard Welsted, another victim, published *One Epistle to Mr. A. Pope.* This poem had a preface
in justification, wherein Pope was accused of attacking inof-
fensive authors, of being actuated by malice and avarice, and
also of being the cause of the personal abuse in the *Miscellanies* of 1727 as well as in *The Dunciad.* It was here declared also that Swift never saw the *Profund* until it was
published and that Arbuthnot had wished the satire to be
general and all names to be omitted.[8] The *One Epistle* itself
indicted Pope for plagiarism, lack of originality, and empty
copiousness, and sneered at him as appealing chiefly to ladies
of society. The authors paid their respects to "Quack Arbuthnot", deplored the association of Gay, whom they admired, with Pope, asserting that Gay "gives his foes his
fame, and bears their sins," raked up the old story of Pope's
imposition on Broome, and ended with denunciation of Swift
for sacrificing all his sacred duties to his love for Vanessa.

Smythe was soon made to realize afresh what it meant to
incur Pope's hatred. A frontal assault of this fashion demanded retaliation, and received it in a series of prose
articles and epigrams beginning in the *Grub-street Journal,*
number 19, May 14, 1730. The first entry is in the form of
a letter[9] signed "Jemmy M—r Sm————," wherein the
"author" declares that he will be more scurrilous and dull
than anyone else. He will abuse Pope and Arbuthnot personally, because they have not abused him. "We [Smythe
etc.] call ourselves gentlemen, because one is the son of
an alehouse keeper, one the son of a footman, and one the
son of a ————." The defense was further maintained in

[8] The author continues, however, "I cannot indeed say much in praise
of some performances which appeared against him, and am sorry that
volunteers entered into the war whom I could wish to have been only
spectators. But the cause became so general that some gentlemen who
never aimed at the laurel grew poets merely upon their being angry. A
militia in case of public invasion may perhaps be thought necessary, but
yet one could always wish for an army of regular troops."

[9] Ascribed in the *Memoirs* to "A" (Pope), as are also the "Answer"
in 20. and the epigrams in 21. These are the first ascriptions to "A."

the next issue by specific rebuttal. Here are disposed of the charges that the Duke of Buckingham since becoming acquainted with Pope had stopped payment of a pension to Charles Gildon and that the Archbishop of Canterbury had censured the poet. The defender asks various direct questions in connection with other charges: Has Pope ever spoken in friendly fashion to or of the infamous Colonel Chartres? Was he ever at variance with Fenton? Did Broome complain of Pope's treatment of him in regard to the money derived from the translation of the *Odyssey*? Has Pope ever discouraged any young writer of merit? Was he ever lewd, drunk, in debt, etc.? Was he ever avaricious? The writer declares that whoever can prove these things shall receive the panegyrics of all the Grubstreet Society. In conclusion he speaks of the malicious denomination of Swift and Arbuthnot as Pedant and Quack. Still another long blast came in number 21, this time from Russel ("M").

The Theobaldians who had been driven out of the field the last campaign by the publication of the Dunciad opened this at the beginning of this month with the publication of the One Epistle to Mr. A. Pope. An abstract of the contents of the preface to this epistle, sent us by a Popeian was published in our Journal, May 14. In the Daily Journal of May 16, was published the following epigram by a Theobaldian.

> Of all thy short lived progeny this last
> Has met with harder trials than the past.
> With rueful eyes thou view'st thy wretched race,
> The child of guilt and destined to disgrace.
> Thus when famed Joan usurped the pontiff's chair
> With terror she beheld her new born heir.
> Ill starred, ill favoured into birth it came,
> In sin begotten and brought forth with shame.
> In vain it breathes, a lewd abandoned hope
> And calls in vain th' unhallowed father, Pope.

We should be glad to hear the names of Mr. Pope's short lived progeny, all those children whom he owns being to our sorrow alive and in good health; we likewise desire to know what the epigrammatist means by a lewd, abandoned hope.

In our last of May 21, N. 20, we offered a reward to any person who would attest the truth of any of those facts there mentioned, and which had been charged upon Mr. Pope in the One Epistle. To which we have hitherto received no answer. But instead of it in the Daily Journal, May 23,[10] there is a complaint against us for publishing in our last Journal (which is false, for it is our last but one) the contents of the preface above mentioned. Wherein they charge us with saying that one of the authors is the son of a w——. In our Journal there is no more than the son of a ——; the w is added by the complainant himself, no doubt upon good reasons.

The observation about the genealogy of the three gentlemen was not, we imagined, levelled against the merit of the poem but against the appellation of gentlemen, which the authors had assumed in the preface. We beg the favor of the gentleman who wrote the letter in the Daily Journal to write his next in plain English, for we could not apprehend what he meant by charging us with "pouring out a lying spirit upon the genealogy of the supposed writers" of the One Epistle.

To this skilfully abusive letter are appended two equally scurrilous epigrams upon Moore, contributed by "the Pope-ians," and ascribed to "A".

> Moore goes two years, and then alas produces
> Some noisy, pert, dull, flatulent abuses.
> So some stale, swoln-out dame, you sometimes find
> Has been at last delivered but of—Wind.

> To prove himself no plagiary, Moore
> Has writ such stuff as none e'er writ before.
> Thy produce, Moore, is like that Irish Wit
> Who shewed his breech, to prove 'twas not besh——.

Then followed a series of epigrams and short prose squibs on Moore-Smythe which constitute perhaps the cleverest and most virulent of the *Journal's* essays in persecution. They are a revelation of the extent to which literary men of the period were willing to let themselves go in the matter of personalities. The first of these, is an advertisement in number 23: "Last Friday at the Prince William Tavern, a very modest young gentleman alias Moore, alias Smith, who

---

[10] This article in the *Daily Journal* for May 23, 1730, accuses Pope of malice in attacking the descent of the supposed authors of the *One Epistle* and also offers alleged instances of plagiarisms by him from Garth and Dryden. The *Daily Journal* was often the channel for letters hostile to Pope and to the *Grub-street Journal*. The appendix to *The Dunciad* charges Moore-Smythe with authorship of several letters and notes against Pope in the *Daily Journal* during March and April, 1728. According to a note in the *Memoirs* the author of this particular letter was Curll. Moore was also threatened with an attack in the form of a second *Author to be Let*, which was advertised several times in the *Journal*, 21 ff. See Lounsbury, p. 379, and Carruthers, p. 279.

had been concerned in a libel against an eminent physician had the correction of the cane bestowed upon him by a relation of that physician, which correction he received with exemplary patience and resignation" ("A").

In number 24, we find "Mr. J. M. S———e" ridiculed about his whipping and "catechised on his One Epistle to Mr. Pope" in the epigram—

> What makes you write at this odd rate?
> Why, sir, it is to imitate.
> What makes you steal and trifle so?
> Why 'tis to do as others do.
> But there's no meaning to be seen!
> Why, that's the very thing I mean.[11]

In the next issue one learns that Moore-Smythe was stung into an appeal to the law, for there is an epigram "On Mr. M—re's going to law with Mr. Gilliver. Inscribed to Attorney Tibbald."

> Once in his life M—re judges right:
> His sword and pen not worth a straw,
> An author that could never write,
> A gentleman that dares not fight,
> Has but one way to teaze—by Law.
> This suit, dear Tibbald, kindly hatch,
> Thus thou may'st help the sneaking elf,
> And sure a printer is his match,
> Who's but a publisher himself.[12]

These lines are preceded by a note to the effect that Gilliver was "served only with a rule requiring him to shew cause why an information should not be granted; which he will do next term," and are followed by an abusive personal description of Moore-Smythe, and information that he has lost his mind and wandered off. This last invention is further developed in number 26 in a long illiterate letter[13] addressed to Moore-Smythe by his "uncle," Dr. Moore, the

[11] This epigram was by Samuel Wesley, and was adapted for use here by changing the original "sirs" of the second line to "sir," and an original "rant and ramble" in the third to "steal and trifle." (Compare *ante*, p. 34, n.)

[12] A sly charge of plagiarism, in allusion to the borrowed lines which had made Pope Smythe's enemy. This epigram was ascribed to "A."

[13] This letter would seem to be Pope's, but in the *Memoirs* it has no ascription. The "answer" and epitaph in 29 are ascribed to "A," as are also the items just noted from 25.

famous "worm-powder" quack. The "uncle" upbraids his
"nephew" for having so little to do with his family, com-
miserates with him over the state of his health and wits,
and then informs him that the cause is worms, and can be
removed by a course of the worm powder.[14] In addition
there are epigrams with appropriate satirical comments—

> Said Christ, the man that's pure in heart,
> And means no ill, for heaven may hope.
> But sure, the bard's not worth a fart,
> Who nothing means, says Master Pope.
> Critics and casuists, speak your mind,
> Is S—e for Heaven or Hell designed?
> Answer.
> Blest may the *man* be, by believing,
> The *poet's* hardly worth the saving.

and, ascribed in the *Memoirs* to "A",

> A gold watch found on cinder whore
> Or a good verse on J—my M—re
> Proves but what either should conceal
> Not that they're rich, but that they steal.

—the last being doubtless, like other allusions to theft, intended to recall again to the reader's mind the original cause
of Pope's enmity.

Three weeks later, in number 29, came an "answer" to
the letter from Worm-powder Moore. Herein J.M.S. is
made to declare that he has always been against wit since he
found wit against him. Now he always has recourse to law
when wit is against him. He admits that now he can live
only with his relations, and studies law. As for fearing God,
"I cannot yet bring myself to it; I have still some bravery
left toward him." He insists that he never wrote five lines
of his own in his life, and that no one thinks he is a wit—
even his own friends deny it the morning after. The only

[14] Interesting comment on this letter by a fellow sufferer appears in a
note from Theobald to Warburton, reprinted in Jones, *Lewis Theobald*,
p. 274: ". . . I have only to tell you that the Grubstreet continues to
make a devil of our friend Moore. They have placed him in too ridiculous a light by inditing a whole letter to him from Worm-powder Moore,
who calls himself his uncle, and requires him as a madman to put himself under his care; and cautions him against falling under the hands
of a graduate physician, who wants the management of him. They besides renew the charge of cowardice so strongly against him, that, I
confess, I should choose to have two broken arms rather than be so
stigmatized in print. . . ."

person who accuses him of being an author is Captain Gulliver;[15] anyone who reads of his travels can judge of his credit. As for Pope, "It is true I did go with something against P—pe (or rather like a puppy carried it to and fro in my mouth) these two years and upwards: but . . . got nothing by it, and had not got that neither, but for my good friend Mr. Welsted."

Apparently it was now decided that J. M. S. had been sufficiently belabored, for the *Journal* published, to mark the conclusion of the episode, an epitaph on the victim with the concluding phrase, "ex nihilo nihil fit." Nothing more appeared until number 41, when readers were reminded that he was "a young gentleman lately deceased," that the editors had already published his epitaph and promised to say no more about him. Still, if his ghost appears at Westminster next term [to prosecute the *Grub-street Journal*] means will be taken to *lay* him.[16] One may conclude that nothing came of the lawsuit, however, as there was no further reference to it, and he was allowed to rest in peace. In number 44, he was included with Duck, Cibber, Moore and Dennis among the commissioners of the Grubstreet Society to name the laureate. The editors ask their readers not to be surprised at seeing a dead person in the list—the ode "in Monday's Post-boy must have been written either by him or the Rev. Mr. Eusden, likewise deceased: certain it is that no man *alive* could write such a one." The only notice that he received hereafter was by way of announcement six months later in number 65 that he had settled in Staffordshire and spent his time in making "pretty copies of verses upon persons and subjects that occur hereabouts," one sample of which "pretty copies" is presented.[17] There is also, in number 73, a passing allusion to "the incomparable J—M—S—."

[15] Gilliver, the *Journal's* printer.

[16] Ascribed to "M" (Russel).

[17] In 66 appears the following epigram "On Mr. James Moore's pretty verses . . . printed in our last Journal."

> What makes for once, Squire Jemmy's Muse so toward?
> Mere joy to see a cousin of Ned Howard.

This is signed "Bavius", but in *The Memoirs* is ascribed to "A" and may be by Pope, though certainly there is no especial encouragement in the style to believe it.

Pope's vengeance for the *One Epistle* fell almost altogether on the head of Moore-Smythe, although the chief author was apparently Leonard Welsted. In the appendix to *The Dunciad* it is asserted that part of the poem came out in folio in 1731[18] "under the just title of Dulness and Scandal," but this latter piece contains nothing more than echoes of the earlier one. There are enough of these echoes, however, to suggest common authorship. In any event, probably because his part in the poem was underrated,[19] Welsted's share of the abuse fell on Moore-Smythe's head, and he figures in the *Journal* only as one of the Theobaldians who come in for occasional contemptuous allusions. He is, for instance, made the author of an illiterate letter (a device Pope seems to have used frequently) published in number 40, wherein he asks the *Journal* to print all the epigrams the Dunces send in. Pope ("A") replied that this must be considered with caution, for the sake of both parties. It is significant that the later *Dulness and Scandal* drew little fire; Pope was no longer regularly using the *Journal* as his mouthpiece.[20]

----

[18] There is in the British Museum a copy dated 1732. "Of Dulness and Scandal. Occasioned by the character of Lord Timon in Mr. Pope's Epistle to the Earl of Burlington. By Mr. Welsted. London, 1732." *Dulness and Scandal* is most abusive of Pope, but concentrates chiefly, unlike the *One Epistle,* on him and does not attack his friends. A typical abusive line is—

Inglorious Rhimer! low licentious slave!

There are occasional parallels of thought or material between the two poems, but not identical lines. The closest parallel in phraseology is—

One Epistle, p. 18—For thou wert born to damp each rising name
And hang, like Mildews, on the growth of Fame.
. . . Low lewdness, unexcited by desire.

Dulness, p. 6—O born to blacken every virtuous name
To pass like blightings o'er the blooms of Fame
. . . Lewd without lust. . . .

[19] Seven years later, in *The Memoirs of Grub-street,* there is the note: "This person [J. M. S.] reported himself author, but was only a publisher; it being written by Mr. Welsted and others."

[20] Note, however, in 106, a brief query ascribed to "A," concerning false Latin in *Dulness and Scandal*: Did Welsted understand Latin, or were the "second and third" editions an imposition, so that he had no chance to correct it in them?

During the period of the *One Epistle* Matthew Concanen also suffered from Pope's pen in the *Journal*. He had the temerity to publish as *The Speculatist*[21] a number of *Essays Moral and Political, Serious and Humorous* which had appeared in the *London Journal* and the *British Journal* from 1725 to 1727. Two of these stirred Pope's ire: "On Pope's Miscellanies, November, 1727," and "On Frauds of Booksellers." In these essays Concanen accused Pope and his friends of abusing Congreve and of inducing other authors to father some of their scurrilous productions, and intimated that Curll ought to feel honoured at being satirized by pens which had attacked Marlborough and Addison. Although these scandals were old ones, Pope evidently thought it worth while to resent them. Accordingly there appeared in the *Journal,* numbers 32, 35, and 38, a series of three articles[22] on *The Speculatist* and Concanen. The first is in the form of a satirical letter to "the Speculatist. Mr. M—w Con—n-n," and is signed Will Slyboots. It suggests to Concanen that it is well for the low classes of writers to think whether they have any reputation before they undertake to justify and defend it, implies that he has worked hard to build a reputation and that no one ever accused him of modesty, and finally asks him to mark with an asterisk those papers which were intended humorously. The second article is headed by four lines from *The Dunciad,* Book II, beginning "True to the bottom see Concanen creep." It is a savage, direct attack on Concanen. It declares that the *Speculatist* is nothing but a patchwork of old material revamped from the *London* and *British Journals,* names C-nc—n as author and calls him a scurrilous liar. It disposes of accusations or "lyes" about Pope, especially that he had often been "concerned with booksellers in jobs and frauds." In reply to the charge that Pope and Swift had abused Congreve it declares that the remarks to which Concanen took exception were published at Congreve's own desire. The notes to *The Dunciad* are quoted to

[21] The British Museum has a copy of the second edition, 1732.
[22] All ascribed to "A."

the effect that Concanen was "an anonymous Slanderer and
Publisher of other men's slanders" on Dr. Swift, to whom
he had particular obligations, and that this was known to Dr.
De[lan]y, and can be proved by other men also. Finally, that
"said C-nc—n is an immoral man is what every reader ought
to be told; that he is a dull one is what every reader can find."
In the third article, Pope returned to the more usual satirical
and ironical vein, and wrote a letter purporting to be from
Concanen, "being an explanation of his first of September
8th." Concanen's "first" letter referred to had appeared in
the *Daily Journal,* September 8, 1730. He there asserted that
he had been attacked with malice and virulence by the *Grub-
street Journal,* and answered categorically the charges made
against him. Most of these answers were nevertheless weak
or evasive, and a fairly correct impression of them is given
in Pope's satirical "second letter" in the *Grub-street Journal.*
Concanen did deny effectively, however, any obligation to
Swift, who "expressed some intentions to serve me, which he
declined at the next visit I paid him," and declared that he
had no further relations with the Dean. In Pope's "second"
letter, Concanen is made to excuse himself for statements in
the first on the ground that he had said the same things three
years before, that he merely said "he heard so" not that *it
was so,* that in his Irish vocabulary *often* and *once* were
equivalent, that he had never used scandalous or foul language of Swift, but had merely called him a lampooner,
impudent, malicious, poisonous, and so forth. It ends, "I
desire you to publish this paper, which must be true, for it is
my own account of myself."

   In the Pegasus column in this same issue the editors declared that they were impartial in the controversy, and that
they themselves would have been willing to publish Concan-
en's letter of September 8, had he sent it to them in manuscript, and Pope ("A"), in commenting on the episode, concluded: "We return him therefore to that obscurity he
desires, with no other mark of distinction than what the
[Dunciad] has set upon him, for having the boldness to at-

tack his betters, unprovoked." This brief expedition of Pope's against Concanen was concluded with this third article, and Concanen received no further notice from the *Journal,* until his appointment as Attorney General and Advocate General in Jamaica. This good fortune, having been noted in a news item in number 138, was satirized in an epigram[23] a fortnight later, in number 140, "On the new Attorney General"—

> Come, Dunciad authors, come to dinner all,
> C—'s made attorney-general.
> Think not this honor a mere act of grace;
> His noble talents justly claimed the place.
> For all Attorney Generals till of late
> Were ever famed for legal Billingsgate.[24]

Moore-Smythe and Concanen are the only two Dunces who suffered concerted and consistent retaliation from Pope himself in the *Journal.* That Pope was personally responsible for the articles and epigrams against them we have the best evidence that there is in ascribing authorship to any material in the *Journal;* that is, the signatures in *The Memoirs of Grub-street.* As far as one can judge, these articles on Moore-Smythe and Concanen constitute Pope's most important contributions to the *Journal.* In gauging his connection with the paper, this fact is significant in view of the very slight bulk of the material in comparison with the whole, and of the number of much lengthier controversies which could have had very little, if any, interest for Pope. Indeed, even the later quarrels with victims of *The Dunciad* appear to show

[23] An interesting sidelight is thrown on the editorial methods of the *Journal* by the reply to a complaint of the author of this epigram that it was not published as he sent it in, but was "most scandalously altered." In reply it is admitted that it was altered to improve the versification and also the sense. Notice is also served that unless a piece is submitted with a real signature, "we shall take the liberty to alter, if we think there is occasion, as being the properest judges what may be convenient or inconvenient for us to publish." See *ante,* p. 14.

[24] Nichols, V, 534, draws from Akenside some interesting details as to Warburton's partisanship with "Theobald, Concanen, and the rest of their tribe." "In his intercourse with them he treated Mr. Pope in a most contemptuous manner, and as a writer without genius." Later Warburton explained away his intimacy with Concanen as a youthful error. He also said that Concanen married great wealth and came back to England "of so scoundrel a temper that he avoided ever coming into my sight."

merely that the *Journal* was always hostile to Pope's enemies and glad to attack them. During the first year or so Pope quite possibly instigated and directed the attack on notorious Dunces like James Ralph, Theobald, or Dennis, but the signatures in *The Memoirs of Grub-street* show that most of the lampooning was actually done by other pens than his.

The early attacks on James Ralph, for instance, are by Martyn or Russel, that is, they are signed in the *Memoirs* either "B" or "M." The first ones, by Martyn, are not personal, but merely satirical literary criticism. Yet of course it is not too much to surmise that Ralph's being a Dunce was the initial cause for his distinction here, and in fact Pope's interest and the *Journal's* bias soon came out clearly in an article by Russel, which is quite as "Popeian" and personal as Pope's own attacks on J. M. S. or Concanen.

James Ralph,[25] an American, and most famous as an early associate of Benjamin Franklin, had not appeared in the original Dunciad but had been so hardy as to publish *Sawney, an Heroic Poem Occasioned by the Dunciad,* a crude satire on Pope, which had effectively secured him a place in subsequent versions, and of course made him fair prey for the *Grub-street Journal.* The first mention of Ralph is in number 5, in Martyn's essay on Miltonic verse, where it is stated that in digression, which is one of the ways of imitating Milton, Mr. Ralph is very happy. His poem on Night is all digression. ". . . he begins . . . with telling us, that when the sun goes down, night arises, and then it is either dark, or star light, or perhaps moon light. *Meanwhile* (that is, as I take it, in the space of one night)

> . . . revolving time with restless toil
> Through all the seasons turns the circling year"

—a comment, which, however prejudiced in its source, leaves one doubtful as to Ralph's poetic abilities. Ralph soon attracted the notice of the *Journal* again with an entertainment called *The Fashionable Lady, or Harlequin's Opera,* which

[25] For an interesting essay on this picaresque hero, see R. F. Dibble in the *Nation* (New York), October 13, 1926.

Martyn reviewed in number 16. Martyn describes it as an imitation of *The Rehearsal*, or a very silly thing in the same manner, except that it contained no parody. He holds up to contempt the similes, the wit, and the "elegance" of the language. Of the songs he says, quoting a line from the piece itself, "they are worse than a psalm at an execution, or an owl at midnight." To this criticism Russel[26] added a list of specimens "of polite and sensible language," the author having told his patron in the dedication that the play was "an essay to entertain politeness and good sense." *The Fashionable Lady* was again attacked in number 21 in an unsigned letter with notes by the editor. In the letter Ralph is spoken of as "one who would have lived and died in obscurity, had it not been for the ingenious author of the Dunciad, who left him to be hooted at by the Owls." This personal attack Russel continued in the comments with which he elaborated his letter. He repeated Pope's old remarks upon Ralph, to wit that "the learned Mr. Ralph" was said by Pope in *The Dunciad* to have written

a swearing piece against Dr. Swift, Mr. Gay, and him; that he once praised himself highly above Mr. Addison in wretched Remarks upon that author's account of the English poets,[27] printed in a London Journal, September, 1728, that he was wholly illiterate, and knew no language, not even French; and that being advised to read the rules of dramatic poetry before he began a play, he smiled, and replied, 'Shakspeare writ without rules'. Now though this account be very improbable, yet supposing it true, it carries in it a real panegyric on this gentleman by a tacit acknowledgment of his extraordinary parts. Without which a person not understanding any language but English, and consequently not thoroughly understanding that, could never have raised himself to that eminence as to be the inventor of a new species of poetry, *a pindaric ode in blank verse;*[28] a species so sublime that not one person has had the presumption to imitate him therein.

[26] Signed "J. T." Ascribed to "M," as likewise the letter and notes in 21.
[27] Addison's *Account of the Greatest English Poets. To Mr. H. S. 1694.*
[28] See in the *London Journal,* September 14, 1728, an article demonstrating the superiority of blank verse over rhyme, with praise of Ralph's new ode, *The Muses Address to the King.* The author speaks of softness and sublimity of style, and the fineness of the sentiments of the *Muses Address,* and says no one "ought to be prejudiced against this ode because of the novelty of its manner, for it must show a fine genius that can succeed so well in a new and untrodden path." The *Journal* refers

Further personalities on Ralph appeared in number 30, apparently on information that he had attached himself to the *Weekly Medley*. A letter from "Jemmy Friendly, Secretary to the Weekly Medley," and beginning with the lines from *Hudibras,* "A squire he had whose name was Ralph," and so on, states that the writer has been ousted from his position by "Jemmy Ninny Hammer, that modest, sweet (or as some say) smockfaced, self worshipping prig." The writer encloses with his own another letter signed "J. Ninny Hammer, alias J. R." and addressed to the *Weekly Medley,* offering to become its secretary, provided he can manage it freely, and will not have to insert anything by Swift, Pope, or Gay. Another attack on Ralph followed only after an interval of two and one half years, in connection with unfavorable criticisms of Gay's *Achilles* in the *Daily Courant.* In number 165 Bavius reports,

It is not without reluctance that we comply with the request of a gentleman whom we take to be at least as well informed as the author of a letter and of a short copy of verses concerning the opera of Achilles in the Daily Courants of last Friday and of this day. By two verses in the latter . . . it is evident that the author is a latent member of our society. The gentleman's request is that we would refer the author to the decree pronounced against him by the sovereign judge of Parnassus, Dunciad, Book III, verses 159-160, and to the remarks thereupon. . . .

These scattered allusions to Ralph may be justly regarded as echoes of Pope's war on the Dunces. They are none of them, to be sure, by Pope, but they continually refer to Pope and *The Dunciad,* and all but the last were written during the first months of the *Journal's* life, while Pope was not only contributing but doubtless keeping in close touch with the editors. The final item seems to be one of those very occasional reminiscences of the original policy of the *Journal,*

to this matter again in 120, in connection with "freeing the lesser parts of poetry from that barbarous and Gothic tyrant, rhime. . . ." "The learned Mr. Ralph undertook this some time ago in his Muses Address to the King, an incomparable Pindaric ode in blank verse of which proper notice has been taken in our Journal. The success of which specimen of this new species of poetry was so great that no person has presumed to imitate it."

which became less and less frequent after its first year. As a matter of fact, Ralph was a much more prominent butt for the *Journal* during its later years than he was at first, and yet the later attacks on him seem to have no connection with, or interest for, Pope. They are made, not on the basis of allusions in *The Dunciad* and Pope's old grudges, but rather on current indiscretions by Ralph seized upon as openings for profitable controversies, and treated quite independently of old scores.[29]

Early in 1734, Ralph turned his hand to a series of architectural essays on London buildings, publishing them first in the *Weekly Register,* and then in a pamphlet entitled *A Critical Review of Public Buildings.* The editor of the *Journal* evidently scented in this presumptuous undertaking a fruitful source of controversy, for he published in number 230, May 23, 1734, an attack on it. The author, who signs himself "Atticus", asserts that the architectural critic "discovers in his laborious survey just as much skill in architecture as is about sufficient to qualify a man for a freemason." He cites as especially irritating such stock critical phrases as "preserves a fine keeping," and the airy way in which Ralph had praised or condemned by wholesale and had suggested improvements and alterations.

The *Weekly Register* accepted the challenge at once by publishing a counter-attack and a general rebuttal. This the *Journal* summarized and answered in number 232 in its Pegasus column. The author of the *Critical Review* declared that his work had always been well received and that "this very pamphlet has been fathered on some of the noblest and most eminent names in the kingdom." Like most angry opponents of the *Journal,* he then reverted to the subject of its early history. Originally, he declared, it had "owed its whole prospect of success and reputation . . . to an opinion that was artfully circulated through the town that Mr. Pope and Dr. Arbuthnot were concerned in it as authors." According

[20] For a theatrical quarrel in which Ralph became involved, see numbers 174, 177, 178, 179; and *post,* Chapter v, p. 212.

to the *Journal*, the utmost that ever was imagined was that
Pope and his friends had at times contributed short pieces—
never that they had been "constant authors." "If by *artfully
circulated* it is designed to insinuate that there was no foundation at all for such an opinion, what grounds has he for that
insinuation? Is he certain that neither of those persons wrote
anything in this paper at its first outset? If he will believe his
brother, Budgell, one of those gentlemen has been concerned
in it even at its last outset." Then, after an equivocal discussion of mistaken rumors as to authors, with many rhetorical questions, the editor goes on to dispose of the *Register's*
charge that the *Journal* "was timed critically in the heat of
the *Dunciad* controversy" to make Pope's connection seem
plausible. This, the editor asserts, is untrue, since the heat of
that conflict was already over, numerous editions of *The
Dunciad* having appeared, and the pamphlets of the victims
having perished for want of buyers. He quotes the *Register*
further to the effect that the *Journal* has subsisted on "mere
love of scandal" and "the hope of something malicious one
week to make amends for the dulness of another." To all
this was appended an epigram on "The Grubstreet Architect,
Statuary, Painter, etc.," suggesting that he had found all his
material in Bailey's *Dictionary*.

The following week began a systematic and devastating
analysis of the *Critical Review*. Ralph had remarked at
length on some pictures by Amiconi at Powys House, and
Bavius was able to demonstrate that he had mistaken a picture of the Seasons for Morning, and two pictures of the
story of Judith and Holofernes for David and Abigail and
Antony and Cleopatra. These slight errors were likewise com-
memorated in epigrams, one in this issue and one the following week (number 234). The second one, which was probably by Russel (Maevius), follows equivocal dallying with
the *Register's* charge that the *Journal* was malicious and exhibited sense only when it was helped out by a chance correspondent. It runs—

> The dame so fair, the chief who rough and stern is
> Designed for Judith were, and Holofernes.
> The critic, spite of Scripture, fain would have it
> Painted for Abigail and smooth young David.
> To please 'em both, I'll own each understood
> His art:—and then the piece is bad and good.
> 'Tis a fine Judith as the painter wrought it;
> But a damn'd Abigail, as the critic thought it.

Allusions to this *faux pas* continued at intervals, and were often combined with answers to reiterated charges by Ralph that the *Journal* was malicious and underhanded, was surreptitiously the organ of Pope, and so forth—points that the *Journal* apparently considered valuable as advertising, else it would have ignored them.[30] Ralph aided in keeping the controversy alive by the most futile and absurd attempts to explain away or minimize his mistake, saying for instance that one couldn't have always at his elbow "one of those Rotine [*sic*] Historians who show the Hospital at Greenwich, the tombs in the Abbey, or write the Grub-street Journal, to enlighten these obscurities and hinder a man of imagination from using it where it has no business."

The *Journal's* favorite weapon of burlesque and parody was also invoked, especially in "A Critical Review of the Buildings, Statues, Vases, etc., in Grub Street" by "Vitruvius Grubeanus" in number 236. Among other points there is here suggested an improvement in barber poles, in phrasing which closely follows Ralph's—

I cannot deny myself the pleasure and *vanity* of making public an improvement which I have long since planned for reducing our barbers into a better *gusto* with regard to that long party-coloured column which their profession obliges them to exhibit to view. If this column was placed *horizontally,* even then 'twould be absurd in a great degree, but as it is mostly *oblique,* it is not only highly so in itself, but also spoils the *keeping* of the whole street. I would therefore have it erected perpendicularly at two yards distance from the door, at the edge of the paved stones, and it would have all the *surprising effect of a wreathed obelisk.*[31]

[30] Note especially 235, 237 (where Bavius plays with Ralph's reference to the story of Judith as coming from church history), 238, 245, 252.
[31] Another phrase typical of Ralph's architectural style which occasioned some mirth in the *Journal* was "squares octangular."

For some three months Ralph's name went unmentioned; his anonymity was respected. Finally, however, in number 244, he was called by name and compared with Perault, who gave up poetry to become a great architect, while Ralph—

> —with his head so foul and muddy
> Two noble arts at once would make his study,
> And, vainly thinking he excells in either
> Shows plainly to the world that he knows neither.

Other epigrams followed: one (number 248) reminiscent of a great scene in *The Dunciad*, the other (number 252) a rather pointless squib "On poet R—ph's studying of painting and architecture." The first is on the text from Ralph himself, "I own myself much pleased with the design of filling up Fleet-ditch"—

> Ask you why R— so triumphs in his mirth?
> The cause is plain: Fleet Ditch is stopt with earth.
> Henceforth not Pope, nor all the Popes alive
> Shall souse the bard, or make the critic dive.

In its ridicule of Ralph's absurd pretensions the *Journal* was in its own natural vein, and it made the self-appointed critic ludicrous enough. Not satisfied with this, however, it undertook to dispose of Ralph's pamphlet in serious and weighty fashion point by point, and to establish a satisfactory substitute. To this end it began in number 237 a series of articles by "Mr. Hiram," which, despite their judicious and formal discretion, wind their weary way through the columns of the *Journal* for nearly nine months. In most of the numbers during this period Mr. Hiram's name is prominent, but he came to a summary end in number 271. Although the usual note "To be continued" was attached to his installment in that issue, nothing more was heard of him. Doubtless the paper's readers had long since grown restive and had demanded his cutting off. At any rate the controversy died at this point, and except for a poem in number 287 wherein Walter Harte is defended against an attack by Ralph, and one or two other casual instances, Ralph's name disappeared from the *Journal's* pages.

There is nothing in this later attack on Ralph to show that it was inspired by Pope. It seems rather to be a new and independent controversy arising out of the simple fact that Ralph had once more made himself fair game. As a matter of fact the only two occasions in its later history when the *Journal* obviously entered into quarrels as Pope's organ were at the time of his squabble with Lord "Fanny" Hervey late in 1733, and of the scandal in 1735 over Curll's publication of Pope's letters. And it is noteworthy that the *Journal* devoted very little space to either of these quarrels.

Lord Hervey had allied himself with Lady Mary Wortley Montagu in her famous war with Pope, which is said to have resulted from the "immoderate fit of laughter" wherewith she had rejected Pope's love. Pope retaliated venomously in the lines on Sappho in his imitation of Horace's *Satire* II, 1 of February, 1733. This drew an immediate reply in the *Verses addressed to the Imitator of Horace. By a Lady.* Apparently Lady Mary was assisted in this piece by Lord Hervey and others.[32] At any rate Lord Hervey carried on the campaign in *A Letter from a Nobleman at Hampton Court to a Doctor of Divinity,* a feeble but venomous attack on the poet, which Pope countered with the vigorous prose satire *A Letter to a Noble Lord,* November, 1733.

It was at this point that the *Journal* became useful. In number 205, November 29, 1733—almost exactly the time of publication of Pope's *Letter*—the *Journal* printed a statement that Hervey's authorship of *The Letter to a Doctor of Divinity* had been denied in the *Daily Courant* of the twenty-second, and that the newspapers had been enjoined from connecting his name with it. The *Journal* evinced little respect for the noble lord's privileges, however, for in its next number appeared *Advice to a Nobleman,* consisting of applicable lines from Ben Jonson's *Poetaster,* beginning "Fannius, hold up your hand."[33] In number 207 the significance of the

[32] See Elwin and Courthope, V, 255 ff. and 423 ff.

[33] This scene from *The Poetaster* was reprinted in *A most proper reply to the Nobleman's Epistle to a Doctor in Divinity. To which is added Horace versus Fannius, etc.* Published by J. Huggonson [the *Journal's* bookseller]. 1734.

advertisement in the *Daily Courant* of November 22 was carefully analyzed. It was reprinted verbatim, as was also an assertion in the *Craftsman* of December 8 that it was "a pitiful equivocation" intended to prejudice the proprietor of the epistle. The attempted defence in the *Courant* was the vaguest of evasions, its obvious point being that the paper wished to apologize and avoid the penalty of using Hervey's name without permission. The *Journal* ironically declared itself forced to believe the author some latent member of the society whom the world had honored by ascribing his work to Lord Hervey, "so eminent for the most extraordinary parts and learning," and reprinted from the *Epistle* the section containing the chief slanders of Pope. In number 209 appeared what is apparently a contribution from a disinterested and impartial observer, a vapid and sentimental plea for peace and harmony. The writer declares his neutrality, and denies personal acquaintance with either Pope or Hervey. He deplores the fact, nevertheless, that the one remaining Parnassian should be attacked because of "some few ill-natured lashes," and concludes with an idealistic demand that Hervey forget his animosity, scorn controversy, and write poetry which shall raise him to the level of Pope.

In these few comments consisted the *Journal's* support of Pope during the heat of the quarrel. There followed, however, from time to time echoes and reverberations testifying to the fact that Hervey, as one of Pope's enemies, was *persona non grata* with the *Journal*. In number 216, some two months later, were listed among the effects of a deceased author, "Brother Fannius," "A Satire on Mr. Pope, with some allusions to an ape, and several ingenious conceits of a like nature." Hervey's enrollment among the Dunces of Grubstreet was again noted in number 223 in an epigram by "R. S.", quite probably Richard Savage, "To a noble Lord on his late most incomparable poem"—

> Most noble peer, your ever charming verse
> Delights the more, the oftener you rehearse.
> To your harmonious strains all others yield
> Like bending corn when winds breathe o'er the field.

> Right honorable bard, exalt thy lays
> From princely rising to majestic praise,
> Then shall the world, in spite of envy see
> The laureate's lofty odes outdone by thee.

Again, a full year and a half later, in number 287, came "Fanny, or Poetry and Paste, a Tale. Inscribed to Mr. Pope." The argument of this narrative is Fanny's love affair with the rustic Trulla. Fanny hangs about the ladies all day and is allowed the greatest intimacy because he is considered harmless. Cupid finally shoots him, however, and he falls in love with Trulla, whom he woos closely, but without arousing her enthusiasm. In the face of her indifference he undertakes to rouse her with his verses, though all his friends have told him that they are worthless, and that his attack on Pope shows his brains to be addled. Still he reads them to her, and throws her into a profound sleep lasting well into the next day. Then she rushes off to her baking and uses the poems, which he has left in her lap, to line her pie and tart dishes. But the verses are so heavy that they keep out the heat and ruin the pastry. Hereupon Trulla raises such an outcry that the neighbors and Fanny rush in, and Fanny explains that Phoebus has merely taken his revenge on the nymph for her abuse of his poetry. This fails to assuage her grief and anger, and she beats him over the head with a ladle—

> And pelted him with dough along
> Low skulking through the hooting throng.

The next year Hervey became once more a subject of contemptuous ridicule in the *Journal*. In number 352 appear two epigrams, one "To the E. of B. [the Earl of Bathurst] asking who writ the verses against him"—

> You wonder who this thing has writ
> So full of fibs, so void of wit?
> Lord! never ask who thus could serve ye
> Who can it be but fibster H—.

—and the other "On the L— H—, by another hand"—

> Of charms most lady like possest,
> With not one useful talent blest;

> How handsome let your glass set forth
> And all mankind, how little worth.

The following week brought a reply to this "doggerel on
L— H—" in the form of a couplet to be found on the sign
"to a farthing pie house in Moorfields, of a couple of mon-
grel curs snarling at the moon"—

> Since I am high and ye are low
> Ye barking dogs why bark ye so.

To this the editors of the *Journal,* refusing to leave the last
word to a partisan of Hervey, appended another epigram,
the last shot they were to take at him—lines on a person
who admired Hervey's bust at the sculptor's—

> The sculptor praised,—and praising laughed,
> A pretty figure I profess,
> This is Lord Fanny's head, I guess.
> How happy, Rysbrack, are thy pains!
> The life, by G—d — it has no brains.

Aside from Hervey, Edmund Curll, the most notorious
and scandalous bookseller of the period, was the only person
against whom the *Journal* took up the cudgels in Pope's
behalf during its later years. Curll was of course an inveterate
enemy of Pope, and during the first year of the *Journal* his
name is bandied about in its columns much as are those of
other Dunciad heroes. It should be remembered, however,
that Curll was an object of almost universal reprobation;
his name appears everywhere in the satirical literature of the
period and in the other newspapers. He was apparently an
Ishmael against whom all the literary tribe were eager to
raise their hands.

During the *Journal's* exuberant and gay first months, he
was used as a peg for satire in the history of the burlesque
election of a bookseller to the Grubstreet Society. This began
with a long letter in number 4 from "Kirleus," actually written by Russel, asking for the position. The burlesque discussion which resulted in his defeat and the choice of
"Captain Gulliver" did not appear until number 15. In that
discussion Kirleus' election was opposed by Orthodoxo be-

cause of his activity in circulating lewd books, to the point
that literary filth had come to be called Curlism.[34] He had
found a friend, however, in Pruriento, who proved the great
use and value of such books to the human race as a means of
increasing offspring. Pruriento also argued that even Curll
must provide for his family. The pamphleteer members were
reported as opposed to his election as bookseller, but thought
him worthy of election to the society. Bavius himself pointed
out that probably Kirleus would refuse the post anyway,
since their bookseller would not be allowed to vend obscene
or irreligious books. Finally "Captain Gulliver" was elected,
partly it was said because of the influence of friends in
Dublin.[35]

Two months later, in number 24, appeared a notice that
Kirleus resented the unfavorable action of the society, was
publicly showing disrespect, and had even written an abusive
letter to the *Daily Journal* of May 23.[36] The editors pointed
out, however, that, after all, the proceedings had been very
much to Curll's honor, for had the society not elected him a
member? Moreover, they now voiced their approval of his
removing from his "literatory" books of antiquities, and keeping only biography, secret history, poetry, and the like. As
he looked at these volumes he ought to call to mind their real
authors and realize his obligations to the society. Certainly,
"he would find all his wealth and reputation in the world
were originally owing to his acquaintance with our members,
who were still willing to contribute to the advancement of
both."

Like all the other papers, the *Journal* made fairly frequent
reference to Curll's peculiar professional activities. Among
these, his sale of salacious literature came in for occasional
notice. For instance in number 12 one of the editors, in
commenting on a letter, says, "The readings which this

[34] It is said that N. Bailey "philologos" has failed to record "Curlism"
in his *Etymological Dictionary,* though he has been at pains to collect
most of the obscene words used by the dregs of the people.
[35] As Carruthers points out, a humorous allusion to Swift.
[36] In connection with the *Journal's* attacks on James Moore-Smythe.

learned gentleman mentions have been restored in the accurate editions of my Lord Rochester's poems, published by the learned Kirleus, which are the most compleat and are used by the venerable mothers of Drury Lane in their families."[37] More frequently he is satirized for his ventures in "secret history," that is in scandalous biography and gossip, and "last wills and testaments."[38] In number 29, the *Journal* appended to a notice of Fenton's death the remark, "I am informed that the learned Mr. Kirleus has the life of this gentleman (who was a great enemy to our society) lying by him, which he will speedily publish with some posthumous pieces of his, and according to custom, a true copy of his last will and testament." In number 167, Curll's life of Robert Wilkes, the comedian, is shown to be made up altogether of material stolen from other books, and to contain prominent advertisements of other lives, "printed for and most of them supposed to be written by Mr. E. Curll." Here too in an epigram Sarah Malcolm the murderess is consoled with the promise of having "C—l record your life in prose and rimes." Similarly in number 184, a garreteer who is hard pressed "for a little of the ready" offers for sale his literary stock in trade, "wholesale or retail—including some dozens of last wills and testaments—and lives of remarkable persons not yet dead (all these bespoke by Mr. Edm. Curl)." In number 147 also, two printer's devils discussing the state of the profession, remark on a certain printer's becoming "a much more famous biographer than Mr. Curl himself," and refer to "copies of last wills and testaments, which are always added to the Curlean Lives and Memoirs, only to swell the volume." The general opinion concerning the hacks whom Curll employed in his "literatory" to grind out all this grist appears in a brief but trenchant notice in number 13. The *Journal* quotes the news item, "On Sunday

---

[37] Note especially in 105 a list of advertisements of obscene books with comment on Curll's proprietary right in the art of ingenious advertising.

[38] The *Journal* printed in 123 a versified will, to which Russel ("M") appended advice to Curll, suggesting that he turn the wills to be published into verse on the pattern of this one.

THE ART AND MYSTERY OF PRINTING
(From Number 147)

died at his lodgings at Charing Cross, Duncan Campbell,[39] the famous dumb fortune teller," to which the *Journal* had to add, "This is the second of the writers to Mr. Curl's chaste press who has died within a small compass of time. Mr. Goodburn made his exit lately at Tyburn, and Mr. Campbell was decently interr'd not far off, at Paddington."

Various tricks of the trade of which Curll seems to have been past master are occasionally cited. He is accused in number 107 of "republishing" an old edition—"These transactions [Henley's *Oratory Transactions*] are it seems only republished, a word of great propriety invented by Mr. Curle, who scorns to put off an old edition by putting on persons a new imposition under the title of a new impression." The suspicion with which his offerings were regarded by the public receives (number 273) sarcastic comment in a catalogue of "The Lover's Auction," listing packets of love letters with the note—"E—d C—l is to take notice that he won't be admitted to be a bidder at this sale, lest the world should suspect the genuineness of these letters, if they should ever come to be printed." The same criticism is implied ironically (number 316) in a defense of Curll against the charge of imposition in connection with his publication of Pope's letters. It is said that he has always prefixed his name to every book he ever published, besides "a pretty picture of the initial letters E C curiously interwoven in cyphers," and that he cannot be charged with deceiving any one purchaser, since no one in the kingdom who sees Mr. C——'s name on a title-page but will be "from that circumstance enabled to form a perfect judgment of the book."

Pope's hatred of Curll may have accounted for the earlier attacks on him, especially in the burlesque contest for the post of Grubean bookseller. The *Journal* was also of course acting directly on Pope's account when it rushed to attack

---

[39] Famous as one of the subjects of Defoe, who had once done much to revive his languishing fame.

Curll on his publication of Pope's letters.[40] In number 275, the *Journal* together with several other papers printed Pope's advertisement:

Whereas E. C. bookseller has written to Mr. P— pretending that a person the initials of whose name are P. T. hath offered him to print a large collection of the said Mr. P—s letters, to which E. C. requires an answer: This is to certify that Mr. P— having never had, nor intending ever to have, any private correspondence with E. C., gives his answer in this manner. That he knows no such person as P. T., that he thinks no man has any such collection, that he believes the whole a forgery, and shall not trouble himself at all about it.

Nevertheless, the affair grew into a public scandal involving appeals to the courts of law and the House of Lords. The *Journal* called attention to it from time to time in news items quoted from the dailies, and in scurrilous, not to say obscene, verses abusing Curll.[41]

Finally, as a last shot, it published in 315 a letter directly charging Curll with imposition and giving cause for the ironical defense in number 316 quoted above. This letter, which is signed "D.L.", opens as follows:

The scandalous practice of prefixing the names of celebrated Writers to the mean performances of those who cannot otherwise impose their Trash on the world, has, of late, so much prevailed, that it is highly to be wished some method were discovered, whereby a stop might be put to such unfair proceedings. No one, has, I think, suffered more in this way, than the inimitable Author of the Essay on Man, nor has any one been more audaciously, or more frequently guilty of it than C—. If the considerations of his impositions on the publick be not of sufficient weight, it is methinks but an ill requital for the pleasure all men of sense must receive from Mr. P's incomparable Writings, to countenance such vile behaviour in a Book-seller. How unjustifiable is it (to speak in the mildest term) thus to prostitute an Author's name to three Volumes of Letters, the first of which Mr. P. has publickly disowned, and the two last can, on no other ground be ascribed to this Author, but the insufferable assurance of the Publisher of them.

[40] For the story of Pope's tortuous course in his intrigue to get Curll to publish these letters without seeming himself to have any hand in the transaction, see Elwin and Courthope, V, 283 ff., and also VI, 419-48. An earlier episode of much the same nature is referred to in 64. (See *ante,* p. 32.)
[41] In 290 and 293.

"D. L." then goes on to show that the second and third volumes constituted a miserable imposition on the public. These latter volumes, he says, contained practically nothing that Curll even pretended was Pope's, but were filled with thefts from various sources and with trash from Curll's own correspondence; and as for the promised fourth, that might be judged by its predecessors. He concludes:

Let now any candid person judge whether such proceedings are not deservedly cryed out against. The success of the first Volume has too much elevated this Re-publisher; yet had he again been elevated to a higher degree, and again displayed his assurance in a more proper place, it would be but giving the Devil his due; and I doubt not but he will meet with it, when he pyrates the volume Mr. P. has promised the Publick, as he has insolently declared in print he will do.

This letter is dated, "October 28, for then 'twas written, but till now mislaid"—the date of publication being January 8, 1736.

Pope's name, it is true, appeared occasionally in the *Journal's* columns throughout the whole period of its existence, but it was only during its first year or so and in the sporadic outcroppings of its original policy—the quarrels with Hervey and Curll—that it showed itself devoted especially to the poet's interests. And it should be noted that these two later quarrels, when viewed in perspective and compared both in bulk of material and in animosity with other campaigns the *Journal* was waging at the time, seem utterly insignificant. Doubtless the readers of the *Journal* soon after 1730 forgot to think of it as Pope's mouthpiece or agent. To them these later attacks on Pope's enemies probably seemed of slight consequence. As has been remarked before, Pope must have been chary of having his name coupled with that of an organ so notorious for its violence and ruthlessness. These facts are especially noteworthy in view of the well established tradition that the *Journal* was simply and merely his organ and had no other grounds for existence.

CHAPTER III

BENTLEY'S *MILTON* AND THEOBALD'S *SHAKESPEARE*

To chastise Moore-Smythe and Concanen, Pope himself came down into the arena. Both had been guilty of personal reflections against him, and their correction he took into his own hands. There can be little doubt that his resentment against Lewis Theobald as the author of *Shakespeare Restored* was as great as against a man like Moore-Smythe, but nevertheless he seems to have left him, together with Richard Bentley, who was preparing his edition of Milton when the *Journal* first appeared, to be dealt with by others.[1] One need not conclude, however, that Pope held himself entirely aloof when Bentley and Theobald were concerned; he probably had much to do with instigating and supervising the campaigns against them, especially at the beginning. It is true, of course, that these attacks lack the interest that attaches to direct contributions by Pope. On the other hand, Bentley and Theobald are far more important than men like Moore-Smythe or Concanen, who are remembered to-day only as the butts of Pope's derision. Bentley is still famous as one of the greatest of English classical scholars and critics, and Theobald as the first and one of the most distinguished critics of the text of Shakespeare.

Both Bentley and Theobald were old enemies of Pope's. They had felt the lash of his satire and had been enrolled among the Dunces as types of dogmatic, pettifogging critics, who applied yardsticks to the works of great creative artists like Milton and Shakespeare, and who judged poetry violently and without understanding or penetration. Against Theobald Pope had especial reason for disgust on account

[1] A letter on Theobald in 40 is ascribed to "A" in the *Memoirs*. Of course Theobald was included also in the list of would-be laureates of 1730, over whom Pope made merry. It should be noted that Mr. Lounsbury ascribed to Pope a number of items in these quarrels on what is apparently an assumption of internal evidence. It does not seem unreasonable to assume on the other hand that Pope thought it safer to keep somewhat aloof from the *Journal*.

of the controversy over the poet's edition of Shakespeare. Theobald had attacked Pope's work as a critic, had published *Shakespeare Restored,* and had so far presumed as to go on with a complete edition of his own which was to reveal the errors in Pope's and supersede it. He had made himself obnoxious to one who never forgot or allowed wounded pride to heal. Pope hated Theobald as an enemy in the common field of criticism, an enemy, moreover, whose success had been only too disconcerting. And for both Theobald and Bentley he felt the natural disdain of the poet for the "pedestrian" and unsympathetic critic.

In the 1730's the great Richard Bentley was an old man, but he was by no means overcome by time. He was still active and productive, and thus potentially a good object for attack. Apparently he took no formal notice of the jibes at his criticism, but in spite of this the Grubstreet writers found great delight in dissecting his emendations of Milton, which, it must be confessed, were their legitimate prey. And if they did not have the satisfaction of embroiling Bentley himself in controversy with them, they did draw answers from some of his adherents. Although the edition of Milton was not to appear for nearly two years, it was known to be in preparation, and some of Bentley's emendations seem to have been public property. The attacks in the *Journal* began as early as the ninth number, in a letter signed "Zoilus"[2] and dated Cambridge, March 1, 1730. The letter opens with words of approval for the new *Journal,* and then presents satirical emendations of Milton. For "secret" in the phrase "the secret top of Oreb" Zoilus would substitute "sacred"—actually one of Bentley's own emendations. He objects to "adamantine chains" on the ground that chains could not be made of adamant, and offers instead the reading "in Adam and in chains," which, he is assured, "frees us from all obscurity immediately." Among other suggestions, he makes one in regard to the famous line—

So thick a drop serene hath quenched their orbs,

[2] A nickname for Bentley. This letter was by Martyn ("B"), who seems to have maintained a close contact with affairs at Cambridge.

where he is of the opinion that "serene" really should modify orbs—"orbs serene"; and the passage, "And on his crest Sat Horror plumed," he emends to "Sat Horror plumb." He then concludes as he had begun—"Pray my good friend, let me have your Journals every week, for I shall not trouble myself with any other newspaper." This burlesque succeeded in drawing a *bona fide* answer and a serious defense of Bentley's critical method. In number 12, "Philarchaeus" declares, "If the Doctor whom you are pleased to call Zoilus should publish his corrections of Milton you would see how far that author is from being *clean* [*i.e.* of corruptions]." Philarchaeus declares that the Doctor has hundreds of emendations of Milton. One of these reputed changes, "swelling gourd" for "smelling gourd" *(Paradise Lost,* VII, 321) he justifies at great length and with elaborate critical apparatus. This writer receives one of Bavius' usual compliments, to the effect that he has "as well the true style as the penetration of a critic," and is assured that if he were to go on with his work he would doubtless be of great aid to Zoilus and to Theobald. After a lapse of three months a second letter from Philarchaeus appeared in number 25, listing a number of errors "of ignorant or supine transcribers or publishers" noted in a critical study of Book I of *Paradise Lost.*

These "errors" make it plain that Philarchaeus was in Bentley's confidence or was even acting as his agent,[3] for the second and third revisions were included in Bentley's edition. They have, moreover, survived in later texts. The lines emended are as follows—

I, 451—Ran purple to the sea, *supposed* with blood [Bentley: suffused]
   673—That in his womb was *hard* metallic ore [hid]
   703—With wondrous art *found out* the massy ore [founded]

[3] Philarchaeus gives the impression of being rather an affected and foolish admirer of Bentley. For instance he contributed to 49, as though it were of great significance, an anecdote about Bentley's telling three lawyers he had had to advise him that they were like the three in Terence (*Phormio,* II, 3) since after all their debate, he was less certain than ever—all this to illustrate the value of writing down striking passages in one's reading.

Philarchaeus states that he intends to submit similar discoveries in Book II, and insists, "We shall never see the moles and warts in learned authors removed unless we read *more B—ana,* and suspect that no page is free from the mistakes of ignorant transcribers, typographers, and editors, who are frequently corruptors, rather than correctors, of new editions." Maevius in his comment follows a course somewhat unusual for him, of commending an adversary's point. He gives sincere support to the last emendation, *founded* for *found out,* and even prints another change said to come "from the mouth of a very *great man.*" Nevertheless, he advises all *little men* to forbear such audacious hypercriticism. The use of such criticism, he maintains, is well demonstrated by Philarchaeus, "but to alter whole words, solely by conjecture, without the least foundation in the text, we cannot think allowable." He then becomes ironical and facetious over suggested readings for VI, 512 ff.[4] In these early attacks on textual criticism the most significant fact is perhaps the discussion of Bentley's emendations before their publication.

These specific discussions now came to an end, but were followed by a number of satirical allusions to Bentley and his criticism. A humorist from Trinity College, writing on "Sunday afternoon in chapel time," offers (number 35) an emendation "of that no less jugulating than titillating satirist, Butler." Another correspondent, aiming especially at

[4] The passage as a whole reads:—
                         [they] saw beneath   510
    The originals of Nature in their crude
    Conception; sulphurous and nitrous foam
    They found, they mingled, and, with subtle art
    Concocted and adusted; they reduced
    To blackest grain, and into store conveyed.   515
He is especially ironical over the change of 514 to
    Concocted; then with charcoal they reduced.
He also mentions one of the *clarissimi* who suggests the reading of the preceding lines—"Conception; sulphur, charc and nitrous foam / They found—." Bentley emends this passage and does insert "chark," but line 513 he reads, "They pound, they mingle, and with subtle art." These contributors evidently knew of some of Bentley's emendations, although not accurately.

Theobald, alludes (number 37) sarcastically to translators of classic poets into English prose. "Poor Milton himself," he says, "has not escaped their hands." A poor doggerel poem in the same number makes Bentley one of the aspirants for the nettle, the critic's crown, and refers to his never being in chapel.

For nearly a year hereafter Bentley suffered no annoyance, but the approaching publication of the *Milton* gave point to a renewal of the attack. One "S" in number 82, obviously with Bentley in mind, attacks the whole tribe of critics, who, he says, look chiefly for mistakes and errors and are fond of voluminous notes. By way of burlesque he concocts critical material on the first lines of *Paradise Lost,* giving various readings, and emending and collating manuscripts. He even discusses that crux, "the sacred top of Oreb." A letter from "P. Dulman" appeared the next week in answer to a query by "S" concerning lines in *Paradise Lost,* IX—

> —or to Ceres in her prime
> Yet virgin of Proserpina from Jove.

Dulman offers "Yet virgin, or Proserpina from Jove" and declares, "I think this reading yields a clear sense, is in Milton's manner, and I doubt not but it came so from his mouth."

Then in number 87, Bentley's friend Philarchaeus writes again that having had a sight of the first sheets of the new *Milton,* which Bentley had "communicated to several of his friends," he had been particularly pleased with the revision of *Paradise Lost,* I, 157—

> Fallen cherub, to be weak is miserable
> to be here
> or here to dwell

He suggests, "If you can't refuse it I hope you'll commend and applaud it. But I see you are no great friend to emendation criticism." This letter is answered in number 89 by "Philonous," who admits that while he does not know whether the emendation suggested is really Bentley's, he thinks it is, "for 'tis perfectly agreeable to his taste and spirit." He then makes it clear that the argument in support of such a change was futile nonsense.

This encounter was followed in number 98 by a burlesque from Zoilus—an emendation of *Chevy Chace*—

> They kissed them dead a thousand times
> When they were clad in clay.
> cold as clay

—on the ground that the original is not sensible, and that the northern pronunciation of *cold* is *cald,* and that the word might have been so spelled, thus deceiving a southern printer. Moreover, he declares, the new reading fits better into the whole context and gives "a fine idea of the warm affections of the wives, who so lovingly embraced and kissed their husbands, 'when they were cold as clay'." There were also several epigrams,[5] among them one in Latin, "Homerus Bentleii ab igne servatus," and another article (number 106) from Philarchaeus, combining fulsome praise of the *Grub-street Journal* with testimony to Bentley's success as an elucidator of Horace.

As soon as Bentley's new edition was actually in the hands of readers, there began a continuous, sustained attack, detailed and reasoned discussions being interlarded with satirical epigrams, burlesques, and personal allusions. The preface revealed itself to be especially vulnerable. The first shot in the controversy, a letter by "J. T."[6] in number 108, undertakes quite successfully to demonstrate the absurdity of such statements in the preface as that Milton used an amanuensis not only because he was blind but because he was "obnoxious to the government, poor, and friendless"; and that there was a "secret history" of the writing of *Paradise Lost* which accounted for the supposed errors. Another correspondent,

[5] See 99, 100, 101. These are all reprinted (unascribed) in the *Memoirs,* and the second, beginning "Did Milton's prose, O Charles, thy death defend?" is included among the nine epigrams ascribed to Pope by modern editors.

[6] Probably Russel, who sometimes, according to the *Memoirs,* used these initials as a signature. This letter, however, is not reprinted in the *Memoirs.*

"A. Z.," in number 113, which was devoted almost entirely to the *Milton,* continues the attack on the preface. To prove the interfering hand of an editor, Bentley had relied on four passages which are changed from satisfactory readings in the first edition to what he considered unsatisfactory ones in the second. A. Z. contends, however, that these changes are desirable; he maintains that they conform to their Biblical originals and to the general sense of their context. In one case Bentley cites, as evidence of corruption of the text, a necessary scansion of Michael in three syllables, claiming that Milton used it as a dissyllable, an argument which A. Z. refutes quite adequately by listing a number of lines where Michael, as well as Uriel, Raphael, and other similar names, are trisyllabic.[7] That the *Journal's* sarcastic temper was occasionally impartial is indicated by an editorial comment. A. Z. prefaces his refutation of Bentley with the statement that he has read no remarks on the *Milton* but those in the *Journal,* and that as he is engaged in making some himself he "avoids being led into other men's notions"—a statement which draws from the editor the dry remark that after he has written his ideas down he would do well to compare them with other people's. This number also contains a second communication from J. T.,[8] declaring that his arguments in number 108, though they have been answered, have not been refuted. In this letter he refers to *Milton Restored,*[9] which he had evidently seen since his letter in number 108, as the

[7] The *Journal* subjoins a note to A. Z.'s letter saying that various other correspondents have pointed out the fact that Michael is often used as three syllables. In "Pegasus in Grubstreet" the editor mentions various other letters received regarding the Milton controversy and speaks of having "completed what we thought sufficient to overthrow the greatest part of the Doctor's preface; the foundation upon which all his conjectural emendations are built. As we design to go through the whole poem in a methodical manner, we desire our ingenious and learned correspondents to make their observations on the twelve books in their proper order, and not to proceed in a desultory manner, forward and backward, from one to another."

[8] Russel again?

[9] *Milton Restored and Bentley Deposed* (1732). In this letter, J. T. mistakenly takes Bentley to task for dating the first edition of *Paradise Lost* 1667 instead of 1669. The earlier date is of course correct, as A. Z. noted in 116.

source of some of his present argument. According to him the contention that Milton was "poor, friendless, and obnoxious to the government" he had so answered as to contradict it and destroy its usefulness. Moreover, the statement that *Paradise Lost* was sold to a *poor* printer was false; it was sold to Simons, who was well-to-do. Bentley's statement that Milton never read what he had dictated was likewise false; for how could he have made the changes which Bentley asserts that he made in the second edition if the poem had not been read over to him? In the same way, considering Bentley's argument that the later poems were correct because the poet was in good standing and had a good printer, J. T. asks why Milton did not employ a good printer and supervisor for the second edition of *Paradise Lost,* which appeared in 1674, after *Paradise Regained* in 1671? Still another damaging assault on Bentley's preface was made in number 116 by A. Z. Bentley had remarked, ". . . this poem has for sixty years time passed upon the whole nation for a perfect, absolute, faultless composition." A. Z., however, recalls Addison's criticisms of Milton in the *Spectator,* and adds that Bentley quotes them several times. He also points out that Bentley will base an argument on the fact that Milton aimed rather at "strong expression than flowing numbers," whereas in another place it suits him better to argue on the basis of Milton's genius for music. He then concludes with caustic remarks on the pretension of a man who will undertake to rebuild a whole poem. This, he says, will not increase Milton's fame, and if Bentley's end is to increase his own as a poet (Bentley had declared that under his hand the poem would be "wrought up to its highest perfection") he might better write original poetry.

For a time hereafter the controversy lapsed almost entirely into satire and personality, but it came back at last in number 131 to serious consideration of Bentley's work. In a lengthy essay it is clearly shown that many typical emendations in Book I had no foundation except in Bentley's own peculiar taste, and were not needed to improve or clarify the sense. In

some cases, as "the secret top of Oreb," which had been frequently discussed, the writer shows that the original word is
justified by the circumstances of its use or by implication
from biblical passages. Most of the first page of number 137
is also devoted to an analysis of emendations, which are
occasionally treated humorously. For instance, of Bentley's
emendation of "night-foundered" to "nigh-foundered" (I,
204), "Mr. Conundrum" remarks, "The critic in this place
was certainly nigh-foundered, if not night-foundered." The
weakness of Bentley's reliance on such arbitrary reasons for
emending as that a certain passage "does not reach up to our
author's usual exactness" is also illustrated. Bavius' expressed
intention of going through all twelve books, was, however,
never carried out, probably a fortunate circumstance for the
Journal. A further discussion of instances by Bavius himself
in number 146 proved to be the last installment of this sort
which the *Journal* published.

This matter, for the most part direct and serious in its
point of view, was enlivened and relieved throughout its
whole course by a good deal of satirical humor, ranging from
pure personality to the more effective method of parody and
burlesque. Personal animosity crept into the controversy
almost at once. In number 110, Bentley and his supporter
Philarchaeus were both savagely mauled, for the sake of
Horace, by a correspondent signing himself Horatianus.
Bentley is declared to be a murderer of Horace as well as a
violator of Milton, and Philarchaeus is scornfully convicted
of callowness and affectation, by his allusions to his friends'
country-houses, his condescending praise of the *Grub-street
Journal,* his silly pretense of delight in Horace (in number
106), and his fondness for French phrases and classic citations. As for his emendations of Horace, it is said, he would
realize, if he knew any Latin, that the lines needed no emendation. Bavius apparently saw the possibility of an interesting diversion here, for he appended footnotes which seem, at
least, impartial, and encouraged both correspondents to continue their quarrel—"their arguments shall be presented to
the public in this paper with the greatest impartiality."

Various correspondents brought up the question of Bentley's fitness in the matter of poetic temperament to undertake such a labor as the present one. In connection with "A. Z.'s" strictures in number 116 on Bentley's assumption of his own poetic taste and his ability to raise *Paradise Lost* "to its highest perfection" appeared an epigram in the same vein. Bentley had somewhat smugly applied to himself in his preface Vergil's lines referring to himself as a poet in his friends' esteem—

> —Sunt mihi carmina; me quoque dicunt
> Vatem pastores; sed non ego credulus illis.

Upon which one of the "Grubs" remarks quite aptly—

> How could vile sycophants contrive
> A lie so gross to raise;
> Which even B——y can't believe
> Tho spoke in his own praise.

Bavius (Russel) followed the same line of attack in number 118. He compares statements from Fenton's edition of 1730 with Bentley's, remarking that Fenton is "at least as famous for his poetical genius as Dr. Bentley." He notices Bentley's declaration that forty years before he would have suppressed these notes, fearing for his rising fortune, and is of the opinion that it would have been wiser even for a person of Bentley's mature age to have done so, especially in view of the confessedly hasty nature of the work, which Bentley had sent to press as soon as it was written. Finally, he declares that Bentley is "a very learned critic, but never imagined to be a poet," that he has "acted more like a pedagogue than a critic," and has treated "the heroic poem of the great Milton like the exercise of a schoolboy." To this article is appended a letter from Zoilus, which, as Bavius points out, reveals by burlesque the ease as well as the futility of applying Bentley's method to any poem. Zoilus takes Book IV, lines 677 ff. and writes a note on them *more Bentleiano*—

'Millions of spiritual creatures walk the earth'—Indeed! Millions! so many could not walk together in Paradise, which the author must mean by earth, unless 'gods met gods, and jostled in the dark.'

Besides, so many singers would quite deafen Adam and Eve, or else deprive them of all sleep and distract them. Read it, therefore, as the author gave it, *Several.*

Again, Bavius made light of Bentley's poetic endowments in an epigram in number 122, "A word to Mr. Conundrum; Quaere, whether Dr. Bentley's Paradise Lost would not be Milton's Paradise Regained."

The more purely personal side of the attack was stressed again in two letters by "A. Z." in number 125, dated April 13, and April 28, on Bentley's vainglorious statement that he had written the notes on Milton *ex tempore.* This boasting, it was said, was of course merely for Bentley's own glory and the catching of compliments, although it made little difference, as Bentley was so cocksure that he would never revise a first impression anyway. It might, however, be asserted on the authority of Dr. Ashenhurst that Bentley had told as much as eight or nine years before of making notes on Milton. A. Z. also turns spitefully upon Bentley and asks without much pertinence why the critic, who had been favored so highly by Church and State, should extol the morality of Milton, who was so bitter an enemy to them. A. Z.'s second letter, dated April 28, is a much less effective piece of criticism. Here he maintains that Bentley has evoked the idea of an editor merely to save himself from censure; he wished to attack the poem and thought it less dangerous to lay its faults on an editor who was a mere phantom than on Milton himself. He thinks that all the violent language Bentley applies to the editor should recoil upon himself, and recalls that Bentley did much the same thing in a paper war of 1721, when he attacked Dr. Colbatch for a book known to be written by Dr. Middleton, and expressed himself in billingsgate so violent that it was censured by the University authorities. A personal animus against Bentley and a desire to blow old quarrels into flame is also made evident in a clumsy epigram published in this same issue in allusion to the ancient controversy between Bentley and Boyle.

Toward the end the controversy tapered off with a few

scattered epigrams, verses, and short parodies or burlesques. The reason for an emendation of *bold* to *old* in I, 127, was explained (number 137) by a similar emendation of "the learned Johnstonus" in *The Ode of Tom Bostock,* and the same writer suggests an emendation of *Chevy Chace,* increasing "exactness of phrase," and revising the rime to fit—

> A bow he had bent in his hand
> Made of a trusty tree [yew]
> An arrow of a cloth yard long
> Full to the head drew he [he drew]

In number 153 an instance is cited of three lines in a manuscript turning out to be merely instructions of a transcriber to a printer, and not, as had been supposed, a part of the text. Upon this there is the comment, "The impertinence and ignorance of amanuenses, hackney writers and printers, etc., are intolerable. The learned Dr. Bentley has justly exposed them in his famous edition of Milton."

This was the last shot in the quarrel, but one gets now and again in later issues an echo of it. In number 229, in an attack on Theobald's *Shakespeare,* Bavius refers to "Bentley's (the greatest literal critic now alive) pretended matters of fact [and his] extraordinary liberties" with Milton. A writer calling himself "Torrentius" in a discussion of emendations suggested for a difficult bit of Horace (number 266) refers to "the ornate manner of the operose Bentley," and "B. T." in number 329 praises Bentley's emendations of the classics and takes his part against Bishop Hoadley, who called the critic a blockhead. He might be "proud, conceited, and tyrannical," but certainly he was not a blockhead.

The attacks on Bentley are much more successful than those on Theobald, for obvious reasons. Bentley brought forth a widely heralded edition of Milton devised on absolutely false principles and crying to be exposed. It was exactly the sort of production for which the *Grub-street Journal* sought, and the editors fell upon it with delight as a perfect object for criticism by methods varying from direct frontal attack, as in the examination of the preface and specific emendations, to burlesque and parody. And to these the editors added, as was their fashion, the weapon of personal attack, although the ease with which other methods could be applied made resort to this one less necessary and less frequent than usual. Where abuse of the book itself was so easy, and moreover so legitimate, why turn to the author himself? It should be noted, however, that the *Journal* and its correspondents were by no means alone in recognizing the weaknesses of Bentley's edition. A modern bibliography[10] of Bentley lists seven contemporary pamphlets exposing its errors or satirizing it. One of these, entitled *A Review of the Text of Milton's Paradise Lost. In which the chief of Dr. Bentley's emendations are considered,* runs to two hundred and eighty-seven pages of systematic analysis and is, as a matter of fact, quoted freely by Bavius in his remarks on the *Milton.* When one remembers the arbitrary principles on which Bentley worked, and grasps the implications inherent in such a remark of his as that reason and good sense were worth to an editor more than a hundred manuscripts, it is not surprising that his hostile brethren found his *Milton* such a happy hunting ground.

In Theobald's case, on the contrary, the work the *Journal* would have liked to demolish was too sound and staunch. Theobald's *Shakespeare* was quite a different story from Bentley's *Milton.* Hence, the attack upon Theobald, which was essential for Pope's sake and because of Theobald's old alignment with the Dunces, was forced into more personal channels, and was thus much less pointed and damaging than had been the one on Bentley.

The *Journal's* first allusion to Theobald's *Shakespeare* came in Philarchaeus' first letter in number 12, where, in dealing with Bentley and Milton, the writer turns to a general consideration of literal criticism. He says that apparently Shakespeare is in a worse condition and fuller of false readings than any of the ancients, judging from the work of

[10] A. T. Bartholomew and J. W. Clark, *A Bibliography of Richard Bentley, D.D.,* 1908. Note also J. W. Mackail's Warton Lecture, *Bentley's Milton* (1924), in *Proceedings of the British Academy,* vol. XI.

Pope and Theobald. "If there was half as much nonsense and absurdity in Aristophanes or Sophocles as is yet to be found after all Pope's and Theobald's labors in almost every page of Shakespeare, I am sure they would be far from deserving the admiration and praises they have had for so many ages." Moreover, not only Shakespeare, Milton, and Waller, but "all our best poets are full of false lections." Bavius proposes that since things are so desperate, this writer go on with his criticism and help Zoilus (Bentley) with Milton, Theobald with Shakespeare, and Maevius with Waller, and let it be seen how these editions would surpass "those of our inveterate enemies, Mr. Pope and Mr. Fenton, who have injuriously encroached upon a province which has by a prescription time out of mind, peculiarly belonged to the gentlemen of our society."

In number 37 appears a letter signed "B. T." which Bavius prints in spite of a declared lack of agreement with its author. "B. T.", who later joined the forces against Bentley, attacks prose translations of the classics and says he hears that Theobald has in hand a translation of Aeschylus, in spite of the failure of his *Aristophanes,* "and although he has peoples' money in his pocket for his emendations of Shakespeare.— But I ought to add, indeed," he continues, and at this point one imagines Bavius parting company with him, "that I hear he intends to give us the text of Shakespeare as well as notes, as soon as he can bring matters to bear; a work his very enemies will, I believe, allow him to be capable of." The same charge of accepting subscriptions and making no returns is repeated in number 40 in a burlesque illiterate letter probably by Pope himself.[11] During the contest for the laureateship which took place in the autumn of 1730 following Eusden's death, frequent sarcastic allusions were made to Theobald's poetic aspirations, and his name was coupled with those of the other poetasters who were considered ambitious of the laurel—such men as Welsted, Cook, Stephen Duck, and James Moore-Smythe. This whole group was frequently

[11] Ascribed to "A."

subjected to the contemptuous satire of Bavius, as well as to cutting epigrams probably by Pope.

Upon the publication of his *Shakespeare,* Theobald of course brought upon himself more individual attention, although doubtless not so much as the *Journal* would have liked to pay him, considering the importance of his work and his direct rivalry with Pope. The comparatively small amount which the *Journal* published and its obvious difficulty in finding specific points that were really vulnerable bear sufficient witness to the difference in quality between this work and Bentley's. The first attack came from "A. H."—possibly Aaron Hill[12]—in number 143, a sarcastic criticism of two emendations, *Venus and Adonis,* Stanza 142:

> Soothing the humor of fantastic wits [Theobald: wights]

and *Titus Andronicus,* Act II, final scene:

> And might not gain so great an happiness
> As half thy love. [Theobald: have thy love].[13]

A. H. takes occasion to refer to "the learned and never enough admired Mr. L. T.," and ends,

Upon mentioning these two emendations to Mr. Conundrum he said he feared Mr. T. was but a half-witted critic, and immediately repeated two lines from Harlequin Horace. At more leisure I perhaps may examine this emendator a little farther; at present (to use his own words) upon a careful perusal of his criticisms, I dare warrant that any person of moderate sagacity may furnish out a large crop of errors.[14]

Whatever the truth of the last statement, the "large crop of errors" was never furnished out for the *Grub-street Journal.* As a matter of fact, this represented the only effort of the *Journal* to pick flaws in Theobald's emendations of Shakespeare.

[12] Later, during the quarrel with the *Prompter,* Hill is spoken of as a former contributor.
[13] The second of these emendations seems to have been accepted by modern editors; the first has not.
[14] For the two lines alluded to, see *Harlequin Horace,* p. 12:
Theobald in mail complete of dullness clad
Half bard, half puppet man, half-fool, half-mad.

Finding the emendations too difficult to deal with, Theobald's critics sought a more vulnerable point of approach in his introductory essay defending the general principles of verbal criticism. Here he had quite needlessly cited eight classic passages where the method might usefully be applied.[15] An anonymous writer in number 220, after slighting remarks on emendation in general and the presumption of critics who referred to their work as "Bentley's Horace," or "Theobald's Shakespeare," proceeded to criticise one of Theobald's typical emendations in his preface, the change of σῶμα to ὄμμα in a passage from Platonius.[16] The writer attacks this emendation, introduces pictures of Greek masks (the subject of the passage), and suggests instead, σόμα a reading which he maintains makes the passage clear. He concludes, "Let not Mr. Theobald say (as critics of his rank are very jealous) that this is making a face at him [a pun on the subject of masks] for we protest it is no way intended for a picture of Mr. Theobald, but only of

[15] Theobald himself admitted that he inserted them to support his reputation as a scholar. See Jones, *Lewis Theobald,* 169.

[16] Theobald's preface (p. lv) reads as follows: "The author is saying, that, in the old Comedy, the Masks were made so nearly to resemble the Persons to be satirized, that before the Actor spoke a Word, it was known whom he was to personate. But, in the New Comedy, when Athens was conquered by the Macedonians, and the Poets were fearful lest their Masks should be construed to resemble any of their New Governors, they formed them so preposterously as only to move Laughter; ὁρῶμεν γοῦν (says He) τὰς ὀφρῦς ἐν τοῖς σορπώποις τοῦ Μενάνδρου κωμωδίας ὁποίας ἔχει, καὶ ὅπως ἐξεστραμμένον τὸ ΣΩ͂ΜΑ καὶ οὐδὲ κατ᾽ ἀνθρώπων φύσιν. "We see therefore what strange Eyebrows there are to the Masks used in Menander's Comedies; and how the Body is distorted, and unlike any human Creature alive." But the Author, 'tis evident, is speaking abstractedly of Masks; and what Reference has the Distortion of the Body to the Look of a Visor? I am satisfied, Platonius wrote; καὶ ὅπως ἐξεστραμμένον τὸ ̈OMMA: i.e. "and how the Eyes were goggled and distorted." This is to the Purpose of his Subject: and Jul. Pollux, in describing the Comic Masques, speaks of some that had ΣΤΡΕΒΛΟΝ τὸ ̈OMMA : Others, that were ΔΙΑ͂ΣΤΡΟΦΟΙ τὴν ̈OΨIN. *Perversis oculis,* as Cicero calls them, speaking of Roscius." The word σόμα, suggested by the writer in 220, does not appear in the standard dictionaries of either classical or Byzantine Greek. It might be thought that he had στόμα in mind, but he makes it clear that he means σόμα.

his criticisms." Another correspondent, "N. A.", contributed to number 229 a much fairer letter—"The late edition of Shakespeare is such an one as, I think, will give the highest pleasure to all lovers of that poet; and at the same time must forever silence all the little wits who abuse literal criticism." He is of the opinion that Theobald has shown the necessity for this sort of work, although he might have spared the Greek instances in the preface, which are occasionally inaccurate. In support of this statement he points out weaknesses in Theobald's argument for one of his emendations in the carved inscription on a Greek votive tablet.[17] "Upon the whole I think Mr. T. had not the least occasion to call in assistance from Greece in order to maintain the title he so incontestably possesses of the best English critic." The *Journal* printed this letter in spite of its favorable attitude toward Theobald, but Bavius added a comment which as far as possible minimized any satisfaction Theobald might draw from it. He asserted that Bentley was doubtless the greatest literal critic living, and that his method with *Paradise Lost* had been shown to be absolutely false. Theobald had notwithstanding attempted to excuse him by giving a wrong account of his aim and purpose, and had then followed his example. Bavius then lit upon Theobald's eight "flagrant instances" from the Greek and declared that all but three of them could be exploded, and that even those might upon close examination suffer the same fate. He also called Theobald to book for treating manuscript and carved inscriptions in the same way, and for failing to consult the antiquarians, Spon and Chishull, who were authorities on such matters. This comment by Bavius is perhaps most noteworthy for its seriousness; from beginning to end there is no hint of satire. Moreover, it drew an answer signed "Lewis Theobald," an unusual instance in a paper which conducted literary and other quarrels anonymously or under pseudonyms, and whose adversaries rarely answered directly and openly, preferring

[17] Theobald alluded to the controversy over the Greek inscription in two letters to Warburton dated July 11 and August 27, 1734. See Jones, *Lewis Theobald*, pp. 330, 333.

rather to make use of some rival publication, and in any case to withhold their own names. Theobald admitted errors in regard to the votive tablet, but explained fully and satisfactorily how he came to fall into them.[18] He then gave "N. A." some information of which the latter was ignorant, likewise telling Bavius of his intention and desire to submit another letter on the emendation ὄμμα. Theobald's tone in this letter is distinctly unpleasant. He had clearly the better of the argument, but while he grudgingly admitted N. A.'s courtesy, he was at the same time offensive, seeming to be most interested in proving lapses on the part of his opponents. Toward Bavius this attitude was perhaps justified, but N. A. had treated him with the utmost consideration. In fact, Theobald's rudeness was resented by N. A., who complained of it in "Pegasus in Grub-street" in number 234. Bavius, however, who had long been an ardent and aggressive wrangler, was doubtless untouched by Theobald's retorts. He merely turns to a side issue, declaring—

I could not but wonder, that after so long a publication of our Journal this new and learned correspondent should mistake in the address of the preceding letter, directing it to the *author* of the Grub-street Journal, as if this paper were written by any one particular author. And I am apt to suspect that Mr. T. designed it as a slight toward me by way of revenge, for my supposed spleen to him, of which he unjustly complains. It is true that this paper *has been the vehicle* for several tho not *all reflections levelled at him.*[19]

Bavius' further remarks are somewhat conciliatory. He disavows spleen toward Theobald and promises to print any letters as ingenuous as this last. He cannot, however, resist the temptation to point out lapses in Theobald's Latin, as well as what he deems a wrong account of the word *Bosporus.* In number 234 Theobald's promised defense of ὄμμα was forthcoming with an overwhelming flood of citations to show that the passage in question involved the idiomatic use of the singular *eye* for *eyes,* a use common in Greek, Latin, and English. He also refers with utmost scorn to his op-

[18] See Jones, *Lewis Theobald,* p. 199.
[19] Theobald's phrases.

ponent's sneers at his work as "a masterpiece of trifling and vanity." Theobald's argument here was too strong for Bavius to refute, although he made the attempt.

Thus the only criticism which the *Journal* was able to advance against Theobald's *Shakespeare* lay in an assault upon two single emendations, and upon the classical passages used as illustrations in his preface. And in his defence of the latter, Theobald forced Bavius to meet him with direct and serious criticism, and then won a conclusive victory. In fair fight upon the current issue the *Journal* had little success.

The only point indeed where the *Journal* had any success at all was in a sly, humorous note attached to an advertisement in number 218 of *Verbal Criticism, An Epistle to Mr. Pope occasioned by Theobald's Shakespeare and Bentley's Milton*. In this advertisement Lawton Gilliver, the publisher of the poem, and likewise of the *Journal* itself (according to Lounsbury, he was forced by Pope to pay Mallet twenty guineas for the poem) after taking great praise to himself for mentioning "what is said in dispraise" of a piece he was publishing, is made to "own ingenuously to the town" that Theobald had declared in the preface to his *Shakespeare* that "he could see for his part no manner of conceit, wit, or joke in the poem here advertised." This was followed the next week (number 219) by a letter to Mr. Bavius signed by Gilliver:

Though it may seem presumption in me who am only a seller of books, to invade the high province of one who says he is a restorer of them, yet when Mr. Theobald finds that I do it more out of friendship to him than to myself perhaps he will treat me more mercifully than he does the author of a late epistle on Verbal Criticism by me printed. That Epistle indeed has put him grievously out of temper, insomuch that he affirms positively the author is a baboon, a pedlar, and that his wit is as thick as Tewkesbury mustard.

This is then elaborated with a dissertation on *Tewkesbury Mustard* with learned allusion to support an emendation to *custard*. It was only in this lighter vein that the *Journal's* attacks on Theobald had much success.[20]

[20] Jones in *Lewis Theobald*, p. 194, n. 3, inadvertently speaks of this letter as signed by Mallet instead of Gilliver. Lounsbury (*First Editors*

It was not for Russel and his associates to overcome
Theobald as a critic. They were able, however, to find two
weak spots in his armor. During the contest for the laureateship in 1730, Theobald's aspiration to the laurel had subjected him to the sarcasms of Bavius and even Pope himself in a series of notes and epigrams which cut much deeper
and keener than anything that could be said of his *Shakespeare.*[21] The *Journal* also made some capital of Theobald's
unfortunate declaration that he had discovered a lost play
by Shakespeare, *The Double Falsehood.* In number 97, the
Journal, which somewhat earlier had been persecuting
James Moore-Smythe, whom it had "convicted of death,"
drew up a bill concerning the writings of all those similarly
"convicted." In this bill was inserted the clause "Provided
nothing shall be construed to prejudice L. T— Esq. . . .
in any right or title which he may have, or pretend to have,
of affixing the name of William Shakespeare . . . to any
book, pamphlet, play, or poem hereafter to be by him . . .
devised." In the next issue the same charge is imputed again
in a passage from *Modern Poets*—

> See T— leaves the lawyer's gainful train
> To wrack with poetry his tortured brain.
> Fired, or not fired, to write resolves with rage
> And constant pores o'er Shakespeare's sacred page.
> Then starting cries—I something will be thought
> I'll write—then—boldly swears 'twas Shakespeare wrote.
> Strange! he in poetry no forgery fears
> That knows so well in law he'd lose his ears.[22]

These campaigns against Bentley and Theobald represent
the *Grub-street Journal's* two chief excursions into the field
of textual criticism. In both are to be discovered its typical
personal prejudices in favor of Pope and against his enemies.

---

of Shakespeare, p. 448), says it was "manifestly written by Pope, with
the possible assistance of Mallet, though the wit displayed in it did not
require a conjunction of the abilities of the two."

[21] See *ante,* Chapter ii.

[22] For the authorship of *The Double Falsehood,* see Lounsbury, pp.
145 ff. and Jones, *Lewis Theobald,* pp. 101 ff. The authorship is doubtful;
it is almost certainly not by Theobald himself, but has been ascribed to
Shirley and Massinger.

They doubtless underlie and motivate all the argument and discussion. In the criticism of Theobald's *Shakespeare,* there is unfortunately little to be found but a futile animosity.[23] In Bentley's *Milton* on the other hand the editors lit upon a work not unworthy of their treatment, and in spite of motives which were probably not too noble, they may fairly be said to have performed a desirable work of the sort for which the paper was ostensibly and legitimately intended.

[23] In 227 appears the prose description of the literary garretteer which was to suggest Hogarth's famous plate, *The Distressed Poet,* two years later. It has been conjectured that Hogarth's picture, and hence this passage in the *Journal* also, were attacks on Theobald, but Mr. R. H. Griffith, who has discussed the point at length thinks it doubtful, since at this time Theobald was known much less as poet than critic, and was by no means poverty-stricken. (See *The Manly Anniversary Studies in Language and Literature,* Chicago, 1923, p. 190.)

CHAPTER IV

QUARRELS WITH OTHER PERIODICALS

The *Grub-street Journal* was an Ishmael among its brethren, the other periodicals. Its comments on them were continuous, and never friendly or conciliatory. In fact, it elected most of their editors or authors members of the Grubstreet Society, thus identifying and linking them with Pope's Dunces. For instance (in number 74) several members are accused of absenting themselves from meeting, and even abusing "our Society," among others O[sbor]ne, W[alsingha]m, the Orator and the [Weekly] *Register*. Of the last the writer declares, "But we could not but be surprised at the desertion of our Register no longer ago than last Saturday; who he [*sic*] had made so many repeated declarations that he would never engage in the petulance of party." In number 46 it replied in doggerel verse to an attack in *Fog's Journal,* and then, having waited in vain for *Fog's* to answer, published three weeks later verses which it suggested might have been used by its opponent. Hardly a number lacks a more or less damaging allusion to a rival among the dailies and weeklies, and with several of them the *Journal* carried on pitched battles of major importance. Nothing gave it greater pleasure than to predict the approaching death of another newspaper, or to record that event when it actually occurred. For instance, as early as number 8 one may read, "Last Wednesday night died at his lodgings in the Old Bailey, the Morning Post, a painful member of our society. He was a young gentleman naturally of a weak and crazy constitution." His history is sketched and his various names reported. The cause of his death is said to have been a combination of atrophy and consumption, and toward the end, it is declared, he grew delirious and spoke in Welsh,—this in allusion, if one is to judge from a quotation, to a case of bad "pieing" by a compositor.

In the next number, 9, is noticed in a similar style the death of the *Post Man,* who had been given up to "riddles and cramp questions" and whose "sedentary life soon hurried him to his grave." What seems to be the implied decease of the *Weekly Medley* is reported in number 27, where that paper is advertised as "strayed"; ". . . he speaks broken English interlarded with French and Latin, and frequently tags the ends of his sentences with rime."[1] A circumstantial account is also given (number 382) of the death of the *Daily Journal:* He had grown old and could no longer find his way to coffee houses. Hence he made an arrangement with the *Prompter,* who was very lame, that they should make use of each other's eyes and legs. But finally the *Prompter* died of a bad fall, and his place was taken by a cousin, the *Occasional Prompter,* who was too heavy to carry well, and also suffered a fatal fall which was the end of both. In one issue, number 288, were joyfully recorded the deaths of four colleagues; following obituary verses by Maevius on the *Bee,* came the note :—"The last week proved fatal to the offspring of some of our most eminent members, the Free Briton dying on Monday and the London Journal and Daily Courant on Saturday." On occasion the *Journal* sardonically took up the duties of these defunct brethren; witness the announcement in number 39 that the *Weekly Medley,* which had been publishing a weekly list of new books, "having vanished away instantaneously," the *Journal* would undertake the task, "being convinced of the usefulness of that design."

The most fertile ground for attack on the papers lay in their inaccurate and misleading, not to say false, reporting of news. As a writer calling himself "Histrio-Apris" remarks in number 317, "It is a distinguishing mark of news

---

[1] A foot note in the *Memoirs* states that the *Medley* lasted a year and a half, and that it began with two columns in English and two in French, but finally changed to three of English. In numbers 29 and 30 the *Medley* is made to answer, explaining that "he" had been crippled by a Grubean, "J. Ninny Hammer, alias J. R." [James Ralph]. This letter is answered by Bavius, who says the Society knows the *Medley* is dead; hence his letter must be forgery.

writers to exceed their subject; they by a peculiar felicity even

De magnis majora loquuntur.

Their chief excellence, he maintains, lies in fiction, and they show great skill in working up the truth with embellishments and surprising circumstances. In practically every issue the Grubstreet editors were at pains to insert at least one collation of various reports of a given bit of news. The divergence thus illustrated is ridiculous in the extreme. A correspondent in number 182, "Democritus," submits a burlesque news column divided into domestic news, diseases, casualties, imports, exports, and foreign news—a mass of items ranging from the fantastic to the commonplace and unimportant. In number 184, Bavius himself comments at length on the newspapers. They are, he says,

remarkable, and particularly those which make their appearance every morning in the week except on Sundays, and yield a most grateful entertainment to the curious. These five papers, like five stately fountains, are continually pouring out streams of fresh occurrences which from time to time quench that ardent thirst after news which still returns and inflames a true British palate. And as the sources from whence these occurrences flow are secret and hidden like the springs upon which fountains are erected, so they are likewise as inexhaustible as those; in both which respects the justness of the comparison is still more conspicuously evident.

He analyzes the "domestic advices," "some of which are written more in the prophetic than historical style," so that what should constitute one item, "may furnish out a decent paragraph . . . for two or three days together," and help the necessary multiplication of articles.

He also describes in numbers 187 and 188 the various styles of reporting. To illustrate the frequently pretentious manner of the journals, he submits a list of high flown phrases from the *London Journal* to show that "the dignity of the subject can warm the coolest reasoner and insensibly elevate the gravest prose into the most rational, because unriming poetry." It is their untrustworthiness and irresponsibility, however, that he finds most reprehensible. He speaks of the "positive style," which he says needs no explanation, and the "dubious style," indicated by the openings, *We hear, We are informed, It is said,* and so forth,—useful in case of news which turns out later to be false or is known at the time to be false, but which the writer wishes the public to hear. Experienced readers, he suggests, never really believe such items.[2]

The universal carelessness in the reporting of deaths makes sport for a clever satirist in the Pegasus column in number 260:

> There is no privilege in which the authors of our daily and weekly papers may more justly glory than that of the power of life and death. Whom they will they send to the grave, and whom they will they restore to life again. . . . The Archbishop of Canterbury, who, God be thanked, is still living, has often with pleasure and surprise read in these papers the account of his own death.

The writer speaks of the innumerable generals and other notables killed off and then resuscitated by the papers, and recalls with glee how Bickerstaff inhumanly dispatched "poor Partridge untimely into the other world, in spite of his teeth and his own assertions to the contrary, solemnly protesting that he was not only alive some time after, but even at that very time when the advertisement of his decease was published." It then transpires that the immediate occasion of the satire was an announcement in the *Daily Post-Boy* and the *Daily Advertiser* that Dr. Cockburn (actually, the late Dr. Cockburn) was to preach before royalty. The reverend gentlemen had also been revived by the *Courant* as Coobourn, and with a strange living. The royal preacher was in reality the Rev. Dr. Cobden, and—"It is great pity but he [Dr. Cockburn] should now be suffered to sleep quietly in his grave."

As late as number 401, the *Journal* continued to harp on the irresponsibility of news writers. In reference to a notice that Joshua Ward would devote two "public days" at his

---

[2] Later, in the preface to the *Memoirs,* he says that newsgatherers were paid by space for news, that their foreign news was full of errors in translations, and that "scarce one article of domestic news in ten but what is false, either in whole or in part."

hospital at Pimlico to the dispensing of medicine to the poor, the *Journal* asserts sarcastically that this is a likely story, since the patients at the hospital had all been turned out two months before, and the building closed. Similarly of a notice that a monument in the Abbey had fallen: "The invention or credulity of the collectors of news is very great. There is not the least truth in any part of this account; but it is like the story of the person's lying all night with his bowels out, whom the crows hovered round to devour, inserted in the Daily Advertiser, August 22."

Intermingled with these frequent sarcasms on the exaggeration and falsities of the news writers, are also comments on the triviality and silliness of much of the news. The bulk of the news, in fact, consisted on the one hand of murders, suicides, and other crimes of violence reported with as many horrible details as the writer could discover or imagine, and on the other of the activities of the socially great presented in minute detail and with the most deferential formality. In number 190 one finds an analysis of this latter category.

First, it is said, come the doings of the royal family, whether they are dining at home or abroad, whether they walk, ride, or go on the water. Such news is valuable since it informs the public that the royal family is in health, and also since it gives entertainment to those of low station. Second come the activities of the nobility; their entertainments, births, deaths, and comings to town. At first glance such matter may not seem important, but it is very useful to tradesmen, who thus know the proper time to solicit custom or the payment of bills. In the third place, (and with the most sarcasm) one finds preferments in church and state. Thus the public sees how well the younger sons of gentry and nobility are provided for, as well as the dependents of some few great men, and learns of the elevation of men of great parts, never heard of before.

For the general reader, the news items are probably the most interesting section of the *Journal*. A large proportion of them were chosen for their sensational interest, and the lurid cast they give to life in the 1730's is more than romantic. The callousness, not to say the brutality, of the age is reflected in the gusto with which all the details of horrible accidents, suicides, and crimes are spread abroad for the edification of the public. Doubtless such material was reprinted in the *Journal* for its intrinsic value in attracting readers. An item in number 10, for instance, which is keyed no higher in its pitch of horror than others to be found in almost any issue, would surely have yellow journalistic value in any age, though it could not ordinarily be so vividly presented. A surgeon having opened a vein in what was thought to be a dead body, and having carelessly left it open, "The next day he [the corpse] was found really dead, but with his legs drawn up, and a cold sweat on his face, with a large quantity of blood in his coffin."

Such crude horror was collected in all the dailies; the chief distinction in the *Journal's* news columns lies in the collation of news items, for sarcastic comment on which Russel's vitriolic pen was unusually well fitted.[3] Indeed, the cold cynicism of many of these collations and notes is, at first anyway, appalling. Would it be possible for instance for a news writer in any later age to report the death of a child, and then add calmly, as the *Journal* does in number 3, "This is the very child that was said to have died above a month ago; and was buried in the same grave with his mother, by several newspapers"? Or to remark (number 349) upon the death of twenty-five people in Edinburgh, poisoned by ratsbane in bread,—"They will have no occasion to take Dr. Ward's pill"? More fitting subjects for his wit were, however, legion, and on the whole these columns furnish a great deal of highly amusing information and comment on the life of the time. One could cite innumerable comments as neat as

---

[3] In the earlier issues many of these notes were written by Martyn ("B"). That Russel's cynicism was not altogether peculiar to him is shown perhaps by such a comment as the following in number 2, by Martyn. Of the news that a woman had been found dead in a coach house "among old lumber," he says, "The learned Dr. Zoilus [Bentley] thinks that there is an omission of the copyist in this place, and that we ought to read among *other* old lumber."

Last week the Assizes ended at Salisbury, when 4 persons received sentence of death; 2 were ordered to be transported; 1 was burnt in the hand for sheep stealing; and Rob. Bullock and Daniel Croker (the latter a Hackney Writer from Chancery-lane, who in this dearth of business had strolled down to Bath, and stole a Barber's waistcoat) were convicted of petty larcenies, and order'd to be whipt. *D P.* — This Hackney Writer from Chancery-lane *had better have stayed here, and turned* Political Writer.

Two young children of —— Haffel, of Lincoln's-Inn‘ Esq; who were lately inoculated for the Small pox, at his house in Bedford-Row, are since both dead. *D P.* —— *They are now secure from the* Small-pox *in the common way.*

In the News Papers of the 2d inst. it was invidiously insinuated, that most of the cloaths worn at Court on his Majesty's birth-day, were French silks; which is so far from truth, that by her Majesty's Royal encouragement to the manufacturers to invent new patterns, the making of gold and silver stuffs, and the richest silks, is brought to such perfection in England as has never been excelled by the French; and all the Royal Family, and most of the Nobility and Gentry, did do honour to the Manufacturies of their own country, by appearing in them on that joyful occasion. *DP. — I did not see this circumstance about* the French silks *mentioned in any other* News Paper of Mar. 2. *but the* LE.

Yesterday a poor woman, who I suppose got up to ride, Fell out of a dust-cart, and immediately died.

WEDNESDAY, *March* 15.

The Hon. Mrs. Mary Vane having last week resigned her place of Maid of Honour to her Majesty, the Hon. Mrs. Martha Lovelace, only Sister to the Right Hon. the Lord Lovelace, we hear is appointed to succeed her in that station. *D P.*

We hear that the books and papers belonging to the Charitable Corporation have been discovered, and found concealed under a floor in a house in Broad-street. *D J.* —— *It is strange, they should be* be found concealed, *after they had* been *discovered: but this happens sometimes.*

On sunday last the Envoys from Algier went to Windsor, where they dined, saw the Castle, and return'd in the Evening to their Lodgings in Suffolk-street. *D P.*

Yesterday, on a man, and boy, by coaches put out of breath,

The Coroner's Jury sate : their verdict, *Accidental death*. P.

TYPICAL NEWS ITEMS
(From Number 115, March 16, 1732)

that in number 7 on an obituary notice in the *Craftsman* concerning the relict of Admiral Hosier, "This lady, who has been so often mentioned in the newspapers, sometimes as alive, sometimes as dead, is, I believe neither; there never having been any such person in the world."[4] Moreover, the sarcasm wherewith the editors, especially Russel, brought together and displayed the wildly divergent accounts of the same incident by various papers was certainly well employed, and should have been useful in checking the irresponsible and careless fabrications of the news hacks. Considering the nature of the newspapers and the newswriters, however, one can hardly imagine that such criticism had much effect on them.

When we remember the quality of the journalists themselves, we are not surprised at the material they produced. Apparently writing for the periodicals was one of the lowest and least desirable employments of that despised class, the hack writers. There is little doubt that Martyn and Russel themselves, Martyn a botanist, and Russel a clergyman and scholar, regarded the *Journal* as hack-work, or at best as a temporary side-issue. Allusions to journalists and reporters are almost uniformly contemptuous; their calling was one of last resort for literary starvelings. The figure in the following account in number 407 is representative. Some verses on "The political State" were brought to the *Journal* by a messenger who paid a half crown for their insertion. The editor of the *Journal,* thinking the verses might be made to apply satirically to his enemies the magazines, rewrote the title to include their names.[5] The messenger thereupon returned and demanded his half crown back, which was given him out of pity for his meagre appearance, and with the hope that his principal allowed him to keep it as a porter's fee in addition to the other half-crown he had got for writing the verses. In addition are furnished descriptive details of

[4] The writer goes on to explain that there was a Mrs. Dian Pritchard, who claimed to be the admiral's widow and heiress. Occasionally such items were rather effectively turned into doggerel verse.
[5] See 405.

"the grim Rime-carrier," doubtless intended to reveal his identity.

The payment of the half-crown in this instance is significant. It is doubtless true that the papers paid for some of the material they published, since the bitterest complaint against the magazines was that they stole material which the original publishers had had to pay for. Still it is clear that for a consideration they would insert notices and articles, which appeared not as advertisements but as having editorial approval and sanction. A case in point is the history in number 410 of a letter against the law restricting the sale of spirits. This letter had originally been taken to the *London Evening Post,* which demanded two guineas to insert it. The author then got it printed in the *Grub-street Journal,* number 407, and paid the *London Evening Post* three shillings to advertise it. The *Post* never printed the advertisement and thereby laid itself open to attack on the ground of failing in its original pretense of desiring to be serviceable to the public and of being attached "to Liberty and the country interest."

Among the attacks on general methods of writing news and articles for the journals are to be found a great many fulminations against particular papers. On the whole the *Journal* avoided politics, yet it came into occasional conflict with its colleagues on political issues, especially the excise, for which it had a virulent hatred. In general, however, it waited for a chance to quarrel until a paper, in an interval between political campaigns, perhaps, should have committed itself on some points in the arts or sciences. For instance, in number 193, Maevius (probably Russel) contributes an ironical panegyric of "Walsingham," editor of the *Free Briton.* This person had declared that many who had only slight talent in art or science had gone far through education and encouragement. Maevius asserts that some, even, who were unsuitable because of the lack of proper education have gone far, and then cites Walsingham himself as one who without any real education has been practising the arts of politics and rhetoric the last three years, and has now taken up painting and sculpture. Then, in an ironical panegyric, he dissects an article from the *Free Briton* on the sculptor Rysbrack and attacks readers who have declared the article "an undigested heap of highflown tautologies," and have accused the author of "setting up rhetorical figures on the wrong end," of being illogical, ungrammatical, inaccurate, and especially of committing one egregious blunder which ruined the whole article. Attached are "annotations on the Free Briton" by Bavius, pointing out the errors in question. This was followed in number 196 by a direct attack signed "P. P—re." This correspondent wonders how enough copies of the *Free Briton* are sold to pay the printer, and thinks the chief reason must be the amusement derived from guessing at the meaning of Walsingham's sentences. P—re also compares Walsingham to a pickpocket for reprinting Cato's Letters and Temple's Essays,[6] and thinks, from the delay in his death, which is expected momentarily, that he must be like one of those consumptives who linger on indefinitely.

During the same period, late in 1733, the *Journal* also published a number of satirical attacks on "Francis Osborne,"[7] editor of the *London Journal*. In number 180 appears an attack, signed "Anglus," on his logic in a political argument, and in number 195 another by "The Witch of Endor" on the weakness of a pronouncement wherein Osborne had denied any religious attachment, claiming to be for all sects and against none. The Witch points out inconsistencies and derides Osborne's boasted independence. "Mrs. Osborne's" patron, it is asserted, lately gave her two places. one of which she sold for £1100. The aspersion of the "Mrs." evidently suggested a letter in number 201 :

[6] The custom of reprinting perfectly accessible and well known material was not uncommon. Naturally it was done in lean times.

[7] This was Thomas Pitt, who commonly suffered from the perversion of his pseudonym into "Mother Osborne." He was generally regarded as being in the pay of Sir Robert Walpole. See Nichols, *Literary Anecdotes,* III, 649, where he is spoken of as writer of the *Gazetteer.*

Mr. Bavius—Whereas Mr. D'Anvers[8] and yourself, have, either erroneously or maliciously misrepresented me as a woman, by calling me Madam, Mrs., Goody, Dame, and Mother Osborne, this is to certify to the public that I am no woman, but as much a man as either of you: nay, I am so far from having an effeminate countenance, that I look as fierce as Hamilcar, and can swear like a trooper. I hope you will show your impartiality by communicating this to the town in behalf of your injured Francis, not Frances, Osborne.

This same point is further exploited in number 226 in a satirical fable by "J. T."[9] on a Mrs. Osborne, who, having failed in an attempt to influence her milkman's vote, not only took away her custom but refused to pay his bill. Editorial comment on this fable asserts that their brother Osborne is hardly to be distinguished from the old lady, and then launches a series of innuendoes against his political sincerity.[10]

Against the magazines, the *Gentleman's* and the *London*, the *Journal* was especially bitter, for it regarded them as subsisting almost altogether on stolen goods. In number 168 the *Journal* reviewed sarcastically and at length their history. The cause of their invention was ironically declared to be the partiality of the post-office, which assisted some papers and hindered others. To remedy this defect and to bring order out of the chaos of newspapers, was established the *Gentleman's,* now two years old. A year or more later was born the *London Magazine,* which imitated its elder brother closely and thus precipitated a bitter quarrel between them.[11]

[8] "Caleb D'Anvers," editor of the *Craftsman.*

[9] Initials sometimes used by Russel.

[10] Note also, among others, an attack (340) on *Fog's* and the *London Evening Post* for publishing false stories about clergymen, on the *Post-Boy* for printing verses stolen from the *Grub-street Journal* as the composition of some Dublin wit (328), on the *Universal Spectator* and *Whitehall Evening Post* for somewhat similar offenses (179 and 204), and on the *Daily Journal* in connection with a theatrical quarrel (367 ff.).

[11] Although the *London Magazine* reprinted a great deal from the *Grub-street Journal,* including many of the same articles as were taken by the *Gentleman's,* the *Journal* did not hate it so fiercely as it did the *Gentleman's.* In March and April, 1733, the *London Magazine* reviews the *Journal's* charges against the magazines with evident delight in the assault on the *Gentleman's.* In September, 1734 (III, 487), the *London*

The important fact about both, Bavius continues, is their piracy. This charge was answered with a *tu quoque* by the *Gentleman's,* in an advertisement which the *Journal* prints in number 169. Bavius (in numbers 171 and 172) retaliates with a finespun distinction between upright and downright piracy, and points out that the *Gentleman's* is accused only of the latter. He also makes the point that fully half his *Journal* is original material. He defends himself rather unconvincingly by stating that the spoils of the *Gentleman's* are much greater in amount and reiterates that the *Journal* contributes an element of originality in its collation of news items from the various papers.

This defense Bavius repeated in number 210, in answer to a letter in which the *Journal* is referred to as "the original of all abbreviators of news." He pointed out that the practice of taking news from the dailies was an old one but that it had not been usual to tell the source, or to present the various divergent accounts of the same event. The magazines continued to be a thorn in the side of the papers and provoked many complaints.[12] Indeed their thefts were spoken of in the preface to *The Memoirs of Grub-street* as one of the chief reasons for the decline of the paper. The *Gentleman's* took formal notice of this complaint when it summarized the introductory essay from the *Literary Courier of Grub-street:*—"The late Grubean Secretary, blind to his own faults, and prejudiced against our Magazine, to its success attributed the decay of his Journal. With the same view, he reprinted several charges against us in his Journal

Magazine published verses on "Cavius and Bavius"—Cavius being Cave, of the *Gentleman's*—

> Cavius and Bavius differ but a letter ;
> Compare their works, you'll understand 'em better.
> If Bavius dulness pleads, 'tis with design,
> But Cavius birthright pleads in every line.

[12] These complaints continued to appear in later years of the *Journal.* In March, 1737, under poetical essays, the *Gentleman's* reprints from the *Daily Journal*—

> Gainst filchers hear the pert Grubeans rail !
> Yet their own practice weekly is to steal.
> (To blab a secret, and enhance their shame)
> They filch the property of those they blame.

of December 22,[13] though they had been proved false in our Magazine for May last." As a matter of fact the frequent abridgements by the *Gentleman's* of Grubstreet articles was a compliment the *Journal* could ill afford to accept. While it bears witness to the *Journal's* popularity, it very probably in time tended to reduce its circulation; obviously many patrons would stop subscribing if they could find the best of it condensed in a magazine. The *Journal* may well be granted some sympathy in its hostile attitude.

These various squabbles and skirmishes with other periodicals, however, were of slight importance beside the major campaigns against the *Weekly Register,* the *Hyp-Doctor,* the *Bee,* and the *Prompter.* These battles, especially those with the three last papers, were sustained and continuous and almost extravagantly virulent.

The *Weekly Register* seems to have survived, except for a few stray issues,[14] only in the pale reflection of its abridgements in the magazines. In its own day its enemy the *Grubstreet Journal* frequently called it "obscure," and Eustace Budgell says of it in the first issue of his *Bee* (February, 1733), "The Weekly Register . . . has been on foot some time, and has perhaps been less taken notice of than it deserved; we have seen some good things in it, and hope our Bee may now and then get a little honey from it." Good reason for the *Journal's* hatred of the *Register* from the beginning appears in a dialogue between printer's devils (number 148[14a]). The Grubstreet devil says to the one from the *Register*: ". . . your master had better never have undertaken that paper, which he published at first in opposition to my Grub-street Journal almost on the same model and on the same day, but he soon found that would not do, and changed the day to Friday, which proving unlucky as the other, he

---

[13] The last issues of the *Journal* reprinted in installments the preface to *The Memoirs of Grub-street.*

[14] In the Yale Library. There seems to be none at all in the British Museum, and an appeal to several special students of newspapers in England has proved unfruitful.

[14a] *The Grub-street Journal Extraordinary,* a special number, published October 30, 1732.

passed on to Saturday." The *Register* appeared for the first time on April 19, 1730,[15] and although the *Journal* frequently prophesied its decease, continued to exist until late in 1734, when the disappearance of its name from the list on the front cover of the *Gentleman's Magazine* would indicate its final collapse. Its editor is alluded to by the *Gentleman's Magazine* as "Mr. Birch,"[16] probably the "Tim Birch" who is the subject of several contemptuous remarks in the *Journal*; but the author of the attacks on the *Journal,* "A renegado who has been very illiterately scurrilous in an obscure weekly paper called The Weekly Register" was revealed by Bavius in *The Memoirs of Grub-street* as "Mr. D. Bellamy."[17] James Ralph was also one of its writers; he contributed to it his rapid *Survey of Public Buildings.*

Early in 1731 the *Register* published a series of attacks on the *Journal.* It gave a satirical etymology of the word *Grub,* and spoke of ridicule as a vice which was "contagious, and runs through the whole people; it wanders everywhere, like an ignis fatuus, and is only at home in the Grubstreet Journal." The authors of the *Journal* are said to have "undertaken the drudgery of invective under pretence of being champions for politeness."[18] It also derided the plan of the *Journal,* and especially its use of prints, "that the decoration may atone for other deficiencies, and children admire what men would not read." In August, 1731, it renewed the assault. The *Journal,* it said, was in the pay of the opposition, with *Fog's* and the *Craftsman.* A taunt that the *Register's* scheme had been stolen from the *Journal* it calls an "impudent assertion"—"Their [the *Journal's*] scheme consists chiefly of scandal; every man of candour might be ashamed of it." It cites instances of the *Journal's* low tone—its "maliciously prophesying the death of the Register in May last," and its low shift of printing the picture of the Lord Mayor and the

---

[15] See Nichols, *Literary Anecdotes,* IV, 95.

[16] II, 612.

[17] Bavius especially ridicules "his great morality and religion," and derides his projected edition in ballad metre of "fifty select moral Tales and Fables."

[18] *Gentleman's Magazine,* I, 12, and 69.

arms of the City Companies. It announces that its own sales increase steadily, and "'tis not in the power of the authors of the Grubstreet *with all their popularity to say the same.*"[19] Another criticism "against the Grubstreet authors" is noted by the *Gentleman's Magazine,*[20] but the only part reprinted consists of remarks on false prosody in a Latin poem on the Lord Mayor.

The climax of the quarrel was reached in the *Register's* issue of July 8, 1732,[21] under the heading "The Grub-street Journal Censured"—

The Grub-street Journal has long subsisted very oddly, universally condemned, and yet universally read, conducted with the most consummate dullness and infamous scurrility; a political or religious controversy has been its author's daily bread for a month together;[22] and when the town has been sick of the subject, scandal and defamation have taken their turn, and are indeed the life of the paper. At its first outset, the authors of it insinuated[23] that they fought under the banner of a celebrated poet, who then had a controversy with his minor brethren, and we fancied that the Dunciad and the Grub-street Journal were derived from the same original, and therefore no wonder that the paper was established e'er the cheat was discovered. Hence the scribblers of that paper took the liberty to abuse every gentleman whom Mr. P— had exposed in his Dunciad. And who were these formidable censors of the age? Why, a set of little physicians, non-juring parsons, and pert booksellers, such ignominious low scribblers that they openly offered their paper to be the vehicle of scandal, and if any gentleman complained of his being ill treated, the publisher replied, "The paper was at their service the same way."

This forthright bludgeoning continues with an expression of surprise that "their infamous libels have not been answered with a cudgel rather than with a pen," and an assertion that the immediate cause of the present diatribe was the *Journal's* attack on the author of *The Modern Husband,*[24] "a gentle-

[19] *Gentleman's Magazine,* I, 340, 368. (Italics inserted.)
[20] *Gentleman's Magazine,* I, 424.
[21] *Gentleman's Magazine,* II, 844.
[22] The *Journal* did not, as has been said before, go in for politics.
[23] The *Journal* never gave the least hint that Pope was connected with it. The first official implication to that effect is in the preface to the *Memoirs.* The writer in the *Register* may mean that they insinuated it in private conversation.
[24] Henry Fielding. The *Gentleman's,* which evidently found this squabble amusing, reprinted a good deal of the *Journal's* criticism of *The Modern Husband.*

man as much above their reputation as genius, who has too much sense and spirit to contend with so contemptible an adversary."[25] To this the *Journal* retorted (number 141) with charges of plagiarism in the *Register* and with contemptuous allusions to its authors, emphasizing as usual their obscurity.[26] This concluded the quarrel with the *Register* itself; although the *Journal* later criticized at length Ralph's *Survey of Public Buildings,* which appeared serially in the *Register,* it passed by the paper itself and concentrated its fire upon Ralph.

Most of the victims of the *Grub-street Journal* were scarified in its columns for a time, and then left in peace to forget and to heal their wounds. A quarrel like that with the *Bee* and the *Prompter,* or with such Dunces as James Moore-Smythe or James Ralph, flamed up in the bitterest of personalities for a few months or perhaps a year, and then subsided and yielded place to some newer controversy. The reason is obvious. In most cases the quarrel sprang from some immediate provocation like the publication of a satire or the cropping out of a scandal like the one over Tindall's will,[27] and when the utmost interest and life had been abstracted from it, like juice from a squeezed orange, it was dropped, and the editors cast their eyes about for a fresh one.

[25] The *Gentleman's Magazine* speaks of this article as a reiteration of an earlier attack. "Dr. Quibus" of the *Grub-street Journal* is said to be "the old fellow who shows the tombs at Westminster," since they have the same way of joking. He is also said to resemble one of his predecessors who remarked, on seeing a scaffold fall with a couple of laborers, who lay dying at his feet, "Blessed are the dead that die in the Lord; for they rest from their labour, and their works follow them."—A piece of grim humour of which the *Journal* would have been quite capable.

[26] The *Gentleman's,* which had a grievance of its own against the *Register,* annotated the *Journal's* phrase, "an obscure weekly journal"—"He means the Weekly Register, the printer of which he charges in another place with inserting a poem from a Grub-street Journal above a year old, and with taking most of his copy from other papers. The said printer some months since asserted in his paper that the undertakers of the Gentleman's Magazine slily endeavoured to obtrude their book, which had been subsisting eighteen months, in the room of one printed by him, which had not then been in being so many weeks. This we took no notice of before, because of the obscurity of the paper and the inconsistency of the assertion. For the same reason we overlook with contempt some other derogatory reflections, which carry with them their own conviction."

[27] See *post,* p. 136 ff.

The chief exception to this rule was that extraordinary and unabashed mountebank, the Orator John Henley. It may be said that he was a natural object for the *Journal's* satire, since he was already ignominiously enrolled among the number of the Dunces, but it is doubtful if this fact had much to do with the case. Henley was in truth almost the richest vein that the editors of such a paper as the *Journal* could hope to discover for exploitation. During the whole period of the *Journal's* existence and long after, he was continually and brazenly in the public eye. With his pen and with his own voice he was continually roaring his own praise, or propounding some strange opinion in religion or science which cried out for satiric attack. Moreover, what is even more to the point, he undertook to be versatile, and explored many fields, so that he was continually furnishing new sensations of a fresh flavor, and thus helped to keep his opponents from becoming uninteresting and hackneyed. Hence it is not surprising to find his name continually in the *Journal*. There is no period in the paper's history except at the very beginning when he is not held up to ridicule for one extravagance or another. In fact the custom of lampooning him was continued during the brief life of the *Journal's* sequel, the *Literary Courier of Grub-street*.

The *Journal's* only significant allusions to Henley during 1730 consist of brief sarcasms upon his assurance. In commenting[28] on one of Henley's typical puffs that he was to compete "for the prize of the next question in the French Academy," Bavius remarks, "That he has assurance for such an attempt is what no one will doubt; that he has the capacity is what everyone will."[29] This was followed in the next issue by an ironical disclaimer to the effect that the preceding reference had been inserted by a person who happened to be at the printing office when the paper was composed. It had not been authorized by a member of the Grubstreet Society, none of whom would have ventured such a remark, since Henley's

[28] Number 36.
[29] Ascribed to Russel.

capacity "for any such attempt or undertaking whatever" was beyond doubt. This sounded a note on which the _Journal_ was to harp frequently in later years, but at present the editors did not seem to be interested in coming to loggerheads with the Orator.

On December 15, 1730, however, Henley launched the first number of that strange semi-weekly effusion, the _Hyp-Doctor,_ in which he remarks, "Caleb [D'Anvers] is my Harlequin, Fog my Boot-catcher, and Dr. Quibus [one of the imaginary editors of the _Grub-street Journal_] is my knight of the pestle, or as the vulgar has it, my apothecary." In the second number, apropos of Bavius' attacks on Cibber, just elected laureate, he says—

> Bavius is hypt at Colley Cibber's bays
> And IS a duller fool than those HE only plays.

War between Henley and the _Journal_ began in good earnest in the _Journal's_ issue for March 11, 1731, number 62, and raged hotly during the rest of that year and the early months of 1732, Henley on his side fighting back in the columns of his _Hyp-Doctor_ and in the advertisements, chiefly in the _Daily Journal,_ of his _Oratory Discourses._ Whether the discourses themselves fulfilled the promises of their advertisements, it is now impossible to say. In its issue for March 11, 1731, the _Journal_ published an "Essay on Impudence," of which Henley was palpably the subject. Henley at once advertised that his next subject for public discourse would be an apology for wit and that he expected one Dr. M[artyn] who called him impudent in print, to dispute on that problem. Consequently the next Journal contained the comment,

I wonder Mr. Henley should make an unnecessary apology, and that he should be offended at being called impudent, since it was plainly showed in our last that impudence comprehends all qualifications. . . . If the problem intended be either whether Mr. Henley has wit or whether he has impudence, I deny that either is a problem, and consequently any matter of dispute.

Russel ("M") declared that he could not guess whom Henley was referring to in his "M——," and in the Pegasus column filled in the gap as "Mitchell." In the *Hyp-Doctor* for March 23, 1731 (number 15), Henley then published "A letter from Johnny Martin (once a Book-keeper, now a botanist and snail-picker)"—animadversions on a Grubstreet article on political weather—and speaks of low uses for which he reserved "the ingenious Mr. Gilliver's, Dr. Martin's and Mr. Russel's Weekly productions."

In the next issue, in a description of certain "birds", he says,

Under the scarecrows were listed the cuckoos, who sits [*sic*] on other birds eggs; these represented Gillivers, who hatch all from other author's papers: There was a runt with the name R—l on his side; he and a black Martin kept close together: they lived upon catching flies and eating spiders, . . . a Tomtit that set up for a mighty songster and warrior; the letters on his side were Pope.[30]

In the same connection he reveals R—l in the note "Runt Russel, one of Gilliver's news brokers."

In number 21, the "Grubs," as Henley called the Society at the Pegasus, are said to have "sent to pygmy P-pe to be their president," and are again accused of stealing their material. In number 23, Henley professed to give "part of the character of two Grub writers." The first of these is Pope, attacked for his corrosive malice and his physical deformity, but "his bow, as his back informs you, is too weak, and his arrows too short and blunt." The second is Russel—

A mouse-eaten shred of an author who was once a go-between to two doctors of the holy league, when Friar Bungy's dance was playing, and the Duke of Ormond wrapt his sword in Irish wool to prevent its being run on the French; he then wrote a poem (as he says himself, for none else knows the secret) called the Impeachment; which just appeared like Bateman's ghost in a white sheet, frighted the house with a dismal groan and vanished. He was of the college of Magdalen unconverted, before the legion was cast out of her, and as the devil has his name from false accusation, he is a descendant from the expelled tenants. . . . but it is impossible to cut him or his wit shorter than they are.

This is indeed a cryptic style, but the general intent is plain, as well as the fact that Russel is accused of political activity

---

[30] Allusions to Pope appear also in numbers 4 and 8.

at the time of the Duke of Ormond's ill-fated escapade of 1719. The allusion to Magdalen and its Jacobite, non-juring tendencies is probably a mistake of Henley's ; Russel is clearly recorded a member of University College. In this same article are references to an attack on "Robert Stephen's book." It will be remembered[31] that Thomas Martyn speaks of Russel's having been concerned with his father in a new edition of that work.

The attack is more general in number 31, where it is declared, "The Grubs, who are the sediments of sense, the dregs of the cask, have robbed two pamphlets and three papers last week to serve them up cold and mangled barbarously, in their two-penny ordinary,"—this in a list of the shortcomings of the newspapers. Thus Henley's jibes run on, with remarks on the history and the mental and physical qualities of Pope, Martyn, and Russel, and declarations of the rottenness of the *Journal,* and its always imminent dissolution. In number 38, Henley tells his readers that

the worm eaten vessel that has been carrying the Grubs over that dreadful gulf, the long vacation, is at present sinking, as appears from their late unfortunate squeak complaining to the world that they cannot get their papers into the country. . . . They are now pumping for life in a foul hold and leaky bottom. . . . Poor Grub! Can nothing be done for him. . . . We shall have these Journal daubers in a short time stationed at the corner of Whitehall Gate to cry buns and penny-books together.

A letter signed J. Pelle in number 48 announces "credible information that the beginner of the Grub Paper as it is called was a papist, Mr. P—pe, who intended it to continue his Dunciad, where he says very courtly—Dunce the Second reigns like Dunce the First. That the main writers have been two professed non-jurors, M—n and R—l." After accusing the *Journal* of theft in number 54, and referring to Bavius as "small-hopes," Henley turned his attention in number 56 to Martyn.

I had a footman named Martin. I called him Martin Mar-all; he thought himself privileged to wear my castoff jests, as well as my livery; and at last the rogue stole a pocket-book of my minutes, ran

[31] See *ante,* p. 40.

away from me, and has been murdering my original jibes ever since in a society called the Grubs, that is the worms, the Grub-worms. Picking such worms from herbs and salads he calls botany. These worms peep out in paper, but the last snow before Christmas killed multitudes of them, and the rest are in a very poor starveling condition.

In number 59 comes Henley's own account of the origin of the *Journal;* he declares it to be an imitation of his own highly successful *Chimes of the Times,* from which the Grub editors took "not only his scheme, but his thoughts, and racked and mangled them in their paper. . . . The goods are found upon these plagiaries and buccaneers." He also gives a fantastic genealogy of the editors—"Martins the shrub and Russels the dwarf-elder," and insists that as they could get no book advertisements for their paper they had to fill space with advertisements of their own. In the same tone is the statement in an issue of July 11, 1732, that when a *Grub-street Journal* was put with "a newt, the author of it," in a vacuum pump, it swelled up and looked like Dicky R-s-l, and puffs appeared of Vida's Latin poems,[32] and so forth, and "Rare Plants" by Dr. M——n. Plagiarism is again charged in number 84, where various stolen articles are described as being seen through a magic telescope in the rooms of Dicky Russel in College Street, Westminster; and in number 87 it is asserted that the *Journal* exists only to "make fritters" of news; everything in it is false—the last issue ends with a false fact, namely that it "was never scandalous, whereas Scandal is and ever has been the length, breadth, and depth of it: it requires a very large cavo-fango to cleanse the mud of that excremental paper." In number 88, Henley imitated the *Journal's* usual statistics on the *Hyp-Doctor* with "Casualties of the Grub-street Journal for the month of July last," and in succeeding issues makes passing allusions to the editors, notably in number 92, "non-jurors, as MARTYN and RUSSEL," and in number 94, where he asserts that Runt Russel gets half a guinea for writing two *Journals.*

The personal attacks on Russel continue. Number 100

[32] An edition by Russel. See *ante,* p. 43.

is given up to a fantastic description of the *Journal* and its vices, and reasserts that the writer's real name is Dicky Russel of College Street, Westminster, and that he comes up to Temple Bar every Thursday, "like a wet weazel creeping and jumping along the skirts of a common sewer to take the air." Various details of his private life are disclosed;—he keeps a boarding house for boys of Westminster School (number 101); he was once a supporter of Sacheverell (number 105); he is a non-juring clergyman of North Street, Westminster, late of College Street, was once the author of a poem called the Impeachment, and is now working on "Stephanus's Thesaurus and bales of Barnabas's Epistles"; he is a "runt in criticism, as in stature" (number 110); he shows his lack of scholarship in his attacks on Cibber's odes (number 112). After this, however, the strife died down; and except for a very occasional comment, as when proper notice was taken of Runt Russel's assertion that the *Hyp-Doctor* was an "unintelligible, neglected paper" (number 128) and he was alluded to as "a broken, non-swearing but all-lying parson of North-street, Westminster" (number 152), his name disappeared from the insane columns of the *Hyp-Doctor*.

These characteristic utterances in the *Hyp-Doctor* Henley supplemented with his even more fantastic advertisements. For instance, in the *Daily Journal* for March 23, 1731, Henley advertised his attack on Martyn in the *Hyp-Doctor,* number 15, and again in the *Daily Journal* for March 27, he added to his advertisement the note:—

We, the wits and poets undermentioned did not design in our last advertisement against the Hyp-Doctor to detract from his merit which we acknowledge, but only to sell our own heavy trash . . . to vent our ill humor . . . in the foul language which is our element. . . . As we are only apes of humour we can't help being mischievous. L. Sillicur and A.[33] Ruselle.

Similar outbursts appeared in the advertising columns of *Fog's Journal* for April 10 and several succeeding issues,

[33] Misprint for R?

where Henley announces especially a refutation of Martyn's botanical ideas. His defense against his detractors will, he says, be postponed until Wednesday in Easter week, "when the town may, God willing, depend on something very particular, especially as to Dr. M—s definition of a plant." He also promises, in *Fog's* for April 17, a defense, "especially against the atheistical, obscene reflections of some enemies, after which will be a specimen of his philosophy on Mr. M—s first botanic l—e,[34] proving it erroneous and inconsistent, from the aloes to the stinging nettle, that he has not botany imPLANTed in him." Henley also made fantastic and cryptic allusions in his advertisements in the *Daily Journal* to a "battle of the birds" at Richmond, e.g., "We, the apparitions, sprites, and stuffed mawkins of a buzzard, runt, etc., slain in the Battle of the Birds last Tuesday, humbly and unfeignedly retract"—and there follows an apology to the *Hyp-Doctor* signed by the strange company of "Jigguni-bob Gilliver, Skewball Scoggin, Runt Russel, Bear Garden Bickham and Company."[35] Neither did Henley hesitate to impute to Pope an interest in the encounter, and accordingly to load him with outlandish abuse. He speaks of discussing "the whim that his writings are not his own, yet good for nothing," "his Amours,"[36] "the falsehoods of Alexander Pope, Esq. of Twickenham; the assistance reported by one Mr. Savage on that head."[37] Henley also seems to have suspected Dr. Arbuthnot as a conspirator against him, for in one of his strange utterances he lights upon the latter's "late essay on aliment and physic."[38] It was Russel, however, that he seems to have regarded as the head and forefront of the

---

[34] *The first lecture of a course of Botany being an introduction to the rest.* By John Martyn, F. R. S. 1729. This lecture bears the imprimatur of Hans Sloane, P. R. S., and is the lecture referred to in the *Journal,* 67 (see *post,* p. 128).

[35] Who "Skewball Scoggin" was it seems impossible to say. "Bear-Garden Bickham" may possibly have been James Bickham, later junior tutor of Emanuel College, who was "a bold man, and had been a bruiser when young". Nichols, *Literary Anecdotes,* VIII, 420.

[36] *Daily Journal,* April 21, 1731.

[37] *Daily Journal,* May 5, 1731.

[38] *Daily Journal,* May 11, 1731.

cabal. The abuse of Russel is continuous; evidently all the few details of his history and his customs which were discoverable, and some which were only guessed at, were set forth in an attempt to discredit him and the *Journal*. In an advertisement in the *Daily Journal*, May 11, it is said,

We hear the oratory subject for tomorrow evening . . . will be the Lady of the May, with the history of the Silly Curs continued in a challenge to Mr. Russel, who is hired to revile Mr. Henley weekly; the said Russel's principles, the reasons for his caluminating [*sic*] Mr. Henley as well as others by name, and particularly his parts, learning, and honesty, brought to the Touchstone.

Again the next day, he refers to "the ninnies hackneyed to rail at Mr. Orator, particularly that go-between Mr. Russel, the Runt, his principles and mean, ungenerous practices against Mr. H——, . . ." In his mouthings from his Oratory tub, Henley probably outdid even his written effusions in the *Hyp-Doctor* and the *Daily Journal*.

During all this chatter in the *Hyp-Doctor* and Henley's advertisements, the *Journal* had continually irritated Henley with ironical pin-pricks. While Henley turned all his attention to exposing the personalities of the Grub writers, the *Journal* on its side dodged his imputations or met them vaguely, but retorted with damaging suggestions concerning his character and abilities. It followed up the attacks in numbers 62 and 63 with a parody of Henley's advertising style[39]—

Shortly will be published in prose and rime after the manner of Satan's Game Cock whose name begins with a *Hen* and ends with a *Ly*.
  I. Whether all the felons that have been hanged at Tyburn for five years past were not honester and handsomer men, juster both in action and speech, and better grammarians, than the bull-beef orator.
 II. Whether to praise the same people for twopence be right That once were abused for twelvepence a night.
III. Whether this news could of being acceptable fail: We have a general peace, and H—— is in jail.
        N.B. Is not he a silly cur
           To abuse Lawton Gilliver?

[39] In number 64.

Succeeding issues of the *Journal* abound in allusions and retorts of a similar nature. In a burlesque almanac for April, blustering weather is prophesied for All-fools day, the final ravings of "an eminent Grubean orator . . . he will die the 29th."[40] Of a "Curlean" advertisement that the *Hyp-Doctor* "will not be sold shortly under double-price," the *Journal* insinuates that it is probably true—it won't be sold at all. It notes a repetitious issue of the *Hyp-Doctor*,[41] and asks if the imposition on Christians of cabbage "twice-boiled, cold, and without any vinegar" on a Saturday in Lent is according to "Apostolic Constitution and Canons."[42] Henley's style is said to serve as a model of baby talk for nurse-maids, and the possibility of turning all the *Oratory Discourses* into rime is canvassed.[43] There are frequent plays and retorts on Silly Cur, Henley's name for Gilliver, publisher of the *Journal*. To Henley's attempted sarcasms on Martyn's botanical lecture the *Journal* replied,

Mr. President said he took the person hinted at under the name of Dr. M— to be one who had published a pretended Lecture of Botany about two years ago, under which pretense he had scandalously abused several members of our society, in his allegorical definitions. That of a Plant in particular he always took to be levelled at the character of Mr. H.

Then follows a detailed explanation of the allegory of Henley and the Plant.[44] Henley is reported[45] to have taken three or four papers of Dr. Quibus' Cephalic Snuff, which threw him into a fit of elocution and removed a large brainworm similar to the one James Moore-Smythe had suffered from.[46]

[40] See 65. In 122 is copied a news item falsely reporting the death of a member of Parliament named Henley, with the comment "This was Mr. Orator Henley: Mr. Auditor Henley [the M. P.] *We Hear* is still alive, tho in a weak condition."

[41] Number 15.

[42] Number 65.

[43] Number 66.

[44] Number 67. This lecture of Martyn's was of course a serious professional production, although the application to Henley is burlesque. The phrases quoted from it in mock seriousness in 67 appear exactly in the lecture as Martyn originally published it.

[45] Number 70.

[46] See *Grub-street Journal*, 26, and *ante*, p. 62.

To Henley's complaint that the *Grub-street Journal*—"murderer of all decency," did not even spare his deceased father in its assaults on him, the *Journal* replied with the statement that it had not cast the least reflection on his father, "unless it were one to mention him as the father of such a son."[47] A "Blind Orator" was invented to serve as a rival to Henley, and was praised for his modesty, simplicity, lack of avarice, and so on.[48] A news item that Henley had bravely driven off two foot-pads, was capped by Russel with the couplet (number 87)—

> Illiterate rogues who thus attacked th' Orator
> Cantabit vacuus coram latrone viator.

These squibs and many others like them were accompanied by several more detailed analyses of Henley's weak points. For example, in number 69 the *Journal* abridged Henley's own account of his life published in his *Oratory Transactions*[49] and signed "A. Welstede." A few italicized quotations served sufficiently to reveal the absurd assurance of this biography—e.g., "Mr. H. has given in his youth *more demonstrations* to the public of his desire to improve himself and the world than *all his antagonists* put together." The *Journal* adds, "The scandalous author of the Dunciad, an inveterate enemy of our whole society, has set this eminent member in another light," and quotes *The Dunciad,* III,

> But where each science lifts its modern type,
> Embrown'd with native bronze, lo, Henley stands,
> Tuning his voice and balancing his hands.
> How sweet the periods, neither said nor sung!—

The author of the earlier "Essay on Impudence" also returned to the charge in number 71, with a leading article in ironical praise of all Henley's various exhibitions, and then to prove finally that Henley deserved "the palm of effront-

---

[47] Number 79.
[48] Numbers 78 and 84.
[49] *Oratory Transactions, No. 1. To be occasionally published by J. Henley, M. A. London, printed in the year 1728.* The second item is "A Narrative by Mr. Welstede." Pope pretended to confuse "A. Welstede" with Leonard Welsted. See *Dictionary of National Biography.*

ery," reviewed his French and Italian grammars, thus exposing his complete ignorance of his subject. It appears clearly that he transcribed from other books and often coupled a translation with the wrong original. For instance, "Date melo—Send it to us."[50]

Although the attack was prosecuted most vigorously during the first three years of the *Journal,* it was never allowed to die down. Statistics of "hyp-Oratorical Puffs" were regularly presented for each month,[51] and epigrams both in verse and prose were sufficiently frequent to keep the Orator continually before the *Journal's* readers. Indeed in its last gasps, the paper took up the quarrel again with all its original animosity;—the six final numbers are replete with jibes at him.

From beginning to end, Henley's assurance and impudence were emphasized as his distinguishing characteristics. That is of course the purpose of the regular monthly puff-statistics. Apparently the *Journal* never missed an opportunity to prick the bubbles of reputation which Henley was continually trying to inflate. Late in 1732[52] he had the impertinence to write a defense of his *Discourses* wherein he claimed the approbation of three learned men—Dr. Baker, Bishop Hutchenson, and Montfaucon.[53] In the *Journal* it is made clear that the letters from these three all deal with Henley's grammars, were written years before he established his Oratory, and that, as it was, they contained no recommendation

---

[50] *The Complete Linguist, or, an universal grammar of all the considerable tongues in being . . . Collected from the most approved hands. To be published monthly, till the whole is perfected.* London, 1719-1721. 7 numbers from Spanish to Chaldee. These grammars are the thinnest kind of compilation. The *Grub-street Journal's* quotations and instances are accurate. The French grammar consists of 63 pages, octavo, in large type. It ends, "A master, dictionary, reading the best authors, practice, and conversation will supply the remainder."

[51] Note in 160, "A bill of Hyp-oratorical mortality for the year 1732. . . . all these, both puffs and advertisements, died immediately after birth, having in vain cried out for help, and had nothing Christian at their first appearance or exit, neither baptism nor burial."

[52] See 153.

[53] The *Journal* made the typical corrections, *Mr.* Baker and Bishop Hutchinson.

or favorable criticism, but were merely formal and conventional letters of acknowledgement. It is also demonstrated that the eminent men whose approval Henley had claimed in his preface had in reality never recommended him at all. What, for example, Henley had called "an attestation in favour and recommendation" by Bishop Burscough resolved itself into his employment years before as an assistant preacher (number 156). The limits to which Henley's effrontery carried him are indicated by the advertisement in *Fog's Journal*—"As bishops and people now own the oratory is the only true religion of Britain, the scandal of a few desperate enemies is not worth notice;"[54] upon which the *Journal* remarked, "I wonder my brother will prostitute his paper to be the vehicle of such an impudent lie."

Although Henley ceased after a time to reply to the *Journal* in the *Hyp-Doctor*, he continued occasionally to argue with it at the Oratory and in his advertisements. In number 154 and the following issues the *Journal* managed to work up a squabble over Henley's generally peculiar manner of expression as illustrated in his advertisement in *Fog's Journal*, "In the Scripture, the rule of preaching, are above a thousand burlesque passages, which renders it strictly religious in its turn." The *Journal* declared this "as irreligious as ungrammatical and nonsensical," and in the ensuing squabble, Henley reiterated some of his earlier personalities concerning Russel, which drew the rejoinder (number 158): "Mr. H's affirmation that Mr. R. is writer of the Grub is not only false in itself, but likewise contrary to his own repeated assertions, in which he has ascribed that paper to several persons whom he has defamed with false and scandalous imputations, for which it is probable they may hereafter call him to an account."[55]

That the *Journal* and its editors fixed themselves in Hen-

[54] See 177. In 197 is an account of a challenge by Henley to all bishops and divines to argue with him at his Oratory.

[55] A similar squabble took place some four years later on the subject of the word *pridial*. Henley had now founded The Gentleman's Proper University. See *376, 377, 378*.

ley's memory is clear from his pamphlet, *Why, how now,
Gossip Pope,* published later, when the paper had long
been dead. He refers to it as "a continuation of the Dunciad
transposed," and speaks of "Mr. Savage surnamed the Half-
hanged,[56] one that continued your prose Dunciad in the
Grub, with Russel the non-juror that wrote the Impeachment." Of the *Journal* itself he says it "was the offspring
of your muse, and a sweet-tempered babe it was." Like many
other victims of the *Journal,* Henley makes Pope's association with the paper the reason for its attacking him,
although Pope had probably almost severed his direct connection with it by the time the continuous attacks on Henley
began.

The large amount of Henley material in the *Journal*
bears eloquent testimony to the character of the victim. He
was always active, absolutely and recklessly brazen, and ever
about to undertake some new venture that proved more
ridiculous than his last. He richly deserved the sarcasms in
the *Journal.* There has been some attempt to present Henley
as a genius gone astray, but very few of the arguments to
this end are sustained by enough evidence to be convincing.
Indeed, the statements of "A. Welstede" (Henley himself)
have been taken at their face value to prove Henley's eminence as a schoolmaster and a scholar.[57] It does appear that
Henley was a clever youth who was regarded by university
tutors with some favor, but he was always obstreperous,
and showed early signs of a charlatanism which soon passed
all bounds. His stronghold lay in his combination of tireless
energy and invention with superb impudence. Certainly by
1730 he was a thoroughgoing fraud and a proper butt for
the not too gentle shafts of the Grub writers.

The *Journal's* quarrel with Eustace Budgell and Aaron
Hill, or, in other words, with the *Bee* and the *Prompter*
took another tone. Henley was regarded as a low, ignorant

[56] A few years earlier, Savage had been condemned to death for a
homicide, but had been reprieved through interest in high quarters.
[57] See especially the *Retrospective Review,* Series I, XIV, 206, and I.
Disraeli, *Calamities and Quarrels of Authors,* (London [1881]).

mountebank, and the attacks on him, though they were violent enough, generally betrayed a tinge of condescension and tolerant contempt. Such a tone was out of the question in dealing with Aaron Hill, and even with Budgell, in spite of his unbalanced intellect. For Budgell, although he was bombastic and extravagant, was not a mountebank, and when stirred to frenzy by the heat of battle spoke with marked directness and force. Consequently the controversy which began with the *Bee* and continued with the *Prompter* was especially savage and bitter. Budgell, and later Hill and his colleague Popple, wrote as plainly and strongly as they knew how; in fact they frequently rivalled Swift in the robustness of their invective. The *Journal,* on its side, while it fought as usual from behind a screen of anonymity, and employed its ordinary weapons of irony and cold sarcasm, at times evinces an interest in its retaliation which smacks of actual hatred. As a result, among all the *Journal's* major campaigns this is perhaps the most ruthless.

Budgell's name had appeared several times in the earlier issues of the *Journal,* but the paper's attitude toward him had been amused and indifferent rather than definitely hostile. The publicity it gave him was not, however, of a desirable sort, and it may be supposed that a saner person than the erratic, half-crazy Budgell would have been at least somewhat resentful. As it was, he seems to have held no grudge, for in the first number of the *Bee,* in a descriptive catalogue of his various contemporaries, he says, after granting the *Journal* the first place in its particular class, "The person thought to be at the head of this paper is Mr. R———l, a non-juring clergyman. Mr. P———e and some other gentlemen are likewise suspected to have wrote some pieces in it. Whoever the authors are, they have shown upon several occasions that they want neither wit nor learning."

The *Journal's* earlier allusions to Budgell concern his political activities, but stress especially the question of his sanity. For instance in "Pegasus in Grubstreet," in number 16, one reads, "We are informed that Eustace Budgell, Esq.,

appeared on Tuesday at St. James, where without any introduction he presented a memorial to His Majesty, and afterward made a surprising speech to him, in which among other
things he complained of the present ministry."[58] A letter
from Swift to Pope, January 15, 1731, seems to represent
the usual attitude his acquaintances took toward him. Swift
says he has heard

> . . . lately from Mr. Budgell, the direction a feigned hand, and
> enclosed to Mr. Tickell. He desires I would write to some of my
> great friends in England to get him into the House of Commons
> there, where he will do wonders. What shall I do? I dare not answer
> him, and fear he will be angry. Can nobody tell him that I have no
> great friends in England, and dare not write to him?

The *Journal* also published a number of letters[59] in a dispute between Budgell and one William Piers, a former opponent of Budgell's in a lawsuit over a piece of landed
property. The resumption of their dispute was due to Budgell's statement of his case in his pamphlet, *A Letter to Cleomenes, King of Sparta.* Piers, in the *London Evening Post,*
June 12, 1731, declared this statement to be absolutely false,
and intimated that Budgell's suspected insanity was the best
excuse for what he had written. This letter the *Journal* reprinted and with it an answer by Budgell, wherein he represents Piers as a tool used to embarrass him in his public
career. He declares that Piers, like his other opponents in
lawsuits, is supplied with money for this purpose. He hopes
that no one will ever have to undergo such unheard of persecution as that he suffers, but asserts that if he dies in confinement he will leave memoirs behind him. Twice again he used
the *Journal* as a channel of reply to another letter of Piers
in the *Daily Courant,* July 22, 1731. The burden of these
letters is the wickedness of Piers and the martyrdom of Budgell:—Piers is dishonest; he is the tool of "those who 'assist
him and skulk behind his name," that is, the political forces
in league to destroy Budgell; he is hypocritical and only
feignedly pious. Budgell himself, on the other hand, is per-

[58] See also numbers 20, 39, 56.
[59] In numbers 78, 82, 83.

secuted just as the patriot Pulteney was, trying to do his poor country a service. "The best of it is, the whole world sees through these plots." The *Journal* took no side in this quarrel, but merely allowed Budgell to express himself and to make apparent his delusions of grandeur and persecution. It is hard to believe, however, that it had much sympathy with him, in view of the remarks about him published earlier, as well as two later sarcastic comments,[60] in both of which his name is linked with Henley's. The first is an epigram on a projected pamphlet by Budgell—

> I think the booksellers of Mr. Budgell
> For his and their own reputation judge ill
> To blow his works about with puff on puff
> As if they were Hyp-Oratory stuff.

The second noted the aptness of initiating Budgell into masonry on a Saturday and Henley on a Sunday—"As the gentleman of the law was initiated into the mysteries of masonry on the Jewish sabbath, the burlesque orator of the gospel was initiated on the Christian. . . ."

When Budgell decided to join the ranks of the magazine compilers and publish the *Bee*,[61] he enrolled himself among those whom the *Journal* regarded as its active enemies. If he still had any uncertainty as to the *Journal's* regard for him,

[60] See 122 and 167.

[61] The *Bee* seems never to have been a flourishing venture. The *Journal* continually gibed at its feebleness. The following gossip from the *London Magazine,* May, 1733, is corroborative: "Mr. J., one of Mr. Budgell's drawn in Gulls (alias Partners) did honestly declare to Mr. H., another Gull before a large company of booksellers at a public auction in Paternoster Row, that after sending out no. 2 of the Bee they were most of them returned him the next day, with a prohibition from his customers to send no more. He further added that 'He himself perceived it was such sad trash and a piracy so barefaced, that he was ashamed of being concerned in it; and neither could nor would encourage so scandalous a practice any longer.' This was verbatim Mr. J—s speech to his brother H. and the company. Mr. M. [another partner] soon found out the fraud . . . and threw up his share of the Bee at the third number." There follows an analysis of Budgell's charges of persecution by the Stamp Office. See also in the *London Magazine,* IV, 383, verses "On the Death of the Bee," giving a satirical account of its sickly life and the various expedients to keep it alive, including "Tindal's golden drops," and referring to its costume of "party colored clouts from Grubstreet stolen."

it was soon rudely dispelled. The growing animosity of "Grub writers" toward the compilers who "thieved" from their original contemporaries is reflected in an epigram[62] "occasioned by frequent puffing of Bees and Magazines," which compares the regular journals to "passengers robbed, stripped, and murdered." They also commented caustically on a puff of the *Bee* in the *Daily Post-Boy:*—" 'The Bee which was published Saturday last (if we are not much mistaken) carries a sting in his mouth and his tail too.' I believe WE, the compilers of the Bee are much mistaken, since a sting and a puff seldom issue from the same mouth, whatever they may do from the same tail."[63]

Then, in October, 1733, the *Journal* threw itself with all its vigor into the quarrel over the will of Dr. Matthew Tindall, the deist. Dr. Tindall, dying at an advanced age, was found to have made Budgell his heir in place of his nearest of kin, his nephew, Nicholas Tindall.[64] This fact led to an acrimonious public dispute, in the course of which appeared a pamphlet against Budgell, *A copy of the will of Dr. Matthew Tindall with an account of what passed concerning the*

[62] See 186.
[63] See 189.
[64] In number 73, the *Journal* had noted that the author of *Christianity as Old as the Creation* (one of Tindall's latest works) was dying of consumption and taking the last desperate remedies—"country air and asses milk," and had commented (item by Russel, ascribed to "M"), "I fear this prescription will have little success, it being a change only of air, and not of diet."

Nicholas Tindall seems to have been best known before this episode as translator of de Rapin's *History of England*. Nichols, VIII, 267, notes a public letter by William Duncombe (1728), criticising Tindall's style, "which is certainly none of the best." The *Journal* (138) advertised a new edition of the work (1732), and from April to December, 1736, it was the subject of an almost continuous controversy, which ran off into an independent discussion of Scottish antiquities. It is also the subject of remarks in the preface to the *Memoirs*. "Monsieur Rapin, so often extolled both by the *Craftsman* and the *London Journalist* [sic] as a fine historian, is very concisely characterized by the late *Free Briton* as the dullest of dull writers. And truly if a multitude of mistakes and blunders be any indication of dullness, this character cannot be charged with injustice." The writer (Russel) goes on to say that it had been made clear in the *Journal* that in fifty pages there were sixty errors, chiefly in the translation of Latin sources. In proportion, he says the whole work would contain two thousand; hence Rapin's prodigious popularity was mere Bibliomany, and he a Grubstreet author.

same between Mrs. Lucy Price [Tindall's housekeeper], *Eustace Budgell, Esq. and Mr. Nicholas Tindall.* The circumstantial account of Tindall's death contained in this pamphlet was very damaging to Budgell. On the whole it makes a strong case for a fraudulent will, and Budgell's answer, *A vindication of Eustace Budgell, Esq. from some aspersions thrown upon him in a late pamphlet,* is a weak and vague defense against it.[65] The *Grub-street Journal* was interested in the affair on both Tindall's and Budgell's accounts. Tindall, as one of the leading deists, was anathema to the highly orthodox Russel and had, in company with his confreres, Woolston, Collins, and others, been frequently held up to derision in the *Journal.*[66] Hence the scandal over his death and will was seized upon and exploited to the full. Budgell too, being a notorious figure and having incurred hatred as a thieving magaziner, was doubtless regarded as excellent prey when he got into a tight corner trying to play the rôle of Tindall's heir.

The *Journal's* first shot was a leading article (number 199):

The death of the late *great* Dr. Tindall (as the *great* Mr. Budgell styles him about ten times in one letter) gave occasion to the publication of the last will and testament of that famous Christian freethinker . . . and of Memoirs of his life, etc., by the *great* Mr. Curll, who, by a prescription of a *great* many years justly claims it as his *great* privilege to publish the lives of all *great* men together with copies of their last wills and testaments. Notwithstanding which long prescription the *great* Mr. Budgell, though by profession a *great* lawyer, took *great* offence at the publication both of the last will and the memoirs, upon which has ensued a very *great* quarrel between these two *great* men.

Following this comes a derisive comment on Curll's materials and his style, which the writer, "Giles Blunderbuss," main-

[65] According to Nichols, V, 161, the author of this pamphlet was William Webster, the "Richard Hooker" of the *Weekly Miscellany.* The author of the other pamphlet was N. Tindall, himself. Nichols, V, 516.

[66] See *post,* Chapter vi, p. 234. One amusing instance of ridicule of Tindall occurs in 68, where in a summarized attack on Collins and Tindall, the latter is spoken of as "Richard" with the footnote that his *Christian* name was Matthew, but having renounced his *Christian* name, he might as well be called Richard.

tains is modeled on Tindall's own. In the next issue a wood-
cut of a scene at a hair-dresser's, The Art of Trimming, is
interpreted by Bavius to represent various objects of the
Journal's satire. One group, he declares, consists of the persons involved in the Tindall scandal—Mrs. Price, who wrote
the will, Mr. Curll, N. Tindall, the doctor's nephew, and
Budgell. The latter is shown with passages from his pamphlet in his mouth, trying to compensate the nephew for the loss
of his inheritance. A month later[67] the Journal began a systematic analysis of the facts in the case, pretending impartiality and purporting to represent both sides, but probing
mercilessly the damaging weaknesses and vague evasions of
Budgell's defense. In the next issue came Pope's brilliant
epigram, which drove Budgell into a distracted rage—

> Great Tindal's gone, the Lord knows how or whither:
> To heaven we hope. 'Tis said Budge sends him thither
> To vend his wit. How so?—The Bee by this
> Will prove the Doctor's apotheosis.
> Thus canonised by Budge, sure all men must
> Confess, he died like Socrates the just.
> Fair Lucia[68] this attests—she saw him rise
> By G—d, by Bees transported to the skies.
> The fact, the phiz, the name in gold shall shine:
> Th' Athenians thus stamped Socrates divine.
> The oath and emblem's just: Rome's senate thus
> Made Gods of Caesar and of Romulus.

In his fury at these lines Budgell gave vent in the Bee to
a confused and long-winded denunciation of the Journal for
accusing him of murder. In reply the Journal (number 207)
explained away the charge with great gusto: "The compilers,
or rather chief compiler, in the worst sense of that word, of
a weekly pamphlet (consisting of servile piratical transcripts
from the works of others . . .) having charged our 205th
Journal with an abominable falsehood, it was thought proper
to represent this matter to the world in the fairest manner."
There follows a crushing set of ironical resolutions passed
by "the Society," after the laughter at "reading this tragi-

[67] In number 204.
[68] Mrs. Lucy Price, the housekeeper.

comical accusation of us" had ceased, in which is presented
a most colorless and innocent interpretation of the lines.[69]
Budgell is, moreover, accused of writing his own defense in
the *Bee*; his brain, it is affirmed, is turned by his "great
learning," and he wrote his long vindication of himself
merely to demonstrate his own great talents and swell the
Bee with ten original pages on nothing. This led to more
recriminations in the *Bee*. Budgell complained of assault
"without the least provocation in a most scandalous and
barbarous manner" and resorted to personalities about Russel. To these the *Journal* (number 209) replied with sarcasms on the *Bee's* descent to personalities, and its general
contempt for the clergy as unpatriotic, grasping, and dishonest. It also sneered, "If the late Dr. Tindall had left his
works and all his money to a priest, I should indeed have
taken it for granted that his will must have been forged,
or that he was out of his senses."

The *Journal* was not content, however, with insinuating
that Budgell had done away with Tindall. As soon as his
fury had had time to subside, they ingeniously suggested
that he was possibly Tindall's natural son. He had foolishly
inserted in the *Bee* (number 37) a poem in praise of adoption, where he proclaimed

> An ass may be an heir by Nature's rule
> And the philosopher transmit the fool . . .
> On reason's basis Budgell forms his claim
> And Tindall still survives, but in his name.

The *Journal* (number 214) pounced on these lines with
some of its own—

> —Since Nature's laws, as old as the creation,[70]
> Work stronger than revealed—in propagation;
> In Budgell's name how Tindall may survive
> My Muse will humbly her conjecture give.

[69] For instance, that the allusion to Socrates was merely suggested by
the *Bee's* own phrase, "Socrates did not meet death with more courage
and presence of mind," and that the *thus* at the end referred only to "a
similitude between the titles conferred upon Caesar and Romulus after
their death and those pompous eulogiums on the Doctor, so often repeated in the Bees."
[70] An ironical use of a deistic phrase.

Some act perhaps that god-like man had done
Might make this more than his adopted son.
Philosopher and fool thus, two in name
Reason's and Nature's heir may shine the same.

Such sneers and innuendoes drew from the furious Budgell further vehement defences of himself and equally vehement attacks on Russel and also Pope, who, it was intimated,
was the real cause of his "scandalous and barbarous treatment." In his desire to tear off his opponents' mask and
reveal their malice, he wrote for the *Bee*[71] "A Letter from
the authors of the Bee to Russel, a clergyman living in
Smith's Square, near the Horse-Ferry, in Westminster, and
the reputed author of the Grubstreet Journal." He asserts,

We are informed that you are a parson, that you have but a mean
fortune and no preferment; that you rent a house in Smith's Square,
near the Horse-Ferry in Westminster;[72] that not one of all your
neighbors either visits you or esteems you, and that the only visible
way you have of getting a livelihood is by taking some young gentlemen to board in your house, who go to Westminster School.

He demonstrates his own righteousness by the fact that he,
though he is the only writer for the *Bee* whom the *Journal*
or "its poet" [Pope] ever attacked, has declined to print
several satires on both the paper itself and the poet. Nor
does he disdain to puff his own abilities as satirist and poet.
The same number of the *Bee* likewise contained "A second
letter from the authors of the Bee to Parson Russel," in
which was included "An Essay upon Envy." In his next
issues Budgell carried on the war by printing several letters
chosen from the great number received sympathizing with
him for his treatment by the *Journal*. One writer points out
that the *Journal* has even attacked the memory of "the great
Mr. Addison," and has never yet "commended and spoke well
of any one man but of Pope the poet, for which there can

[71] See the *Bee*, IV, 72.
[72] Information which drew from Russel an epigram (209) to the effect
that where logical argument with the *Journal* was impossible, an opponent
might well resort to such personalities as "reverend master; or parson,
or priest," cry out "Wounds, Blood and Murder," and tell "a story of
poison, Smiths Square and Horse Ferry."

be but one reason." Another believes that the writer of the epigram "Great Tindall's gone" must be a monster in his soul and hopes that when discovered he will be found to be a monster in his body also—obviously an insinuation of Pope's authorship. In reply to a correspondent who offers to send in anecdotes about "the Parson and his Poet," the *Bee* says that though well posted about them already it will accept the offer. The *Journal's* statement that it had by no means accused Budgell of murder was also reprinted together with a minute analysis of the epigram to show that such was nevertheless its intention. Notice was then served that the discussion was concluded, but that the *Journal* might possibly expect public revelation of the lives of its writers.

The *Journal,* for its part, had no intention of closing the matter. On the contrary, it entered into a long serial history of Tindall's last days and the writing of his will. The will itself was printed with an ironical defence of Budgell's explanations of it. It was noted that the amount of the estate was far less than the bequests, with the comment, "There was some secret mystery in this affair, without any priestcraft."[73] Suspicious points such as the matter of a bond which Budgell had given Tindall, and the unusual spelling *Tindal* in the will, were also emphasized. The gist of the implied charge against Budgell was that he had managed to insinuate himself so far into the Doctor's favor by agreeing with and supporting his doctrines that Tindall had lent him large sums of money and had made him his close confidant and adviser, to the exclusion of his nephew and natural heir, Nicholas Tindall. It was suspected, moreover, that he had abused his intimacy and taken advantage of Tindall's weakness of mind at the last to forge a new will by which he became the heir. The Doctor's housekeeper, Mrs. Lucy Price, the "fair Lucia" of Pope's epigram, was implicated as Budgell's accomplice. The articles which set forth the detailed evidence for these suspicions, and which of course have a distinct bias against Budgell, form the body of the attack, but are relieved and

[73] Another ironical use of deistic phraseology. See 206.

garnished with numerous short squibs and personal epigrams. Thus Budgell was stung into a renewal of his personalities against Pope and Russel, and in consequence came retorts in the *Journal* about Budgell's egregious vanity, his doubtful sanity, and the dullness and piratical methods of the *Bee*. As a result the quarrel had become, even before it reached its height in the interference of the *Prompter,* the most virulent in the *Journal's* history. The personal allusions in the *Journal* range all the way from the comparatively innocent stanza in a poem advising an old maid searching for a husband to pretend to wealth (number 212)—

> Then may you see more happy days
> In being B—s wife.
> When dead, his Bee shall buzz thy praise
> And C—ll shall print thy Life.

to the devastating epigrams hinting that Budgell had murdered Tindall, and was his natural son, and Maevius'[74] savage "Short, but good advice to E. B., Esq." (number 220)—

> Answer to facts alleged, nor think to mask all
> Calling thy brother grubs, knave, villain, rascal.
> What if these names seem just?—yet if the stain
> Of testamental ink uncleansed remain
> Of thee the wicked world as wrong may judge
> And add those titles to the great Squire Budge.

Tindall also was made the butt of epigrams. He is said to have destroyed the Testaments after they had stood for hundreds of years, and, the world having learned from him, his own testament stood but seventeen days. And when Budgell, with many trumpetings of his own and the Doctor's greatness, offered medals as prizes for poems on Tindall, the *Journal* professed interest in the symbolical representation of the Doctor on them (also in number 220)—

> Ha! what strange figure's this, thus oddly clad?
> The whore of Babylon, mounted on her pad,
> The seven headed beast in Revelations,
> Of harlots mother and abominations?
> No, 'tis the beast, but not the scarlet whore,

[74] Probably Russel.

> A doctor standing where she rode before.
> A doctor!—How! I swear it is like no man
> 'Tis rather some old visionary woman.
> Nothing but smock and gown has this old hag on;
> Who muttering seems enchantments o'er the dragon.
> 'Tis Dr. Tindall, *learned, godlike, great,*
> Has driven his once loved mistress from her seat
> Where light revealed outfacing with his own
> Pope Mat now shines superior to Pope Joan.

On the award of prizes in this contest, the *Journal* (numbers 225, 226) reported the results and discussed the poems, since it seemed that the authors were "latent members of our society." The first prize poem received especial attention for its bad Latin.

Budgell's replies to this persecution were directed almost altogether against Pope. He burst forth in another "Letter from the authors of the Bee to Parson Russel, living over against St. Anne's Church near the Horse Ferry in Westminster," wherein Russel is told that he is odious to mankind, but must nevertheless have been persuaded to this present malicious course by "the Poet, your helpmate." "The raging envy of this poor creature toward every man whose writings have made him eminent is now become so obvious and notorious to all the world that he is better known by this part of his character than by his works." There are further comments on "the villain your Poet," "the little envious animal," "the Parson's black petticoats" and "the pygmy size of his Poet," and other similar matter intended to cast down opponents and assuage the wounds of Budgell's inordinate pride.[75] These outbursts in the *Bee* make it clear that even now Pope was regarded, by Budgell at least, as the main force behind the Journal, and that Russel was considered merely a willing and malicious tool in the hand of a malicious master. Budgell's critical attitude toward Pope is clearly reflected in his remarks on the *Epistle to Dr. Arbuthnot* and *The Characters of Women* (*Bee*, number 103):

[75] See the *Bee,* numbers 52-61. In 61, in commenting on an advertisement in the *Journal* nominating Budgell for Parliament, the *Bee* declares it a malicious banter of Pope's, and says that the poet had probably heard that a great man had promised Budgell a place in Parliament but had broken his word.

We cannot help saying that as Mr. Pope is at present in his declining years, we think that spirit which formerly appeared in some of his pieces is almost extinguished: In the two pieces last mentioned, tho there are some good lines there are others extremely low and obscure. His very rhimes are not always what the French call rich, and his versification has not that harmony which it formerly had. We may possibly give some instances in a future Bee to prove what we assert.

The final installment of the *Journal's* account of Tindall's will was published in number 231 (May 30, 1734), and marks the end of the first phase of the quarrel, extending over a period of eight months. Except for an occasional prick, Budgell was now allowed to rest in peace for something over a year. Slight allusions to him and the controversy appeared occasionally; for instance, in a proposal for rebuilding Grub-street in number 289, it is suggested that the dome of the capitol be shaped like a beehive and assigned to Budgell, "tho the place will be but small, 'tis not unlikely by the time it is built, 'twill be big enough to hold himself and all that will be left of the Doctor's money."[76] The *Journal* showed no intention, however, of renewing the quarrel until it reprinted in number 294 a deistic composition by Tindall, "The Philosopher's Prayer," as "uttered by the Dying Bee," and then, "in order to give it some other recommendation, . . . thought proper to tag it with rime."[77] A fortnight later came a second provocation, in the form of an attack on infidels, especially Tindall, running off into side thrusts at Budgell and the *Bee*. The question is asked why, since the witlings of the *Bee* show such respect for Addison, they do not refute his Christian writings. There are also contemptuous remarks on Budgell's puffs of himself, on "The Philosopher's Prayer," and the bad Latin in one of the odes on Tindall. In number 298 came further criticism of the "Prayer," and in number 300 a letter and verses "On the Deists' Scheme of Fitness," and notice of a long puff[78] "by late authors of the

[76] For other allusions, see 232, 256, 275.
[77] See *post*, p. 234 ff.
[78] In the *Post-Boy*, September 16 and 18, 1735, and the *Daily Journal*, September 17.

Bee" charging the *Journal* with false quotations from "The Philosopher's Prayer." Upon these the *Journal* retorted in its usual vein, and published "A Soliloquy of Pufferus Secundus" (that is, Budgell, Henley being Primus) making the point that since Budgell couldn't answer the arguments against the "Prayer" he would make the most of a few insignificant misprints in the *Journal's* version. In succeeding issues (302-313)[79] the fire was maintained; the *Journal* reprinted various prize poems on Tindall and called attention to their bad Latin. One of them (in number 311) is declared to be a riddle, and the hope is expressed that since the *Bee* has given one medal for it, it will give another to anyone who can elucidate it. It also printed an accurate version of the "Prayer" as well as a ridiculous one in verse, and annotated one of the Tindall odes with remarks on the scandal over the will. It was announced that Orator Henley, who had derided the "Prayer" on its first appearance, had praised it in a special oration, and even announced a second on it, but, being taken to task for inconsistency, had rambled off into a discussion of King William's landing at Torbay and the benefits of the revolution. The final shot at Budgell and his prize poems came in number 313 in the lines—

> What is't to me if Tindal flies
> Or proudly tramples o'er the skies?
> What tho' it be (I hope 'tis so)
> His fellow breathes not here below.
> Yet still his scorn of gold was vain
> For he (as I now) wrote for gain.
> His country's love, what was't but gold?
> For that he faith and honour sold.
> Gold was his god. And (to be free)
> Give but, dear Budge, the prize to me,
> I Tindal's steps will straight pursue
> And even write in praise of you.

[79] In 311, "Jack Nab" says roundly, ". . . the world grows cursed tired of your contest with the Bee writers; it must be sure for want of other matter that you take such pains with a defunct drone. . . . For my part, as I take in your paper and never read a Bee in my life, I look on myself as two pence out of pocket when instead of a cheerful entertainment I see the first page of your paper filled with the Philosopher's Prayer."

The only later mention of Budgell came upon his death in May, 1737, by suicide, with a coroner's verdict of lunacy (number 386). The newspapers reported that he had been very uneasy over a cause soon to come on at Westminster, upon which the *Journal* commented "This cause at Westminster Hall, we hear, related to the late Dr. Tindal's will."

The point of Budgell's guilt in connection with Tindall's will seems never to have been satisfactorily cleared up. So much minutely circumstantial evidence was produced against him, and his own defense was in comparison so vague and unconvincing, that it is hard to believe that the will was a legitimate one. Budgell was nevertheless so unbalanced and so wildly erratic that the spectacle of his baiting by the *Journal* is rather unpleasant. This scandalous quarrel, with the frenzy of excitement which it threw him into, must have been, as the newspaper reports suggest, a last straw to cause his suicide.

Although the *Bee* expired in the summer of 1735[80]—the *Journal* printed obituary verses on July 3—the quarrel did not die with it, but was carried on even more heatedly by the *Prompter,* which came to the defense of "The Philosopher's Prayer" in the autumn.

The semi-weekly *Prompter,* which was the organ of Aaron Hill and William Popple and was devoted especially to the theatre, had been on excellent terms with the *Bee* from the very beginning. Indeed, the *Bee* had paved the way for alliance by declaring of the *Prompter's* first issue that it "seems to be much better wrote than the Universal Spectator, the Grubstreet Journal, and other papers which have of late attempted to divert the town"—an expression reflecting the change which controversy had made in the *Bee's* originally complacent attitude toward the *Journal.* The *Prompter* had managed to run through nearly one hundred issues without falling foul of the *Journal,* except for one slight encounter on the subject of harlequinades, which had led to no especial

---

[80] For some time after its death its editors still advertised it for sale, and inserted notices in the newspapers complaining of malicious treatment. See *Grub-street Journal,* 304.

bitterness. In its ninety-eighth number, however, it sprang with surprising boldness and vigor to the side of the *Bee,* now practically defunct, in the squabble over "The Philosopher's Prayer." Under the heading "Qui Bavium non odit, amet, tua . . . " appeared a violent assault on the *Journal.* It opened promisingly, "There is a meanness in some minds," and continues with allusions to "a set of obscure writers" and "these reptiles," who "only censured the Prayer because it was wrote by the late Dr. Tindall and recommended by Mr. B—", a statement which contained more than a grain of truth. It also maintained that there was nothing in the "Prayer," "but what not only a tradesman, or a gentlewoman, or a porter, or a cook maid, but even the whole bench of bishops and body of the clergy might with great devotion and on bended knees repeat."

In this same issue and those following during the next four months the *Prompter* carried on a campaign against the *Grub-street Journal,* which showed in the matter of personal abuse a good will and fluency which even Bavius himself must have envied. For a vocabulary of opprobrium, one may search the pages of the *Journal* in vain for a collection of words and phrases to exceed those of the *Prompter.*[81] The quarrel after a time turned, however, into a tiresome squabble over Latinity and theology, until it broke out on the *Prompter's* side into shrieks of triumph over what it termed the defeat and forced resignation of Bavius.

The opening attack was followed in the *Prompter* (numbers 101 and 102) with a burlesque of the *Journal's* methods with the "Prayer." After a sarcastic allusion to "the very great talent" of "the little fry at the Pegasus," it analyzed ironically in the *Journal's* manner a prayer of Cleanthes, and announced,

[81] Apropos of the *Prompter's* fluency in abuse, appeared in 311 the complaint: "It is very remarkable that all those apostatizing members from our society, whose ignorance, immorality, or impiety in writing has been exposed in this Journal have made use of the very same double method in their own defence" (that is, discussion of petty detail and personal abuse of the Grub editors).

Whereas the author of the Daily Gazetteer has published a versification of the prayer of an ancient philosopher called Cleanthes, contrary to the right and title which the learned Bavius has to versify all philosopher's prayers whatsoever, this is to acquaint the public that the said Bavius is determined to prosecute the aforesaid publisher according to the extremest rigor of the laws now in force, to secure the property of the subject.

In numbers 105 and 107 the *Prompter* resorted to verse, both Latin and English, "In effigiem doctissimi Bavii, aedi suae in via Grubstreet dicta, loco Pegasi, praeponendam.

> Pollebam Juvenis, studio sine divite vena
> Cum Pater, incertus, clerum, faceretne, poetam,
> Mallebat clerum. Clerus—nolente Minerva
> Versiculos facio, atque hebdomadalia pango.

and the following adaptation from *Henry IV*—

> In faith, dear Grub, you have been much to blame!
> You must needs learn, my Wag, to mend these faults;
> Defect of manners, want of government;
> Pride, haughtiness, opinion, and disdain.

The word *clerus* in the Latin epigram gave rise to endless disquisitions on Latinity as well as to the bandying back and forth of charges of disrespect and lack of reverence for the clergy.

The *Journal* was indeed throughout the quarrel continually pressing the charges that the *Prompter* was deistic and hostile to the church and its clergy, while the *Prompter* on its side consistently denied, excused, and explained away such accusations. The *Prompter,* deistic in its sympathies, yet had no desire to appear as a detractor of the clergy, or an opponent of orthodox religion. Its explanation (number 108) of *clerus* was as follows:

The word clerus is used by Pliny for . . . a worm or grub that got into bee hives and infected the honey. Allusively to this kind of occupation in Pliny's Grub the epigrammatist thought it might with great propriety and beauty be used as a name for such a little poisonous grub as the reverend drayman of the hebdomadalian dung-cart [Russel, of course], and in this sense of the word could not be understood (but by Bavius himself whom I have charity enough to suppose mistaken in his application of the word) to mean the clergy in general.

This apology was enforced by a further onslaught on Russel, in number 112, for his unclerical activities,

Of all the hot-headed and ignorant bigots this age has produced, none has distinguished himself in this wrong method [*i. e.* defending religion by pulling down reason] so much as the Reverend Drayman at the Pegasus; whose employment (to observe it en passant) in writing Grub-street Journals is just as becoming the function of priesthood as was his who employed his time in inventing gun-powder; the one being made use of to destroy the bodies, the other the characters of men. This mixture of priest and scavenger, this motley composite of sacred and profane . . . this artful hypocrite and cold designing traitor . . . the Vicar of Grub-street.

In the *Prompter,* number 120, Pope too is branded as a libeller of the clergy in his translation of Horace, and accused of leading all the *poetae minores* who ape him, to follow in his footsteps.

Other issues were also dragged into the dispute. "T. B.", who contributed several anti-Grubean letters to the *Prompter,* criticised Pope for defects in style in *The Dunciad,* tautology, for instance (number 108), and again (number 111) enlarges on his career as a libeller. More pertinent is the direct attack on the *Journal's* manners and methods in controversy, to which, with two epigrams, the whole of number 107 is devoted. Between personalities and Latinity, however, "The Philosopher's Prayer," which was the original bone of contention was at times almost lost sight of. A pretense of discussing it was maintained, nevertheless—the *Prompter* defending it as a high and noble utterance, and the *Journal* contending that it was epicurean and atheistical and denied the very being of God (number 320). Bavius on his side cited the doubts and reservations implied in Tindall's numerous *if* clauses as constituting a denial of religious dogma (number 324), and examined the *Prompter's* attributes as a philosopher and a Christian. These he declared contradictory; for the *Prompter,* while seeming desirous of acceptance as a member of the Christian community, still denied all Christian dogmas and preferred apparently to be called a philosopher rather than a Christian (number 326). This side of the argument, like the one over the Latin, at length lapsed into pedantry, and became a hairsplitting wrangle over points of religious dogma.

The *Journal* stuck to the point at issue no closer than did its opponent. On both sides the chief desire was of course to discover a weak spot and score a hit. An exposure of improper motives was more important than the true meaning or value of "The Philosopher's Prayer." The *Journal* at the outset had recognized the entrance of the *Prompter* into the quarrel by accusing it, in "A Dialogue between Prompterus and Pufferus Secundus,"[82] of taking up the cudgels against a well known opponent merely to attract attention:

Prom. I've advertised and puffed this thing of mine
      In vain: tho got to number ninety-nine.
Puff. Write 'gainst the Grubs; 'twill give it a new motion
      If you'll defend my prayer's profound devotion.
Prom. 'Twould fill, to answer all their damned reflections
      Three Prompters. *Puff.* Snap at two or three objections
      This still has been my way. In puffs I'll bully,
      And tell the world, that you have answered fully.
      Thus my last Bee, by puffing repetition,
      Is flying in *another new edition.*
Prom. Another? That's the third. Pray, how is't reckoned?
      It never heard of, much less saw, the second.
Puff. N'importe. If 'tis a new edition, brother,
      Tho there's no second, surely 'tis another.

The *Journal* also selected as a vulnerable point of attack the practice of reprinting extracts from the *Prompter* in the *Daily Journal,* which was published by the same printer. This trick of the trade was duly emphasized in "An egregious puff in the Daily Journal paraphrastically illustrated" (number 307) and an epigram voicing objection to buying the *Prompter* for twopence and then the *Daily Journal* for three halfpence only to find that

> these twins of different name,
> Prompter and Daily Journal are the same.

The same point was made again in the epigram (number 316)—

> A beggar blind, with legs and feet supplied
> A lame one riding on his back as guide.

[82] Budgell again. See 304.

> Thus Daily Journal, stumbling in his track
> And puffing, bears the Prompter on his back.

It was also suggested that the somewhat similar practice in the *Bee* of issuing "three editions" which were in reality only one was probably defended from the Bible—"The last shall be first," etc., (in number 307).

As to personalities, charges of impudence, ignorance, and so forth, the *Journal* was quite justified in replying with a *tu quoque,* and asking who in this matter had the "greater occasion for shame and confusion." As a fair specimen of its own powers in this way it offered in number 310 an epigram which hit off cleverly the various points in the quarrel, and recalled one embarrassing episode in Hill's career—his futile promotion of a speculative scheme to manufacture beech-oil—

> In quiet let Tindal's adopted inherit,
> Complain of great men and his own slighted merit.
> Let him rail, let him rail, be eternally railing
> At priests and the Christian religion's prevailing.
> Let the Prompter, his second, too take up the cudgel
> And weakly and formally vindicate B—l.
> If the gospel e'er suffer from two such infectors
> The world must be crazy or Beech-oil Projectors.

In the midst of the campaign, which apparently was to run on interminably with arguments over *clerus* and theological quibbles, the *Journal* suffered a major casualty in the resignation of Bavius. This the *Prompter* jubilantly hailed as a signal for its victory, declaring, moreover, that the defection of Bavius had led to a dissension in the Grubstreet camp over the choice of a new commander.

The baton, [the *Prompter* says (number 123)] by the spies I have among them, I am informed, will be conferred on another Reverend Militant, who having served a long time under that renowned commander, the experienced Bavius, has acquired as consummate a knowledge as his predecessor. It is yet a doubt whether he will carry it (tho the odds are very much for him), being opposed by the Honest Yorkshireman[83] who has lately given some proofs of his

[83] Doubtless Henry Carey, whose ballad opera, *The Wonder! An Honest Yorkshireman,* was acted at Drury Lane, 1735. See *Biographia Dramatica.*

capacity in the Grubean way, and made two or three attacks that
have been very much applauded by the learned society. But unless
Bavius resumes the baton in order to prevent a division, it is most
probable the election will fall on the Reverend Doctor, celebrated
for his performances in the last Prompter but two, and better known
by the name of the Man of Taste,[84] than his own.

Bavius refusing to retire at once from public disputes, the
Prompter issued (number 127) the announcement that
"Whereas the ghost of the deceased Reverend Captain Bavius
continues to walk and haunt the old place of his abode, these
are to acquaint such whom his reappearance may be disagreeable to, that care will be taken to lay him, after he has walked
to the end of the Philosopher's Prayer."[85] But in number
128 appears an obituary notice—

The Reverend Captain, deceased, having already finished his short
course, and lain himself, now sleeps with his fathers. His behaviour
in dying showed even death could not cure his itch of nibbling, as
long as he had a tooth in his head. But, as he lived, he died.

> Thus by the chimney fire a monkey lay
> And in death's agonies remembering play
> Crawled o'er to puss, who slept on t'other side
> And having bit his tail, came back and died.

Even now Bavius refused to rest in peace, and number 133,
with the heading "Rest, rest, perturbed spirit" is devoted
entirely to reiterations of the charges against him, in the
course of which it is said that the *Gentleman's Magazine* for
January has two Russello-Grubean articles by Bavius. This
seems to be the final echo of the battle over the Philosopher's
Prayer, except for the criticism of a correspondent who has
noted in the *Prompter's* manner "now and then a little oozing
from the Grubstreet common sewer, to the great annoyance
of all lovers of cleanliness" (in the *Prompter,* number 137).

With the passing of Bavius and the accession of a new
editor, probably James Miller, the *Journal* came still more
bitterly into conflict with the *Prompter* over a new bone of
contention, which soon distracted interest from "The Philos-

[84] James Miller, author of the comedy, *The Man of Taste* (see p. 198).
[85] The *Prompter* thus took a leaf from Bavius' own book; it was in
such phrases that the *Journal* had made sport of James Moore-Smythe.
The trick was of course not an original one, witness Swift.

opher's Prayer." Miller and William Popple of the *Prompter* were the authors of two new rival comedies, *The Man of Taste* and *The Double Deceit,* which now became the subject of a violent altercation.[86] Each made the most of his position as an editor to cry up his own play and damn his opponent's.

Charges of plagiarism, the organization of cabals, and so forth, were bandied back and forth, and the new quarrel was soon going as vigorously and merrily as had the one before it. In its turn it too became an exchange of personalities, this time between Popple and Huggonson, the printer of the *Journal*. During this controversy the *Journal* also made a slight side excursion against Aaron Hill's theories regarding amateur acting, but as little came of it, the latent attempt to start another line of disagreement was soon abandoned. It is quite probable that readers of the *Journal* found these squabbles, and particularly the one over the "Prayer," extremely boring. Such is the impression to be gathered from a letter in number 325 asking the *Journal* "to give over pestering your readers with disputes about a damned play and a damned prayer." The *Journal,* however, retorted virtuously that it did not consider it out of the way to give a little space now and then to a defence of natural and revealed religion "against the wicked insinuations contained in that prayer and against the weak and wicked arguments published . . . in vindication of it." Moreover, this letter, it is suggested, comes with a bad grace from one who, the editor thinks, is himself a contributor, and whose work they have even gone so far as to publish as their own! As far as the "Prayer" was concerned, little more was said about it; the "damned play", however, still flourished as a topic of discussion.

One of the most interesting phases of this varied controversy between the *Journal* and the *Prompter* was the question of Aaron Hill's participation in it. Hill was certainly hostile to neither side before the quarrel. He had been a contributor to the *Journal* and was on good terms with the *Bee*.[87] Never-

---

[86] For a detailed account of this quarrel and criticism of Hill's theory of acting see *post,* Chapter v.

[87] See Dorothy Brewster, *Aaron Hill.* Carruthers in his life of Pope summarizes this quarrel, 282 ff. He says (287) that a long prose obituary

theless, the *Prompter* was his; Popple's influence in it must have been secondary. That the *Journal* held Hill responsible is clearly evident from its sarcastic allusion to Beech-Oil Projectors, its turning of the attack on his theories of acting, and the more or less veiled personalities directed against him continually in the discussions of the Philosopher's Prayer and the two rival plays. Hill's attitude toward these personal allusions is manifest in a somewhat surprising letter to Richardson, March 6, 1735.[88]

I have observed from many angry and indeed unjust personalities in the Grubstreet Journal pointing grossly at me that I am misrepresented by the author or authors, as the defender of the Philosopher's Prayer and disliker of the Man of Taste; not to mention other mistakes which they seem often to be led into about me.

As you know that I have nothing to answer for on either of these two heads, having never seen any of those papers till I read them in the published Prompters, I should take it as a favor if you will immediately find means to undeceive the gentlemen concerned. I am ashamed to give you this trouble, but am altogether unacquainted with any of them myself: nor do I know who is their publisher.

It is very disagreeable to me to find myself ill-treated upon such mistaken grounds of resentment; and it would be more so to be forced into a necessity of defending myself publicly. I have always been an enemy to these personal bickerings among writers, and wish well to them all with a sincerity, that (of how little service soever it may be) does not at least deserve to be treated unkindly.

I shall be very much obliged to you if you can find some way to let this be known to the gentlemen, whoever they are, that they may no longer misconceive, Sir, your most obedient, humble servant, A. Hill.

It is rather difficult to accept literally all of Hill's statements here. He was the chief editor of the *Prompter,* yet he disclaims all responsibility for large sections of material and even asserts that he had never seen them until he read them in print. Neither could the statement that he knew nothing of any of the *Journal's* editors, or even the name of the pub-

of a Mrs. Butler of Sussex which appeared in the *Journal,* November 28, 1734, was by Pope. Hill inserted in the *Prompter* of December 8 laudatory verses to the author of the obituary, who, he believed, was Pope. These lines, Carruthers says, were later ascribed to Pope himself. Cf. Griffith, *Pope: Bibliography,* p. 262.

[88] In the Foster Collection in the Victoria and Albert Museum. This letter is quoted in part in Dorothy Brewster's *Aaron Hill.*

lisher, be quite ingenuous. The *Prompter* and the *Bee* had both for some time been naming and describing Russel as definitely as possible as the editor, and the name of the publisher, to whom communications might be sent was, as in all papers, clearly printed at the end of each issue. The most probable assumption is perhaps that Popple was the chief mover in the quarrel, and that Hill preferred to have him carry the weight of the abuse. The whole letter sounds as though it were a formal diplomatic note to the editors of the *Journal,* which Hill wished Richardson to convey to them in order to avoid the trouble or possible discomfort of dealing with them himself. That he was as innocent and ignorant of these long continued personalities as he claimed to be it is difficult to believe. He would seem to be doing much as Pope did with the *Journal* itself, disclaiming responsibility when he found it irksome. That the note accomplished its purpose is clear from a statement in number 325 (March 18, 1735)—

We have been likewise assured than an ingenious gentleman, formerly our correspondent, and at present generally thought to be one of the chief authors of the Prompter has declared that he never wrote anything concerning the Philosopher's Prayer or the Man of Taste, that he never saw any of the papers on those subjects till after they were printed, and that he entirely disapproved all the personal scurrilities in them levelled at the supposed authors of some pieces in our Journals.

This was indeed making the most of Hill's statement and stretching it to cover all possible ground. It is noticeable, too, that there is no hint of conciliation in the *Journal's* notice, but rather satisfaction in receiving apologies and explanations from an opponent who was admittedly in the wrong. The impression is confirmed by an editorial note in the *Journal* six months later. In number 352 was published "Of the praise of tobacco, or the smoker's epitome. Mr. A. H——'s style imitated," with a note "See his Actors Epitome and the Dedication to Zara." The forty lines of this poem were full of phrases apparently in burlesque of Hill's style, especially in his advice to actors. They also had a postscript wherein the *Journal* was charged with having "injudiciously attributed to Mr. P—— what in reality concerned Mr. H—— and *sic vice versa.*" The *Journal* declared two weeks later:

This charge is entirely groundless, for most of his allegations are brought against the paper called the Prompter, considered in a personal capacity, to which as a person are justly reputed indiscriminately the mistakes and ill conduct of the two authors, who are both answerable for everything which appeared in that paper, not under the character of any correspondent, but in that of the Prompter. And as to some things which are particularly attributed to one of those authors, none of them in reality at all concerned the other.

The *Journal* was not one to forget and forgive, nor are there many instances of its eagerness to grasp an outstretched hand. Another interesting side-light is thrown on the quarrel by a letter from Budgell to the editor of the *Prompter* dated February 8, 1735-6.[89] Budgell here complains that the *Prompter* had acknowledged his letters very tardily, and had also criticised them for being fragmentary and incomplete.[90] He goes on,

A gentleman much my superior both in parts and learning [an unusual admission for Budgell] . . . sent you a letter long since with the Universal Spectator enclosed in it. This gentleman (as I thought at least) showed in a very masterly manner how flagrantly the Spectator and the Grubstreet Journal, though they both condemned the Philosopher's Prayer, had contradicted one another. He showed how much the layman excelled the Parson [Russel] both in candor and good breeding, and I own I cannot still help thinking that nothing could more mortify the Grubstreet Drayman than your publishing my friend's letter. . . . I presume I need not tell you how much Bavius triumphs on your silence, nor how many adversaries your espousing the Philosopher's Prayer had drawn upon you besides the Drayman. . . . I should think that nothing would more contribute to make your paper taken notice of than so many little curs barking at you, if with a few lashes of your whip you sent them yelping home to tell their story and make their complaints to their brothers. . . . A. B.

[89] See British Museum, MSS 37232, f. 137.
[90] *Prompter,* January 27, 1736, "The letters signed A. B. are both, tho late, come to hand. If the author will extend himself in some of the subjects he recommends he will find due regard will be paid to them. Hitherto they have been, more properly speaking, hints, without execution."

Appended to this letter is the illuminating note—"Sir—You have all the letters that came to my hand. Surely this should be signed E. B., who knows no end of his Philosopher's Prayer. S. R. [Samuel Richardson]." Evidently Budgell became wearisome even to his friends and allies.

The *Journal* was able to enjoy the last word in these quarrels and to crow over its adversaries, for it survived them both. The *Bee* seems to have died a lingering death; in the *Journal's* following number, 300, there are frequent allusions to the fact that the *Bee* had ceased its buzzings, except for issuing what it called new editions of its last number. The *Prompter,* which survived the *Bee* by about a year, was upon its demise the subject of an exultant editorial of more than four columns (number 350), in which a sarcastic résumé of the whole quarrel is preceded by the announcement, "On Friday the second of July last died the *Prompter,* an apostatizing member of our Society, who taking no warning by the fate of the *Weekly Register, Bee,* etc. imitated their conduct by showing a particular enmity to our *Journal.*"

CHAPTER V

LITERARY AND DRAMATIC CRITICISM

The professed purpose of the *Grub-street Journal* was a literary one. According to announcements at the beginning, to reiterations of policy from time to time in the heat of various controversies, and to Bavius' history in the preface to *The Memoirs of Grub-street,* the *Journal* was intended first of all to serve the cause of literature. It was to reveal the unnoticed or hidden excellences of good books on the one hand, and on the other the stupidity or imposture of bad ones. Although it dealt during its course in nearly all sorts of wares, it did in reality keep literature, taken in a broad sense, its leading interest. It might betray an occasional warmth against the excise, undertake a crusade against a quack doctor, wrangle over a point of theology, or fill its columns with Addisonian moral essays, but it did cling with more or less fidelity to its avowed purpose as a champion of literature. In pretense at least it regarded itself as a defender of literary ideals in its quarrels with Bentley and Theobald and in its assaults on the newspapers and magazines, which it accused of demoralizing contemporary periodical literature.

Of course the spirit of the *Grub-street Journal* was essentially combative and pugnacious. It soon became evident that while it might talk generalities about putting down the impudent or uplifting obscure geniuses and reviving forgotten classics, what it really existed for was to ferret out weaknesses, detect errors, and expose false motives. Moreover, one can never shake off the impression that the *Journal* is neither ingenuous nor disinterested. It was apparently delighted rather than disappointed when it found something to attack. In addition there is always the underlying possibility of personal complications. This is obvious, of course, in the case of the Dunces. Theobald, for instance, was pilloried chiefly because he was objectionable to Pope, and the various books which suffered in the *Journal's* columns were often clearly the objects of personal rivalries, between either authors or booksellers. Of plays this was even truer. The difficulties of getting a play produced, the prevalence of claques and cabals in the theaters, the jealousies of actors, all combined to interfere with genuine criticism. The criticism of a play became almost at once a series of angry shrieks and recriminations between rival authors and their friends. The result is often amusing and lively reading, but it is interesting far less as indicating the critical point of view of the period, than as illustrating and exposing its literary manners and practical methods—it is quarrelsome and personal.[1]

The *Journal* carried on numerous sustained quarrels extending over a period of months, quarrels like those over Bentley's *Milton,* which stand out distinctly in the paper's career. Apart from these, however, it kept up a steady fire on less important productions, noticed perhaps in only one or two numbers.

Of real literary criticism, the discussion of the principles of literary art, or aesthetic and artistic analysis of individual works, there is in fact very little to be found in the *Journal*. Occasionally, to be sure, one comes upon a detached bit of comment which in its point of view is disinterestedly critical. For instance in number 54, "Thomas Didymus" summarizes the battle between Aeneas and Turnus in the *Aeneid,* Book

---

[1] This has of course been continually illustrated in the preceding chapters, but another typical instance at this point may not be superfluous. In a series of letters concerning a verse satire, *The Dramatic Sessions,* in 241, 242, and 243, the poem was savagely attacked by "The Laesos", and its author, "Scriblerus Theatricus", tried to evade responsibility by declaring that the poem, having been refused by the *Grub-street Journal,* had been brought out by a bookseller, much to the author's surprise and with many unauthorized changes. This merely brought down a second savage attack by "The Laesos", who said he had not originally mentioned all the faults of the piece since he considered his job as difficult as cleaning the Augean stables. The whole plan of the poem, he says, shows a "blundering genius," and he expresses his contempt for the cowardice of an abusive writer who, when taken to task, avoids blame by fathering his own abuse on some unknown person who is declared to have made changes in the text.

V, to show that it reflects little credit on Aeneas, and has a decidedly anticlimactic effect, coming, as it does, at the end of the main action. Or again, in number 386, one "R. S." appears in defense of Tasso's pastoral play *Aminta,* which had been adversely criticised in the *Guardian* (28) as being unpastoral in language, sentiment, and so forth. R. S. objects to the point of view of the critic who had disparaged Tasso and had also praised highly an English pastoral in the broadest Somerset dialect. He points out inaccuracies in the *Guardian* articles and is sustained in his charges by the Grubstreet editor. It is perhaps indicative of the contemporary taste that R. S. should object to the use of such names as "Rager" and Cicely in the dialect of the English pastoral. Of philological interest there is also a trace, as in a letter (suggested by the *Spectator,* number 135) proposing an academy for the standardization of English, with the *Journal* as temporary guardian of the purity of the language. To illustrate the proper work of such an authority the writer brings up the case of *never so much,* which though very old and practically universal, ought to be "sifted out" of the language and replaced by *ever so much.* Another and more interesting suggestion appears in number 213, in a petition of "H" for recognition as a letter. The author contends that such recognition has been denied chiefly because of the lack of an H in the Greek alphabet, the symbol H merely representing Eta. He remarks upon the fact that H as a letter had existed in the older Greek in such forms as HO and inveighs against the use of *an* before words with an aspirated initial h or an initial u like that in *universe.* "All the world says, and therefore should write, *a union, a unity."* Clearly the writer was a man in advance of his age; the reforms he sought are hardly complete two centuries later. Again, Martyn ("B") in number 26 collates an obscure passage in Urry's *Chaucer* with Caxton's edition, and notes that the earlier reading is perfectly clear. But such stray scraps of criticism are few and far between, and are almost lost sight of in the great bulk of the literary and dramatic discussion, which, practically all of it, impresses itself on the reader as being personal in its motivation. But doubtless Vergil's technical skill in narrative, Tasso's style, or the propriety of *never so much* or *an universe,* seemed altogether too tame to serve as anything more than convenient filler.

There is only one notable exception to this general conclusion. During the *Journal's* early period there appeared in it a series of four articles on *Hudibras* signed "M. J." (numbers 39, 41, 45, 63). The purpose of the writer is to bring out the excellence of the poem. He shows little independence of idea or imagination, and says little that a reader of average intelligence would not notice at once by himself,[2] but the articles are in general amusing because of copious quotation from the poem itself. They consist for the most part of a description of the two main characters, Hudibras and Ralpho, the group of comic figures at the bear-baiting in Canto II, and a running account of the action in the first two cantos. He begins by declaring *Hudibras* a new type of poem. He rejects the denominations *burlesque poem, mock heroic, mock epic,* and comes to the brilliant conclusion that it can only be called *Hudibrastic.* He then proceeds formally to lay down rules for Hudibrastic composition, and to show the nature of its action, characters, and language. His most interesting point is made at the end of the fourth article where he points out Butler's ridicule of epic machinery, e.g., Pallas descending in the form of rust and preventing Hudibras from firing his pistol, and Mars bringing the bear for him to fall on when he is unhorsed, and so preventing him from being brained in the fall. M. J.'s remark that Sir Samuel Luke was the original of Hudibras brought the information from "W. H." in number 53 that:

There was when Butler wrote Hudibras, one Colonel Rolls, a Devonshire man, who lodged with him and was exactly like his description of the knight; whence it is highly probable that it was this gentleman and not Sir Samuel whose person he had in his eye. The reason

[2] He says, nevertheless, towards the end, ". . . though perhaps I have said nothing new to some of your readers . . . I flatter myself that I have set some things in a light in which some of your readers have not yet considered them."

that he gave for calling his poem Hudibras was, because the name of the old patron Saint of Devonshire was Hugo de Bra.

Additional annotation of this sort the *Journal* encouraged with the comment,

We think ourselves obliged to this gentleman for this little hint; and we shall be glad if any other persons who can clear up any obscurity in that author will, through us, communicate their illustrations to the public.

These articles on *Hudibras* are, however, the only extended instance of impersonal and dispassionate criticism in the *Journal's* whole history. It much preferred apparently to deal with living authors, and to denounce rather than commend.

Many of the *Journal's* attacks on current productions may be ascribed to its deep seated suspicion of the booksellers. Toward dictionaries, cyclopedias, and histories, it seems to have cherished a special hatred, doubtless with some justice, for they were often hack-work pure and simple, mere re-compilations of old material foisted upon the public by booksellers who could find no better grist to grind or wished to parallel the successful ventures of their competitors. In numbers 170, 172, and 175, for instance, a proposed new edition of Stephens' *Thesaurus* is duly revealed in its proper light by a writer signing himself variously "B. T." and "Calliopius",[3] who having given instances of the new editors' stupidity asks scornfully who they are. His attack is supported by Bavius, who guarantees the accuracy of his citations except at one point. In this case it may be pertinent to note that Bavius, or Russel himself, had been for some time engaged on a new edition of this work. Another more significant instance is the attack at this same period[4] on the prospectus of a new *General Dictionary*. A correspondent, "A. B.," shows that the editors make promises they do not keep and that they attempt to establish a number of false impressions. He examines as a specimen their article on

[3] In the third article, signed Calliopius, he says that the first two were from the same hand, and implies distinctly that it was his.
[4] See 171, 178, 179, 182.

Eastern History, to prove that they had not, as they claimed, consulted original Eastern writers, but had taken all their material from d'Herbelot's *Dictionary,* including with the rest all of his many errors. A.B. also points out the excessive cost of the new work. The editors defended themselves in one of the dailies by charging A.B. not only with distortion of facts, misrepresentation, and so forth, but also with an interest in a proposed translation of Bayle's *Dictionary,* which would compete with theirs. In reply A.B. insists on his accuracy and justice, offers to adduce as many instances of error as may be desired, but equivocates as to his interest in the Bayle. Hereupon "The Authors" of the *General Dictionary* repeat their defense, declare that A.B. is unfair and malicious, and that the Bayle contains as many errors as their work. This encounter has all the appearance of a squabble between competing booksellers, each of whom is trying to secure public favor for his wares at the expense of the other.[5]

A similar but more protracted quarrel took place in the *Journal's* columns between the booksellers Cave and Watts over rival translations of Du Halde's *History of China.*[6] It is significant that this discussion from beginning to end is concerned with the ethics of the booksellers—with such matters as respecting prior rights, living up to promises made to subscribers, and so forth. The fact that the bulk of the material supports Cave against Watts indicates the *Journal's* side in the affair. The controversy is, however, altogether in

[5] *The New General Dictionary.* 10 vols. 1734-8. There is another edition of the same date in five volumes by Des Maizeaux, which seems to be the one followed by later editors. This controversy suggested a letter in 182 on the value of an index to Bayle. The writer submits a sample index to the article on Adam, intended seriously, but very amusing in its phraseology. Among the editors was "T. Birch," but he was Dr. Thomas Birch, and not the "Tim Birch" of the *Weekly Register* (see Nichols, V, 560).

[6] See *Grub-street Journal* 354 and 363 ff. A more important bookseller's quarrel is hinted at in Gilliver's advertisement of Pope's collected works, vol. II (280) : ". . . B. Lintot having the property of the former volume of poems would never be induced to publish them complete, but only a part of them, to which he tacked and imposed on the buyer a whole additional volume of other men's poems."

the form of correspondence; there is no official or "editorial" pronouncement. It begins with a defense by "A. B. C." of Cave against Watts—a declaration that Cave's prospectus appeared first, and that he intended to include much material that Watts was omitting. Then "P. L." (number 363) attacks Watts's translation, declaring it an imposition and a misrepresentation, since it omitted plates, maps, and even whole chapters, and was in addition wretchedly translated, and mangled in its proper names; in fact, was stuck full of blunders of all sorts. What looks suspiciously like free advertising of Cave's edition appears in number 364 in a number of extracts submitted by a correspondent for the sole reason that he had enjoyed reading them—passages dealing with the duties of man and wife, of friends and relations, and with the government of a house and the apartments of women. P.L. returned to the attack in number 365, listing the serious omissions in Watts's edition, and pointing out that Watts's advertisements would lead the public to think it was getting a complete work. This same issue contains the only statement from the other side, a letter from Watts himself denying that he had supplanted Cave, and maintaining that he had undertaken the work after a long period of waiting in vain for Cave's promised translation. As for the omissions he was charged with, he argued that Du Halde had originally loaded his *History* with much useless lumber in the way of irrelevant description and maps which were quite incomprehensible to a European. These he had omitted as useless, and as making the book too expensive to be popular. In number 367 P. L. developed in detail his charges concerning the spelling of proper names and general inaccuracy, and in number 368 the episode was concluded with a jocose epigram reprinted from the *Daily Advertiser*—

> If thou has spirit, Cave, proceed
> And for no sculptures[7] spare.
> Convince us you in China deal
> But Watts in earthenware,

[7] An allusion to the illustrations and maps, which Watts was accused of suppressing to save expense.

and with Cave's advertisement that his edition would begin to appear February first in installments of eight folio sheets for one shilling. He also promised an absolutely complete work, and in a note described the shortcomings of the rival work and announced that he would reprint and distribute gratis the letters which had appeared in the *Journal* and the *Daily Advertiser*.[8]

Any suspicion that Cave was consistently supported by the *Journal,* however, is contradicted by a warm controversy over two rival astronomical essays which began in number 369 immediately after the Cave-Watts quarrel. Here there appeared a direct charge by one Thomas Wright that George Smith of York had plagiarized his "scheme of the late eclipse." Smith replied in number 371, asserting the originality of his scheme, which he declared to be new, and deriding Wright's as being forty years old. He also spoke of his rival's impudence and supported himself with numerous technicalities—to all of which Wright replied two weeks later in a strongly personal vein with charges of weak evasions and shifts.[9] In the meantime the *Gentleman's Magazine* had published Smith's scheme, and came in, in number 375, for a drubbing from "Phil Filch", who threatened to expose Cave for publishing a piece of work supposedly by an unknown George Smith of York, but really copied from Wright. The former astronomer was now defended in his turn in number 376 by "Phil. Aret." who asserted positively not only the existence of George Smith of York, but also his superiority to Wright in the field of astronomy. This correspondent also defended the magazines,

[8] Two short criticisms (184 and 190) of Chamber's proposed *Cyclopaedia* offer an instance of less biased criticism. The writer, while in sympathy with Chambers, considers his project of collecting materials by general invitation impractical since scholars will not turn in material they have worked out for themselves. He also takes exception to various other details of the work, but thinks it on the whole extremely important, as such compilations form the basis of a library. He believes that money should be spent to get together the proper authorities to work on a monument of this sort.

[9] Advertisements of both pamphlets appear on the back page of number 370.

declaring that he himself had never objected to having his articles in the *Journal* taken over into them. In spite of a letter in number 377 signed by Smith himself and refuting certain technical charges made by Wright, Phil Filch again denied in the following issue, number 378, that Smith existed, insisting that he himself knew nothing of him, though he knew York well, and that acquaintances in York to whom he had written had never heard of such a person. He also asserted that he did not know Wright either, and that he was interested merely in exposing Cave's plagiarisms. The whole affair came to an inconsequential end in number 379 with a letter from "Tom Tell Troth" declaring that Smith's scheme was stolen from the work of an Italian, Manfredi, and offering to prove it by documents. One is finally left to draw his own conclusions as to the existence of Smith and the respective merits of the two schemes.[10]

These various quarrels are typical of the *Journal's* excursions into what might be called the secondary, not to say tertiary, fields of literature. Such attacks were very probably dictated by the antagonism of the editors and correspondents of the *Journal* toward their natural enemies the booksellers, except in a case like the Cave-Watts quarrel, where Cave had obviously enlisted the services of the *Journal* on his side. The booksellers were of course thoroughly sordid and commercial in their system of hacking, and these attacks may be taken as laudable attempts to expose a vicious practice. Yet even the *Journal* could see the possibility of another point of view. In number 214, "Jeremiah Gimcrack" tells the story of his relations as a young author with a bookseller. He says that though his work was successful he never had income from it, the returns being all swallowed up in charges for expenses in printing and *et caetera's*. Bavius comments on

[10] Note also an attack on a school edition of Persius by a schoolmaster named Sterling. This edition had been exploited as illustrating a new method for the easy acquisition of Latin; as one ironical critic said, a method which was to make all England happy. Apparently the brilliance of Sterling's idea consisted chiefly in the rearrangement of verse in prose order. See 370, 372, 375, 378.

this letter oddly enough in support of the bookseller, who, he says, advanced money at the beginning, and was doubtless justified in his various charges for *et caetera's*. Moreover, Bavius contends, many young writers overrated the value of their work and the extent of its sale; in fact booksellers were sometimes ruined by authors, as well as authors by booksellers.

In general, however, booksellers might look for little sympathy in the columns of the *Journal*. Quite characteristic of the usual attitude toward them is an attack (number 247) on a current device of selling books to the poorer classes by printing them in sixpenny installments. The writer scoffs at the professed philanthropic motive of this scheme, and declares that it is not in any case for the good of the poor, who need their money for food and clothing. He even goes so far as to assert hard-headedly, "I used to think that nineteen in twenty of the species were designed by nature for trade and manufactures; and that to take them off to read books was the way to do them harm, to make them, not wiser or better, but impertinent, troublesome, and factious." According to him, booksellers and compositors get together in clans and do so well with weekly pamphlets that a genuine author has little chance. The Knaptons, for instance, who were publishing a translation of Rapin in this way, were expected to make between eight and ten thousand pounds from their venture.

Of any sort of plagiarism or piracy the *Journal* was always especially contemptuous. Its own sense of self-righteousness in this respect appears strikingly in its reply in the Pegasus column of number 246 to a request that it reprint, in an extra sheet if necessary, the Tatlers and the Spectators, a project to be undertaken in the interests both of amusement and morality. Bavius points out that to reprint books already in circulation would be not only unjust and piratical, but also impractical, especially in the present instance, where the papers suggested were very easily obtainable. When hard pressed for material, however, the poorer newspapers did actually reprint books chapter by chapter.[11]

Throughout the *Journal* one finds, as might be expected, a conservative and pessimistic attitude toward current literary production and the taste of the age:—Writing in general is bad, but is tolerated by the low culture of the time, and despite the valiant and bitterly fought battles of such guardians of art and taste as the *Journal* itself, probably little improvement is to be hoped for. Although there was doubtless truth enough in such a point of view, the general impression it creates is one of bitterness and disappointment in the writers themselves; as though they themselves had offered the public the bright flame of true literature, and had been passed by unnoticed and unrewarded. A strikingly typical illustration of this attitude appears in a letter by "H. W." in number 149 on *Scribendi Cacoethes*. H. W. decries the existence of the crowd of scribblers who sink the deeper, the higher they try to soar. No man, he says, safely enough, can be a writer unless he has genius, yet a writer should not give up hope merely because his work is not popular. Some writers are too conceited—they raise their readers' hopes only to dash them; while others, discouraged by a recognition of their limitations, give up all effort. The careful writer will be encouraged by men of sense, although he may not meet with universal applause. Still, the general taste of the age is bad; it supports noise and nonsense, and "a man who can furnish a loose poem, or an atheistical discourse, is preferred to a solid reasoner or an impartial historian." Such a diatribe, it would seem, might slip easily from the pen of

[11] An interesting instance of barefaced plagiarism is related in 356 by John Colson, the author of a *Comment* on Newton's Method of Fluxions. A certain "Dr." Philip Nichols, alias Charles Rhodes, who had been expelled from Cambridge for various offences, among them the stealing of books, had imposed on various people, including Colson, had got his hands on some of the manuscript of the *Comment* which was at the time in press, and had undertaken to get it published beforehand. He did apparently succeed in inducing some unwary bookseller to publish the book, and Colson gives a list of errata in it to prove definitely that the whole work, errata and all, had been plagiarized from him, Rhodes not even having taken the trouble to correct errata in the reprinting.

an orthodox literary critic in almost any sophisticated age. Its sense is repeated continually in the more scathing personal attacks of Bavius and of the numerous literary correspondents of the *Journal*. It is, however, cast into a more original and humorous mould by one signing himself "Scriblerus cum Dasho," in a history of the excise on Dulness (numbers 172, 174, 176, April and May, 1733). This history tells in chronicle style of the thwarted attempt to substitute an excise on Dulness for the one on wine and tobacco. It opens with the elaborate date "In the seventeen hundred and thirty-third year, in the third month of the said year (Colleius Kiberus being Laureate of Great Britain, France and Ireland; Johannes Oldmixonus Historiographer and Edmundus Curleius Biographer in chief of the said dominions)." The author proceeds to explain the excise as it was and to detail all its evils, especially its effect on *courage and policy;* that is, among soldiers and the disputants in the coffee houses. He then tells of the scheme to change the excise from wine and tobacco to Dulness. The manufacture of this commodity, he explains, flourished exceedingly at this period, in spite of the stamp tax and the tax on paper. The numerous dealers in it (among them the writers of newspapers, the booksellers, and the laureate) were at once aroused, formed a combination against it, offered up burnt sacrifice of their wares to the Goddess of Dulness, and succeeded in thwarting the whole scheme.

The sum of such material as the foregoing—the discussion of individual books or of literary and critical questions and conditions—is altogether surprisingly slight, once the personal attacks on Bentley, Theobald, the newspapers, and its various other enemies are excepted. Of dramatic and theatrical matter in the *Journal* there is on the other hand a great plenty. This is of course what one might expect. Since the drama in the 1730's was still the most popular form of literature, and the London audiences were being continually regaled with new performances of all sorts, including not only the legitimate forms of tragedy, comedy, and farce, but also pantomimes, operas, and nondescript entertainments, it is not surprising to find continual reference in the *Journal* to the theater and its affairs. This material is most interesting perhaps as a reminder that the problems of the practical theater are perennial, and that the mutual relations between authors, players, managers, and audience give rise in one age as well as another to difficulties which are, it would seem, beyond solution. There is the actor's struggle for independence from the manager and his insistence that he is the keystone in the dramatic arch, and on the other hand, the manager's firmly fixed intention to direct his property, the theater, and his employees, the actors, as he sees fit. There is the outcry from one portion of the audience against the obscenity of the stage, and the debasing of what ought to be a great instrument of education into a mere channel for vain, frivolous, and even degrading shows and entertainments. There is the protest against foreign artists and performers; the English-speaking world has always depended on them, and is always inveighing against them and fulminating patriotic encouragement of native talent. And there are also the complaints of authors regarding the mutilation of their plays, and the poor taste and lack of discrimination in audiences which condemn masterpieces. These perennial subjects for discussion are raised as often in the columns of the *Journal* as they are in those of a modern periodical.

As far as the theater was concerned, the period was, of course, a mediocre one. The plays produced were, taken altogether, worse than mediocre; the most successful author writing for the stage was Henry Fielding, and his forte lay elsewhere. Nor were there any actors of really first rank; nearly all the names that are remembered at all today—Cibber, Kitty Clive, Rich, Macklin—are associated especially with comedy and that largely of the broader type. The names of Wilkes and Booth are hardly to be put into the category with Burbage, Betterton, or Siddons. Still, it must be said that the level of acting as marked by the better actors was probably much higher than that of the authors who furnished them with new parts. In view of such conditions, distinguished criticism, either in current comment or in discussion of general dramatic principles and ideas, was hardly to be hoped for. At any rate it failed to appear, quite possibly because there was so little to stimulate it. The material in the *Journal,* then, is interesting, not as being distinguished or brilliant, although it is very often lively, sharp, and brisk, but rather as it furnishes a sort of typical cross-section of dramatic history.

On the whole, the idea that stands out most clearly and that is most frequently reiterated is the somewhat academic one that the taste of the age was distressingly corrupt. The audience, according to the critics, was uneducated and unrefined, and its natural tastes were gross and low. It rejected or was indifferent toward the fine classical tragedies and the warmed-over Restoration comedies which were prepared in great numbers for its delectation, and guzzled at the trough of "entertainments", pantomimes, and shows offered it by those who were willing to pander to its tastes. As a result the stage was abdicating its high mission and debasing itself into a sink of corruption, both moral and artistic. Maevius, criticising *The Humours of Oxford* in numbers 6 and 7, notes sarcastically that the author has taken care not to leave out of his dialogue "the fashionable ornaments of pruriency," and, by placing them in the mouths of characters where they would be least expected, has increased the interest and surprise of the audience. The correspondents on this subject display all the fanaticism one would expect. "Theatricus" (number 135) ascribes the degeneracy of the youth of the time to the degeneracy of the stage with its ridiculous, stupid, obscene, and infamous plays, and characteristically proposes a board of censorship with power not only to reject the improper, but to require the presentation of the edifying. Another writer, anonymous, (number 202) in a letter "Of the use and abuse of the stage," deplores the current quarrel between actors and managers[12] and declares that both sides

---

[12] See *post,* pp. 214 ff.

should have spent their energy raising the standard of the theater. In his opinion there were too many theaters, especially since they competed with each other only in singing, dancing, and immorality. Practically all the stage was perverted, catering to the lower passions in its attempts to attract the vulgar crowd, with a resultant deplorable effect on the young. Still another letter in much the same vein, advocating a moral and artistic censorship of the theater, appeared in number 221. The writer contends that under wise regulation the stage would be highly conducive to the public benefit. He discusses the regulation of public health by the state as an analogous situation, and wishes that Parliament might "erect a society of the most ingenious and polite persons, through whose hands all performances for the stage should pass before they were exhibited to public view." Then worthy citizens might let their wives and daughters go to the theater without fear of corruption! "Nothing that was not improving would be suffered to appear; morality and good breeding would be inculcated, and true wit and humor, the pleasing vehicles of instruction, would, by a noble emulation amongst our writers at length arrive at such a standard as must in a little time render the English taste the most refined of any in the world." Now, he complains, the ladies seem to hear with pleasure "the grossest obscenities," and he expatiates with special horror on a performance of Carey's burlesque, *Chrononhotonthologos,* to which people of the highest quality crowded, deriving great enjoyment from its improprieties. He quotes objectionable lines from the songs which were received "with smiles from the fair and loud applauses from the gentlemen." Still another moralist, a self-styled "Cato" (number 315), who had been outraged by the immodest dancing of a Mlle. Roland, complains that matters have reached such a pass that if the play has no harm in it it is accompanied by two or three immodest dances, and followed by "a farce which teaches no good lesson to our wives, sisters, and daughters." A later contributor (number 352) in a crudely ironical letter even goes so far as to assert that the sole purpose of the theater is pruriency and a stimulation of business in the adjacent houses of ill repute in Drury Lane.

Although it is hard to believe that the editors of the *Journal* could really have been shocked at the liberties which dramatists took in dialogue and situation, their chief indictment of Fielding's comedies in one of their most important theatrical quarrels was for obscenity. The *Journal* had devoted little attention to Fielding's earliest plays,[13] *The Author's Farce, Tom Thumb,* and so forth, but in 1732[14] it undertook a frontal and sustained attack on him for his immorality.

This quarrel, like many others begun in the *Journal,* finally involved several other papers, and gradually degenerated into personal attacks, and inquisitions into opponents' motives, intelligence, and general character. It began with a single, detached letter from "Dramaticus" in number 117, but broke out into a steady fire of correspondence and editorial denunciation ten weeks later in number 127, after which it kept the center of the *Journal's* stage for nearly three months. The plays abused were the *The Covent Garden Tragedy, The Modern Husband, The Old Debauchees,* and *The Mock Doctor,* especially the two first. In number 117, Dramaticus,[15] who says he saw *The Modern Husband* at its first performance and has since carefully read it over, declares that the play is neither diverting nor instructive, and that Fielding has no true notion of comedy. He condemns the characters as thin, silly, and unoriginal, and says that although he did note an occasional good touch he had to wade through filth to get it.

This attack, however, was mild as compared with the storm of righteous indignation which burst upon the un-

[13] See however 17, 18, 23, 38, 75. In 75 appears a notice signed Bavius addressed to all the members of the Grubstreet Society asking them to assemble to see the first performance of *The Grubstreet Opera,* and orders the author, "Scriblerus Secundus" (Fielding), to have a large chair for Bavius in a front box.

[14] See 117-141, March 30-September 10.

[15] A frequent correspondent. See 112, et cetera.

fortunate *Covent Garden Tragedy*.[16] A correspondent calling himself "Prosaicus" (number 127) tells of being taken
by a friend, "a man of pleasure," to see *The Covent Garden
Tragedy*. He was deeply shocked at the characters produced,
and could only conclude that many of the audience did not
understand what they were seeing, namely, "a dull representation of the most obscene characters in life." Were this
acceptable, any Drury Lane bully might make a humorous
poet. The success of such a piece will, he declares, indicate the
low taste of the town; it is "the most dull, obscene piece
that ever appeared on a public stage."

Prosaicus was outdone in his indictment by Dramaticus
(number 128), who, upon seeing the first performance of
the play, believed that "Such a scene of infamous lewdness
was never brought before on any stage whatsoever." The
managers, he thinks, might as well take the audience to a
Drury Lane bawdy house. He describes himself as a rejected
author, who is forced to think that his plays were not bad
enough to suit the taste of the town, but he declares that if
the public wants such stuff, he could not (God forbid!)
undertake to write for it; nothing could justify such an out-
rage on decency.

These righteous outcries in the *Journal* drew forth spirited
defenses in the *Daily Post,* mingled with the usual counter
attacks and personalities. Apparently the *Daily Post* had
been Fielding's special avenue of publicity. In it had appeared on June 16, 1732, an obvious puff-preliminary of
The Mock Doctor:

[16] Apparently in retaliation for attacks on *The Modern Husband,* Fielding made several slighting allusions to the *Journal* in *The Covent Garden
Tragedy*. The Prolegomena contains burlesque criticism of the play by
ignorant critics, one of whom qualifies as an expert on the basis of his
having read the *Craftsman,* the *Grub-street Journal, The Rape of the
Lock,* and parts of a history of the King of Sweden (*Charles XII,* by
Voltaire). He also says he thought *The Modern Husband* "a good play,
till the Grub-street Journal assured me it was not." There is also an
illiterate and pompous "Criticism on the Covent Garden Tragedy, originally intended for the Grubstreet Journal," the style of which may be
judged by its reference to "Aristuttle" and "Horase." In the text itself
appears one allusion to the *Journal*; in Act I, Scene i, a pimp is told—
    For thou hast learnt to read, hast playbills read,
    The Grub-street Journal thou hast known to write.

We hear there is now in rehearsal at the Theatre Royal in Drury Lane a new farce called The Mock Doctor or The Dumb Lady Cured. The piece of Moliere from which this is altered and adapted to the English stage is justly esteemed to contain the purest and most natural humor that has appeared in any language. As the Old Debauchees (which is not long enough in itself for a whole night's entertainment) has met with great applause in the town, the author, lest it might suffer by the addition of any old worn-out entertainments, has permitted this performance to come on at a more disadvantageous season than he at first intended.

Then, in answer to the *Journal's* onslaughts there appeared on June 21 in the *Post* and also in the *London Evening Post* a "Letter to Dramaticus, alias Prosaicus, alias Bavius, alias, etc., etc., etc.," and signed "Theatre Royal Ale-House, from —your No very good friend nor admirer, Mr. Wm. Hint, Candle Snuffer." "Hint"[17] begins by maintaining that when such a set of scribblers as the Grubstreet writers set up as critics, anyone, even a candle-snuffer, may be an author, and that even he, Hint, may answer a critic of his own rank, who has had a *place* and a *play* refused. He charges the *Journal* with ungenerous motives in its attack, since *The Covent Garden Tragedy* had been withdrawn at once, and had been published only as a defense against the earlier attacks upon it. He points out further that vicious characters upon the stage are not an innovation, and declares the real occasion of the *Journal's* animosity to be the lines in which it had been mentioned contemptuously. He then turns personal, saying that Dramaticus, alias Prosaicus, should have supported his points with quotations, and that it was easy to see from his writing why his play had been refused. Moreover, he continues, as far as the *Journal* was concerned, its own success was a greater proof of the low taste of the age

---

[17] Quite possibly Fielding himself. The manner is not unlike his, and he is later alluded to as "Hint." Or it may have been Theophilus Cibber collaborating with Fielding (Cross, *History of Henry Fielding,* I, 133). In 130, Russel ("M") implies that Hint stood for these two together (see *post,* p. 177), but in 136 (see *post,* p. 180) he states definitely that Hint was Fielding. He says here with obvious bitterness that Fielding had "inveighed bitterly among his acquaintance against the *Grub-street Journal,* representing the authors of it as a set of paltry, ill-natured, and ignorant scribblers."

than was that of *Hurlothrumbo*. To "Hint's" effusion Bavius retorted the very next day (number 129, June 22) in his most acrid style. He reprinted from the *Daily Post* a notice that *The Old Debauchees* had succeeded, and went on to say that the *Post* had also announced the favorable reception of the "damned Common or Covent Garden Tragedy."

We hear they were both illuminated by Mr. Hint, Candle-Snuffer, who finding the latter fit only to be acted in the dark snuffed out the candles. Hence it has only stunk, but has not been seen since. This gentleman has written a learned defence of both, in which it is evident that some sad comi-tragical Grubean had both a finger and thumb.

In this same issue appeared a letter from "Poeticus," asking if Dramaticus' failure to prosecute his attack for the last ten weeks (since number 119) was due to his having had his play accepted, and in case this was so, enclosing "verses of recantation" for him to sing to the manager of the theater.

Poeticus' hint that the *Journal* and its correspondents were losing interest in the squabble was unfounded. The next issue of the *Journal* contained three items dealing with it. Prosaicus reappeared with a promise of regular remarks on all new productions, and for a beginning chose *The Modern Husband,* of which "scarce a scene . . . but what betrays want of judgment, or, to use softer terms, manifests at least the author's hasty way of writing." Fielding, he says, should be encouraged by his success with the town to take more pains. On the other hand, at least he cannot be charged with puffing; doubtless he had had no hand in a puff of *The Old Debauchees* in the *Daily Post* for June 16. The second item is an answer by A. B. to Hint's letter. A. B. replies to Hint's defense of Fielding against the charge of indecency, that while such characters are doubtless legitimate, appearing even in Roman comedy, still an author need not depend solely on that class, and such offensive action as Fielding shows is unnecessary. He protests that he is unbiassed against Fielding personally, and fails to see why the objects of his satire should resent it—it is so dull. As for citing passages to prove indecency, Hint's challenge to Dramaticus, there was no need to do so; any passage illustrated it, as would appear if the play were published (as it had been, according to Hint). And finally, in the third item, Dramaticus defends himself and the *Journal* against the charges of Hint, and reasserts the vileness of *The Covent Garden Tragedy*. He declares that though he had thought at first Hint had no real existence, he had come to change his mind; Hint's letter was exactly such as a candle-snuffer might write. The *Grub-street Journal,* he continues, can stand such phrases as "a set of scribblers giving laws to the theatre," for words of this sort have been applied before by the same kind of critics to "the wittiest papers, from the *Tatlers, Spectators,* etc., down to the *Grub-street Journal."* Whatever Hint may say, the fact remains that the *Journal* "is, in the opinion of the town, a paper that contains much real wit and humor", and from now on will be increasingly useful in attacking enormities on the stage. For his own part, he doubts whether his play would have been rejected if the managers had known who he was. He thinks his papers have been well received, and is willing to let the town judge of his dramatic ability from his discussions here; his play had been rejected as being "sensible and pretty, only not theatrical." As for the subject of the present quarrel, the lewdness of *The Covent Garden Tragedy* is plain enough, and need not be read into it. Such characters and action as Fielding uses are improper; and the same might be said of *The Beggar's Opera,* though that had wit to redeem it.

Here also appeared a typical Grubean contribution savoring strongly of Russel, a certificate signed with the mark of William Hint, declaring that he had not written the letter he had been credited with, and that he had always thought Fielding's plays either above his comprehension or beneath his notice. He further deposes that it was written by Fielding and C[ibber] together at Mrs. —ld-m's. The editors then express doubts concerning the authenticity of this certificate, which might be forged; certainly Hint's letter had been written with more spirit than Fielding's and Cibber's letters dedicatory. On the other hand, there was the possibility that they wrote better over the name of a candle-snuffer. At any rate, they continued, one member who had read *The Covent Garden Tragedy* thought its lewdness exaggerated, but suggested that a thorough explanation of it would increase its sale among the ladies of Drury Lane.

In the meantime the *Comedian*[18] had been enlisted in Fielding's service, and in 132 Dramaticus again appeared to point out the falsity of its logic in excusing the young author on the ground of haste and in glossing over the deficiencies of *The Modern Husband,* simply because it had a few good points. As for statements that Fielding had taken the controversy lightly, Dramaticus hints at a violent meeting with Gilliver, the *Journal's* printer, and a near approach to blows "at which it was thought the Bookseller, as usual, would have had the advantage of the Tragedian." Here Bavius also comments on the faulty logic of the *Comedian,* and likewise writes, over the name of "Miso-Clericus," an ironic attack on *The Old Debauchees,* which he takes as an assault upon all the clergy. He cites lines in the play on the vices of priests and concludes ironically, "Priests of all religions are the same." The play is, he says, an addition to the mass of literature—prose, verse, and cartoons—on the story of Father Girard and Miss Cadiere; now "a Gentleman of a surprising genius wrought it into a play." Russel, as always, was here resenting a possible affront to the clergy.

The charges of immorality and obscenity were vigorously renewed in number 133 by a new correspondent, "Publicus." The latter goes so far as to declare that the abolition of the

[18] A new paper edited by Thomas Cooke, and hostile to Pope. In its second number, May, 1732, appears an attack on Pope's *Epistle to the Earl of Burlington.* Its third contains "Reflections on some modern plays," a defense of Fielding's *Modern Husband* as superior to other current plays, and its sixth an epigram on Fielding, the persecuted—
    When Grubs and Grublings censure Fielding's scenes,
    He cannot answer that which nothing means, etc.
In a note to 132 in the *Memoirs,* it is said of the *Comedian* that it lasted eight months, and that its sale never paid for paper and print.

stage is as much to be wished as that of brothels, and asserts that managers hire their authors with the express purpose of insulting the common sense and modesty of their audience. For horrible examples he singles out especially *The Covent Garden Tragedy* and *The Old Debauchees,* and speaks of their having been defended by "pander newspapers" after they had been condemned by the town. Against *The Covent Garden Tragedy* especially he reiterates the old charges of obscenity and grossness, and in citing examples to prove his point apologizes to Bavius for having to defile his pages with such filth. *The Old Debauchees* he also lashes for its coarse, foolish dialogue and its impiety and immorality. He declares, "When such things as these are suffered on the stage, 'tis no wonder there are so many whores and pickpockets in the streets," and says of Fielding, ". . . his pen is not only void of wit, manners, and modesty, but likewise of the most common rules of poetry and even grammar." This diatribe was supported by an epigram signed "F. N."—

> 'Tis strange you say in this refined age
> That brothels, bawds, and whores adorn the stage.
> I think 'tis not. They justly law the scene,
> Don't Drury Playhouse stand in Drury Lane?
> And own you must; tho void of wit, or art
> They naturally write and act their part.

In the next numbers the bombardment continued unabated. In number 134, Dramaticus divided authors into two classes, the venal and the gentlemen, describing the first as those who write for profit only, and abandon an unsuccessful play without defense to save a more successful one, as Fielding had done with *The Covent Garden Tragedy.* He also refers again to the lack of judgment among the managers and the rejection of his own play, and presents as a logical axiom the statement that a gentleman with leisure should write better than "any venal poet, that lives only by the numerous productions of his too-often-drained brains." The following week, apropos of the controversy, appeared the letter by Theatricus already referred to,[19] railing at the immorality

[19] See p. 171.

of the stage and suggesting a rigid censorship, and also a
reply by Dramaticus to a "Dramaticus Senior" of the *Daily
Courant* for July 29. The latter had written an elaborate
and dull defense of a third person who had been defending
Fielding in the *Comedian* and whom Dramaticus had accused
of bad logic. In these letters the quarrel departs from its central point and becomes involved almost entirely in discussions
of methods of debate and of proper logical processes—a not
uncommon occurrence in the *Journal's* quarrels. Fielding
himself now took up the cudgels in his own defense, writing
as "Philalethes" in the *Daily Post* for July 31,[20] and was
immediately answered in the *Journal* by "Publicus." Philalethes, having declared that *The Old Debauchees* had met
with as great applause as was ever given "on the theater,"
was reminded that the audience of the third night was so
small it had to be dismissed. Moreover, Publicus points out
the weakness and irrelevance of Philalethes' argument in
merely complaining that speeches had been torn from their
context, and in presenting "an account of the birth, parent-
age and education of the writer [Fielding]." Publicus, however, like the other debaters, wanders from his point and
betrays a characteristic personal animus in dissecting scornfully such phrases of his opponent as *on the theatre* and
human wish [for *humane*], and in declaring that the success
of *The Mock Doctor* was due altogether to its acting, "everyone agreeing that 'tis as ill written as well acted." This
answer to Philalethes was supplemented by one of Russel's
pointed but remarkably clumsy epigrams—

> Charged with writing of bawdy, this was F—'s reply—
> 'Tis what Dryden and Congreve have done as well as I.
> 'Tis true, but they did it with this good pretence,
> With an ounce of rank bawdy went a pound of good sense.
> But thou hast proportioned, in thy judgment profound
> Of good sense scarce an ounce, and of bawdy a pound.[21]

Russel himself, in fact, now struck out with both fists. For
the next issue (number 136) he wrote a résumé of the con-

[20] This letter has been reprinted in full by Cross in *The History of
Henry Fielding,* I, 135.
[21] Signed Maevius, and ascribed to "M" in the *Memoirs.*

troversy. In powerful and savagely bitter invective he refers to Fielding as "a venal and venereal poet" and defends the *Journal* against its detractors. He likewise published in the Pegasus column of the same issue an ironical defense of *The Covent Garden Tragedy* against the unfair attacks of Prosaicus, Dramaticus, and Publicus, and proves the quality of the play by summarizing the action and citing typical lines in such a manner as to intensify their objectionable qualities.[22] The next week he continued his attack with comments on Fielding's Prolegomena to the same play, wondering whether the playwright was pretending to satire in his remarks therein on *The Rape of the Lock,* the *Craftsman* and Monsieur Voltaire, and pointing out a garbled passage from *The Dunciad* with lines from another author attached to it.[23] In the course of this analysis most of Fielding's earlier plays are alluded to disparagingly. The generally hostile attitude of the *Journal* to Cibber and Fielding and all their concerns is also made evident in this issue in an epigram praising ironically "Miss Raftor [Kitty Clive] on her success in acting Polly Peachum"—

> By Hint and Keyber formed to please the age
> See little Raftor mount the Drury stage.
> Fenton[24] outdone, with her no more compares
> Than Gay's best songs with Hint's Mock Doctor airs.
> Lament, O Rich, thy labours all are vain—
> Hint writes and Raftor acts in Drury Lane.

The quarrel came to an end with a criticism of Fielding's current plays by Prosaicus;[25] and in number 141 an extended answer by Russel to Philalethes' "slanders" against the *Journal,* and two final epigrams, one "On a poet's pleading the example of Congreve, Wycherley, etc. for writing of bawdry," to the effect that Fielding, who follows the masters only in "their smutty strain," may be set right by the boxes

---

[22] The résumé is signed "Bavius" and the second item "B. B.," but both are ascribed to "M." Russel omitted the citations when reprinting in the *Memoirs.*
[23] Compare p. 174, n.
[24] The original Polly.
[25] In number 138. This letter is quoted extensively by Cross (I, 140).

on the ear dealt him by Bavius, and the other on the acting of *The Mock Doctor* at Smithfield under the title of *The Forced Physician*. In his final remarks Prosaicus bestows grudging and qualified praise on *The Mock Doctor*. He says he is unaware how much credit is due to Molière, but thinks that it is "an entertaining farcical piece," and as for the acting, that alone would not have saved it if it had been altogether bad.[26]

Hereafter one runs upon a few widely scattered allusions to Fielding, but in its later years the *Journal* made no sustained attack on him. There appear (number 179) verses[27] addressed "To a Gentleman who had bound up some of Swift's and Pope's poems with one of F—s plays," and described "as censuring an author who has long been enlisted among the Grubs"; in a denunciatory character sketch of a flirt (number 268) the writer announces, "I will venture to say there is not a woman in England of this character but what has ruined more young ladies than either the Charitable

[26] In addition to the usual remarks on imitation and indecency, Prosaicus says he defers to Fielding's birth, but that birth does not entitle him to claim wit—he would have no poet "pique himself on his family or his school." The *Journal* itself would not go so far as Prosaicus. It had copied a note (130) from the *Daily Post* and *London Evening Post* concerning performances of *The Old Debauchees* and *The Mock Doctor,* to the effect that the *Medicin malgré lui* "bears the best reputation of any petit piece in the French language, and many good judges allow the English farce is no way inferior to the original"; and then commented sardonically, "These good judges are certainly members of our society, and I hope the world will take their words that the author is no way inferior to Molière."

[27] Say wretch, what enmity, what rage
    Could thus provoke thee to profane
      The pure inimitable page
    Of Pope and our unrivalled Dean?

      .   .   .   .

    Thy F—'s labours thus to save
      Extremely elegant and nice is,
    Like wise Egyptians from the grave
      Preserving carcasses with spices.

    In this position be assured
    He's more conspicuously undone,
    For Mercury's but more obscured
      By being placed too near the sun.

Corporation[28] or Beau Fielding"; and a sharply worded notice that Mr. Pope had not been present as had been stated, at a performance of Fielding's *Pasquin,* and "we think it very probable that a person of his uncommon sense and wit will not have any curiosity to see it acted at all."[29] At this time[30] also the *Journal* printed a long attack on *Pasquin* over the signature "Marforio."[31] This article is an analysis with frequent quotation to bring out the lack of aptness and even the confusion and nonsense of Fielding's allegory. The opening paragraphs are carefully veiled and to an unsuspecting reader would seem to be genuine praise, but the writer grows bolder and more obvious as he progresses. His chief resentment seems to be against Fielding's satire on the professions, especially divinity.[32] On the whole, it would be hard to deny that the *Journal* displays a strong bias against Fielding. Its few allusions to his first pieces are in the sarcastic tone which it used of most new and unknown writers, and its abuse of his plays of 1732 was occasioned, one cannot help thinking, by the satirical allusions in *The Covent Garden Tragedy* to the *Journal* itself. The quarrel opens with letters from a number of pseudonymous correspondents with whose outraged sensibilities the *Journal* finds itself so much in sympathy as to give them at first publicity, and later the support of frequent and lengthy editorial utterance of a most caustic nature. As has been said before, the editors of the *Journal* may have had artistic or academic objections to "obscenity" in stage literature, but one can hardly believe, considering their own way

[28] See Nichols, II, 14—One of the fraudulent financial schemes of the time, "for relief of the industrious poor, by assessing them with small sums upon pledges at legal interest." The *Journal* allowed a considerable amount of space in its columns to an exposé of it. (See numbers 127 ff.)
[29] See 329, and also 331 for further comment on the same point.
[30] In 330 and 332.
[31] In *Pasquin* Fielding had attacked the nondescript theatrical entertainments in which Rich specialized, and Rich had retaliated with a satire called *Marforio*. Rich had, by the way, refused *Pasquin*.
[32] Allusions to Fielding may also be found in 150 "Scriblerus Secundus," and 203, although this latter may be simply to the mountebank Fielding of Smithfield with whom the more famous Henry has been confused, sometimes purposely by contemporary satirists, but inadvertently by later historians.

of writing and their discrimination in editing, that they were actually shocked or offended. Anyone familiar with the manners and methods of the period will realize that Fielding had probably his unfortunate allusions to the *Journal* to thank for the very considerable drubbing he received in its columns.[33]

Who all his assailants were it is impossible to say. Russel's authorship of numerous articles and epigrams signed Bavius, Maevius, and B. B. is revealed in the *Memoirs*. Russel was quite probably also the Marforio of the attack on *Pasquin*; this would be indicated especially by the writer's sensitiveness and resentment toward satire on the clergy. On the other hand the insinuation by Fielding's defenders that Prosaicus, Dramaticus, and the rest, were mere disguises for Bavius or Russel is certainly not to be accepted. None of them writes like Russel, and the most important of the lot, Dramaticus, revealed himself almost conclusively to be Sir William Yonge. This gentleman had theatrical ambitions, had collaborated in an entertainment in 1730, and was the recipient at just this time of a tribute called *Of Modern Wit. An epistle to the Rt. Hon. Sir William Young.* Dramaticus is continually harping on the fact that he is a gentleman, that his work would be accepted if he cared to exert personal pressure, but that he writes merely for pleasure. Moreover, he says (number 119) "I cannot conclude without returning my brother C— J—n[34] thanks for his kind epistle to me." The only epistle noted in the lists of new books and pamphlets which could possibly fit the case is the one just mentioned.

[33] Verses in *A New Miscellany* by Swift and others (1734) show the esteem in which Fielding was held by Pope's circle of friends. The lines are in obvious imitation of the *Profund*, and the association of the future novelist with Concanen, "J. M. S.", etc., is of obvious significance —Fielding was to be damned as a Dunce.

> . . . when you rashly think
> No Rhymer can like Welsted sink,
> His merits balanced you shall find
> That Fielding leaves him far behind.
> Concanen, more aspiring bard
> Climbs downward, deeper by a yard.
> Smart Jimmy Moor with vigour drops;
> The rest pursue as thick as hops.

[34] Charles Johnson, the hack tragedy-writer.

This quarrel with Fielding is from one point of view the most important of the *Journal's* excursions into dramatic criticism. The list of the *Journal's* victims connected with the stage contains no other name of equal rank with Fielding. Most of the theatrical and dramatic criticism in the paper is, as has been said before, valuable chiefly as illustrating current methods of criticism and the typical taste and points of view of the age. The Fielding material, however, has an additional importance. It helps to make clear the process by which Fielding acquired that false reputation for youthful immorality so completely exploded by Mr. Cross. It was an easy step for the hostile critics to pass from the conception of an exuberant young playwright charged with writing immoral and even grossly obscene plays to a conception of him as one who was merely photographing the regular background of his own experience and picturing the life he himself led. How for instance would a contemporary reader interpret the remark about ruining as many young ladies as the Charitable Corporation or Beau Fielding? Clearly comment of the sort which appeared in the *Journal* played its part in building up for the dramatist and future novelist a picturesque but unfortunate reputation which has been accepted by all his biographers from Arthur Murphy down to the present day, when it has finally faded away under Mr. Cross's careful scrutiny. At any rate *The Covent Garden Tragedy,* the most "objectionable" of Fielding's plays, is no more immoral or improper from a modern point of view than the usual Restoration comedy or the imitation of it which passed current in the 1730's. The usual comedy, however, was "elegant"; Fielding occasionally presented the same materials with a characteristic direct frankness and realism which were not, one must admit, "elegant."

The only other representative of the theater who suffered sustained attacks in the *Journal,* and whose name after two centuries is still remembered with much interest, was the ubiquitous Colley Cibber. Pope had of course treated Cibber with contempt before the *Journal* ever appeared, and he continued to do so after its day, and until his own death, but there is little in the assaults on Cibber in its columns to establish the impression that they were written or personally inspired by Pope, as were those on Ralph, Moore-Smythe, and Concanen.

Endowed with a faculty for making himself continually ridiculous whenever he abandoned the field where his genius lay, thick-skinned and insensitive, and yet of so much individuality and character as to appear a unique figure, Cibber was excellent game for the *Journal*. In one guise or another he was continually before the public, and could usually be counted on, like that mountebank, Orator Henley, to do something to arrest attention. If he was not acting, he was writing another birthday or New Year's ode in his function as poet laureate, or he was displaying his talents as a manager or playwright. There is to be found in the *Journal* some interesting criticism of Cibber's acting from as unfavorable a point of view as possible, but it was with Cibber as poet and especially as poet laureate that the *Journal* delighted to deal. As a comedian at least he was too clearly an acknowledged success; but as a poet he could find few critics so uncritical as to approve his efforts.

Of Cibber in his proper sphere as a comic actor, the *Journal* could find little to say. His success in certain parts, notably the fops of Restoration comedy, had become historic. For instance, in a controversy over the merits of a new actor, Stephens,[34a] "Somebody" (number 253) begins with a grudging admission of Cibber's excellence "in a few comic parts," but this was satisfactorily explained by his enemies as being not acting at all, but purely a presentation of his own natural character. Thus the anonymous writer of an epigram in number 47 asserts—

> 'Tis no hard task the reason to assign
> Why fool and knave in C—'s action join.
> Full of himself, half way he never stops;
> His fops are villains, and his villains fops.

[34a] An amateur. See Genest, III, 456 f.

And another in number 211, in an epilogue to Terence's
Eunuch—

> Let C—r by his coxcombs gain applause;
> Live, as he acts, and be the thing he draws.
> The many various fops his writing apes
> Are but himself in just so many shapes.

The same attitude is reflected in an epigram by Russel in
number 73—

> To Kneller Dryden writes, Some bear the rule
> Thus thou sometimes art forced to draw a fool;
> But so his follies in thy posture sink
> The senseless idiot seems at least to think.
> But thou, Gisoni, with sincerer art
> Hast drawn the laureate in his noblest part.
> As in his New Year's Ode, in thy design
> The thoughtless Fopling shines in every line.

On the other hand, of Cibber venturing unwisely into the
realm of tragedy, they could speak in more direct censure.
"Somebody," in the letter just noted, after admitting Cibber's limited excellence, attacks him scathingly for his acting
of tragic roles. Speaking of Colley's interpretation of Richard III, he says,

How does our laureate acquit himself? When he makes love to Lady
Ann, he looks like a pick-pocket with his shrugs and grimaces, that
has more a design on her purse than her heart; and his utterance
is in the same cast with his action. In Bosworth Field he appears no
more like King Richard than King Richard was like Falstaff, he
foams, struts, and bellows with the voice and cadence of a watch-
man rather than a hero and a prince.

And of his liberties with the text Somebody cites as an example the change of "Inspire us with the spleen of fiery
dragons" to "Inspire us with the rage of angry lions." Of
his Iago, the writer goes on to say, "Our laureate when he is
working up Othello to his ends, shrugs up his shoulders,
shakes his noddle, and with a fawning motion in his hands
drawls out these words, 'Good name in man or woman,' . . ."
Anyone would, he says, see through him, and Othello must
be supposed a stock or a fool, not to. This attack drew an
indignant reply from "Outis", who declares that Cibber "is

allowed by all gentlemen of true judgment (and therefore Mr. Somebody is not one) to perform every character . . . which he represents, extremely well." Then with the usual freedom of controversial manners he labels Somebody a "vile scribbler" who had obviously been hired for the purpose, and with the proceeds would "fill his belly, as empty as his head."[35]

It was in the field of poetry, however, that Cibber shone with a particular unconscious brilliance to the *Journal's* complete satisfaction. There is a steady stream of humorous comment on his appointment as laureate, and the burlesque discussions of his occasional odes—especially those for the New Year—became a regular institution from the first. His poetical utterances were regarded from every angle—his language, meter, and rhyme were minutely dissected for humorous effect, and his allusions were challenged, as were even his grammar and spelling. His two most famous blunders (which were not committed in his function as poet laureate)—his spelling *paraphonalia* and his remark that one of the actresses of his company had in a certain rôle "outdone her usual outdoings"—were worn threadbare; regular allusions to them may be counted on. For instance, in regard to the news that Mrs. Oldfield's performance of a new rôle was "surprising," one of the editors remarks (number 10), "I would rather have expressed it in the words of our learned Mr. Cibber, Mrs. Oldfield has outdone her usual outdoings," and in "Verses occasioned by Mr. C—r's erecting a booth in Smithfield," published in number 190, Maevius (Russel) says that there will shine the modern British Muses—

[35] Bavius, in comment on this controversy, derided Outis' letter and declared that as far as writing for half-crown dinners was concerned, Outis was more likely to do it than Somebody—moreover, Outis' letter was not worth a half crown. See also "The Modern Poets," in the *Journal* 98 cited below. Note also Brewster, *Aaron Hill*, p. 126: "Cibber, under the pseudonym of Outis, had been expressing in the *Grubstreet Journal* a very favorable opinion of his own abilities." The *Journal's* criticisms of Cibber's acting were paralleled by Hill in the *Prompter*. In 321 "Outis Junior" explains that "Outis" is not "Is out" as the *Prompter* had explained, but is the Greek for "Nobody," i.e., the antagonist of "Somebody."

> Adorned with all their grand Paraphonalia
> To celebrate our annual Bacchanalia.

The "outdoings" and "paraphonalia" were indeed, two of the most familiar jokes of the period—practically all the literary or dramatic satirists[36] were bound to make use of them sooner or later.

The *Journal* of course made as much capital as possible out of the scramble for the laureateship which followed upon the death of the incumbent, Eusden, in the autumn of 1730. In the campaign for the place, Cibber's name does not seem to have been publicly discussed. His appointment came as something of a surprise, and it was only after the actual announcement of his selection in number 48 that the satire on him began. As one writer puts it (number 52)—

> But guessing who would have the luck
> To be the B— day fibber;
> I thought of Dennis, Theobald, Duck,
> But never dreamt of Cibber.

In number 49 the *Journal* reported in equivocal phrase his reception at court, agreeing "that he is a grand and consequently a famous comedian, and very comical author," said it did not doubt "but that this new preferment will make him more justly celebrated than ever," and inserted in following issues[37] numerous epigrams at the new laureate's expense. By far the best of these is Pope's famous squib —

> Tell if you can which did the worse
> Caligula or Gr—n's Gr—ce?[38]
> That made a consul of a horse
> And this a laureate of an ass.

[36] Or even political. Note, for instance, *Fog's Journal,* January 9, 1731—"We are informed that Keyber comes on pretty well in his spelling, and by the time he begins to read a little he will be initiated into the society of political authors . . . and as he has the happiness to be provided with all the Paraphonalia of a Whig hackney it is everybody's opinion he will do his patron as much honor and service as the best of them."

[37] See 50, 51, 52, 53.

[38] Grafton's Grace, The Duke of Grafton.

which Maevius (Russel) capped with another question. Considering the present state of society, the stage, and poetry, he asks—

> Who better than an ass with laurelled pride
> O'er authors, actors, audience can preside?

Most of these epigrams are mediocre or worse, but one possibly is clever enough to be reprinted —

> Court fools and poets once illustrious lived;
> With different titles graced distinct they shone;
> But both are now so scarce, 'tis well contrived
> To join a poet and a fool in one.

The attacks on Cibber the laureate were regular as long as the *Journal* lived. It never failed to reprint his New Year's and Birthday odes with a running comment of mock annotation and discussion, and with epigrams and numerous chance allusions.[39] Reference to him was in all tones, ranging from derisive condescension to savage contempt, and all the devices of satire, burlesque, and parody were employed at one time or another. The writer of a letter (number 55) on his first ode remarks, "So unexpectedly raised to so high a dignity, so envied by all the wits, no wonder he has herein

---

[39] For instance, in the usual notes on the New Year's ode for 1733 (162), it is suggested that in one place where the verse made nonsense, error must have crept in through the carelessness of an amanuensis or proofreader—a palpable hit at Bentley and his theories of Miltonic criticism. In this same issue appears a discussion of his allusion to the Muses as "Sicilian sisters," to which the *Journal* became fond of referring. In 161 and 162 it is noted that Orator Henley has changed the subject of his quarrel with the *Journal,* and run off to defend Cibber and the phrase "Sicilian sisters." A correspondent in 150 writes an anecdote of a poet named Choerilus of the time of Alexander, who sang that hero's praises in odes and birthday songs, but so badly as to give offense. He was ordered a piece of gold for every good verse and a lash for every bad one, his final reward being three pieces of gold and three hundred lashes. In *Hooker's Miscellany* (202) the editor remarks by way of preface to one of Cibber's birthday odes, "We shall observe that the said ode may be said to be better than some former ones of the same author, and has fewer faults; because it is *shorter.*"

Russel ("M") began his satirical attacks on the New Year's Ode in number 2 with a criticism of Eusden's ode for 1730. He begins, "It presages no small happiness to our society to have the New Year opened before the most august assembly with this incomparable ode, composed by one* of our most worthy members. . . . *The Reverend Mr. Laurence Eusden, Poet Laureate." The foot-note (*) appears only in the *Memoirs.*

outdone his usual outdoings." In a letter (number 74) on
"the Keybers"—a spelling to which the *Journal* among others
was much given—is sung the poetical glory of both Colley
and Theophilus; and in Latin verses (with English translation) the fact is deplored that the envious wits should deny
poetical gifts to so great a comedian, and the prophecy is
made that one day he shall hand on the laurel to his son
"formose Theophile," "by right hereditary, poet born." One
"John a Nokes" (number 104) says,

Our laureat's last ode so much exceeding his former in the unintelligible sublime, I have restored it to its true reading, after the
Theobaldine manner, for the benefit of the public. . . .

> And for the which, when that as once it was
> Not to be so, but furthermore likewise,[40] *etc.*

. . . If you put the ode itself in a counter column you'll find the
meaning of both exactly the same.

In the same way, Bavius (number 202) applies Horace's
touchstone by reducing the last birthday ode to prose to see
if the sublime language still shines forth, and declares that
"upon changing the order of the words, they lose nothing of
their loftiness." In number 106 a letter from the Elysian
Fields tells of Cibber's declaring before Apollo his rights to
the laurel. He is made to present his "works"—his plays—
which Apollo rejects, the writer intimating by the way that
most modern plays are kept in a library by the temple of
Cloacina near the foot of Parnassus. Cibber is finally given
a drink of Hippocrene to test his poetic quality, with disastrous effect. In number 209 the device of comparison
also yields fruitful results. In a categorical examination of
the physical and mental qualities and the careers of Cibber
and "Mr. Carpenter, poet-laureate . . . and deputy bell-man
of the city of Hereford," it is pointed out for example that
Mr. Carpenter is a shoemaker by trade, and Mr. Cibber a
cobbler of Corneille's and Molière's old shoes. The official of
Hereford finally comes off best and it is concluded that he

[40] For other burlesques, see 106, a New Year's Ode, not in "the Cib-
berine style," but translated into English; and 312, "Tobacco, an Ode,
in humble imitation of the manner of our excellent laureate, Colley Cibber, Esq., designed to be set to music."

may be held the better man. A somewhat similar device is used in number 210, where the new year's verses by the St. James bellman are reprinted in connection with Cibber's ode for 1733, with the remark that they are equally the entertainment of the polite part of the town. Again in number 305, the *Journal* published a doggerel birthday ode with the author's note, "As the author of these verses is not the laureate, I hope they will escape censure. A private man, unpensioned, has, I think, a right to be spared upon such an occasion. It is enough for him to mean well, let the execution be ever so indifferent."

In quite another strain are the direct assaults which appear occasionally, as for instance in "The Modern Poets" (number 98), where he is taken to task for his attempts to imitate Congreve and to write odes and pastorals, as well as to play tragic parts, and in number 245 where Russel speaks of—

> Thy crazy muse, unfit for praise or satire,

and adjures him—

> Be not so lavish of discordant rime
> Nor claim our scorn before the proper time.
> To dullness and contempt thy title clear
> By odes stands well asserted twice a year.

Still another (number 213) speaks of his range between high sounding and grovelling nonsense, and tells him—

> . . . thy excellence
> Consists in darkness. Then go on, and spread
> Darkness around thee each revolving year.
> Let others boast of perspicuity,
> Thine is the praise to be completely dark.
> Cimmerian darkness was a proverb once;
> Cibberian darkness is a proverb now.

The same idea appears (numbers 150, 151) in connection with a letter censuring Cibber's impiety in beginning one of his odes "Let there be light," which drew forth the comparison with a puppet show in which the master cried "Let there be light" and—"Punch enters with a farthing candle." Appended is the commentary:

Let there be light, th' Almighty said.
A blazing glory shines
And o'er the universe was spread
Except on C—r's lines.

Nor did the more private and less professional activities of the laureate escape the *Journal's* notice. It reprints (number 181), for example, verses on his being expelled from the House of Lords, describing his affected condescension there and advising him if he wished revenge to avoid satires and to frighten the Lords with his odes. When he announced his intention of leaving the stage, the *Journal* remarked (number 170), "It is below the dignity of a poet laureate to continue an actor," and it also commented (number 115) on his "usual eloquence" when he spoke at a stockholders' meeting of the South-Sea Company, in which "his stock is large."

Its hostility moreover extended undiminished to his son, who seems to have been regarded as a smaller and more absurd edition of his father.[41] The *Journal's* contempt for Theophilus Cibber is illustrated by its description (number 121) of the cast of "A Lapland Entertainment" at Drury Lane, in which the parts were taken:—"The Bear by Father K-b-r, The Monkey by his son, bare-faced, the stag by ditto with a most illustrious frontispiece." All the cast "out-did their usual out-doings." When Theophilus ventured his play, *The Lover,* the *Journal* was prepared to believe the worst of it. It reprinted (number 54) a letter of his to the *Daily Post,* dated January 8, 1731, explaining that the play was entirely his, that his father had had nothing to do with it, that although he had "some tolerable opinion" of it, his hopes rested chiefly on the indulgence of the town. Upon all this, the *Journal* remarked, clearly in Russel's style,

[41] For instance in an "Ode to the Poet Laureate" by Maevius, (doubtless Russel) in 203, ridiculing all his activities, appears the Recitativo—
With equal might our laureate and his son
Through town and court their glorious course have run.
Far as the sire his borrowed scenes extends
The sire-like son his face and stature lends,
And the same jokes th' industrious bard compiles
Our player repeats to raise our grins and smiles.

I fear this young gentleman has too much timorousness, piety and modesty to succeed in this degenerate age. Fearing lest the world should impute some part of this play to his father he declares him entirely unaccountable for any one good as well as bad or indifferent line in it. As his own opinion of it is only tolerable to himself, it may possibly prove intolerable to others, but let the appearance on the stage by means of false light be what it will, the light of an author of a *moderate* (indifferent) *new play* can be but darkness.

Of the first night, the *Journal* (number 55) said, "This evening Mr. Theob. [*sic*] Cibber's play called *The Lover* was acted which proved a tragi-comedy, both in itself and in the consequences, it occasioning the drawing of blood in the pit. The success was so dubious that it was uncertain whether the hisses or the claps were more numerous. The epilogue was received with universal applause, either because it was the conclusion, or because of the truths told him in it by his wife."[42] Upon the news in the *Daily Courant* that the play was attended by "great applause" the *Journal* tartly remarked the next week, "Applause is here taken in a literal sense for clapping of hands, but intermixed with almost continual hisses and a great variety of other noises."

Some time later, during the quarrel between the actors and the patentees at Drury Lane,[43] a correspondent "Musaeus" holds Theophilus, whom he calls "the Ancient" or "Pistol," responsible for the trouble. He concludes, "Upon the whole, I can discern no other motive for this rebellion, but that Theophilus Cibber, Comedian, had resolved to be the Lucifer of the stage; and I don't understand why he has not so much title to claim the laurel when his father dies, as to succeed to the management while he is living."[44] The

---

[42] "The Epilogue, spoken by the author and his wife." The lines referred to are as follows—

Now I suppose you'll find your work is done;
Did not I say—you were your father's son?
Be what it might you play, the town would game it,
That your bare name were half a cause to damn it.
Experience to your cost will show you now,
Who wears the wiser head—your wife or you.

[43] For a brief summary of this quarrel, see Brewster, *Aaron Hill*, 118.
[44] For other allusions to Theophilus Cibber, see 132, 162, 164, 180, 186. For the letter by Musaeus, see 187.

Journal, however, does not seem to have felt the same animosity toward Theophilus' wife, Miss Arne, sister of Thomas Arne. In verses on the occasion of their marriage, dated April 30, 1730, but not published until May, 1734 (number 228), the usual ridicule is meted out to Theophilus, but she is given credit for "her beauty, her fortune, her sweet little voice," and in general is treated with benevolence.[45] Moreover, in a dispute which arose late in 1736 when the manager assigned the part of Polly in *The Beggar's Opera to* Mrs. Cibber, although it was one of Kitty Clive's great successes, the *Journal* seems rather to sympathize with Mrs. Cibber. It even went so far as to allow space for a letter actually signed Theophilus Cibber wherein that gentleman pointed out that the dispute was entirely between Mrs. Clive and the manager, and that Mrs. Cibber was not implicated in it. He added further that she was fully conscious of her youth and inexperience and never pretended to rival Mrs. Clive.[46]

The thrusts of the *Journal* at the laureate and his son, were, as has been noted before, more or less in the fashion. Cibber was generally regarded with more or less good-natured contempt, allowance first being made for his ability as an actor, and his son seems to have been thought of as one who aped his father, and had inherited the latter's weaknesses without a great share of his ability. Both were credited especially with vanity and extreme effrontery. Theophilus apparently could be goaded into indignant and noisy replies to the sallies of their enemies, but the more seasoned Colley seems to have accepted all taunts with calm and placid indifference. Indeed, he says himself, "After near twenty years having been libelled by our daily paper scribblers, I never was so hurt as to give them one single answer."[47]

---

[45] See also 321, for "To Mrs. Cibber, An Ode"—on seeing her as Indiana in *The Conscious Lovers.*

[46] For this quarrel, see numbers 361-368.

[47] See Cibber's *Apology,* edited by R. W. Lowe (2 vols. London, 1889), I, 44, n. 1. The complacent vanity of his disposition displays itself in his remarks on Pope's enmity toward him. "When I therefore find my name at length in the satyrical works of our most celebrated living author, I

The attacks on Fielding and the Cibbers are perhaps the most interesting and important of the *Journal's* bickerings with theatrical celebrities. There was another campaign, however, which the paper engaged in with equal vigor and gusto, and in which its personal interest was even more intense, its squabble with the *Prompter* over William Popple's comedy, *The Double Deceit*. The personal animosity between the *Journal* and the *Prompter* had been rendered unusually bitter by their long continued controversy over Matthew Tindall's will, and "The Philosopher's Prayer," so that when occasion offered a new bone of contention, both parties seized it with a fierceness which would otherwise demand explanation.

Popple had had, it would seem, rather unfortunate ambitions as a playwright. In 1734 he had had produced a piece called *The Lady's Revenge*,[48] which expired after dragging out a short but weary life of four nights. The author in his preface explained that partisan and unfair tactics had hurt the play, but insisted that it had not failed but had been withdrawn for fear of trouble with a hostile claque. This

never look on those lines as malice meant to me (for he knows I never provoked it) but profit to himself: One of his points must be to have many readers. He considers that my face and name are more known than those of many thousands of more consequence in the kingdom. That therefore, right or wrong, a lick at the laureat will always be a sure bait, *ad captandum vulgus,* to catch him little readers. . . . But as a little bad poetry is the greatest crime he lays to my charge, I am willing to subscribe to his opinion of it." The same attitude is to be seen in verses from the *Daily Journal,* March 26, 1736, "Epigram on the writers of the Grubstreet Journal"—

>Of old when the Grubs attacked Colley Cibber
>As player, as bard, as odaic wine bibber,
>To a friend that advised him to answer their malice
>And check by reply their extravagant sallies,
>No, no, quoth the laureat, with a smile of much glee,
>They write for a dinner, which they shan't get from me.

To which the *Journal* replied in 327—

>Since the Laureat, quoth Dactyl, is resolute bent
>Not to answer our malice, that we may keep Lent,
>Let him fling up the Bays and return to the stage
>And try as an actor to charm the dull age.
>For if he writes on—o'er a glass with good cheer
>We shall feast on his odes, I am sure, twice a year.

[48] *The Lady's Revenge, or The Rover Reclaimed. A Comedy* (London, 1734). The prologue and epilogue were both by Aaron Hill.

feeble apology of Popple's in his preface met with vigorous
analysis in the *Journal.* "Atticus" (number 215) denied point
blank Popple's assertion that the play had been damned by a
cabal, and declared that the bulk of the audience had been
sympathetic until they discovered that the play was poor. He
then undertook to disprove categorically Popple's statements
that the audiences of the second, third, and fourth nights were
in general favorable, and even went so far as to say that
on the last night the actor Quin quieted the audience only by
promising that the play would not be repeated. Popple's side
was taken by two of his friends, of whom one, "Terentianus,"
answers Atticus unconvincingly (number 216), and the
other, "Candidus," attempts (number 218) a formal critique
of the play, discussing the unities, consistency of character,
and so forth, a defense which Bavius analyzes point by point.
That the controversy might have run on indefinitely is indicated by Bavius' explanation (number 221) that letters received could not always be published because of lack of space.
In addition to those already printed concerning *The Lady's
Revenge,* the editors had received a long defence by Philalethes[49] and a longer letter in ridicule by Drawcansir. But
as the play had no success and was of little interest, the editor
was told, according to Bavius, to shut off the correspondence. Some time later, Atticus had sent in a second letter, and
"Baviophilus" a criticism of Bavius' answer to "Candidus"
in number 218. This letter was not published, but Bavius did
answer some of its contentions. Baviophilus, however, in
spite of his name, returned to the charge with such an abusive
letter that Bavius could not let it pass. Accordingly, in number 224 he announced the receipt of Baviophilus' second letter, and printed it without comment.[50] The style of this letter
is indicated by the following extract:

Exert all the wit you and your fraternity are masters of, to expose
the attempt of a gentleman who had a mind to try his genius in the

---

[49] Possibly Fielding. He had used this pseudonym.
[50] The particular point on which they were at odds was whether "the
man of pleasure" in the play, who repents at the end and marries the
heroine, is sufficiently repentant.

dramatic way. . . . Be advised in time, and let not your vanity make you imagine nobody has any sense but yourself or that a play must be bad because you write against it.

He further insists that Bavius finds fault for its own sake, wilfully mistakes the sense of passages, and gives false turns to them.

The *Journal* in this campaign had indeed been definitely hostile to Popple, and it is not surprising to find the quarrel renewed when he came out with another play, *The Double Deceit*,[51] a year and a half later. This second phase of the quarrel had, however, additional motivation. The chief point at issue was Popple's plagiarism from James Miller's comedy, *The Man of Taste,* of the dramatic device of having two footmen appear as their masters. Since the quarrel over *The Lady's Revenge,* Popple had become one of the editors of the *Prompter,* which in its violent squabble with the *Journal* over Eustace Budgell and Tindall had shown itself a most outspoken enemy; moreover Miller, it is supposed, had taken Russel's place as chief editor of the *Journal,* when the latter resigned at the end of 1735. It is not surprising then, that the statements on both sides were extremely warm, and that they soon developed into personalities and recrimination.

The quarrel seems to have got well under way privately, for the first utterance in the *Journal,* which appeared rather significantly on the day *The Double Deceit* was to be given a second trial, speaks of it as though it were well established. The author of the letter, who calls himself "Neitherside,"[52] explains that while he does not consider *The Man of Taste* a good play, he thinks *The Double Deceit* a worse. Moreover, he says, Popple's play was thought to have been produced before *The Man of Taste* merely to forestall a charge of plagiarism, and now after a lapse of time is to be presented again. The device in question, which after all went back to

[51] *The Double Deceit, or a Cure for Jealousy. A Comedy.* By William Popple, Esq. (London, 1736)—Prologue by Aaron Hill.
[52] He says, "I am neither an enemy to Mr. P—le nor a friend to Mr. M—r: I know neither of them but by their writings; and these lines entirely flow from my love to justice and impartiality." See 322.

Molière, was said by Popple's adherents to have been stolen from *The Double Deceit* for *The Man of Taste,* notwithstanding that Miller's play, though produced later, had been put into rehearsal first. In addition Mr. Popple had done everything he could to injure Mr. Miller, yet in spite of all efforts *The Double Deceit* had been so poorly received—it took only £30 the first night and £5 the second—that it was withdrawn. Neitherside also taunts Popple with his earlier absurd excuses for the failure of *The Lady's Revenge.*

This letter, of course, belies its author's claim of impartiality in its obvious espousal of Miller's cause. The next week Neitherside published another letter in the *Journal* to the effect that he had attended a performance of *The Double Deceit* and had seen it receive the fate it deserved. He then quotes entire a handbill given out to each spectator :

Whereas the writer of the Grubstreet Journal has printed a letter in his paper of this day vilely misrepresenting Mr. P—le in every light in which he considers him, and tending manifestly to injure him in his character both as a gentleman and an author, and whereas it is evident that the publishing of that letter was deferred to this day (it being dated the 17th inst.)[53] in order and with a design maliciously to create a disturbance at the playhouse and prepossess the audience against *The Double Deceit* to the very great prejudice of the author, these are to desire such of the audience as may have read the aforesaid letter not to give any credit to the allegations therein contained till they shall have seen Mr. P—le's justification, which he will print with all convenient speed.[54]

Neitherside then declares that he is a *bona fide* correspondent and not "the writer of the Grubstreet Journal," that his charges had been against Popple only as an author (which was hardly true), and that the letter, which was dated the seventeenth, could not have been published before the twenty-sixth,[55] and for various other reasons could not possibly have been written especially to appear at a critical moment

[53] Number 322 was published February 26. According to its date the letter might have appeared on February 19, in 321.

[54] There is also a note in which Popple denies having charged the gentlemen from the Inns of Court with having caused the failure of *The Lady's Revenge.*

[55] Still the *Journal* was able on occasion to print articles received the day before publication.

on the day *The Double Deceit* was to be acted. He declares
that his letter had been called forth not by Popple's mediocrity as an author, but only by his puffing of his play beforehand—"he might have been annually damned without any
animadversions from me"—and asks how his letters could
have caused the play to fail. In this same issue is reprinted
from the *Post* the news item that *The Double Deceit* was
acted before a splendid audience including members of the
royal family, but that the author, "perceiving . . . a determined resolution [on the part of certain persons] to breed
a disturbance . . . occasioned . . . from an invidious letter
inserted in Thursday's Grubstreet Journal," chose to withdraw the play rather than gratify them. This feeble defense
got its quietus in the comment: "Mr. Conundrum conjectures
that the true reason of this gentleman's withdrawing his play
was that the audience would not withdraw till another play
was given out for the next night."

The *Prompter* on its side had been puffing *The Double
Deceit,* answering the *Journal's* charges against the play,
and disparaging *The Man of Taste*.[56] As usual, however,
its remarks ran off onto the subject of the *Journal's* manners
and even such an irrelevant matter as its origin. The
Prompter intimated that Neitherside was Miller himself,[57]
a suspicion which met an explicit denial in the *Journal's*
statement (number 323) that the gentleman suspected had
no hand in the quarrel, knew nothing of it, and had never
written a syllable in defense of his own play. The *Prompter's*
allegations are then made the occasion for a disquisition on

[56] See the *Prompter,* 137. An advertisement of this issue in the *Daily
Journal,* February 28, promised "a full answer to that insolent, scurrilous,
false, and malicious letter signed Neitherside in the last Grubstreet
Journal wrote with a design to injure a gentleman both in his public and
private character. Its author is supposed to be a clergyman who instead
of employing his time in works suitable to the sanctity of his profession
has already misspent it in writing one damned play and two vile translations from Moliere, and is now making Much Ado About Nothing, on
which occasion, 'tis hoped something will be done with somebody." This
is clearly an allusion to Miller; his ecclesiastical superiors and his enemies held his comedies against him.

[57] See the *Prompter,* 134, for a discussion of *The Man of Taste*; and
for other points, 137 and 144.

its taste in general—its habit of puffing pieces which failed miserably and then damning the taste of the town. It is, in fact, charged with always missing the mark. For instance, *The Man of Taste,* regarded with disfavor by the *Prompter,* ran thirty nights at first and later seven or eight more,— "this Mr. Prompter, sadly remembering the dismal catastrophe of Athelwold,[58] could never forgive."

At this point the quarrel becomes a purely personal affair. In the *London Daily Post* for March 5, Popple, signing himself "The Author of the Double Deceit," denied Neitherside's assertion that he had attempted to injure Miller, declaring that when *The Man of Taste* was acted he did not even know who the author was, and also denying (quite correctly) that in his preface to *The Lady's Revenge* he had charged the Templars with maliciously damning it. This, apparently the letter Popple had promised in his handbill, was cleverly but maliciously dissected in the *Journal,* which inserted in the issue last mentioned (number 324, March 11) a statement over the signature "J. H.,"— that is John Huggonson, at this time the *Journal's* bookseller: "The author of The Double Deceit (in his letter in the *London Daily Post* of March 5) talks much about, and seems to value himself highly on his character as a gentleman, and among other thing says, 'Mr. Neitherside in his first letter asserts two facts of me which in Tuesday's *Prompter* were proved to be false. Upon my applying to the printer of the Grubstreet he told me they should be retracted, which I expected to see in this day's paper.' To which I answer: That I always thought speaking, writing, or publishing of truth had been one grand characteristic of a complete gentleman, but the author of *The Double Deceit* (in causing these words [he told me they should be retracted] to be printed in a public paper) has published an untruth or falsehood; and therefore in my opinion is no complete gentleman. J. H." The clear

---

[58] By Aaron Hill (1731). According to *Biographia Dramatica,* this was his favorite tragedy. It was acted at Drury Lane for three nights. He had tried the same subject in another play, also a failure, some twenty years earlier.

intention of this letter was to turn the quarrel into the channels of a personal wrangle by irritating Popple into further declarations. The device was successful, for in the *London Daily Post* for March 15 "W. P." begs leave, Neitherside not having deigned to answer his letter of the fifth, "to say a word or two to the insolent advertisement of the printer in yesterday's paper on that subject." He then goes on to contradict J. H.'s denial that he had promised retraction, remarks on Quakers' affirmations (Huggonson was a Quaker) and threatens—"if he takes the liberty to sport any more with my character . . . I shall . . . resent it in another manner."

The next week's issue of the *Journal* printed and answered a request "to give over pestering your readers with disputes about a damned play and a damned prayer." In their answer the editors admitted that they did not think it wise to write criticisms of "damned plays," and especially of the two last. They added that the author of one (Miller, of course) did not approve the puffs his play received before it was acted and was now resolved not to defend it. As for the other, criticism of it would be as little regarded as the author's attempt to vindicate it.[59] This *Journal* also contains another provocative note from J. H. to W. P. on the subject of "a complete Gentleman" and a challenge to a duel, and still another appeared the next week (number 326) in a long demonstration that W. P. was "NO GENTLEMAN." This statement is undisguised ragging—for instance it proves Popple a Quibbler and a Blunderer. Furthermore it denies again that Popple had been promised any retraction, and says that he had merely been told that if what he said were true he had been injured, and that if he would send in a statement of such injury either the printer or authors of the *Journal* would do anything proper. Huggonson asserts, however, that Popple had been more anxious to learn the identity of

[59] To this letter is appended the notice of Hill's statement that he had had nothing to do with the letters in the *Prompter* on "The Philosopher's Prayer" and the theatrical quarrel, and disapproved of their scurrility. See *ante,* p. 155.

Neitherside than to secure a retraction; and says he has heard that Popple is about to invoke the aid of the law.

These hints failed to draw further quarrelsome rejoinders from Popple, although they were repeated in number 327,[60] and again, after a silence of six weeks, in numbers 333-336, apparently with the idea that with some prodding Popple could be drawn once more. In the first of these issues the whole affair was summarized and it was announced that the reasons Mr. P—le had assigned for his silence would be examined the next week. The promised analysis proved to be contemptuous remarks upon a fable of the affair, which had appeared two months earlier in the *Prompter* for March 23. The story was of a school boy who, after he had thrown one of his mates in fair fight, had been besquirted with dirty water by his fallen enemy and thereupon ran off saying he was not afraid to be wet, but was ashamed to be dirty. The *Journal,* having paid its respects to this analogue, went on to imply that Popple had written the letters in defense of *The Double Deceit* to himself as editor, "one to acknowledge the justice he was willing to do himself" and "the other to restrain himself" from publishing any more. The *Journal* also took up (numbers 335-336) old points that had been made earlier, exposed errors in some of Popple's mythological allusions, and "odd peculiarities" in his style and grammar, waxed sarcastic over his suggestion that the editors of the *Journal* ought to act like scholars and clergymen, when he himself was an attacker of all believing clergymen, contradicted an inference that Huggonson had not written the "J. H." letters himself, mocked his magnanimous decision to drop the controversy, and finally, in reference to the *Prompter's* theory that the *Journal* had sprung from Pope's design for "Works of the Unlearned," insisted, "This design was not in the least known to those who set up our Paper; nor was the Letter published till near six years after

[60] In a letter from J. H. contrasting with Popple's behavior the "civil, gentleman-manner" of another young man who had been to him on the same sort of errand.

the beginning of our *Journal.*"[61] These delayed shots failed to revive a contention which had had all the publicity it deserved and more. Popple did not reply and the *Journal,* deciding, it would seem, that there was nothing more to be made of the matter, also allowed it to drop.

During this controversy, the *Journal* also came into collision with the *Prompter,* or more properly with Aaron Hill, on another point, although with much less violence and personal animosity. Hill had evolved a theory of acting which he explained at length in the preface to *Zara.* He believed that the only necessity for good acting was natural genius, which should be manifest at once, without training. He was tired of the affectations of acting which "made tragedy forbidding and horrible," but was, he says,

despairing to see a correction of this folly when I found myself unexpectedly re-animated by the war which *The Prompter* has proclaimed and is now weekly waging against the ranters and whiners of the theatre, after having undertaken to reduce the actor's lost art into principles.

He announces that his only motive in presenting *Zara* is to test this theory, but somewhat illogically takes it for granted that he is correct, and that a failure of *Zara* would indicate only a general lack of taste on the part of the audience. The test did result in failure. Mrs. Cibber, who was making her first essay of a tragic rôle and who had been carefully coached by Hill himself, but who was after all a professional actress, made a brilliant success. On the other hand, Hill's nephew, Charles Hill, an amateur, who was cast for the part of Osman, failed totally, and according to a later account in the *Journal* (number 350) was "hissed off the stage."[62]

[61] A pretense or assumption that Pope himself had nothing to do with founding the *Journal,* and that his letters and ideas in general would be unknown to the founders until they appeared in print. The letter referred to was an old one to Gay. See *ante.*

[62] The training of actors was the subject of two letters to the *Journal.* An anonymous writer in 277 suggests that steps be taken to raise the actor's profession to a level with the others. He declares that the requirements as regards appearance, education, manners, and so forth, are so great that men of breeding and family but small fortune should be thus encouraged to enter it. Some such idea seems also to have been in the

This project of Hill's for training up amateur actors is dubbed by a sarcastic writer, "Meanwell" in number 326, a piece of impudence, and Hill himself is designated an "extraordinary Gentleman." According to Meanwell, the appearance of an amateur on the public stage is, more than anything else, a sign of vanity and ostentation. He approves of boys acting at school to gain assurance and poise, but he has no desire to see young gentlemen strutting about on the public stage. The typical sequence of events in such a case, he says, is for a stage-struck amateur to give private performances before his friends, to feed upon their encouragement, then to appear in public with great disaster, which is laid to envy and ignorance, and finally to write fables insinuating that he himself is a horse, the other actors mules, and the pit "a confederate tribe of asses." This letter, like the earlier one concerning Popple, resulted in a personal visit to Huggonson, the printer, by Charles Hill, the outcome of which is indicated in a note the next week:

Inasmuch as I believe C. H. (who, as himself supposed seemed to be the person aimed at in Meanwell's letter in our last journal and as I apprehend, vindicated in the following) was with me to ask such like questions as W. P. had asked me some time before; and seeing C. H. (on my making him such like answers as I had made to W. P.) seemed to be pretty well satisfied, and parted with me in a civil gentleman-like manner, I have prevailed with our Society (who have been always ready to do justice) to order the following letter to be inserted this week, tho it came rather too late, J. H.

The letter here referred to is a defense by "J. English" of the acting of the young gentleman who took the part of Osman in *Zara*. At least the appearance of impartiality is lent by some adverse criticism. The writer says, for instance,

mind of the writer in 184, who advances proposals for a new theatrical college on a vacated site in the Strand. His plans included a central theatre and two wings, one for men's apartments and one for women's. Immorality was to be punished by expulsion, and no student was to be admitted without "a genteel and liberal education." The head of the school was to be a gentleman of the highest attainments, capable of directing the education of young actors, devising scenery, selecting plays, and so on, and the officers might quite happily (and in this he is serious) be supplied from the decayed gentry! Its proponent admits that this scheme is a very grand one, to be undertaken only with the patronage of the throne.

that he at first gave the impression of conceit, but concludes that he showed variety of manner and gave "a just idea of the character." With this conciliatory criticism, the discussion of amateur acting was allowed to drop.

Altogether, there is in the *Journal* surprisingly little criticism of new plays. Aside from Fielding's plays and Popple's, which became the subjects of extended quarrels, the new pieces which the *Journal* bothered to discuss from any point of view can almost be numbered on the fingers of one hand. And moreover, among these there are not more than two or three instances of anything approaching a review. More often than not the comment turns at once, or almost at once, to personal matters or to some subject for which the play itself is merely a stalking horse. Obviously the editors had no intention of reviewing new plays as they were produced. Day by day contemporary playwrights were grinding out new grist for the theaters, but there was as yet no dramatic editor to evaluate their efforts and advise the public. Notice that a new play was on the boards was generally given in the daily papers and copied from them in the weeklies, and, unless the result was a riotous failure, the public was informed in stock formula that it "was acted with great applause, before a large audience including many people of quality." Almost without exception a personal animus of one sort or another can be traced in any of the *Journal's* criticisms. It is also notable that the criticism is regularly unfavorable; even when the *Journal* undertook the cause of James Miller and his *Man of Taste* it found nothing good to say directly of the play itself. Occasionally, however, a pronouncement does seem to be colored by a definite contempt for the play as such, apart from the authorship, or the management or the actors. For instance, early in the paper's career (numbers 6 and 7), Russel exercised his powers of sarcasm to the full against Miller's *Humours of Oxford.* He summarizes the action and declares that the play was intended to expose one of those seats of learning which breed up Parnassians in a classic tradition in distinction

from those geniuses who are able to scorn such a training
and distinguish themselves very early with some surprising
composition. He analyzes the construction and after saying
of the unities, " . . . the author has shown the greatness
of his art in observing the two former, and that of his
genius in neglecting the last," shows that the comedy has
the surprising architecture of two main plots and two sub-
plots, and then in the same ironical vein cites characteristic
detail of the author's language and sentiments. It is evident
that Miller was as yet an outsider; his membership in the
Journal's approved coterie was still to come. *The Humours
of Oxford* nevertheless seems to be treated on its merits,
independent of its authorship or personal connections.

On the other hand, in dealing with *Sophonisba,* a new.
play by James Thomson, toward whom Pope was friendly—
and who was therefore a "Parnassian" and *persona grata*—
the *Journal* avoids the play itself and attacks two pamphlets
about it. In number 11, these pamphlets are advertised, one
an unfavorable criticism and the other an answer to it, both
published by the same printer. The *Journal* over Bavius'
signature[63] also pronounced them to be by the same author—
"Tim" Birch. Thomson himself is referred to as "probably a
profest enemy of our Society"—the usual phrase for the
elect—and the two pamphlets are made a pretext for attacking the newspaper puffs of plays, and asserting the *Journal's*
independence and contempt for all such devices. In this particular case, the *Journal* was doubtless motivated chiefly by
its hatred for Tim Birch, later to edit that "obscure" paper,
the *Weekly Register.* Criticism of Thomson also affected the
Journal's attitude toward *The Contrast,*[64] a burlesque on

[63] The next week, in number 12.
[64] See 70. According to *Biographia Dramatica* it was by Benjamin and
John Hoadley, and was never printed. *The Contrast* is also satirised by
"Philo-Grubstreet" in 73. . . . "Nor need Grubstreet ever fear an enemy
while there is an author of *The Contrast* to defend it. What honours
ought you not to decree to perpetuate his memory who has made such
bold attacks against those formidable enemies, Steele, Congreve, Rowe,
and the immortal Shakespeare, not in the least fearing their wit, nor
paying a decent regard to their Manes."

the model of *The Rehearsal*. An ironical correspondent, "Salisbury Steeple", announces his authorship of the play, since several other people who like himself had no hand in it are letting it pass as theirs. He prides himself on his uncommon ability in exposing, not the bad but the good, and asserts that despite denials the play was intended as a satire on two or three dramatists, among them "that strenuous anti-Grubaean," Thomson. An even clearer case of personal interest is furnished by the criticism of James Ralph's comedy *The Fashionable Lady*. Ralph was of course one of the chief butts of Grubstreet satire during the paper's early period when Pope was actively connected with it. Consequently its tone is not surprising. Preparation for an assault is to be found in number 14, in a comment on notice of its "successful production" : "This excellent play was presented to the Society on Wednesday last, and referred to the consideration of Mr. Bavius." Two weeks later came the results of that worthy's consideration, in an article by Martyn headed "Oons, Mr. Drama, what d'ye mean by such stupid stuff as this? Let me be hanged if I have not been entertained a thousand times better by the Humours of Rustego and his man Terrible at Southwark Fair!"[65] Doubtless Ralph, the Hoadleys, and Miller got fully as favorable criticism as their work deserved, but it is equally beyond doubt that that criticism was unfavorable because they lived outside the charmed circle. Miller indeed, having been able to creep within it, became sacrosanct. Just a year later (59) his manner had become "palpably Parnassian" and in time he may possibly have assumed the mantle of Bavius himself.

Another equally personal passage began in number 108 in connection with *The Modish Couple* by Captain Charles Bodens. In a discussion of modern writers which begins in generalities but soon develops into an attack on Bodens, the writer charges him with undertaking to write for the public though "without wit or humor, without genius or capacity." After a number of epigrams and little squibs, in

[65] See *ante*, p. 68.

the course of which Bodens was called "a military author of a late damned dramatic performance" and "an oppressed brother," the cudgels were taken up by "Dramaticus,"[66] who was chiefly interested in contrasting his rejected masterpiece with *The Modish Couple,* which had been acceptable to the managers but had nevertheless failed. Dramaticus complained especially that though several of Bodens' characters, unlike his, were "unaccountable", his play had been stigmatized as untheatrical. *The Modish Couple,* on the other hand, evidently was theatrical; it had been "licked into the form it now bears, and had the last touches given it by a person in the management of the house, famous lately for several odes, in which he has shown as much poetry as judgment . . ."[67] The situation here is obvious; Dramaticus is writing out of jealousy and resentment toward Cibber and Wilkes, also a manager. The extent to which he nursed his grudge is shown by the fact that in number 119, in a second letter, he defended his point of view in the first, and discoursed at length on the significance of the word "theatrical." In fact the dictum "not theatrical" rankled so deeply that, as has been noted, he was continually recurring to it in his numerous letters in the Fielding quarrel, and it became the subject of remarks in the *Journal.* In number 115, in a letter which sounds somewhat like Russel, but is signed C— J—n (Charles Johnson), that prolific writer of tragedies is made to say that he has written more than twenty *theatrical* pieces, ("tho neither sensible nor pretty") and that Mr. W— (Wilkes, to whom Dramaticus had submitted his piece) "applies that word to the pieces of those authors who have the knack of wriggling themselves into his good graces." To this, Russel ("M") added the sneering comment that "theatrical" might also mean containing parts in which actors might display to advantage their tricks, gestures and

---

[66] In 112. See p. 173.

[67] Dramaticus also attacks *Injured Innocence* (by Fettiplace Bellers, according to *Biographia Dramatica*), which he says he heard was kept going only by the financial support of the author.

grimaces. In number 129 too, "Poeticus" offers Dramaticus a "Recantation Song" to sing to Wilkes. It ends—

> Then friends once more we'll be today;
> Act but my Un-theatric play.

The same hostility toward the Cibbers led to the publication in numbers 164, 165, and 167 of a series of critical articles by "Somebody." Indeed, the author explains that he has no quarrel with the authors whose plays he is dissecting; he merely wishes to disclose the defects of the management of the Drury Lane, just as one might attack a manager for using dancing dogs, without being malevolent toward dogs. He begins by saying he had expected comments on the current plays by Dramaticus, especially since this year they "afford so much room for satire" but supposes the reason for his silence is contempt. He then takes up in succession *The Boarding School Romps, Betty, or The Country Bumpkin,* and *Caelia,* three of the Cibbers' new offerings at Drury Lane. "Somebody's" tone is anything but temperate. Of the first he sneeringly declares that its songs might have been written by a little Miss working her sampler, and its tunes by a parish clerk. He insinuates moreover that the piece had been stolen, like another by the same authors, *The Devil to Pay,* which had been taken from an old play, *The Devil of a Wife.* This latter, which had first appeared in three acts, was reduced by Theophilus Cibber to one, and had had inserted in it four old songs in which the so-called authors had no hand. *The Boarding School Romps* likewise was merely an abstract of Tom Durfey's *Boarding School.* He goes on to foretell similar thefts in the future and suggests as a typical possibility Etherege's *Man of Mode, or Sir Fopling Flutter,* to be enlivened with a few songs and rechristened *The Modish Man or The Fluttering Fop.* The Cibbers, he says, deserve nothing more to manage than a puppet show, and he dubs the author of the two pieces "Fiddle Faddle Filch", and his collaborator "Sly Boots".[68]

---

[68] See *Biographia Dramatica: The Devil to Pay* was published as by Charles Coffey. He and one Mottley each undertook to work over one

In his second article he takes up in the same manner *Betty, or The Country Bumpkin,* which had been kept on the stage seven or eight nights in spite of popular disapproval, and which the author had not presumed to print. He admits that the author had some ability as a musician and that the songs were pretty, but two of them he holds up to ridicule as nonsense. Are such performances, he asks, fit to attract the patronage of royalty and the great, or to train properly the youthful mind? Of *Caelia,* the subject of his third article, he found nothing better to say. The plot, which he outlines, had possibilities, but these were defeated by the author's style, which failed to produce one single memorable speech, although Mrs. Cibber had made her part of the heroine remarkably pathetic. This leads to a discussion of poetic diction, with specimens from Shakespeare and Lee, who were able to make ideas attractive and give them permanence. But, the writer interjects scornfully, the generality of dramatic authors would no more understand what he says of taste than as if he wrote in Latin. Still he insists that *Caelia* was superior to the other plays criticized and enjoyed a greater success. Yet it was denied a second performance.

Who "Somebody" was and what specific grievance he had against the Cibbers it is impossible to say. He was, however, a frequent correspondent, and his hostility toward the laureate and his son and all their concerns is patent. It was the obvious motive for this series of attacks on their latest productions. Moreover, he soon appears again as the champion of Rich, manager of the rival house. In number 174 "No-body", apparently in retaliation for Somebody's articles, attacked Rich's judgment in choosing plays, and his

and one-half acts. T. Cibber then cut it to one act and added one song by his father and another by Rochester. It was successful and furnished Mrs. Clive with her first notable success.—*The Boarding School* [*sic*] *or The Sham Captain* (1733) was taken by Coffey, from Durfey's *Love for Money* and was a failure.—*Betty, or The Country Bumpkin. A Ballad Farce,* by Henry Carey, was acted without success at Drury Lane in 1739 (Genest records performances in December, 1732), and was not included among Carey's works.—*Caelia* was by Charles Johnson, with an epilogue by Fielding. It had no success. (Genest records a performance in December, 1732.)

insistence on having them made over to suit his own peculiar ideas. His ability as a harlequin is allowed but his taste and learning denied, and in addition he is charged with pirating a play belonging to a friend of the writer. No-body was probably the Outis of some three years later, who explained his pseudonym as being οὔ τίς, or Nobody, and who is supposed to have been Colley Cibber himself.[69] He received an answer from Somebody in number 177, in which the latter clears Rich altogether of the charge of piracy, answers ably the other indictments brought against him, and concludes with a comparison between Rich's magnanimity as a manager and the meanness of the Cibbers at Drury Lane. For instance, No-body accuses Rich of rejecting a translation of Voltaire's *Zaire*. In reply, Somebody explains that Rich had never been shown more than two or three scenes from the third act, passages which Somebody ascribes to a brother of Aaron Hill. He also explains away the charge that Rich had stolen a comedy, *The Mock Lawyer,* by saying that the play in question had been stolen from James Ralph, its author, and brought to Rich, who discovered the theft by accident. Rich happening to show the comedy to Fielding, the latter recognized it as Ralph's. Hereupon Ralph is dragged into the quarrel, and asked to explain whether his part in the affair had been an innocent or guilty one. In number 178, Ralph objected (over his own signature) to the use of his name in this controversy, and declared that he had given the play to the person Somebody charged with stealing it.[70] This drew an apology and retraction from Somebody in number 179. Somebody's third contribution to the *Journal* consisted in a series of letters (numbers 254 ff.) wherein he disputed with "Outis" over the talents of the Drurian actor Stephens and incidentally of Colley himself. His position, then, as a

[69] See *ante*, p. 188.
[70] See *Biographia Dramatica. The Mock Lawyer* was by Edward Phillips. According to Somebody, Mr. P. (Phillips) and one C—mbe had each brought a farce to Rich, and he had commissioned them to work their two plays into one. Then doubts arising as to C—mbe's authorship, he was dismissed and none of his material was used.

bitter enemy of the Cibbers and Drury Lane, and on the other hand as a friend of Rich, is clear. Indeed one may guess at a fairly close connection with Cibber's chief rival, for in the letter defending Rich he shows himself possessed of much intimate detail of Rich's life. One need not go so far as No-body, who called him "a vile scribbler" hired to attack, but he may very well have been a sort of unacknowledged but official champion of Rich and Covent Garden. It is also clear enough that he was in favor with the *Journal,* which continually allowed him space and supported his side editorially. This of course was to be expected in view of the paper's inveterate and consistent hatred of Cibber.

Doubtless it was much more interested in him for his hostility toward the Cibbers than for his friendship toward Rich. The *Journal* had little to do with Rich and mentioned him only rarely. On such occasions, however, it exhibits no particular love for him. For instance when he built his new theater it published in number 139 verses beginning:

> While Drurian actors, Rich, with envious eyes
> In Bow Street see th' aspiring fabric rise—

and continuing with praise of Rich, all his undertakings, and all his company, each of whom is mentioned by name. The editors headed these verses, however, "Published not as containing their sentiments, but those of the unknown author whom they are willing to oblige," and admitted to number 144 the distinctly unobliging verses in answer—

> In vain with glowing heart and smiling eyes
> Rich sees his theatre in Bow-street rise.
> In vain with expectation fills the town
> Whilst thou at random knock'st his actors down.
> Thy executing pen, dear Scribbler, sheathe;
> Already thou hast praised thy friends to death.[71]

[71] The only other allusion to Rich of any significance is a defence of him in 376, against an attack in the *Daily Journal.* It is said for him that the machinery he devised for his entertainments showed great genius and invention, that he used his great profits from *The Beggar's Opera* to build a new and convenient theater, and that he revived many old plays. Some of the arguments here were answered in 378 by "Haberdasherus," who was especially disturbed because Rich had raised prices for new entertainments.

At any rate, Somebody's bias is obvious enough. His criticism can no more be accepted as the utterance of disinterested or virtuous indignation than can that of Dramaticus, or Bavius himself. Like them, he has an axe of his own to grind, and is at no great pains to conceal the fact. As one discovers again and again in all connections, it is impossible to find consistently disinterested criticism in the *Journal*. It was an avenue or channel for personalities, and the temper and manners of the time and the motives of the paper itself were such that arguments and discussions, even though marked by some dignity in their beginnings, speedily twisted themselves into personal diatribes. The inhabitants of Grub-street might be interested in abstract and general critical ideas, but they were much more concerned in justifying themselves, and in disclosing to the world the defects and flaws in the talents and characters of their opponents. In this latter field of endeavor they were especially zealous workers.

The anti-Cibberian feeling of the *Journal* is apparent again in its stand in favor of the patentees of Drury Lane in their quarrel with the actors during 1733. The patents being held as private property and shifted about from one owner to another for sale, the actors grew restive, insisted that they were no better than "slaves", and started an insurrection to secure a hand in the management. In this they were led by Theophilus Cibber, a fact which must, in any case, have cost them the *Journal's* support. As a matter of fact, the letters and articles on this quarrel consist to a large extent of attacks on the younger Cibber, or "Pistol". Their tone, while on the whole it shows a bias in favor of the patentees and their vested interests, is not distinctly hostile to the players, except in the case of Theophilus Cibber.

The quarrel was well under way when the *Journal* began to give space to it in June, 1733 (number 180), although the attack on Theophilus Cibber a fortnight earlier,[72] in which he was indicted with great contempt for misdemeanors

[72] See *ante,* p. 194. This letter attacked him for his lapses as manager of Drury Lane and as author of *The Mock Officer,* and for appropriating to himself the parts left vacant by the death of Wilkes.

as author, actor, and manager, may be taken as having some bearing on the more specific discussions later. Two long letters in number 180 present both sides of the case. The spokesman for the actors dignifies his party by declaring that the best playwrights have been actors, for instance, Shakespeare and Otway, and that actors have often been thought worthy of taking part in management, as when Steele joined with him as managers the actors, Booth, Wilkes, and Cibber. He denies the justice of a system which allows a group of individuals to buy a patent outright—presumably for profit —and with it virtually the actors. Such a system, he says, might do for negro slaves, but not for Englishmen. The tendency of such patentees will be to pay as low salaries as possible and to take for themselves all the profits of hard labor and genius, denying encouragement to merit and industry. "It seems to me unjust that the useless and unprofitable members of any society should feed upon the profits arising from the excellencies of all the rest"—an eighteenth century pronouncement of a doctrine which is still "dangerously radical" in its implications! On the other hand, "Musaeus", a defender of the patentees, while admitting that stage tyrants had existed and that authors and actors had been treated like slaves, asserted that the shifting about of the patent interests in the present case had been for purposes of peace and the redressing of grievances. The plan had been for two benign gentlemen to buy one half the patent, "yet one little creature, who was only deputy and representative of his father, was turbulent enough to balk their measures, thwart their designs, and with his single insolence counterbalance all the civility and decency in the opposite scale." Then, Musaeus continues, "to extinguish this meteor," one of the patentees bought his father's share and set the son down "in the same obscure place from whence he rose."[73] This, it was thought, would set everything aright, but the same trouble-maker then stirred up dissension among the players by making them dissatisfied

[73] Cibber's reason for selling is said elsewhere to have been a desire to provide financially for his children.

with their salaries, although the system of the theater remained unchanged from the one they were used to. His
motive in this, Musaeus says, was the destruction of all property value in the patent share his father had just sold, and
his suggested plan was for the players to set up in their own
interest, taking the same salaries as before and dividing the
profits at the end of the season. They were all to be managers,
to judge plays and undertake all other responsibilities. "Like
the drunken sailors in the play they are all to be viceroys,
Pistol [T. Cibber] desired only to be viceroy over them."

Practically the whole of the next issue is devoted to the
quarrel. One writer, claiming impartiality, and declining to
dispute the wisdom or the rights of either side, is really sub-
versive of the players' cause. In humorous and ironic vein,
he thinks it quite possible for the players to start a new
theater of their own—with fifty new churches in London,
why should there not be as many new theaters? A new
theater would probably be put up in a fashionable district,
but why not near the Pegasus, for the advantage of intercourse with the Grubstreet Society? As for the actors, all—
except possibly Theophilus Cibber—were probably sincere
and disinterested, and the actresses merely followed their
lead. The writer reveals his contempt for the actors, however, when he regards the situation from the point of view
of the patentees. It would be quite possible, he thinks, for
the actors to reap advantages from the suggested revolution.
Heretofore very few decent people had become actors; now,
with a fresh start, the patentees could recruit a new company
from the university and the Inns of Court, where many knew
more about the stage than they did of the law. Furthermore
any charity school, he sneers, could furnish a dozen wenches
of more decent education and character, and more health,
beauty, youth, and genius than the common run of actresses;
and one season would doubtless qualify them all for the stage.
An illustration of the case was offered by another writer,
who contributed a passage from Vanbrugh's *Aesop,* which,

he said, offered a close parallel to the present situation.[74] According to the dialogue cited, players "always did and always will hate their masters, though they cannot support themselves without them." Moreover, the dialogue makes the point that the players were dissatisfied for silly reasons, and that they were not thriving or working well together. On Aesop's making this clear to them in a fable, they decide to make peace with the patentees.

From time to time during the rest of 1733 the progress of the quarrel was reflected in letters to the *Journal*. Theophilus Cibber had addressed a public letter[75] to Highmore, one of the patentees, and Musaeus (number 187) undertook a categorical answer to the points made therein. He declared his purpose to be the humbling of Cibber; in fact, his letter opens: "There is one Theophilus Cibber, Comedian, who has lately thrust his person full into the face of the public, and taken much pains to put himself upon us for a person of importance." Musaeus waxed especially sarcastic on Cibber's contention that the actors were the only support of the theater, maintaining on the contrary that they were least of all fit to manage a theater, and also took occasion to illuminate the casuistry and the evasion in the actor's letter. When the affair had attracted enough attention to be satirized at Covent Garden in *The Stage Mutineers,* a new correspondent, "Philo-Musus", in number 189 protested against the new farce as a personal attack and the paying of a grudge not only against Theophilus but his father as well, and asked what difference it made to the town in general, whether Cibber or Highmore won the battle. Still another, "Plain Dealer" (number 198), replied to an attack on the patentees in the *Daily Post*. He declared that Highmore had not bought part of the patent for someone else, and grew indignant over the reference in the *Post* to one of the patentees as "one

---

[74] See *Aesop,* Part II, Scene I. Part II was first printed in quarto, 1697. The British Museum has: *Aesop, A Comedy. With the Addition of a Second Part. Written by Mr. Vanbrugh. The Hague, 1711.*

[75] *A Letter from Theophilus Cibber, Comedian, to John Highmore, Esq.* [1733].

John Ellys," when that gentleman was highly respected, of good family, and a well known painter to boot. Moreover, the share sold to Ellys, according to Plain Dealer, had been offered first to Mills, one of the actors, and had been declined. Plain Dealer also refused to admit as an argument for the actors the fact that Giffard, an actor, was one of the managers of Goodman's Fields, since the notable qualities of his character—modesty and economy—distinguished him from actors generally. The last significant allusion to the quarrel is in the unsigned letter (202), "Of the Use and Abuse of the Stage," wherein it is suggested that both sides would have done better to expend their energy in raising the standards of the stage than in vilifying each other so long and exposing their own "artful tricks."

The friction between actors and patentees, and the attempts to escape established tyranny by the foundation of new theaters, and so forth, are reflected in two letters published in the *Journal* a year and a half later. A bill[76] having been introduced to limit the number of theaters, "Modulus" writes (number 274) ironically that he deplores restraints on theater building, with the consequent closing of opportunity to architects and masons, as also to the dissatisfied clerks, apprentices and broken tradesmen who would fain become actors. He then adds more seriously that in case of such limitation,

---

[76] Apropos of laws regulating the theaters, an amusing burlesque petition of female dancers and actresses against a bill prohibiting plays in houses where liquor is sold, appears in 279:—"We, your humble petitioners do apprehend that it will be impossible for us to perform our parts with any spirit, if this clause should continue," and so forth. Also the punning epigram—

Were drams to these denied, we soon should see
That less dramatic would each drama be.

Another correspondent (327, 328) presents a most remarkable project for taxing theater tickets and using the income for the redemption of seamen who had fallen into slavery among infidels and barbarians. The writer discusses the present low state of the theaters, the general theory of sumptuary legislation, and the taxation of vice and pleasure. He estimates that £84,000 per annum is spent on the London theaters, and argues that a duty on such a luxury to be used in redeeming slaves, whose great sufferings in Morocco he details, would be more proper than some taxes already in force on such necessities as chairs, coals, and candles.

additional laws should be enacted protecting managers and actors against each other, fixing definite grades of actors with their salaries, safeguarding the rights of authors, and also assuring the town against the determination of managers to present unpopular plays, or refusal to give popular ones. Three numbers later another correspondent, anonymous, proposes a referee appointed by law to settle all disputes between managers and actors, with power to fine obstinacy on either part.

In all these prolonged controversies the operation of personal prejudice is only too apparent—Fielding, the Cibbers, and Popple were for various reasons despised or hated by the *Journal*. In Fielding's case, a resentment toward his "immorality" was certainly a factor, the immorality of the stage being of course a perennial and fruitful subject for serious discussion and reforming zeal in all ages. Equally enduring is the hatred of the more serious part of the theatrical world—the writers and purveyors of regular tragedy and comedy—for the merely entertaining—for the easy lure of spectacle and music, and for the potent charm of exotic and strange foreign novelties. The particular objects of these animosities in the eighteenth century were practically the same as at present—the opera, the spectacular entertainment with ballet, pantomime, and so forth, and the invading armies of foreign performers of all sorts.

As before and since, even down to the present, the Italian opera was assailed for its inherent lack of dramatic power, but the chief fault found with it was the extravagant adulation and the "showers of gold" bestowed upon the stars. Especially hateful to the freeborn Englishman was of course the male soprano. Frequently one finds sarcastic comment on the riches accumulated in England by the Italians, notably Farinelli. Typical and representative of all these are the verses in number 284 on Farinelli, of which the following are an excerpt—

> While Britain, destitute of aid,
> Weeps taxes and decaying trade,

Sees want approach with nimble pace
And ruin stare her in the face,
Charmed by the sweet Italian's tongue
In showers of gold she pays each song.[77]

English chauvinism also resented bitterly the appearance on
the London stage of French and Italian actors of other types.
Thus "Patriophilus" in number 254 tears to shreds the work
of a French company at the Haymarket. He saw *L'Avare*
and thought it a very poor performance. He found fault with
the costumes, considered the delivery monotonous and stilted,
and declared that there were only two respectable actors in
the company; the rest seemed to have undertaken a business
for which they were totally unprepared. In the silly entertainment which followed, the actors were so painted that their
faces had the appearance of masks. He concluded that the
company must be mere strollers imposing on the British public or that if they ever had acted in Paris it must have been
in the lowest parts.

Another letter in number 272, signed significantly "True
Briton," criticizes in much the same tone a French company
at Lincoln's Inn Fields. The writer, after explaining himself
as a country gentleman who regularly spent three months in
London for the theaters, says that he found everyone praising the French actor, M. Francisque, and so went to his benefit. He had nursed the hope, he says, that Francisque, by
giving the best plays of Molière, Racine, and others, would
force English companies to reform, and purge the stage of
entertainments, not even excepting *The Beggar's Opera* and
Fielding's burlesques and farces. Although play and acting
were both poor, the theater was crowded. The next day, happening to meet one of the company at a coffee house, he was
told that they acted plays in London for which they would
be driven from the stage at home; that Francisque could do

---

[77] A typical instance from another paper, *Hooker's Miscellany* (119)—
"[there is] nothing now regarded but unmanly tweedle-dums and
tweedle-dees, and the effeminate quavers of a wretched Eunuch's quail
pipe!—A glorious prospect this for our volatile neighbors! Who have
no occasion to apprehend any more Blenheim's or Ramillies from our
quarter, while this infamous taste continues to engross us so entirely."

anything with the English, and condescended to suit their palates with buffoonery and drollery. The French actor had also told him that whenever a nobleman commanded a performance he always asked for a very short play and a very long farce, a disgrace which True Briton thought hardly possible in a nation glorified by Shakespeare, Otway, Ben Jonson, Congreve and Dryden. He ends with an appeal to the ladies to drive out foreign invaders and reform the theater, and a reprimand for the *Prompter,* which had praised Francisque and his company, and had urged the translation of their plays into English. Bavius, in an editorial comment, approved True Briton's zeal against foreign strollers, but tempered his heat with reservations in favor of Francisque and two or three others of the company, who, he said, were considered by good judges to have merit.

Of course there was ample provocation for these letters, in spite of their absurdities and their narrow and ostentatious patriotism. The competition of foreign talent with native,[78] and the lionizing of mediocrity from abroad by an uncritical public has always irked and irritated the dramatic and musical profession in England and America. Doubtless many of the foreigners were mere strollers, as they were accused of being, and were quite satisfied to act the rags and tatters of their repertoires in a slipshod, slovenly fashion for undiscriminating English audiences. Nevertheless the resentment toward them had in it a large proportion of jealousy, and a still greater of hidebound parochialism. Obviously True Briton, despite his protestations, shows himself, as much in his style as in his *nom de plume,* to have the true Anglo-Saxon suspicion and contempt for foreigners. For this spirit in its pure and unadulterated fervor, however, one should turn to "Staunch Old Briton" in number 312, who voices his indignation at the impending arrival of a company of Italian

---

[78] The *Journal* announces the approach of an Italian opera season with the comment: "As this revival of Italian operas is grateful to some of our members [*i.e.* of the Grubstreet Society] who hope to have the translating of them; so it is disagreeable to those greater geniuses who write English operas themselves." See 41.

tumblers and rope-dancers from Paris. He declaims against the "Faronellies, Cuzzonies and Francisques" who have "choused" the English nation of so much money, and hopes that the new band of invaders will be driven from the stage with cat-calls, peas, and potatoes; "if there be an honest, unpolluted Briton left, let him bravely cast the first stone." "Let us drive these vermin from the British stage, and return them to the tumbling skip-frog nation from whence they came." Such letters as these have dozens of parallels in other papers, both daily and weekly. They do not represent the particular point of view of the *Journal* and its following, but rather of that section of the public which hated the foreigners as much as another section petted and idolized them.

The zealots for reforming the theater and restoring it to its ancient dignity lumped the foreign singers and actors with the still more dreadful menace of the "entertainment." The foreigners, after all, made only sporadic and isolated raids, which though mischievous could never prove a mortal danger. The entertainment, on the other hand, was ever-present, and was, or so the serious-minded seemed to think, usurping more and more the place of genuine comedy and tragedy. Bitter complaints about the foreigners were common enough, but they seem comparatively infrequent beside the steady stream of satire and invective against the spectacle, the slap-stick humor, and the elaborate machinery of the entertainment. And naturally along with the cursing of the thing itself came denunciation of the public taste, or lack of taste, which bred it and nourished it into such rank growth. On this subject, as on the foreign actors, the tone of the *Journal* is hardly distinguishable from that of other papers. Its letters and essays are like those in the *Prompter,* the *Craftsman,* or *Fog's Journal.* Those who expressed themselves in print were seemingly united in their detestation of the mummeries that tickled the public palate and made it impatient of plainer but solider food. One favorite attitude, that of righteous sorrow or indignation, is reflected in True Briton's remarks about the noblemen who always ordered a very short play and a long entertainment.[79]

On the other hand, what would at present be called a more "constructive" point of view is taken by one "Scenicus" in number 384. After pointing out that the purpose of the stage is pleasure as well as instruction, he ventures to suggest that pantomimes, rightly managed and on proper subjects, might be as valuable as plays. To illustrate his point he cites a description from Apuleius of the Judgment of Paris —an elaborate scene full of conventional sylvan and pastoral charms, which obviously might be embodied in a pantomimic ballet.

Some idea of the general type of these shows which so offended the dramatically righteous may be gained from a satirical description of them in a letter of "Harlequin Chef d'oeuvre" (number 269). The writer plans, he says, to produce a wonderful entertainment. In this he is encouraged by the favor of the town toward such things and toward the French and Italian strollers. The subject is given as "The History of the Fall of the Tower of Babel," the actors to be giants, and most of the dialogue in High Dutch, but with scraps of all other languages to suit all tastes. When the tower falls it is to turn into sugar loaves, which are to be eaten up by some of the actors. The stage is to be successively an orange grove, a dog kennel, a ship, a palace, a mountain, a windmill, a wheel-barrow, and finally a pleasant prospect of Hell. To all these wonders are to be added the attractions of famous jugglers, dancers, tumblers, and monsters. For his success in such a venture Harlequin says he relies on the well known hospitality of the British nation, and informs the

---

[79] Some indication of the recognition in the theaters, or at least at Drury Lane, that the entertainment was more important than the play itself is given in a letter signed "Haberdasherus" in 340. The writer complains over having to pay two shillings for a gallery seat at an old play and a long tedious performance called in the bills an entertainment. He suggests that anyone who wishes to go out at the end of the play ought to get part of his money back. He asserts that this has been done at Drury Lane for patrons who wished to see a new pantomime, and asks why a similar arrangement should not be made for those who wished to see the play and avoid the entertainment.

nobility that in supporting him they will be in no danger of serving their own countrymen, and besides, will be sure to transmit a favorable opinion of themselves abroad.[80]

In these insular, even parochial, fulminations one senses a spirit which has been ever since more or less rampant; sometimes, it may be said, with very good reason and justification. It is nevertheless a personal, rather than a detached and disinterested spirit, and, as has been continually noted, pervades other provinces where one would much less expect to find it. There is no reason why journalistic comment and controversy on points of art, literary or dramatic, should not be conducted without personal heat, but in the 1730's they very rarely were. The *Grub-street Journal* and its companion journals of a literary turn, as well as the floods of satire that the period produced, beget the impression that criticism and discussion could hardly ever have taken the form of a walk in an academic grove where "cool gales did fan the glade." The regular procedure seems to have been for a writer to gird up his loins, take his pen (and his life) in one hand and a dagger, or more often a bludgeon, in the other, and descend into the hurly-burly and uproar of Grub Street. For the stabs and bruises he was sure to receive—for certainly neither Pope nor Duck nor anyone between was safe from attack—he had to console himself by trying to give better than he took. Slanderous meanness and jealousy are not to be denied, but neither are energy and vivacity, and the bustle and excitement and high color of such a vividly personal age. There was roughness and brutality and very little squeamishness. It was no propitious time for the shy, the sensitive, and the tender, although after all one may ask what age is. Besides, among the survivors are to be found not only such sturdy beggars as the memorable Colley Cibber, but such first rate

---

[80] Satire on the harlequinades and entertainments in prints and drawings was also common. A typical print of this sort, "The New Grand Triumphal Arch, or, The Stage's Story," is described at great length in number 61. This print is in the British Museum (Press Mark:—1868-8-8-3540). By Burineaux after Croquinolet. See also printed catalogue of *Political and Personal Satires*, II: 739, where the *Journal's* description is reprinted in full.

geniuses as Swift, Pope and Fielding. And it is not merely that they survived. In great measure their interest springs from the impact of this life upon them; indeed from the very gusto with which they threw themselves into the thick of it.

CHAPTER VI

THE LAW, THEOLOGY, AND MEDICINE

Although the *Journal's* original and fundamental interest was a literary one, its editors realized from the beginning that the public would hardly support year in and year out a paper devoted to literature pure and simple, let alone the literary quarrels of Alexander Pope. Hence very wisely its projectors planned from the very beginning to give it a general appeal. In their opening announcement they even assigned an editor to politics, although as a matter of fact they never allowed him to function, but even in the preeminently political age of Robert Walpole avoided political propaganda and discussion. If the paper kept its skirts free of politics, however, there were not, first and last, many other conceivable subjects which it failed to probe. Essays and letters on every subject under the sun from the excise to divine providence and back again to specific remedies for mad dog bites or the plague of vermin are scattered profusely over its pages. Much of this refuses to fit into any pigeon hole save *miscellaneous,* but a great deal of it is of a medical or theological turn.

The religious and theological material in the paper may be explained satisfactorily enough by the fact of Russel's profession. A highly orthodox and conservative clergyman without a cure, but of a bitter and combative disposition, it is no wonder that he gave up so many of the *Journal's* columns to discussion in his own field. In addition, from the point of view of readers' interests, such subjects were not ill chosen. It was to be sure the age of Robert Walpole, but it was also the age of the deists. Disputatious free thinkers and apostles of "natural religion" were legion, and their outspoken heterodoxies led continually to fierce controversies with spokesmen of the regular faith—controversies which very easily and naturally slipped into the unrestrained diatribe for which the *Journal* had infinite zest.

Again it was an age of notable quacks, creatures whose assurance and effrontery made them apt subjects for the *Journal's* favorite weapons of irony and sarcasm, and whose widespread notoriety was an asset not only to themselves but also, in a way, to their enemies. As with the theological discussions, the great amount of space given up to medical material, and especially to the exposure of quacks, testifies to a strong public interest in medical theories and in the empirics. The fact that Martyn was a botanical and medical scientist has not the same significance that Russel's profession has in connection with the theological material. Martyn parted company with the *Journal* in its second year, and yet its liveliest and most interesting medical controversies came after that time, especially its campaign against the great quack Ward, which is to be reckoned among its three or four major wars. The *Journal* was, however, a belligerent organism with an eye always out for battle, and the fact that he was a parson did not deter Russel from venturing into alien territory where the fighting promised to be good. Still, Martyn's personal bias may be seen in the botanical and medical criticisms and essays attributed to him as "B" in *The Memoirs of Grub-street.*

The third profession, the law, receives comparatively little attention. There is, of course, no particular reason why Russel or Martyn should have had much to say about legal points, but it is rather surprising that they should not have received more letters on them. Certainly the law has been in general as favored a subject for attack as theology or medicine, and the lawyer as often a target for satire as the physician or divine. Yet for whatever reason it was, the *Journal* did not happen to light often upon the absurdities of legal pedants or the villanies of shysters.

The comparatively few contributions dealing with the law in one aspect or another follow more or less conventional lines and make points that might be predicted. There is satire for instance on the inequality of the rich and poor before the law, on the pomposity of legal writing, and on the knavery of shysters. There are attacks on the excise on liquors, the execution of the law by constable and bailiffs,[1] and the legal worship of tradition and precedent.

During the first months of 1730, as the *Journal* was getting under way, London was agog over the case of the infamous Colonel Chartres, under arrest for the rape of a servant girl. Allusions to the case in the early issues of the paper were frequent, and echoes of it occur even as late as number 393, when appeared Arbuthnot's pungent epitaph on Chartres—"Here continueth to rot the body of Francis Charteris," and so on—done into Latin by a youth of Charleston, South Carolina. The *Journal's* allusions are always deeply tinged with a sardonic contempt; for instance, it reported (number 41) his serious illness at his house in Hanover Square with the comment: "Had the Colonel put on the infallible Anodyne Necklace some time ago, as was generally desired, this dangerous illness had been prevented."[2] This *cause célèbre* was doubtless the starting point of the first two notable legal satires in the *Journal*. In number 10, Bavius published an ironic defense of the rich from the rigors of the law.[3] Opening with a couplet from Garth's *Dispensary*—

> Little villains must submit to fate
> That great ones may enjoy the world in state—

he stated as commonly accepted in belief and practice the principle that the rich should not endure the same penalties

[1] The general impression is of course that the minions of the law were brutal and ferocious, but a contributor to 382 asserts that while the English laws are as good as those of any nation, they are very badly enforced, and thinks that constables ought to be fined for not carrying out their duties more strictly.

[2] The Anodyne Necklace was a widely advertised contrivance of bone beads for the pacification of teething children. It furnished humorists of the period with one of their favorite quips; it is continually used as a name for the hangman's rope. Chartres died within about two years, and a fantastic account of his funeral in Edinburgh appears in 117. A great hurricane having arisen, the populace concluded that the devil had carried away both the body and soul, and thereupon seized the leaden coffin, opened it, beat it flat, "punched it full of holes," and threw it into the grave with six dead dogs after it.

[3] Russel; signed "M" in the *Memoirs*.

for crime as the poor. It was, he said, "more difficult to get a rich man hanged than to save a poor fellow from the gallows." The prosecution of the rich was always attended, moreover, by serious evils. The rich were always forced to spend in prison great sums of money that would otherwise go to honest and industrious people. Their trials were always attended by bribery, forgery, and perjury, and always stamped a lasting mark of infamy upon the defendant. If convicted, he was sure to be degraded from his high station, and could not hope for a pardon, because the conviction would have been for a second offense at any rate, and since any action in his favor would be hindered by the prejudices of the common people against the rich. And, most serious of all, the prosecution and conviction of the great resulted in a loss to the nation of those who should administer its justice and lead its armies. In view of all these regrettable facts, Bavius suggested a law exempting the great from prosecution for murder, rape, and sodomy, crimes committed chiefly by those in the higher levels of society. This savage humor, most certainly Russel's reaction to the circumstances of the Chartres trial, was further developed, especially in its last point, by his colleague Martyn,[4] four weeks later. In much the same vein, but with less fierceness and power, it was argued that a gentleman should never be fined for adultery, since he regarded it merely as a piece of gallantry, having been bred up to "polite and free maxims." Also in case of trial the jury should be chosen from gentlemen of the same station, and bachelors, to avoid all prejudice. As for rapes, they were out of the way of ordinary tradesmen, and the chief point for consideration should be whether the defendant were qualified

[4] Signed "B" in the *Memoirs*. Although Martyn doubtless had the Charteris case still in mind, his chief interest, as footnotes in the *Memoirs* show, was in another scandal, the Abergavenny case. An intrigue between Lady Abergavenny and Richard Lyddell had been discovered in November, 1729, and Lord Abergavenny had been awarded £10,000 damages in court. The affair was the subject of a sensational poem, *Calista to Altamont,* which drew forth Martyn's article in 14, and subsequent verses by Russel ("M") in 19 and 21. According to Martyn, "our greatest adversary [i.e. Pope] had said that the author of this poem ought to be whipped and pilloried."

by birth, education, and fortune for such entertainment. If
found to be so qualified he should be acquitted and the woman
required to live with him if he so desired. Otherwise she
should be sent to a house of correction for refusing what a
gentleman had a right to require.[5]

The execution of the law by its minor officers, a common
subject for attack in contemporary comedies, novels, and
prints also crops up several times in the *Journal*. In one instance the *Journal* championed the cause of a group of gentlemen who clamored loudly from the Fleet, where they were
imprisoned for debt, for redress from the oppressions of the
deputy warden. This personage had been in number 39 the
subject of a humorous letter in which he was ridiculed as the
"tremendous Deputy Warden," but a consistent attack on
him from the pen of one of his prisoners, John Williams,[6]
began in number 59 and continued intermittently for nearly
nine months. These gentlemen's grievance was that although
they had paid regular fees they were not allowed the rooms
and privileges due them, but had been "locked down on the
common side," where they were languishing away. In fact
some, according to Williams, were practically at the point of
death, and in certain cases their distress was so great as to
touch the hearts of their relatives and their creditors, who
had secured their release. The *Journal* gave Williams the
freedom of its columns to express his troubles and those of
his companions, and to answer the defenses of the warden
appearing in the *Daily Advertiser*. To that extent it showed
sympathy with the complainants. It did not go out of its way,
however, to support them editorially, and in one case at least
when it referred to their troubles, it assumed a distinctly
flippant tone. J. W. having thanked the *Journal* somewhat
effusively for its kindness, the editors remark that their publication of J. W.'s current screed was due to "our tender

[5] The next week the *Journal* reprinted the news that a man convicted
of the rape of a child had been sentenced to a whipping and one year's
hard labor, with Martyn's comment, "He was well served, being a person
not duly qualified for those sports."
[6] The verses and letters are signed "J. W.", but finally the name is
mentioned in full. See 59, 69, and 72-96 *passim,* and an echo in 130.

compassion toward Gentlemen in confinement who . . . cannot vent their complaints in any other newspapers," but they hope nevertheless that he will be briefer next time. This tone and the lack of any specific backing up of J. W. with the sarcasm and irony in which Russel at least was a past master, would hardly indicate that J. W. had been able to inspire the hearts of the editors with any particular compassion.[7] The only serious discussion to which the episode gave rise seems to have been a letter (number 93) from "The Seeker" on arrest, especially for debt, pointing out that gentlemen, who would naturally suffer more than others from the hardships of prison life, were not subject to the reliefs frequently granted in case of arrest.

In several other instances the *Journal* accepted communications on the petty extortions and cruelties of prison officials. "Caterpillars" and "hungry miscreants" are characteristic terms applied to these creatures by one "Publicola" in 186, and they are charged with bleeding prisoners at every opportunity and with having discovered ways to evade all the laws for the protection of prisoners. Indeed, this particular writer continues, they have brought their offices into such ill repute and rendered themselves so contemptible that no decent man would become a prison officer. Another correspondent undertakes to demonstrate that the law is "the greatest grievance under which the people of England labor," that it is in effect as irksome as a general franchise. After declaring that at every county assize one might behold parents offering up children, or children parents, to the Moloch of the law, and finding fault with the voluminousness of the law and the advantage commonly taken of it, he settles down to extended abuse of its officers, especially catchpoles and bailiffs. In fact, in the second installment of his letter, he declares that between the catchpoles, who often ruin a poor man, wringing from him twice the amount of

---

[7] The final item in this affair is the announcement in 96 that the suit of John Williams against the warden, for failure to supply a chamber for which he had been paid, had been won, and that the warden had been reprimanded by the court.

the debt which brought him to prison, and the lawyers, who despoil their clients and against whom there is little hope of redress, because of the strong *esprit de corps* of their profession, the case of the wretched prisoner is desperate enough (numbers 223 and 227).

The crime of extortion, the traditional charge against lawyers, is cited against them much less often than one would expect. In 162 is related the history of a lawsuit in which two solicitors, having privately accused each other of knavery and having both of them extorted large sums of money, were finally brought to justice in a trial in which each tried to prove the other the greater knave. In numbers 189, 191, and 192 is a series of three epigrams on the same point. The first deals with a lawyer who after winning a suit for £500, "honestly" let his client have £400, and thought so well of himself that he had the fact recorded on the memorial to him in his parish church. The epigram is as follows:

> Did Damus gain a cause? This should be told
> In brightest letters of immortal gold.
> And did he once restore what he'd laid hand on?
> This well deserves a golden Memorandum.

These lines adapted and with the addition—

> And pity 'tis, since these so fair appear
> But all his deeds were thus recorded here.

—were inserted in number 192. The issue of the previous week had also contained an epigram on a contest between a lawyer and a priest in which both appeared fools and knaves, and a quite characteristic reply by Maevius, or Russel, who was always quick to take offense at any aspersion upon the clergy, to the effect that they might be equal as fools, but one might possibly be a greater knave than the other. The only serious discussion of this vice of attorneys seems to consist in a technical analysis of a recent law to protect clients against overcharge, with the conclusion that in practice the law had been very ineffective (number 355).

Occasionally one comes upon single, isolated letters bearing on the law, which in one way or another have some interest as reflecting contemporary attitudes toward legal institutions. One correspondent, "T. B." (in number 324), who must have been the incarnation of conservatism, submits reasons against the repeal of the statutes on witchcraft, then pending in Parliament. In what seems a thoroughly serious tone, he urges the tradition and the antiquity of these laws, and argues that if they were absurd they would have been repealed before. Another (number 372) suggests that a good law passed under the commonwealth is of interest as proving that bad men may make good laws. The traditional English love of liberty and hatred of oppression is manifest in an attack on a bill against rogues and vagabonds, which is said to convey dangerous powers to magistrates, in fact to savor of the absolutism one would expect in Turkish bashaws. It was probably this same spirit of liberty that prompted an article by "A. B." in number 370 on the various means proposed for regulating the trade in spirits. He is opposed to all drastic measures as being the ruin of vested property of distillers or retailers, and proposes rather to limit the trade, prohibiting sale to women and children and fixing the amount sold to men. In a free nation, he says, mildest remedies are most effective; violent ones, he asserts with some wisdom, stir up determined opposition on all sides, and are justified only as a last resort. In this connection it may be said that the references in the *Journal* to the excise on spirits, gin especially, are uniformly hostile and derisive. Most of them are flippantly contemptuous, as in a ribald ballad, *The Constitution Clap'd* (number 160), and an obituary of the Lady Geneva (number 391). Allusions to the excise, however, are frequent enough to indicate a strong current of public hostility.[8]

It is perhaps worth nothing that all these letters and verses on the law and things legal are scattered and frag-

[8] For the most notable allusions to the excise, see 160, 164, 170, 172, 173, 182, 222, 229, 230, 370, 371, 391, 407.

mentary. With the possible exception of the series of letters against the deputy warden of the Fleet Prison, they are all slight and sporadic. Moreover, they are all outside contributions; the editors themselves apparently were not interested enough either to write themselves, or even to comment at any length on the letters they published. In medical and religious discussions the case was quite different. Bavius—both Martyn and Russel—wrote continually in both fields, and often accepted letters, it would seem, merely for the sake of replying to them.

The numerical strength and the initiative of the deists during this part of the eighteenth century made arguments over their heresies bitter and violent. It was to be expected that orthodox divines and theologians should regard them and their works as anathema. And among the orthodox there was probably not to be found a more conservative defender of intrenched dogma than the non-juring clergyman, Russel.[9] Anything that savored in the slightest degree of heterodoxy was sure of contempt and denunciation from his pen, and the disparager of the clergy of the Church of England might well expect disagreeably incisive argument with a due admixture of personality, in the *Journal's* columns. The height of vituperation to which Russel could rise in a theological quarrel has already been demonstrated in the account of the *Journal's* quarrel with the *Bee* and the *Prompter* over such a deistic document as Matthew Tindall's "Philosopher's Prayer."[10] There is satire and discussion in the *Journal* on other religious issues than deism, but this particular heresy was flaring up so brightly and vigorously during the *Journal's* day as to make all other issues pale and unimportant, and to monopolize for itself most of the current religious discussion.

[9] For instance, to the *London Journal's* attack on the theory that the church is the support of the state, Russel ("M") answered in 116 that church and state never existed very long apart. Also in 120, he prefaced an ironical "treatise" on a bill to reduce tithes (wherein he expatiated on the great wealth of the rural clergy, much in the manner of Swift or Defoe) with the remark that he hoped it would clear the *Journal* of the aspersion of being "favorers of priest-craft."

[10] See *ante*, p. 144.

Anti-deistic writing in the *Journal* is chiefly in the form of direct attack on some particular deist, or even on a single utterance. "The Philosopher's Prayer" just referred to was the subject of one of the paper's longest and most bitterly personal quarrels. Nevertheless, some of the discussion of deism in general is almost as vivid and sensational, although not focussed on an individual person. The *Journal* and its contributors seem to have regarded deists as outlaws, and deism itself as beyond the pale. There is no such thing as an unbiassed, reasonable analysis of its principles. On the other hand, the blasphemous absurdity of deistic ideas is taken for granted and they are mentioned only as evils to be uprooted, while the deists themselves are presented as compounds of foolishness and downright knavery and wickedness, creatures unworthy of any consideration whatsoever.

An anti-deistic letter representing religious argument at its worst appears in number 139. The author rages in impotent futility against the unorthodox who undertake to answer the unanswerable arguments of the orthodox, refusing to recognize the impregnability of their opponents and advancing as "answers" books which completely miss the mark. Another correspondent (number 226) attacks those modern infidels who are "ambitious of being nothing," and asserts that their reasoning is altogether opposed to the natural bent of the mind, that their claim of a foundation for their beliefs in basic morality is false and insincere, and that they make proselytes of the giddy and weak-minded. In somewhat the same vein is "The Modern Goliah" (number 196), verses on the free thinker who scorns the soul and the gift of everlasting life, laughs at hell-fire (number 296) and believes in "living and dying like beasts." Still another, whose letter is inspired by the controversy over "The Philosopher's Prayer", and who descends for an example upon Eustace Budgell, "a confident, crack-brained coxcomb", attacks the stupidity of such atheistical writers, and, divided "between indignation and contempt", announces, "I never read any of their trash, any otherwise than as quoted by you." The deists' demand for simplicity and directness in interpretation and their somewhat inconsistent proneness to extensive philosophizing is ridiculed in an epigram (number 311) on a writer who said

> 'Let no one's words be heard but Christ's alone'
> And then he adds ten million of his own.

The *Journal* also published a series of extracts from an old *Discourse of Freethinking,* under the heading "Instances of the chief free-thinkers' skill in the Latin language", to illustrate errors in translation, cases of garbling, and so forth.[11]

Almost the only calm and impersonal approach toward the subject is to be found in the attempt of a writer in number 322 to fathom the reasons for the present decay of learning, especially religious. Is it, he asks, because we have, in our own estimation, conquered all knowledge? For, he continues, we set up to be originals, and take pride in demolishing the opinions of our ancestors. He reminds his readers that the pursuit of riches interferes with learning, and points to Erasmus and Usher as men who avoided wealth lest it come between them and their goal. Pedantry too, he thinks, may have had an evil influence—"From the Restoration we have been polishing learning, rather than making any addition to it"; and finally and most remarkably, he blames "the luxury of the press"—"the natural ardor . . . is stifled by fuel."

With the possible exception of this last letter, these instances illustrate the temper of the *Journal* toward deism. Hatred and contempt are generally intensified when they become focussed on the person who holds an idea rather than on the idea itself. So the attacks on individual deists, though the same in tone, are fiercer and more bitter than those on deism itself; witness again the virulent quarrel over Tindall's will and his "Philosopher's Prayer," which monopolizes so much of the *Journal's* space during its middle

[11] See 275, 276, 279, 281, 284, 288.

period. Although this was its most extensive personal controversy over religious matters, the paper had before made personal attacks in the field of religion. Indeed, signs of Russel's very keen interest in such matters appear almost at once. The early issues of the *Journal* abound in sarcastic allusions to Thomas Woolston and his allegorical interpretations of Scripture, which seem to have attracted at the moment a good deal of public notice. For instance, in number 13, in an attack on an anonymous pamphlet, *The Materiality or Mortality of the Soul of Man*,[12] Russel goes out of his way in a preliminary diatribe to express his contempt for Woolston. Formerly, he says, those advancing new religious ideas relied on style, wit, or new material. It was not so any longer. Woolston had made himself famous by an attack on the miracles—

This invective of his against our blessed Savior consists of such low jokes and such opprobrious language that, if we may form a judgment of the wit of the Galilaean fisherman by that of the fishermen and watermen on the Thames, Judas himself would have written with more vivacity and elegancy against the miracles of his master than the learned and ingenious Mr. Woolston.

A similarly vigorous frontal attack on Woolston was published in number 24, where "Philo-Libertas," with the text "Answer a fool according to his folly," urged the necessity of answering such men as the deist. Woolston's writing, it is said, does not spring "from an honest and sincere desire of removing error, and re-establishing truth. . . ." His works are declared to be "full of malicious reflections, arrogant boasts and scurrilous banters," and it is asserted that

he has treated not only his adversaries but even his subject, the most sacred person and the most sacred things, with a most audacious and blasphemous ridicule . . . the true motive of his undertaking was only to gratify the irregular passions of his own depraved heart.

In a lighter vein, and perhaps more effective, are the frequent interpretations "of current happenings in the Woolstonian manner." Russel undertook to apply Woolston's methods to

[12] In the British Museum, author unknown. The attack on it is ascribed in the *Memoirs* to "M."

a remarkable thunderstorm (number 23) ; he explained the allegory at large, and showed how exactly the letter and the spirit tallied," and also to a report from Rome of a complaint at the furious speed with which the Chevalier St. George had his coach driven through the streets. A correspondent "N. T." (number 27) wrote that he had heard Woolston's confinement in the King's Bench Prison explained away in a coffee house as a mere allegorical statement that the gentleman had bought a suit of clothes too small for him. On visiting the prison, however, he saw Woolston literally—

he seemed to be made up of whim, madness and contemplation; his aspect sullen, morose, and daring; . . . reasoning, swearing, arguing, drolling, all in the same breath. I could just hear him muttering to himself the names of Collins, Tindal, and Jesus Christ; which last he never mentioned but with a seeming contempt or abhorrence.

N. T. goes on to imply that Woolston was an infidel merely because money was to be had by it. When it was finally announced that Woolston had secured a writ of *habeas corpus,* the *Journal* commented gravely: "It is disputed whether this is to be taken figuratively or literally."[13] From the frequency with which Woolston's name appears during the first year or two of the *Journal,* it may well be inferred that he was regarded as the arch-heretic. Others are sometimes mentioned, especially Collins, Tindall,[14] and Whiston,—the opinions of the last are quoted at length in numbers 34 and 36, notably his remark that a nettle was a better evidence of God than the subtlest metaphysics[15]—but Woolston bears the brunt of the attack.

[13] "N. T." becomes "T. N." in the *Memoirs.* For similar satire see 25, 53, 82, 96, 157.

[14] In the long wrangle with the *Bee* and the *Prompter,* Tindall, although lately dead, was by no means spared. The *Journal* published (265) an abstract of a scurrilous pamphlet, *The religious, rational, and moral conduct of Matthew Tindal,* accusing him of various vices which were illustrated in sundry anecdotes and stories. He was made out gluttonous, selfish, ignorant, and overweeningly ambitious. It was said that he had turned Catholic to secure the favor of James II, and though a secret deist had conformed to the Church to save his fellowship. The author even denominated him "an egregious fornicator" and cited instances of his having attempted to saddle his bastard children upon other men.

[15] In quotation from and comment on his life of Dr. Samuel Clarke. In 266 it is noticed that Whiston had denied a prophecy regarding a

The *Journal,* however, did make during its second year a comparatively brief but lively sortie against a clergyman of deistic tendencies, Bowman, the vicar of Dewsbury. This person had inflamed the anger of Russel by a published sermon,[16] *The Traditions of the Clergy Destructive of Religion*—a thesis which, almost more than any other, might be counted on to raise a hornet's nest in the *Journal.* As a consequence number 82 contained the epigram—

> In durance vile while pious Woolston lies
> And death waits near to close learn'd Tindal's eyes
> The priest's hard fortune and the layman's fate
> Seem to presage Religion's ruined state.
> But thou, O Bowman wilt the loss supply
> Of both; and whilst thou live she cannot die.
> To thy due station may'st thou rise much quicker
> And cease to *lye* of Dewsbury the Vicar.

This was followed in number 85 and 87 by a long contemptuous letter railing violently at Bowman for his impudence in daring to attack the clergy, ridiculing his points against the episcopal system, and also detailing a fiction about Phillis, an "itinerant bookseller" who sold copies of the infamous sermon by crying, "Here's a sermon against religion." In numbers 91 and following, the attack was shifted to another sermon defending the miracle of the cursed fig tree. Bowman is convicted of a conceited dogmatism, and phrases from his dedication of the fig tree sermon are held up to derision. In number 93 came an epigram on the sudden cessation of sales of the first sermon and the publication of the second, which is compared to a comet which blazed, died out, fell, and upon examination proved to be a "blasted, barren fig-tree." A correspondent, "Laicus"

---

destructive comet, and in 272 his new *Josephus* was subjected by "Orthodoxus" to criticism for inaccuracy—criticisms which are in turn questioned by Bavius himself. Whiston's arguments in *The Primitive Eucharist Revived* are attacked in 345.

[16] See advertisement of it in number 87. For a slight and not very illuminating account of Bowman see Nichols, I, 457 ff., where is to be found a quotation from "Bomanou Kluthi, or Hark to Bowman," a squib on the notorious fig-tree sermon. The sermon noted above is said by Russel (*Memoirs,* number 85) to have been taken chiefly from *The Rights of the Christian Church* and *The Independent Whig.*

(number 94), who despite his pseudonym conveys a clerical impression, continues the ridicule of Bowman's arguments and indicates that the answers to Bowman's sermons have shown him almost illiterate. The final touch, however, came in a dialogue in number 96, between Bowman and a Quaker, wherein the latter, of a sect especially obnoxious to the *Journal* (although later it had to bear with a Quaker bookseller, Huggonson), calls Bowman, a clergyman of the Church, to shame for presuming it his duty to free Christ from the imputation of unreasonableness in asking the tree to bear at the wrong time.[17]

Russel's interest in this attack is shown by the fact that much of this material was brought together and amplified in a pamphlet called *Grubstreet vs. Bowman* with a dedication "not to the Bishop of London . . . but to a much greater person in his own conceit—Mr. Bowman himself."[18] Still, Bowman was dropped at this point, except for a parting shot some months later (number 137) when Bavius remarked upon the news that Bowman had finished a defense of himself and an address to the English laity: "We do not hear, but we hope, that this Reverend Gentleman has written his defence of himself in English; a language which he seemed to be learning when he wrote his sermon."

In general, as in the attacks on deism and its exponents, the *Journal's* strong bias in favor of all the established institutions of the church, its dogmas and its organization, is only too apparent. There are occasional notes of satire on the corruption of the clergy, but they are comparatively rare and are almost entirely obscured by the fierce assaults on the heterodox. The *Journal* published in numbers 142 and 146 a versified letter from a rector to his curate and the latter's answer, satirizing in a familiar vein the selfishness and materialism of the clergy, with their interest focussed on the

---

[17] The writer cites from the sermon a passage to prove that a symbolic interpretation was possible and that Christ was not unreasonable.

[18] Advertised in 93. Nevertheless, in 102 one "Philo-Vermigeneris" praises the *Journal* for the way it disposed of Bowman, and urges it to collect its material into a sixpenny pamphlet, which should be highly diverting.

tithes and the parsonage, driving their tenants and leaving their churches to the wardens and to miserably paid curates. One also finds occasional notes on some individual clergyman, as the one on an Oxford preacher who was so extravagantly learned in a sermon that the laughter of the congregation could be heard forty yards off (number 196), or the letter (number 224) from a member of a congregation near the Royal Exchange, who declared that his clergyman ogled the ladies from his pulpit and exhibited all the graces of a beau, in a manner "ridiculous, scandalous, and utterly unbecoming a clergyman in his desk."[19] Similarly the parsons of the Fleet, who were said to entice women away from their friends and then force them to marry, merely for the sake of the fee, were brought to the public notice by a correspondent in number 270. The real sympathy of the *Journal* is nevertheless much better shown by the zeal with which it flew to arms against Bowman, and by its hatred and contempt for all dissenters and heretics. In contrast with the anti-clerical passages just mentioned, and much more representative, is the ironical discussion of a pending tithe bill allowing payment in goods. The writer asserts that parsons get huge salaries averaging £80 a year, on which they die rich and leave their daughters great fortunes. On the other hand, squires are known to be men "of great humanity and good breeding, of sound morals and unquestionable learning" and should be given legal aid to make themselves still more like eastern bashaws. Tithes should be made as hard as possible to collect. A gentleman farmer (illiterate) and a free-thinker are quoted as advocates of the proposed measure (number 120). In number 380 "Eusebius Old-fashion" dilates on the general godliness and piety of the clergy, and lays the "great contempt of the clergy—which is so very prevailing at present" to a minority "too much conformed to this world." Russel's zeal in fact often brought down upon his head the personal abuse of the less orthodox—note again the case of "The

[19] Hogarth, and the satirical literature of the time, are of course replete with instances of such characteristics in clergymen.

Philosopher's Prayer"—abuse, however, on which he seems to have thrived. In number 99 appeared a letter of warning against dissenting preachers who came over into the church in search of preferment, with the particular case of a Mr. J—s, a dissenter who hypocritically professed conversion, but acted very badly on not getting the advancement he expected, and went back to his original fold. This drew forth the next week a most violent reply signed "Catholicus," abusing not only the *Journal* as "a vehicle of party scandal, malice, and ill-nature" but likewise, Russel and the clergy of the established church.

I ask [wrote Catholicus] who made you a censor or dictator in matters either civil or religious, you (who as I am informed) are as scandalous in your morals as uncharitable in your censures. . . . You it is certain are a doughty hero for the established church, who are known to be a debauched, non-juring priest . . . Mr. Nu—ll, . . . a bastard son of the dear Church.

This letter, which probably did not inflict great pain, else it had not been printed, received due notice in number 104. The editors easily evaded the personal attack, hiding behind the shifting personality of Bavius, who was both Martyn and Russel. It was described as "abuse of the established church in general and of an unknown person in particular." Nu—ll, which was undoubtedly an intentional misprint of Ru—ll, was interpreted as Numskull, and it was asserted that the person who took upon himself the name of Bavius was not in orders, and never hoped to be—which was the truth as far as Martyn was concerned.

The militant orthodoxy of the *Journal* showed itself most clearly in its abuse of free-thinking and deism, but it was also virulent against other groups outside the pale of the establishment. Occasionally the Presbyterians are mentioned in passing with contempt, but the two sects which seem to have been regarded as especially hateful were the Roman Catholics and the Quakers. Slurs against the Catholics, however, are usually inspired by the traditional English fear and hatred of Popery and especially of the Jesuits, and have the commonplace and casual tone of generally recognized fact.

Yet occasionally one comes upon an anti-Catholic utterance marked enough to attract attention, as in the case of verses (number 194), purporting to be by a Dominican, on a picture of Christ as a Jesuit. The author, whoever he was, declared that he would rather die a Jew than a Jesuit, and asserted that the Jesuits dressed God in their clothes that they might make him hated among men, as they were. The traditional insidious and mysterious wisdom of the Catholics is also recognized in an epigram in both Latin and English on those foolish dissenters who had the temerity to enter into argument with Catholics. The general idea, well represented by the phrase "so may the silly dove attempt the hawk," is that the Catholics are so great and powerful that the only adversaries fit to cope with them are those blessed with wealth, high position, and "pompous titles."

The Quakers had been noticed once or twice in the early years of the *Journal,* and during its last issues were the subject of a heated controversy. In number 126 the *Journal* published a Quaker letter from Pennsylvania in answer to an attack by the Rev. Patrick Smith called a "Preservative against Quakerism." The writer of the letter undertook to demonstrate by ten quotations from Quaker literature that "we . . . are believers in God, in Christ, and of his Church," and consequently not "Deists, Enthusiasts, Hereticks, or Schismaticks." Six months later (number 145) appeared a burlesque Quaker letter signed "Esther Zealous," apparently ridiculing *The Friendly Writer* by Ruth Collins, under the guise of a fanatical repudiation of it as not being good Quaker doctrine. Serious consideration of the Quakers, however, came much later. In 1736, there was before Parliament a bill to release Quakers from tithes, a measure which led to extensive argument on the moral and religious qualities of the sect. The discussion opened (number 330) impersonally enough with an analysis of the legal steps necessary to secure tithes from Quakers, but was followed in number 335 by "A New Ballad on the Quakers Tithe Bill," opening, "A

Quaker is a cunning knave," and charging him with refusal of allegiance to the throne and repudiation of the Bible. A typical stanza goes—

> Our laws and customs Quakers hate
> And never eat minced pies.
> They keep their hats upon their heads
> And think to pay no tithes.

These stanzas giving offense to John Huggonson, a Quaker and the *Journal's* printer, he dissected them phrase by phrase in number 338 and pointed out their "falsehood and ill-will." After this the discussion was allowed to lapse for nearly a year, or until number 386, when "E. O.," a bigoted and unreasonable correspondent,[20] again broached the matter. According to him, the Quakers, though they had more allowance than other dissenters, still cried for further exemptions. Their motives were purely mercenary, and doubtless if all tithes were transferred to them they would accept them. To support the truth of this assertion he tells of a Quaker in Berkshire who farmed the tithes of the parish where he lived, and presents with due horror the absolute truth that "one of the Reverend Bench" employed a Quaker as a steward. He also demonstrated an affinity between Quakerism and deism and voiced a suspicion that there was a plot on foot against all tithes. The absurdities of this letter were adequately exposed in number 388 by "B. J.," a Quaker, who describes the Quakers' bill as a regular, orderly request with nothing strange about it, and points out that no complaint had been made when it failed. As to the charge of deism, that, he said, "discovers a most gross ignorance of their writings." In the next issue (number 389) the Quaker's objections to tithes were also supported by the scriptural citations of an anonymous author. E.O. nevertheless continued his campaign with a ridiculously credulous letter in number 390. He now represented the Quakers as tools of the Jesuits in an elaborate campaign. Rome, recognizing the Church of England as the strongest bulwark in the world

[20] He has a letter in 389 on the insolence and degeneracy of servants.

against its "false doctrines and superstitious, idolatrous worship," had planned to reduce England to atheism as the "best soil for Popery to grow in"—in pursuance of which design had been bred "their Brat, Quakerism." He points out the significant failure of the Quakers, unlike other dissenters, to rail against the whore of Babylon, and their willingness alone among dissenting sects, to allow Catholics to consort with them. This brought another remonstrance from B. J., and led to mutual charges of hot temper, poor logic and judgment, and so forth. In number 393 another correspondent, "A. Z.," came to E. O.'s support, with dark questions as to why Catholics had so much freedom to sell rosary beads and other trappings of Popery, and to maintain so many chapels, and tells in great detail of a Catholic chapel in Philadelphia to which the Quaker authorities of the colony allowed full freedom. He even insisted that the *Journal* had aroused the Quakers' ire and that they had organized in their own defense. This outburst drew forth what is really the most sensible and interesting letter in the whole controversy. "C. V.," in number 395, after condemnation of A. Z. as "a fiery zealot," presented the cause of complete toleration, arguing that if the Quakers of Philadelphia tolerated a Catholic chapel they merely showed their good sense. It was, he said, the wisest course for "a trading nation" like the English, who drew their living from their intercourse with other nations, to be tolerant of all religion, and he ends with the hope that the king will protect all people in the exercise of religious liberty. E. O., nothing daunted, appeared again in number 398 with a series of violent aspersions. He dilated upon the "Blasphemy, Nonsense, and Stupidity" of Quaker writings, even those of George Fox, retailed the history of the Quaker family in Berkshire which had farmed the tithes in its parish for sixty years, and repeated anecdotes of William Penn's connection with Catholics—of his education by Jesuits and of his appearance in Rome in Jesuit costume. As usual, B. J. undertook an answer. He submitted letters between Penn and Tillotson to disprove E. O.'s charges

against Penn's character, and showed the misrepresenta-
tions involved in the Berkshire story; the Quakers concerned, it appears, had collected the tithes without profit to
themselves merely for the convenience of their landlord.
Penn's letters, frank and ingenuous as they were, were of
little avail in clearing the air, for the next week, in number 409, appeared a scornful rejection of them as valid evidence by one "D. D.," who called attention to the fact that
Tillotson had merely accepted Penn's word that he was not a
Papist—"As if the sole declaration of any suspected papist
could be alone sufficient to remove that suspicion."

With this letter the quarrel came to an abrupt and inconclusive ending. The paper was now at its last gasp—it survived only two months more—and many threads were being
left at loose ends. It is noteworthy too that the quarrel was
entirely between correspondents and proceeded without editorial pronouncement. Russel of course had been superseded,
probably by James Miller, a fact which may account for lack
of editorial interest. Indeed, the paper appears on the surface
to be neutral, giving equal advantage to aggressors and re-
spondents, although the mere publication, even without comment, of such abusive and bigoted letters as those of E. O.,
A. Z., and D. D.[21] can in itself hardly be regarded as a neutral
act. The truth probably is that during the last months of
1737 the paper was being kept alive, and no more, and that
the editors had little concern beyond keeping its columns full.
At any rate, they showed very little vigor and animation. In
Russel's day it would certainly have been in line with the
Journal's policy to have backed strongly E. O. and his
confederates.

As has already been said, support of the established church
and the clergy, and attacks on free thinkers and dissenters
so pervade the *Journal* as to give it a definite tone, and to

[21] Both A. Z. and D. D. were former contributors. For instance, in 142
D. D. discourses on loose conversations in coffee houses on political and
religious subjects, and attacks deistic literature. In 385 A. Z. suggests
that Whiston in his edition of Josephus is evading his promises to
subscribers.

submerge all other religious and theological questions. Still, there are a few detached and sporadic letters of religious import which are unconcerned with local partisanships. Of pure theology apart from deistic controversy there is very little, the only notable instance being a series of technical arguments (numbers 134, 136, 137, and 138) on free will and prescience, and the doctrine of judgments. At times the *Journal* gave space to contributors' excursions into church history. Thus in number 121 there is a short letter in defense of "eastward adoration" against what another writer had falsely claimed to be the unanimous belief of all the bishops, and in number 175 appears a letter from "Ecclesiasticus" denying Newton's statement that the veneration of reliques of saints originated with St. Anthony, and declaring that on the other hand St. Anthony took precautions against having his own body preserved as a relique. In number 169 "Philo-clerus" recalls that one of Charles I's last wishes had been that the Church should have restored to it its sequestrated lands and revenues, and that in spite of his known wish, his son had made a grant of £30,000 out of church funds to the Duchess of Portland. Queen Anne, however, had restored all that was left in her hands, and Philoclerus advises all those holding church property to follow her example and return it, since their titles are invalid and they themselves guilty of sacrilege. For the person of Charles I, the *Journal* had a very considerable reverence, as one might expect from Russel's non-juring principles. It generally called attention to the anniversary of his death by epigrams or by some sort of notice, and occasionally waxed sarcastic on the manner in which that day was observed. Chiefly it was indignant over the turning of what should have been a time of mourning into a holiday. In number 266 are verses to the effect that it is kept only by those who have to observe it on account of their offices, and in number 111 the paper even went to the point of printing in parallel columns three sermons on Charles, two of them preached before the Lords and Commons respectively, to illustrate the art of suiting an address to the sympathies of its audience. It also gave point to the device by an epigram the next week—"With your station and audience let your doctrine still vary."

Of satire on the laxity and shallowness of contemporary religious observance the only marked instance—and that is really directed against feminine human nature—is in the description (numbers 174 and 175) of a conference at Scarborough between ladies of the Church and young Quakeresses, to settle their differences. To show good feeling each wore the others' clothes, it being believed that agreement on clothes would settle everything else. In his second installment the writer went on to suggest that the pump-room at Scarborough be turned into a chapel of ease on Sundays, where the ladies might nominate the preachers, the texts be drawn from Dryden, Congreve, and Prior, and the clergy be paid in simpers and curtsies.

Of devout and pious utterance there are also only rare instances; indeed, the *Journal* is hardly the place to look for devotion and piety. In number 230, however, appears "A word of reproof to the wicked and of consolation to the righteous," wherein the writer tells of a vision in which the Lord remarked upon the wickedness of England, his favored nation, and declared that he would not always withhold his rod, although he would still continue to mark with his love the faithful. In the same tenor is a dissenting "Call renewed from the City to the Country" for the abolition of the Test Act. According to its author, any true Christian "cannot but heartily wish that the Lord's Supper may no longer be prostituted to the lusts of men, nor its sacred ends perverted to civil views" (number 325). Equally pious is the indignation of "A. B." in number 334 at fraudulent reprints of the Bible. There are, he says, strict laws against tampering with earthly laws and records, but none against tampering with the utterances of the Holy Ghost. He describes the publication by a "set of pirates" for "filthy lucre" of installments from the Bible, and tells of a corrupt edition called falsely a "History of the Old and New Testament," with stolen annotations ascribed to a fictitious S. Smith, D. D.

Although it cannot perhaps be said that the religious and theological material in the *Journal* is of first rate interest, it is of value as illustrating the attitude of the conservative and orthodox toward contemporary free thinkers, and as showing the special bent of Russel's mind in the discussion of matters pertaining to what was after all, his chosen profession. Russel's regular orthodoxy becomes apparent here as it does in all other connections. It is perhaps strange that in view of his profession, theology, if not religion, should not have figured even more prominently in the *Journal*. The space allotted to it is indeed slight when compared with that accorded to medical affairs, and this in spite of the fact that Martyn, a medical scientist, early severed his connection with the paper. Whatever the reason, medical affairs were, on the whole, strongly stressed, and it should be remarked at once that the *Journal* showed the same point of view here that it did, for instance, in theology. That is, it was chiefly interested in combatting the unorthodox, and in defending regular modes of procedure. There was certainly at this time a great deal of medical satire. England was suffering, perhaps more than usual, from a plague of quacks, and allusions to them in print and in cartoons and caricatures were very frequent. In this connection one need only recall the numerous representations of the quack-doctor in Hogarth, notably in *The Three Oculists* (1726) and in *Marriage a la Mode* and *The Harlot's Progress,* and then remember that there were in circulation scores of other satirical prints of the same nature.[22] A glance at the back page of any of the more prominent newspapers—the *Grub-street Journal,* the *Craftsman,* or *Fog's Journal,* for instance—is also enlightening, for it was the prime function of the back page to trumpet brazenly the praise of the most shameless nostrums, especially those for venereal disorders, and also to announce on occasion the impossible successes of various bone-setters and surgeons. The *Journal* displays exactly the same sort of antipathy toward quacks and

[22] For an extremely interesting description of the most notable of these prints see the British Museum Catalogue of Personal and Political Satires, Vol. III, part 1, p. liv ff.

irregular practitioners as it does toward deists and free-thinkers on the one hand, or the small fry in literature, "the residents of Grub-street" on the other. Moreover, although there is medical discussion of other sorts, it is very slight in bulk when compared with the great amount of space devoted to undermining the quacks.

As was the case with the learned or scientific writer in other fields, the author of medical works fared but ill at the hands of the *Journal*. At first there was Martyn to pounce upon him, exclaim over his ignorance and pomposity, and declare him a shameless plagiary. And later, after Martyn's retirement, reviews in his vein, and it may be of course, from his pen, continued to appear occasionally.[23] As early as numbers 8 and 18 appear articles signed "Ephraim Quibus, M.D." and ascribed in the *Memoirs* to Martyn, which may be taken as a starting point for the more specific attacks which follow. They are directed against medical writers in general and detail some of their typical weaknesses. Most of them, says the writer, are members of the Grubstreet society; they are quite different from their predecessors, who wrote very plainly and simply. A modern writer gives first of all an account of the family and importance of his patient. He is especially addicted to "swelling epithets" and "the digressive style," in which Dr. Turner[24] is a past master. As an instance is cited the case of a suicide, which rambles off into legal aspects and avoids the medical ones. Dr. Quibus is also loud in praise of the "politeness" of Dr. Turner's accounts of

[23] At the very end of the *Journal's* career, in 411 and 412 was published a criticism of the third edition of Dale's *Pharmacology,* signed "J. H. M. Philorthos." The initials in conjunction with the subject would suggest Martyn's authorship.

[24] In number 31 is to be found sarcastic comment on Dr. Turner's revision of an old translation of Sir Ulrich Hutton's treatise *De Morbo Gallico.* The Dr. T—— referred to in 23 is probably Dr. Turner. Apropos of a letter from a clergyman telling a lady how her husband had been murdered by his physicians, it was decided that the letter ought not to be printed, since clergymen were impertinent to pry into the business of another profession, and since Dr. T—— objected to the omission from the account, of the patient's name, age, time and place of marriage, and "forty like particulars." After all it was decided that the malice and impertinence of the letter were really reasons for publishing it.

cases involving unmentionable parts of the body. He likewise distinguishes the "marvelous style", of which striking examples are to be found in the works of one Dr. Nicholas Robinson, who tells of a young half-wit who fortunately suffered a bump on the head which "shoved his brains right," and of a madman cured by a fall of thirty-six fathoms down a well. The second article gives an amusing account of a new theory of physic to be developed by the author, based on the assumption that "all diseases whatsoever owe their origin to animalcules." It is obviously intended as a satire on fads in medicine, the pushing of theories to the farthest possible limits, and was suggested doubtless by speculation on the discoveries of Leeuwenhoek.

The attacks on specific books give a still clearer conception of the weakness of medical writers. Here especially a modern reader can sympathize more unrestrainedly with the *Journal's* usual acid vehemence, for the authors attacked seem to convict themselves with their own pens of the faults they are charged with. In number 41, Martyn presents a specimen of "An abstract of an appendix to a system of anatomy" offered by a candidate for the Grub Society. It is, Martyn says, little more than "a bill of cures performed" and should have been given away gratis, like an advertisement. He also quotes Vergil's description of physic as a "mute art" and suggests that it must have been on a different footing in those days when "physicians and surgeons left their hands and their medicines to speak for them." Still earlier, in number 11, Martyn waxes sarcastic over a new *Materia Medica* by R. Bradley. He rejoices that these lectures, which had been heard by only three or four students, should at last be printed, and in conclusion observes that doubtless the want of such lectures has led to the common practice of studying medicine abroad. He also selects curious instances of Bradley's learning, such as description of certain stones like marble, out of which gold and silver seemed to drop like gum from trees, his translation of *Terra Sigillata Lemnia* as "Cologne's earth" (Martyn states proudly that he had always believed

Lemnos and Cologne the same place, in spite of geographies!)
and his statement, of little medical use, but illustrative of his
learning, that mummy was to be found in the hecatombs
[*sic*] of Egypt. Again, a recent book of anatomy is censured
in number 279 for its approval of vague, uncertain descrip-
tions, which the critic calls obvious and within the scope of
any layman of common sense, and which do not at all merit
the praise that has been bestowed on them, praise which is
here cited as a case of "pride and puffing." In some cases the
attacks on specific books were extended into fairly lengthy
quarrels. One such is the analysis by "Isaac de Duobus,
N. M." in numbers 154 and 155 of *The New Dispensary* by
"James Alleyne". The first charge is directed against the
booksellers, who are accused of using well-known names
with a variation in spelling to attract trade; in the present
case James Alleyne was merely a bookseller's variation of
John Allen. The book itself is then cut to pieces: of six hundred and thirty pages five hundred are transcribed from the
Method of Dr. Quincy, who is first despoiled and then
damned for a dunce, and the only notable addition is a Latin
grammar for young physicians. Moreover, the spoliation of
Quincy was performed without discrimination—often the
best was omitted and the poorest kept, and the whole mangled
and thrown into confusion. In the second installment the dis-
sector went on to declare further the general confusion of
the work—"physic and pharmacy dance over hill and dale
after botany, zoology, and I know not what." Even the index
made the book more intricate. The compiler is charged with
citing conflicting authorities and making them "draw in the
same yoke." "His simples look awry on each other; his table
of contents on itself; his index on the book; one part of the
book clashes with another, and the last with the whole; generals fight with particulars; recipes run counter to reason-
ings; and theory gives the lie to practise." This attack received the support in number 157 and 158 of two other
correspondents, "X" and "N. J.," both of whom pointed
out "notorious errors" in recipes, while N. J. went to the

point of declaring of the book, "Should it be in the hands of the ignorant and unskillful, it may be of the most fatal consequence to the lives of many." Despite such utterly devastating criticism, however, Alleyne's book was not without a defender, for the long letter of "de Duobus" received a categorical answer at once, in number 156. Its supporter insisted that Alleyne was not proved a fictitious name, that the publisher had made it clear that the book was not John Allen's, and that in addition it was actually superior to Allen's. He also denied charges of plagiarism and pointed out, part by part, the sources on which the work was based. In connection with this letter the *Journal* showed its position by publishing a note from Nathan Bailey, denying any knowledge of or connection with the Alleyne.

Finally, after a lapse of three months, when any isolated letter on the subject had become pointless, the *Journal* published (number 172, April 12, 1733) a further defense, dated January 11, consisting chiefly of an attack on Quincy, and asserting that it contained six errors for every one in Alleyne. In this encounter the *Journal* seems to have been performing a real service in warning the public against the inaccurate product of a purely commercial bookseller. The charges against the book are clear and specific; the answers, even when flat-footed contradictions, are not convincing.

A more interesting because more reasonable and straightforward dispute was that over Clifton's *State of Physic,* beginning in number 201. Here there is apparently an honest clash between two systems of medical treatment. "A. A.", the attacker, praises Clifton's style, except for the fault of pomposity, but charges him with insisting too strongly on his own particular method. He criticises especially Clifton's insistence that very little medicine be given, and his objection to it even at the beginning of treatment on the ground of its changing the appearance of a disease and hindering correct diagnosis. This view, A. A. maintains, insults the rest of the medical faculty by its extreme heresy, and varies so far from established practice that it gives its professor the appearance of a quack. "He that opposes a little physic at first, does it in my opinion as if he had hopes to make a better penny of it afterwards." He also ridicules Clifton's belief that Galen and Hippocrates were masters of "fortune-telling", or predicting the outcome of a disease. A. A. was effectively taken to task two weeks later by "Laertius",[25] and called contradictory and illogical in his reasoning, and narrow in his unquestioning approval of *ipse dixit*'s to choke all innovations. A much more interesting defense of Clifton by "A. Z.", unfortunately delayed over two months, is notable for its remarkably modern point of view. A. Z. praises Clifton highly, especially for his warmth and impartial, sincere spirit. Clifton had advocated the modern method of keeping a close record of a disease day by day, a practice which A. Z. defends against A. A.'s sneering declaration that it would be too laborious except for hospitals. Moreover, he considers the administration of as little physic as possible the most natural and reasonable practice, and with reference to the "fortune telling" declares it often possible for a skillful physician to forecast the outcome of a disease (number 213).

More curious than most of these criticisms of books are the expositions of contemporary theories of medical treatment, hygiene, and diet, which crop out from time to time in the *Journal's* columns. Some of these show a native common sense and clear sanity such as mark the letter by "A. Z." just quoted, but most of them are of course amusingly out of date and remarkable chiefly for the cocksureness and dogmatism of their proponents. Many of these articles are obviously by laymen, and laymen who venture to express them-

---

[25] Laertius also has a letter in 256 revealing a natural sympathy with Clifton's general attitude. After observing that as nostrum-mongers are mean-spirited wretches, so those who keep real cures to themselves are no better, he presents the case of his wife, who had suffered much from the "vapors" during pregnancy. The usual prescription of "a cheerful glass" and much diversion availing little, and having observed that the vapors afflicted only the well-to-do, he had her advised to drink only water and small beer, which soon proved a cure. Apparently a man of common sense, at any rate.

selves on such subjects are notoriously cranks and faddists. As such, perhaps they are not entitled to the consideration due to those whose scientific ideas are examined two centuries later. At any rate, these contemporary views on quicksilver, mad dog bite, inoculation for smallpox, the effect of tea and spirits, and so forth, are vivid and interesting, if quite useless from a scientific point of view. A reflection of the current fad for quicksilver as a specific appears in number 190: "Bellum Medicorum" by Democritus. The writer considers the treatment a foolish one, and declares that either the quicksilver is not taken into the system at all, or if it is absorbed through the lacteals, as is sometimes the case, it must produce salivation or even complete mortification, as it had with Booth the tragedian. He relates a merry tale of the misadventure of a patient who had taken quicksilver, compares the remedy with Dr. Hancock's prescription of cold water as a universal specific, which had been laughed down by Gabriel John, and suggests that mercury might be sold as a beverage in the coffee-houses, with the result that ladies might become mercury barometers.

A more serious essay is an attack on inoculation by "Democritus" in 197.[26] It opens with a weighty statement that the practice is of Mahometan origin and can never suit a free-born English constitution. Of late, the writer asserts, peoples' eyes have been opened and it declines. If many of the noble and wise are for it, so are many against it. Till its advocates can justify themselves from the word of God, they do nothing. How many lives have been lost by it! And even the loss of one alone would be enough to condemn it. If I inoculate my son, Democritus continues, and he dies, what can I do but, filled with remorse, go mourning to my grave? It is said that fewer die of inoculation than of smallpox, but —and here his argument becomes more practical—those inoculated are the young and the rich. Among the poor and ill cared for the results would be far different. Finally returning

[26] Also the author of a letter in 187 describing the extravagance and gluttony of a bishop's installation feast in 1470; and of an article on several quacks famous in past generations, in 263.

to his pious point of view, he fulminates against "taking the Almighty's work out of his hands." This sermon has appended to it a destructive history of inoculation, supposedly by Voltaire, and is enforced and supported by an editorial note from the pen of Bavius, declaring that there is no occasion for inoculation, and ridiculing a statement that its efficacy had been successfully established in England.

Another subject which seems to have exercised the thoughts of many was the danger from mad dogs. The most popular remedy seems to have been dipping in salt water, but that having failed, according to "Misokuon" in number 271, one gentleman having been dipped a dozen times and yet having succumbed a month later, it is suggested that the protests of country gentlemen, partisans of the dog's fidelity, and so forth, be disregarded, and that all dogs be destroyed incontinent. This called forth statements from two other correspondents. The first notified the *Journal* (number 272) that the patient whose case Misokuon had cited lived seven weeks after the dipping, that he never lost his reason, and died at last comfortably in bed, not having, as it had been said, dashed his brains out against a wall. The second, "Philaretes" (number 276) replied to Misokuon with a eulogy of canine character, claimed the same consideration for the dog as would be accorded any other race or class, which he says could not reasonably be destroyed because of the misdeeds of individuals, and concludes with verses on a lap dog sent as a present to a lady. The *Journal* also printed in number 385 over the initials "R. M." a cure for mad dog bite consisting of a mixture of liverwort and black pepper administered on four successive mornings in a pint of warm milk, and in addition cold baths every morning for a month and then thrice a week for a fortnight. To this prescription was attached a note signed "P. L." on the care of the wound itself, suggesting that the poison should be extracted and the wound cauterized, a process more important in his opinion than the use of internal specifics.

A number of correspondents also reveal a remarkable mixture of common sense and superstition on the subject of drink. Often these correspondents are reasonable enough on ground where common observation and sense suffice; they are, on the other hand, hopelessly lost when they advance into fields where specific scientific fact is a requisite; from a modern point of view they had no science whatsoever. The matter of spirits, especially gin, was in the 1730's an ever-burning question. The drinking of spirits had spread alarmingly, the excise on spirits was the subject of incessant political wrangling, and the attacks on them, of which the most notable is of course Hogarth's horrible print "Gin Lane", were frequent. The political aspects of the trade in spirits and the excise are very often satirized in the *Journal*. Except for the generally conservative and orthodox attitude of the paper and its opposition to the excise, one might expect to find more discussion in the *Journal* of an evil which was clearly recognized. The only attack on spirits is in number 360, where a correspondent, after congratulating the editor on his late refusal to insert "a lewd poem on Punch," proceeds to quote at length from Cheyne on the evils of drink. It is Cheyne's theory that water is the only natural drink and that the others should never have been invented.[27] Strong drink or spirits was formerly, Cheyne says, considered only as a medicine, and dispensed by apothecaries; a healthy person needs no spirits. It is foolish to say that they cannot be given up without danger; the sudden leaving off of large quantities of wine and "flesh meats" has never shown itself injurious. Those who desire it, however, may be allowed a pint of wine or spirits a day. Those who think liquor aids digestion are mistaken; it rather hinders and impairs it—water is the only "universal dissolvent". It is also a mistake for the wealthy to drink strong wines, of which they are apt to be fond. Their only excuse can be that they get drunk so much the quicker. Cheyne denies, nevertheless, any intention of discouraging harmless frolics or even an occasional "dulce

---

[27] In number 86 appear "verses to be prefixed to the next edition of Dr. Arbuthnot's Book of Aliments." They ridicule Cheyne's ideas on diet.

furere", but he is opposed to the drunkenness which has become epidemic, and to which many ladies even have come by chance. He speaks especially of "drams"; these, he says, should never be given as a cure for low spirits, which will yield rather to "exercise, abstinence and proper evacuations." Punch is next to drams in its evil effects. It is compounded of the most heating and drying liquors made by fire from fermented juices from southern climates, mixed with the juice of oranges and lemons, which have to be imported green and are very injurious. There follows the surprising statement that oranges and lemons are very harmful anyway, even in the West Indies, where people universally get from them in punch "nervous and mortal dry belly-aches, cramps, and convulsions, which cut them off in a few days." He even extends the ban to malt liquors, which he declares as hard for weak constitutions to digest as pork or pease-soup,— "The valetudinary, studious and contemplative, must be contented with a pint of middling light wine a day, one half with, and the other without, water." Doubtless to offset such disagreeable doctrine the *Journal* inserted in the Pegasus column of the same number an extract from Fuller's *Pharmacopia extemporanea* in high praise of beer. Among other good qualities, it is claimed for beer,

It cools and moistens the parched membranes of the stomach; scoureth salt, acrid, bitter, frothy, slimy filth from off the villae and glands, turns it over the pylorus, and leaves a balmy, benign litus instead, to keep all supple and easy. . . . The sweeter, softer and thicker ale is, the more it suppleth, filleth, and nourisheth. The smarter and staler, the more it openeth and detergeth.

Cheyne's ideas on the evil of strong drink are likewise derided (number 371) by "Paul Puzzle-Query" whose arguments smack of trueborn English certainty. Punch, he contends, is a Christian drink; why, when Cheyne is attacking alcoholic liquors, does he not enumerate cider among the British drinks and note the health of the west country people who drink so much of it? He ridicules the idea that fire (in distillation) makes spirits harmful, any more than it does meat or any other cooked food, and charges Cheyne with gross ignorance on the subject of lemons and oranges; the "dry belly ache", he gravely maintains, has declined among the West Indians since they began "to drink plenty of small rum punch well soured with juice of lemon or orange."

Another contribution with a strong patriotic tinge, and all the dogmatic assurance of the amateur enthusiast, appears in number 379. In it "South Briton" explains at length his notions on diet, with special reference to tea. The corner stone of his system is the theory that native food is best; the British should live on what is grown in their own climate. In fact, British hardihood, in his opinion, springs from beef, wheat-pudding, and good ale. In tea, however, he sees the chief danger to the British constitution, possibly complete ruin. After classifying food into the nutritive and the pleasurable (fruits, for instance), he says that tea not only has no nutritive value, but rather is harmful and weakening. "The first time persons drink it . . . it gives them a pain in the stomach, dejection of spirits, cold sweats, palpitation at the heart, trembling, fearfulness." Tea, he adds further, is too great an alterative to be taken safely; it is no longer used for consumptions, as it used to be. But it is also bad in another way:

It were yet mischief enough to have our whole populace used to sip warm water in a mincing, effeminate manner once or twice every day . . . out of a nice tea cup, sweetened with sugar, biting a bit of nice thin bread and butter . . . this mocks the strong appetite, relaxes the stomach, satiates it with trifling, light nick-nacks, which have little in them to support hard labor. In this manner the bold and brave become dastardly, the strong become weak, the women become barren; or if they breed, their blood is made so poor that they have not strength to suckle, and if they do, the child dies of the gripes.

The custom of performing empirical operations on criminals, which is several times recorded in the news columns of the *Journal,* is the subject of a satirical essay in number 53. Herein, apropos of an operation on the drum of the ear by Dr. Cheselden,[28] Martyn offers many suggestions as to the

[28] The *Journal* reprinted in 55 from the *Daily Courant* a defence of this operation of Cheselden's. It is said that Cheselden hopes by perfor-

possibilities of such a practice, apparently with the intention
of laughing it out of existence. In view of his usually scientific and scholarly point of view, his attitude is somewhat
unexpected, although the conservative trend of the paper
might naturally oppose it to such experimentation.

A good instance of the *Journal's* disagreeable attitude
toward any serious discussion of a liberal nature appears in
its editorial comments on an article in number 103 attacking priests for their interference with medical discoveries.
This article, which the writer explains had been suggested
by current attacks on inoculation for smallpox, lists a number of supposedly parallel cases from history. He mentions
the opposition to bleeding in pleuretic cases, introduced by
Peter Brissot in the sixteenth century, which the priests, in
an appeal to Charles V, had denominated "mortal, impious,
and heretical"; to the medical use of antimony, discovered
by a monk who by chance gave it to some hogs, and noting
the effects, proceeded to experiment on his colleagues, many
of whom died (hence the name *anti-moine*); and to quinine,
whose use had been called a mortal sin by a "pert, pragmatical priest." The *Journal*, or doubtless Russel,[29] while
it could hardly help but rejoice at such instances of human
prejudice and bad judgment, was nevertheless irritated by
the attack on priests. It takes out its irritation by declaring
that priests are no worse than doctors, and waxes sarcastic
on the author of the letter. It asserts that members of both
professions are "pert and pragmatical", try to make their
professions mysterious, "and equally endeavor to get numbers and noise on their side."

The paper's scorn for anything new or at variance with
established principle is generally harsh and repellant. In its
satire on quackery, and its consistent campaigns against sev-

ating the drum to restore hearing to those whose drum is diseased, and
an analogy is drawn with "couching" for cataract. Furthermore, it is
hoped that the operation will not be very painful, since the drum consists
of a very thin skin. Yet if it does prove extremely painful, who is there
more suitable to bear the pain than a condemned criminal?

[29] The comment is not reprinted in the *Memoirs*; hence its authorship
is conjectural, although the manner is certainly typical of Russel.

eral irregular practitioners, however, its fierce bitterness was beyond a doubt put to a very good use. The unspeakable fraternity of brazen quacks who infested England at this period, and whose measure may be taken from their own contemptible advertisements, merited richly all the abuse they received in the *Journal* and elsewhere, and in destroying or stunting their mushroom reputations and killing their credit with the people the *Journal* was doing the country a valuable service. It should be remarked nevertheless that consistently from 1730 to 1738 the *Journal* carried on its back page without any apparent twinge of conscience the advertisements of many of these nostrum-mongers. Indeed many of its own advertisers, such as Worm-Powder Moore and the purveyor of the famous Anodyne Necklace, were frequently held up to ridicule. It is hard to say exactly what were the relations between editors, printers, and advertisers, but on the whole it would seem that the printer, who was legally responsible for the paper in cases of libel and the like, also filled up extra space with what advertising matter he could get. Certainly the papers of the period continually surprise one by calmly displaying advertisements of medicines, books, and pamphlets at utter variance with the policies expressed in their editorial columns. Seemingly the editors or "writers" of the paper, as they are called, had little or nothing to do with the advertisements, and in many cases advertisers do not seem to have identified the persons responsible for the "editorial" pages with those responsible for the advertisements. At any rate they often advertised in papers where they were bitterly and consistently attacked.[30] It is hard to conceive of a modern paper carrying advertisements of a patent medicine against which it was conducting a campaign, or, for that matter, of an advertiser who would give it the chance to do so.[31]

[30] The only exception noted in the case of the *Journal* was the withdrawal of an advertisement of two punch-houses in retaliation for the *Journal's* refusal to publish as a contribution "a lewd poem on punch." (See 360.) For the *Journal's* refusal to print for pay a news item favorable to Joshua Ward, see *post,* p. 285.

[31] For a few among many note the following from the *Journal's* back page:—"Mrs. Elizabeth Knell . . . still continues to perform great cures

From its very beginning the *Journal* is full of anti-quackery. In general articles, in sarcastic comments on news items, in satiric poems and epigrams, and especially in extended and continuous assaults on notable quacks, it was actually trying to open the eyes of the public to a very real menace. The satirical use of Worm-Powder Moore in Pope's campaign against James Moore-Smythe,[32] the frequent puns on the Anodyne Necklace, and Woolstonian interpretations of quacks' achievements have already been spoken of. Apparently its columns were always open to an effective assault on quacks or to any damaging evidence against them. The range includes humorous squibs like the sardonic comment (number 45) on an apothecary's hanging himself, "I wonder the apothecary would choose to die by a paltry anodyne necklace, value 4 d., when there was (no doubt) so much poison ready prepared in his shop," or the letter from "Teague" (number 105) saying that he had never believed the advertisement that the children of the King of France had all cut their teeth on the Anodyne Necklace, but that recently he has acquired more faith in it. He relates the story of a woman of one hundred and twelve, Jane Hobbs by name, who had lost all her teeth and had to live on soft food. She took to the necklace and within three months' time "cast her old stumps and has now got a new set of teeth, as good as ever she had in her life. . . ." But at the other extreme from such a parody of the absurd claims made for what was probably a comparatively harmless imposture, are more serious revelations. For instance in number 268 is published "a true copy of a bill for physic given to a child of seven years old for the space of five weeks, by a horse farrier who . . . now works at hedging." This "doctor" had got a diploma of some sort from a court at

in the dropsy, of both sexes and of all ages" (she was a steady advertiser during the first years) ; "Dr. Godfrey's General Cordial," "The original, inestimable, angelical electuary," "Dr. Newman's famous anti-venereal pill," and "Dr. Rock's Tincture for the stone and gravel" (Dr. Rock was continually satirized in the *Journal*).

[32] See *ante*, Chapter ii.

Canterbury, and upon refusal of payment recovered legally £31 10 s. for debt and costs. The bill, which is a long and pretentious one, contains among other items twenty-one purges and "thirty papers of powder." Rapacity in another connection is also exposed by "Philopauperis" in number 365,—that of the irregular men-midwives who demanded even of the poor a fee of five guineas, even though the patient were dead or safely delivered before their arrival.

A number of articles against quackery in general are to be noted. Of these the most interesting in its revelation of contemporary conditions is one by "Aesculapius" (number 205), according to whom the quacks were so successful in taking the bread out of the mouths of regular practitioners as to discourage young men from becoming physicians. "Many quacks swarm in every place, whose bills are daily pressed into people's hands, as they pass along the streets, to invite them to their destruction. And at the same time our newspapers are filled with pocky advertisements. . . ." Aesculapius further maintains that the regular surgeon depends chiefly on venereal patients, "and is hard put to it to get his bread, whilst those ignorant, detestable rascals, the quacks, . . . loll at ease, and live in plenty upon the sins of the people." He also includes in his attack the minor species of bone-setters and blood-letters, the first of whom, he says, work great cures by pronouncing every case either a fracture or dislocation, thus securing great credit for remarkable cures; while the second, who know nothing of the anatomy of the arm, fail to do more harm only through fear and a realization of their ignorance. Bavius' remarks upon this letter, although in the main they support it with irony, are distinctly tinged with his characteristic perverse humor, which cannot resist the opportunity of subtle thrusts at the regular practitioners as well as the quacks. He suggests that possibly the quacks are doing a good work after all, in case the population is too large, and that perhaps something might be done to increase the number of venereal patients to provide for the regular surgeons, though some of the latter have actually thought quacks good for business, as reducing patients to extremities. He also demands ironically why young men should not be brought up as sowgelders and barbers, since these do so well; objects to Aesculapius' strictures on assurance and impudence, which adorn, or at least make up for, a lack of talent; and hopes that Parliamentary regulation of quacks may be avoided, since such a measure would hinder the writing of Grubstreet medical books and cut down the advertising in the newspapers.

"Democritus" contributed to number 263, apropos of the scandal over Ward, the greatest of all the fraternity, the history of several earlier quacks of note—including Dr. Tom Saffold, the heel-maker, Sir Will Read, "mountebank, oculist and sworn operator for the eyes," "honest Roger Grant, the tinker", Dr. Hancock, whose cure depended entirely upon cold water and stewed prunes, and several others.

Still another correspondent, "Machaon", in numbers 278 and 279, considers quackery the particular fad of the present, like the religious mania of ninety years earlier, or the South Sea bubble of 1720, and contends that it should be curbed by law. He cites common law on the subject of unlicensed practice, points out that a quack who loses a patient is guilty of felony at least to the degree of manslaughter, and recalls the cases of several irregular physicians in past times who had been convicted under Act of Parliament. His instances, however, bearing dates as far afield as 1589 and 1602, would lead one to suspect that quacks of the 1730's had little to fear from such statutes, and were left undisturbed by legal process.

Such general criticism of quackery is indeed mild and weak when compared with the more practical attacks on individuals. Of the various impostors mentioned first and last in the *Journal,* the name is legion, but out of the press are to be distinguished especially the great Joshua Ward, and to a less degree Dr. Taylor, the oculist, and Mrs. Mapp, the bone-setter. To these may be added also the "Mad Doctor", who was the subject of a brief controversy toward the end of the *Journal's* career. Ward was undoubtedly the arch-quack of the time; his fame and following were enormous. Taylor was not properly a quack, but rather, as the *Journal* was careful to point out, a regular surgeon who reduced his profession to a commercial business. As for Mrs. Mapp—"the female bone-setter"—her status is clear enough. The attacks on this disreputable crew were made for the most part during the last three years of the *Journal's* career; warfare on Ward, beginning late in 1734, was almost continuous until the end of 1737; and the campaigns against Taylor, Mrs. Mapp, and the Mad Doctor also took place during these latter years.

The brief campaign against the Mad Doctor is to be found in numbers 383, 384, 387. His assailant, "Jack the Giant Killer", after congratulating the *Journal* on its war against quacks and irregular practitioners, repeats the advertisement of the Mad Doctor to cure any kind of mania or lunacy gratis if allowed the use of the patient's name in recommendations. Jack derides this offer and says he is willing to take oath that the cure consists of huge and careless doses of stibium, "a Herculean remedy". He cites instances of the disastrous use of stibium and insists that a regular physician always records his failures and never pretends to universal and complete success. He calls special attention to the promise "to perform a complete cure in all cases of this sort, from the highest mania to the lowest melancholy in less than three weeks' time." He was vigorously answered the next week by "The Advertiser", that is, the Mad Doctor himself, who turned his anger against the *Journal*, which he calls "a common public canal to convey private scandal about the town," and which he reprimands for publishing so violent an attack without investigation. He then turns to the letter itself—"a heap of low, foul-mouthed, commonplace scurrility." The antimony he declares no remedy at all, since even in considerable doses it has no effect on the system. He claims a regular medical education and asserts a willingness to justify himself further whenever necessary. The Grub editors promise him the deference due him whenever he produces better proof of his regularity. The Giant Killer returned to his guns in number 387, asking the Mad Doctor to give his name and address (not one at a coffee-house), as a better way to introduce a real cure than an anonymous advertisement. He also declares stibium to be glass of antimony, a powerful drug, and not mere antimony. The editors explain in their Pegasus column that not so much of this controversy would have been admitted except for the attack on the *Journal* itself. They take occasion, as often before, to deny the charge of scandal, and fail to see any "indecency, dishonesty or immorality" in having given space to the original attack. Both writers, they insist, are unknown to them, and they serve notice that they will print no more effusions on the subject except for pay.

Mrs. Mapp seems to have enjoyed a comparatively brief vogue, at least in the metropolis, and in fact must have been regarded as hardly worthy of continued notice. The tone of the *Journal* toward the "female bone-setter" is almost altogether one of broad personal ridicule, as though her absurdity were to be taken for granted. The first of a series of allusions to her beginning in number 350 consists, however, of a wail from one Thomas Barbour, tallow-chandler. He resents industriously circulated reports that he has been greatly benefited by a certain female bone-setter, and invites anyone who wishes to come and see his leg, to judge her performance, and decide to whom he owes his present unhappy confinement to his bed or chair. Some conception of the lady's fame is also afforded (number 351) by notices from the press that Mrs. Mapp's plate of ten guineas offered for a race at Epsom had been won by a mare called Mrs. Mapp, and also that the celebrity's husband had returned to her and had been kindly received. There is also a squabble (numbers 356-359) over the production of a play at Lincoln's Inn Fields at Mrs. Mapp's request, and the consequent advertisement that she had concurred in the applause. One "A. B." points out that as she is not a person of quality or taste, he fails to see the importance of her concurrence, or any compliment in it to the play or the actors. Further he makes bold to suggest that she had seen the play at the request of the performers, and advises the manager to add her to the attraction of his raree-show and advertise that she may be seen there alive. This drew a wordy, confused reply signed "C. D.", evidently from someone in the management of the theater, fired with indignation at A. B.'s insults to Mrs. Mapp and the managers, to which A. B. replied with reiterations and answers to various special charges.[33]

Notices such as these would indicate that the *Journal* regarded Mrs. Mapp merely as a vulgarly absurd and ridiculous figure, beneath serious notice. Toward Taylor and Ward, on the other hand, its attitude was quite different. Both had to be taken seriously. Taylor was a regular surgeon who was unashamed to resort to a most blatant campaign of advertising or puffing to work up such a practice that his progress from place to place throughout the country took on the proportions, to judge by his advertisements, of an imperial triumph. And Ward, though plain quack, acquired by equally effective trumpeting an even more astounding and disastrous reputation as a worker of miraculous cures. An ironic epigram in number 361, does not, apparently, exaggerate the popular credulity and blind faith in Ward—

> In this bright age three wonder-workers rise
> Whose operations puzzle all the wise.
> To lame and blind, by use of manual flight[34]
> Mapp gives the use of limbs, and Taylor sight.
> But greater Ward, not only lame and blind
> Relieves, but all diseases of mankind
> By one sole remedy removes, as sure
> As Death by arsenic all disease can cure.

In dealing with Taylor and Ward, the *Journal* has, as always, continual recourse to derision, yet it also does both of them the honor to discuss more or less scientifically and seriously the cases which they offer as claims to distinction.

[33] For a description of several cases treated by Mrs. Mapp, see *Hooker's Miscellany*, 190 ff.
[34] Slight, *i.e.* sleight?

In the case of Taylor, moreover, the *Journal* showed more fairness than usual in dealing with impostors or puffers. In number 362 "R. S." denounced Taylor as a quack, cited a case of blindness due to one of his operations, and urged the *Journal* to expose him. The editors, however, rebuked "R. S." sharply. They pointed out that Taylor was not a quack, but only a puffer, a rôle in which the *Journal* had frequently exposed him, and they declared the reports of his blinding people to be absolutely without foundation. They also published in the next issue a defense of Taylor, including his various qualifications, together with an editorial account of a free hospital for the poor he intended to establish.[35]

As the editors reminded R. S., frequent notice of Taylor had been taken in their columns, and his reputation as a puffer must have been well established among their regular readers. More than a year before had appeared (number 293) satiric directions for the ready composition of a treatise on the diseases of any part of the body, suggested by Dr. Taylor's *Treatise on the diseases of the immediate organ of sight*. The writer, "J. T."[36] recommends the listing of as many variations and combinations of symptoms as possible, and suggests a search for underlying causes in the obstruction, inflammation, dilatation, constriction, etc., of arteries, veins, nerves, fibres, etc.; the coagulation, acrimony, concretion, extravasation of blood, lymph, spirits, etc., to be applied in as many combinations as necessary. It would doubtless, he continues, be helpful to quote frequently, especially from Hippocrates and Galen, and to present a

[35] Horace Walpole referred to Taylor as a "mountebank," in a letter to Mann, January 9, 1755. His absurd lectures on the eye, ("the immediate organ of sight"!) are described in a letter from John Palmer to Dr. Ducarel, January 4, 1747, the writer having heard them at Northampton (Nichols, VIII, 399-401). The date would indicate that Taylor was still flourishing, a good example of that most robust of all hardy perennials, the quack or the mountebank. Nichols also prints the full title, which runs into several hundred words, of *The History of the Travels and Adventures of Chevalier John Taylor: Ophthalmiator*, as likewise a description of a print of Taylor lecturing, with an ode attached, "Hail, curious Occulist" (Nichols, VIII, 410, and IX, 696).

[36] Possibly Russel. It appears in the *Memoirs* that he sometimes used these initials.

table of the parts of the body, with their diseases visible and invisible, as many as there is occasion for. He asserts that Dr. Taylor, who furnishes the model, shows a noble contempt for those diseases of the eye whereof Nature has fixed the boundaries and characters, and brings forth, out of the inexhaustible fund of his imagination, a new set of distempers never before heard of. As other useful means to help one up the hill of Fame without knowledge, "J. T." recommends university degrees, loquacity, contemptuous silence, formality, gravity, dealing in the wonderful and the mysterious, splendid attire, and so on. In somewhat later issues (numbers 303 and 307), sport is made of Latin verses attached to a mezzotint of Dr. Taylor, and a long puff of his new operation for cataract is reprinted, as well as an account of an "artificial pupil" which restored sight to a patient blind for twenty years. Notice is also taken of his presentation at court, and of other honors. These puffs were evidently reprinted to serve as targets, for "Peter Queer" (numbers 310 ff.) tears them to shreds, showing that Dr. Taylor has nothing new to offer his profession, and as for the artificial pupil—what does that mean? Taylor found a champion, however, in "Tim Justice", who accused Peter Queer of wanting both wit and manners, declaring that no matter how much fun might be poked at the surgeon and his talk about cataracts, it was obvious that he had made a good many people see. A month later, the *Journal* again took notice of Taylor's activities, this time by reprinting the preface to his treatise on the eye, and in conjunction with it a second blast from Peter Queer. The tone of Taylor's preface certainly gives ground for the charges brought against him. He speaks of his long investigations, of his new method of operating for cataract, and claims the discovery of a cure for several types of *gutta serena,* heretofore considered incurable. He asserts, however, that he intends to make all his discoveries public, as he intends to keep no secrets. Peter Queer's letter, to which is attached a warning that if he wishes to get more letters printed he must make himself known to the printer, is chiefly an attack on Taylor's claims to preëminence as a specialist in diseases of the eye, although his abject flattery of the Queen in his dedication is also held up to scorn. According to the correspondent, Taylor had taken all the valuable part of his book from the work of the French surgeon Petit, mangling and obscuring the material in the process. One instance is cited in which Taylor had copied wrongly and carelessly from Petit, and had never discovered his mistake. This drew an immediate answer signed "J. Taylor", minimizing the error Peter Queer had noticed, and insisting that an operation Peter Queer had said was like one of Petit's, was in fact entirely unlike it, Petit's being impracticable.

Apparently these sporadic attacks had little effect on Taylor's popularity, for the newspapers continued to publish accounts of his successful operations for cataract[37] and to tell the tale of his triumphal progress through England besieged by crowds of patients, until the time of his departure for France to attend "a person of great distinction." Further emphasis on Taylor's advertising methods appears in a letter in number 346. The author, "Fair Play", who declares himself a layman and denies ever having had any relations with Taylor, recounts the case of one of Taylor's patients, who a few days after the operation lost successively the sight of both eyes. The surgeon's fee is given as five pounds. Fair Play, in what might seem an excess of moderation, avers that he does not blame Taylor so much for the failure of the operation as for the puffing which leads incurables—the patient in this case was seventy years old—to believe they can be cured.

Six months later Taylor was satirized as a member of "The Trumpeters Club or Society of Puffers" in which "the present honorary professor is the worshipped Dr. T—r, well known for his various puffs all over the kingdom." The most vigorous and effective assault on the oculist, however, came as a final shot in number 377. After emptying the vials

[37] See, for instance, 331.

of his scorn on Taylor for his puffing and his continual talk of what he is about to do for the public, the writer details the history of his treatment of M. Crozat of Paris, an account emanating supposedly from Crozat's regular attendant, Dr. Biat, who was by appointment surgeon to the king of France. It is asserted that a shining equipage and the good offices of the much impressed Dutch ambassador secured him access to the patient, and that the operation was a total failure, the eye being obliterated as a result of it.

When regarded in the mass, these attacks on Taylor seem considerable, but it should be noted that they came at fairly long intervals and that there was no concerted bombardment of a sort to interfere greatly with a well-established popular reputation. Indeed, in spite of the fact that Taylor was drawn once to reply in his own defense, it seems hardly probable that his business as a remover of cataracts was much interfered with. After all, the charge of puffing or of low professional ethics in the matter of advertising would probably seem to the public mind a negligible one. The *Journal,* it should be remembered, although it did print a few accounts of unsuccessful operations, refused contemptuously to brand Taylor as a quack, and reduced to the level of stuff and nonsense the rumors that he was going about blinding people, rumors which with a little judicious circulation would doubtless have taken most of the triumph out of Taylor's widely heralded tours.

The case of Joshua Ward was quite different. Here the *Journal* had to deal with a pure quack, monstrously influential, and guilty of far more than commercialism and lack of professional dignity. Ward was an ignoramus who apparently had no scruples whatsoever in administering frightful doses of violent drugs to his equally ignorant patients, and who had a genius for advertising which made Taylor's efforts in that direction seem the pink of propriety. The accounts of Ward's methods and the results of his treatment are enough to make a twentieth century reader gasp. Even a professed believer in the incurable gullibility of the human race could hardly understand the astounding success which attended his campaigns in spite of the harm he did.[38] Here the attitude of the *Journal* was unmodified and unrestrained. It stopped at nothing in its attack on Ward. The effectiveness of its attack, moreover, was clear. When it asserted over and over again savagely and bitterly that Ward brought in his train nothing but death, paralysis, epilepsy, and other horrors, and published case after case with the most revolting detail, the public took heed, and for a time at least Ward's practice was reduced to a shadow of its earlier prosperity.

When once undertaken late in 1734, the campaign against Ward was almost continuous during the remaining three years of the *Journal's* life. Indeed, Ward's "Pill and Drop" had devoted to them more space than any other subject in the paper's history. The first shot against Ward was fired by "Misoquackus" (number 257) in an analysis of a widely circulated testimonial given Ward's remedies by the Lord Chief Baron, describing the case of a patient whose ailment had yielded to them after "all which the regular practice of medicine could suggest had been tried unsuccessfully." The writer does not undertake to disclose the weakness of the case here presented, but instead declares his intention of pointing out instances where Ward has caused paralytic disorders, where death has quickly ensued upon, or been hastened by, his medicines, and of proving that the nostrum is a real poison, of a "tribe" he recognizes. He then proceeds to describe two cases of paralysis caused by the Pill and Drop. In one, a robust, middle-aged man, having been greatly disturbed by the Pill, was directed by Ward to take more—a treatment resulting in bad eruptions, paralysis of the lower jaw, swelling of the wrists and insteps, and trouble with the

[38] Ward is described in Nichols, III, 329, as "the celebrated quack who first began to practice physic about 1733; and combated for some time the united efforts of wit, learning, argument, ridicule, malice, and jealousy, by all of which he was opposed in every shape that can be suggested. After a continued series of successes he died December 11, 1761, at a very advanced age."

eyes and ears—a state of affairs finally corrected by the regular physicians. Ten cases of death are also charged to the use of the medicines as remedies for everything from a rash to consumption. In nearly all cases their use was followed by the most violent disturbances of the digestive tract —"it vomited and purged her times without numbering"; "it vomited her thirty-four and purged her twenty-two times." Misoquackus, on a basis of such cases, argues that the Pill and Drop are poison, since they are so very small and yet so powerful, as violent as a like amount of arsenic or sublimate. He further describes five preparations of antimony, all of which produce the exact effects of Ward's remedies. Of one (Crocus Metallorum, or Liver of Antimony) he says it is so violent that "it is seldom prescribed but to mad people and in such stubborn disorders where the fibres require very forcible shocks," and of another, "Mercurius Vitae," that it was the basis of "the Purging Sugar Plumb," a nostrum which had destroyed many children. Finally he comes to the conclusion that the Pill and Drop were made from one or more of these.

The *Journal* evidently published this letter with the intention of opening a lively quarrel, for in number 259 Bavius stated frankly that the editors had expected Ward to reply, either in the *Journal* or another paper, but that since he had taken no notice they would go on with the campaign against him, publishing cases where "indiscriminate use has proved very fatal to abundance of persons." The same issue has a communication from a physician signing himself "Amiculus" explaining why Ward's pills are inactive for a time and then suddenly develop a most remarkable energy, by the ingenious theory that they are coated over by slime in one of the folds of the stomach lining. He also attacks the Pill and Drop because of their prescription as a panacea for everything from hysterics to scurvy, "pox", ague, or phthisis, even in cases where the weakness of the patient made violent medicine especially dangerous.

A week later the whole first page and half the second were

given up to an abridgement of an attack on Ward by Dr.
Daniel Turner. The editors censure Turner for not mentioning them or giving the *Journal* credit for material he had
taken from it, but undertake nevertheless to give his article,
published as a "Letter to Dr. Jurin,"[39] space in their
columns. Turner likewise considers Ward's principle to be
antimony, and not, as some had thought, mercury, and recalls
the fact that several earlier panaceas had been similar in
appearance and action. After admitting the possibility of the
Pill's value in some cases, he declares that it must be avoided
by the weak and by sufferers from rupture, and that the
various diseases in which the greatest claims for it were
made, notably gout, rheumatism, scurvy, palsy, lues, king's
evil, and cancer, are of such nature that the action of the
Pill would be especially disastrous in their treatment. Dr.
Turner also cites cases of cancer of the breast, paralysis, and
other diseases, where resort to Ward's remedies had been
fatal. Of one such he says, "There has been a paralytic case
industriously concealed, and notwithstanding all the application and interest I could make I have been denied admittance
to the widow of the deceased." He ends with a conjectural

[39] *The drop and pill of Mr. Ward considered, as well in respect to
their composition as their operation and effects. Wherein, as there is
great reason to believe, the genuine receipt of both. In an epistle to Dr.
James Jurin, Fellow of the College of Physicians and of the Royal
Society. From Daniel Turner, of the same College of Physicians in
London* (London, 1735). The *Journal* had earlier attacked Turner for
his pompous and conceited style as a medical writer. (See *ante*.) Another attack on Ward which is perhaps worth noting is *An essay for
abridging the study of physic. To which is added a dialogue (betwixt
Hygeia, Mercury and Pluto). Relating to the practice of physic, as it is
managed by a certain illustrious society. As also an epistle from Usbek
the Persian to J— W—d, Esq.* (London, 1735). It is dedicated "To the
antacademic philosophers, to the generous despisers of the schools, to
the deservedly celebrated J— W—d, J— M—r, and the rest of the numerous sect of inspired physicians." The tone of this pamphlet is indicated
by the statement that the student must have an "inexhaustible fund of
assurance, that cardinal virtue." Moreover, "a little sense would not be
amiss . . . [but] impudence alone will do." The "doctor" should have at
least enough Latin to show off, should be apprentice to a country apothecary and learn to make pills and give clysters, and should study anatomy
enough to know, for example, whether the stomach lies in the abdomen
or thorax. According to Nichols, II, 307, the author was Dr. John
Armstrong.

formula of the Drop as butter of antimony and cream of tartar, and the Pill as "glass of antimony", formed with the Drop into small pills, each of a grain in weight.[40] Turner's statement that the Pill was not mercurial was corrected the next week by "Philagathus" in a statement that *butyrum antimonii* was a preparation of antimony and corrosive sublimate, and that in addition he knew of a case where the Pill had led to complete salivation.

These attacks finally drew replies, and the editors could congratulate themselves on having started an inexhaustible controversy, which before it was finished developed all sorts of ramifications, legal, moral, and scientific. The first letter in favor of Ward—according to the editors the only one they had received—was apparently from a Quaker with a strong prejudice against the medical profession. "Obadiah Anticlysterpipus" asserts in biblical phrase that Ward had helped him, together with many others, when the regular doctors could not. As for the talk of poison, he reminds Ward's detractors that opium, mercury, and other such drugs, are not poison if wisely administered, and so it is, he says, with Ward's pills. To the charge that children were given adult doses, he replies somewhat confusedly, "Hold thy peace, thou babler, you are condemned out of your own mouth, for do you not often say, 'Such a thing is so innocent it may be given to a child'?" He also sweeps aside the deaths for which Ward had been held responsible in the *Journal,* as due to inevitable causes, and not to Ward. At last, in number 262, Ward himself addressed to the *Journal* the reply they had hoped for a month earlier. After giving his personal opinion of Misoquackus, who he says he has been told is an apothecary, he proceeds with the ignorant effrontery and assurance which characterize his trade, to dilate on the great number of incurables who die under the regular practitioners' hands, after expending large sums, and to boast that he has attended twenty thousand in the last nine months, and cured many whom the physicians had turned away as incurable. He also

[40] The Drop:—Butyr Antim. ℥ii, Crem. Tartar ℥iv.

produces affidavits in regard to the damaging cases mentioned in the *Journal* and in Turner's letter, to show that other causes than his treatment contributed to death or that the patients took other remedies also, furnished by physicians or apothecaries. Some of these affidavits are ridiculously thin—mere assertions that the signer believes Ward's Pill had nothing to do with the patient's death, but others are more considerable, as for instance one concerning a waitress in a tavern who drank a great deal of brandy and had long been in bad health, and another a mistress of an ale house, "a gross fat woman" who ate hugely and was obliged "in her way of business to drink." Ward also announces loftily that in future he will take no notice of such attacks, that Dr. Turner has not guessed the prescription of his medicines at all, and that two of the cancer patients whom Turner has believed dead are actually alive and in a fair way to recovery. In conclusion he points with pride to the decreased death rate for the past year, which had, moreover, been a very unhealthy one, and thinks his remedies may have contributed "not a little".

Two weeks later came the *Journal's* reply to Ward's letter in an analysis of his affidavits to show that they avoided the issue and were valueless as arguments. The *Journal,* in fact, produced counter-affidavits to the effect that the statements secured by Ward were false and had never been sworn to, tells of Ward's agents giving bribes to secure affidavits, and asks if "J. Lacey", one of Ward's witnesses, is Joseph Lacey, the bankrupt, "lately arrived from the Bastille at Paris."[41]

For the most part, however, the material in the controversy consisted of accounts of cases, most of them of course to demonstrate Ward's quackery, but some few in his favor. In number 264, for instance, "Philanthropos" tells

[41] In 267, the *Journal* offers a detailed account of one of the cases supported on both sides by affidavits. It is alleged that the patient herself and every one concerned believed her violent illness due to Ward's medicines, and that the attending physician considered them the real cause of her death.

of two cases cured by Ward after they had been given up by the doctors, one "a gentleman of ample fortune" cured of "tremblings in his hands and excessive headaches," the other a Mr. Haine, formerly so crippled by rheumatism that he could not walk, but now "restored to perfect health by Mr. Ward's Pill and Drop." A year and a half later, in number 344, the editors implied in a footnote that one Smith, who had become implicated as an agent of Ward, had brought the account of these two cases to the printer and had paid one and one half guineas for their publication. Ward also had access to other papers, notably the *London Evening Post*. One communication (answered categorically by "Iatrophilus" in number 266), maintained that Ward might be graduated a doctor "by the voice of one whole nation," that his medicine could not be called dangerous since its prescription was unknown, that Ward had been treated as a public benefactor in France, that he was very charitable to the poor (in answer to which Iatrophilus asks where he got his fortune, and says he sells one pill for the cost of thousands) and finally that he should not be called a quack.

As one might expect, the *Journal* made use of its favorite weapons of satire and humor to support and vivify its affidavits and accounts of cases. In the Pegasus column (number 262) "Isaac Bickerstaff" becomes witty over Ward's statement that he would treat free of charge only those who had certificates from their parish, and suggests two forms:— "We . . . do certify that N. N., a poor person belonging to the parish of ———— may safely undergo a hundred stools and as many vomits without any detriment to the said parish," and "We . . . do hereby certify that N. N. . . . is fitly prepared to take the pill and drop, having received the sacrament according to the Church of England, and received ghostly absolution and being in charity with all the world," and suggests as apt for Ward's use Othello's lines—

> I would not kill thy unprepared spirit:
> No, heaven forfend, I would not kill thy soul.

In the same issue an epigram by "U. C." offers the Pill and Drop as a convenient means of inconspicuous suicide. The notoriety Ward had attained is attested by the advertisement for Drury Lane (number 265) of "A New Pantomimical Entertainment called the Plot; or Pill and Drop . . . Written by a Gentleman of the Temple," and of a new satirical print (number 270) of "Dr. Anti-Money and his brother, in their proper attitudes illustrated with suitable decorations." The device of humorous comment on news items was also found convenient. A Mr. Hart of Lincoln's Inn, being disordered in his senses, and stabbing his keeper with scissors, the *Journal* remarks, "The account seems false that this gentleman grew disordered in his senses after taking a certain pill; one would rather think he was so before."[42]

Then suddenly the campaign came to an abrupt halt with the notice in number 270 that the *Journal's* printer had been served with a writ from the King's Bench for scandalous libel on account of the attacks on Ward in numbers 257 and 264. No more damaging allusions to Ward were printed until number 278—a period of eight weeks—when there appeared an epigram on Ward's use of writs to quiet those who spread the news of the deaths he caused, and on his attempts to silence anyone who did not praise him. Four weeks later, in number 282, "Dactyl" poked fun at Ward's bringing suit in the King's Bench as "Joshua Ward, Esq." and then changing to the Court of Common Pleas and becoming "plain, downright, honest Joshua Ward." By the following week the editors seem to have regained their courage, for they published an analysis by "C. J." of climatic conditions and bills of mortality, apropos of Ward's statements in number 262. "C. J." undertook to show that the death rate for the year in question was high, though lower than in the year before, and that a tabulation of causes of death could

---

[42] This was doubtless the same Mr. Hart whose case had been described in number 267:—Suffering from a slight cold, he had taken Ward's medicines out of curiosity. Ward gave him four pills, of which he took two. These proved almost fatal, as he fell into convulsions, and then into a coma, and when he began to recover, was for a time nearly blind.

give Ward little satisfaction. He calls Ward's statement "as romantic, foolish, and self-flattering . . . as any the most bare-faced quack ever uttered from his stage." An illuminating note on this letter was presented in the Pegasus column, to the effect that it had been actually printed for publication the preceding February (it was now the end of May) "but in the absence of some of our Society was suppressed by the influence of others; who, being thrown into a panic by the noise of Mr. W's legal pills, in the shaking fit let drop this demonstration of the falseness and ridiculousness of one of his puffs." Obviously the reference to "our Society" is not to be taken in its usual sense; it seems quite clear that the editorial board of the paper in an access of timidity thought it expedient to let Ward rest in peace for a time. There is also to be caught from these lines a hint of dissension among the various editors themselves. The authority with which the editor speaks in number 283 might lead one to hazard the guess that it was Russel who had been absent, and that now upon his return, Ward might expect a renewal of warfare.

At any rate, in the succeeding issue, number 284, was published a very clear and succinct account of the *Journal's* campaign against Ward, and of the victim's suit for libel, although it must be admitted that the *Journal's* attitude is made out much milder than it really had been. As for the suit for libel, the reader is informed that when the case came up the *Journal's* counsel refused to admit that Ward was a gentleman who practiced physic, that he was the author or inventor of a pill, or even, without definite proof, that he was the seller of a pill. Ward's counsel then asking for a delay, it was granted, and on its resumption, he offered to drop the case if an apology were made. Finally, although this was refused, "the original rule to shew cause was discharged."[43]

[43] Carruthers in his *Life of Pope* points out that Ward retained as counsel Fortescue, a friend of Pope's, who appealed to Pope for help in getting evidence in Ward's favor from the physicians among the poet's friends. Roberts, one of Pope's publishers, was a defendant, and Carruthers finds it amusing that Pope got very little evidence against him for Fortescue.

During the next year, however, Ward figured in the *Journal's* columns only sporadically. In number 288 "Democritus" suggests that the present European war be settled by giving the soldiers on both sides three of Ward's pills, that side which withstood them best to be declared victorious, it being the writer's belief that such "bloodless slaughter" was less harmful and more conducive to peace than the ordinary kind. Other and more significant comments appeared in number 311 and 315. In connection with the attacks upon the oculist Taylor, the *Journal's* printer, Huggonson, inserted an initialled note declaring that Taylor had more honor than to deny his own paid puffs, "which one of J. Ward's principal agents did (flatly disowning any knowledge or action in the affair) when he was asked about J. Ward's answer and the affidavits he had procured (which this agent handed to the press and paid me £1, 11s., 6 d. for their being inserted in number 262, against the twelve cases (inserted in number 257) which denial and disownment I take this opportunity to call on J. Ward or his paid agent to clear up if they can—J. H." Further evidence that the *Journal* had not forgotten Ward, but was still keeping an eye on his activities, is offered in number 315. In that issue is quoted from the *Daily Post Boy* the item, "We are credibly informed that Mr. Ward has undertaken to cure the stone by dissolving it in the bladder, and without any pain to relieve the patient." To this the *Journal* retorts: "We are credibly informed that a woman who had confirmed herself to be so cured of a stone which Mr. Cheselden told her she had, did not know him when he went to her to inquire about the story."

In the middle of 1736, the campaign began again in good earnest, quite probably stirred into life by the appearance of a pamphlet against Ward, which the *Journal* found to be an excellent weapon. It was the work of an apothecary, Joseph Clutton, and was entitled *A true and candid relation of the good and bad effects of Joshua Ward's Pill and Drop, Exhibited in sixty-eight cases*. It is quite possible too that

the *Journal* was outraged by reports of Ward's growing
fame, for in number 338 it reprinted from the *Daily Advertiser* a notice that "Joshua Ward, Esq." and eight or ten
cured patients had appeared before the Queen and three
physicians who had examined them, whereupon the Queen
had distributed money and congratulated Mr. Ward. This
the *Journal* suggested was "Mr. Ward's answer (there being
no such person as Joshua Ward, Esq.) to all the fatal effects
of his pill and drop, as represented in the many cases lately
published."

Furthermore, the *Journal* undertook to investigate the
"eight or ten" cases of cures, and reported the next week
that there were seven of them, to be exact, and that none of
them could really be described as a definite cure, either because it was not known what the patient had to begin with,
or because he still suffered from his original trouble, and
could maintain at most that he felt a little easier. One of the
seven cases is described in detail. The patient was "a little
crooked woman" who said she had had a ravenous wolf in
her stomach, which caused her to eat two legs of mutton
raw, one quarter peck of potatoes and two pails of beer at
one meal, but that on her taking Ward's medicine the wolf
"fell down flap into her belly, ever since which she had been
very well." The *Journal* also printed ironic verses on the
"seven wonderful cures," making the point that it was
thought of several patients who were supposed to have been
relieved of the stone that they still had stone in the bladder.
Again in number 341 the *Journal,* in noticing the death after
a long illness of the Earl of Westmoreland, added the information that the long illness was gout, for which the Earl
had taken the Pill and Drop, upon which he "fell into a
bloody flux and died like the late Bishop of St. Asaph."

In number 342 the attack became definitely systematic and,
it must be confessed, somewhat tedious, when the *Journal*
opened its columns to Joseph Clutton, the aforementioned
enemy of Ward, printing communications from him, as well
as long extracts from his pamphlet. Clutton's first appear-

ance in print in the *Journal* was in a long letter of five columns addressed to William Ward, Joshua's brother, and apparently his chief business agent. The two, Clutton and William Ward, were now engaged in a controversy over testimonials and affidavits; in fact, Clutton's communication is in answer to an open letter by William Ward, and consists of argument over minute details of visits to certain patients, and over the motives and accuracy of the two writers. Clutton calculates that if Ward's accounts are true he must make £12,500 a year—and Ward was regularly insisting that he gave away to the poor all that he made. In much the same strain is another letter by Clutton in number 344 in reply to one by John Smith, written, according to Clutton, in collaboration with William Ward. Here are more arguments over minor details and the matter of veracity. Clutton, however, declares that he had attended Smith in an illness, had given him medicine and told him not to take any more of Ward's remedies. Smith had, on the other hand, explained that he must not disoblige Ward, whose medicines he sold in considerable quantities, being in fact a Ward agent, a statement supported by the *Journal* in a note identifying Smith as a man employed by Ward in earlier dealings with it itself. Clutton, indeed, tiresomely pertinacious, pursued his argument with William Ward through numerous columns in numbers 346 and 348.

The *Journal* also kept up a steady fire of case histories, many of them from Clutton's pamphlet, to give the public a true conception of the horrors of the Pill and Drop. Clutton relates the case of a patient who took two doses of Ward's pills, and had one hundred and thirty stools, with hemorrhages, then a sudden and violent dropsy, and died within about ten days of mortification of the bowels. Symptoms are described in the most gruesome and revolting phraseology. In number 345 appears the description of a case of dropsy (number 41 in Clutton's pamphlet). In connection with this case it had been stated in Ward's defense that the patient had improved under his treatment, and *it is believed* would have recovered if he had not taken cold, drunk too hard, and left off Ward's treatment. In reply Clutton points out the weakness of Ward's argument, and says the fact remains that the patient died of dropsy, having taken Ward's medicines till they ceased to have any good effect. In another case (52) published in the same issue, the patient having died after violent purging and vomiting, in spite of apothecaries and physicians who were called in, the medicine prescribed by Ward was examined carefully. According to the report it could be resolved into white, yellow and blue powders, judged by witnesses to be white arsenic, glass of antimony, and blue smalt. In another case (53) published in number 346, a woman had taken one pill and one drop for rheumatic pains. This brought on continued vomiting and purging for ten or twelve days, till she seemed at the point of death. Then, to relieve shortness of breath, she was bled ten or twelve ounces, but was so exhausted of moisture that "there was not a spoonful of serum separated from that quantity of blood." Nevertheless, after many weeks she made a slow recovery.

Many of the cases show the most reckless prescription of medicines by Ward, apparently without any consideration of the patient's disease. In number 349, appears the case, contributed by "A. J." and numbered 55, of a youth who took three pills for "venereal eruptions," and after the usual violent symptoms, died in four days. In another instance (56 in number 350), the patient took Ward's medicines for pimples on the face. The pills having no effect, Ward gave him more, saying, "So much the better." The second dose produced violent illness and the vomiting of blood. Finally, the eruption turned out to be smallpox, and the patient died.

Another case (61 in number 357) of a still different sort is that of a woman with *prolapsus uteri* who, doctored by a neighbor with medicines said to come from Ward, grew worse and went to Ward himself. His treatment—powders, drops, and one pill—made her much worse, so that she could hardly walk. Ward finally told her she had an incurable ulcer and dismissed her. Thereupon she went to St. Bartholomew's where she was easily cured in the usual way by the surgeon Freak.

In fact, Ward seems to have prescribed much the same medicine for everything from rheumatism to smallpox, and in the cases reported the chief results appear to have been almost invariably "purging and vomiting." In number 356 is presented the case of a woman whom Ward gave two papers of blue powder, one of which "poisoned" her so that she was ill for a month. Apropos of the "blue powder" the *Journal* inserts the note: "The publishing so much about Mr. Ward's Pill and Drop being made of arsenic and ratsbane has in all probability caused him to alter the form, though not the nature of his medicine."

The Pill and Drop continued nevertheless to be Ward's chief stock in trade, although patients reported being given "powders" and even a concoction called "liquid snuff,"[44] which was satirized in a burlesque puff in number 351. Herein Ward, who had achieved the title "Restorer of Health and Father of the Poor" is eulogized for his wonderful work, sympathized with for his persecution by Clutton, and credited with seven wonderful cures, of which the following is typical:—Alexander Brownsword, discharged from his regiment because of leprosy, was cured in ten days by a pill each day and by liquid snuffed up his nostrils, and, in the best testimonial phrasing, "all his natural faculties reduced to their pristine strength and vigor."

After the middle of 1736, the *Journal* gave up its printing of case histories, and confined itself chiefly to Ward's manner of securing testimonials and his puffing in general. In number 359 appears the detailed affidavit of James and Mary Gill, whose child, according to Clutton, had been blinded by Ward's medicines. They here maintain that they have been constantly importuned by a man in gray, thread-

---

[44] Prescribed for one M. Rymes of Oxford for deafness. It got down his throat and made him very ill, but failed to improve his hearing. He reports his case himself in 352.

bare clothes, who worked in Ward's shop, to sign affidavits denying the truth of Clutton's statements. Various inducements had been offered them. Many times they had been treated with fish and ale (the accounts and houses are named), and her husband, who had been arrested for debt, told he would be released and maintained if he would comply. They were both, as a matter of fact, brought before a justice of the peace to swear that the child was blind when it was presented to Ward, but both refused. To this was appended the editorial note—"A man in gray threadbare clothes went on Friday on a threatening, threadbare errand to Mrs. Taylor, whose case was published in our last."

Another of Ward's methods is disclosed in numbers 383 and 384. In the first the *Journal* took notice of an item published in several papers to the effect that Ward claimed to have cured 8,300 at his hospital, whereas the hospitals of St. Thomas and St. Bartholomew together had cured only 10,297. This item had been brought to the *Journal* to be inserted for pay, but the editors had refused it, being skeptical of its truth. Still, they declare, unless the regular practitioners take the trouble to deny it, they will publish it free. Apparently no regular physician saw fit to interfere, for the next week the advertisement appeared. According to it, Ward's patients

have been all relieved without the assistance or advice of any physician, surgeon, or apothecary, which shows the efficacy of his remedies as well as the industry of the giver, who alone is able to prepare what is necessary for such members as daily go to him, many of them having been turned out of other hospitals as incurable, or given over by regular practitioners, by whom care has been, and daily is, taken to spread dreadful accounts amongst the people against Ward and his medicines, that few apply to him but at the last extremity, and even then if any die, such death is attributed, with many aggravations, to his remedies, whilst those who suffer under their care are said to die by the violence of the several distempers.

To emphasize their position of the week before, the editors announced that this statement had been inserted gratis, and that they did not believe it, but that if the physicians were silent under such provocation, one might think them like the quacks in that their chief end was money and not their patients' health.

Here as often the *Journal's* attitude seems anomalous. Its editors had waged bitter and really destructive warfare on Ward, in an attempt to ruin his nefarious business, yet merely because regular physicians refused to be drawn into a controversy, they published, with a statement that they did not believe them, Ward's preposterous statistics. Such a policy leads one to the conclusion that after all it was a quarrel and not a principle that the *Journal* was interested in. Ward's own attitude, too, is somewhat interesting. It would be hard to imagine a modern quack or vendor of a patent medicine attempting to advertise in a periodical which was trying to undermine his business, but in 1737 there seems to have been nothing absurd in such a situation.[45] The *Journal's* policy or point of view is indeed hard to fathom. Its campaign against Ward has every appearance of being serious and sincere, and yet as late as number 362, when it had been fighting Ward for over two years, it was capable of issuing what is virtually a disclaimer of any active interest in exposing him. In that issue, in answer to a letter urging it to include Taylor as well as Ward in its attack, it announced, consistently enough, that it distinguished between the two, but then went on to say that it had never undertaken to find out about the Pill and Drop but had simply published such cases as were brought in, well attested, and by known persons, and that no similar cases involving Taylor had been received.

After the publication of Ward's advertisement in number 384, the *Journal* indeed displayed very little energy in his pursuit. This may have been due to a general lassitude and lack of interest on the part of the editors in a paper which in a few months they were to give up, or to their belief that

[45] Note earlier mention of the *Journal's* regular practice of advertising patent medicines, even when it was frequently ridiculing them in its columns.

they had given the campaign all the space it deserved. During the last months of its existence, the only allusion to Ward consisted of a few casual contemptuous sneers at his puffing. The only item of any particular significance appears in number 406, quoted from a northern correspondent of the *London Daily Post:*

> The famous Dr. Ward with his Pill, etc., was at this place when I arrived here this day; he had a coach and six fine horses, three French horns almost continually sounding round the market-place (one of them I knew, as seeing him perform in the playhouse). Here is at least twenty gentlemen's coaches from Durham and the neighborhood; and monstrous crowds of people of all sorts resort to him. But what I mostly observe is the ladies, who are extravagantly fond of him. It is generally reported he has cured by his pill several deaf people as well as rheumatick and the gout and all manner of distempers, insomuch that at this instant there are some hundreds about his lodgings.[46]

The *Journal* attempts to dull the colors of this rosy picture by remarking that it is "exactly in the style of a collector of news," and declaring that it cannot be true since it turns "a famous London doctor into a mere circumforaneous country mountebank."

If this description from the pen of a traveller is to be taken at its face value, it is evident that Ward's prosperity was again at flood tide. It is in fact quite probable that the check imposed upon it by the *Journal's* campaign was a merely temporary one. That there was a check, however, there can be no doubt. Ward would probably never have troubled to sue the *Journal* or to secure contradictory affidavits if his practice had not been curtailed. Moreover, Ward's "literary" legatee, John Page, confesses in the preface to his book on the quack that Clutton's pamphlet, which was reprinted in part in the *Journal,* and must have benefited greatly by Clutton's easy access to the *Journal's* columns, for a time nearly destroyed the sale of the medicines.

[46] To contradict Ward's puffs concerning cures in Yorkshire, inserted in the dailies, "merely for the sake of the ready," the *Journal* (413) gives notice of the death of Edward Chaloner, a gentleman of £3000 a year, from Ward's medicines, and promises a particular account of his death.

Page's book also makes perfectly clear the extent of Ward's impudent assurance. It may be remembered that his enemies had guessed at the composition of the Pill and Drop as being glass of antimony, arsenic, and cobalt, and that Ward had denied directly that they had come anywhere near the truth. Indeed, Page in his preface attacks Clutton for having pretended to discover the ingredients Ward used. Ward's formulas, nevertheless, when revealed by Page, showed that Clutton and the quack's other enemies had been right in believing glass of antimony to be one of his chief dependencies. Unfortunately the fact that this revelation was made only in 1763 deprived Clutton and the *Journal's* other correspondents of any righteous satisfaction they might have taken in it. Page's book carries an authoritative title: *Receipts for preparing and compounding the principal medicines made use of by the late Mr. Ward. . . . By John Page, Esq., to whom Mr. Ward left his book of secrets.* 1763. Herein one finds that the pill was made from four ounces of glass of antimony, and one of dragon's blood, made into a paste "with good sack or rich mountain wine" and formed into pills. The drop was merely one half ounce of glass of antimony to a quart of "the richest Malaga mountain" or sack. The dosage prescribed a pill of about one and one-half grains or half an ounce of the drop for adults, doses to be reduced for children or weak adults. That Ward had other, though less useful strings to his bow than the celebrated Pill and Drop, one may adduce from the inclusion of recipes for such remedies as "the white drop" (a preparation of aqua fortis, volatile salammoniac and quicksilver), "sweating powders" of ipecac, licorice, opium, nitre, and vitriolated tartar (dose: 20-40 grains), and also "fistula paste", "liquid sweat", "dropsy purging powders", "essence for head-ache", and "the red pill". To judge from the cases presented in the *Journal,* however, Ward was relying, at least during the thirties, almost altogether on the undeniably powerful effects of the Pill and Drop. That the *Journal,* from whatever motive, lent itself to a campaign against him, and if only for a time succeeded in hampering and restricting his reprehensible activities, are facts which even the most disapproving must record in its favor.

Doubtless for the special student or scholar the *Journal's* chief interest lies in its connection with Alexander Pope. It is significant as an episode in the campaign against the Dunces, and as revealing Pope's methods in guerilla and underground warfare. The nature and extent of Pope's association with it it is impossible to explain definitely, but what we do know hardly tends to the poet's credit. It seems clearly to have been another of those episodes in his life, which like the "P. T." scandal, to take the most flagrant instance, reflects the less heroic side of his character. Nevertheless, the material in which Pope had a hand, or which was written in his defense, is the core of the paper. The *Journal* is valuable too, of course, for the occasional flashes of illumination it casts on the careers of Pope's contemporaries, more or less notable—on Fielding, Colley Cibber, Aaron Hill, Theobald, Bentley, Orator Henley, Joshua Ward, and many another.

To some degree, perhaps, it is interesting as a monument to Richard Russel, for if it is to be a monument to anyone, it surely ought to be to him. It is hardly the kind of monument a scholar, a commentator, and a conservative parson of the Church of England would probably have chosen, but it will assuredly serve the purpose better than his *Vida* or his "bales" of Barnabas' epistles. They have long since returned to dust, and for them there can be little hope of resurrection. The *Journal* on the contrary began with a generous endowment of life, and that endowment has by no means run out, even yet. For this persistence of life, this vivacity, one should of course return some thanks to Pope, but even more in all fairness to Russel. The "parson" had no mean part in the *Journal* along with Pope at the beginning, and he kept it going at a rattling gait long after Pope had discreetly and secretly disappeared.

But from a broader point of view, the *Journal* has a

greater interest than these. A general reader of historical or antiquarian turn, to whom the intricacies of Pope's secret affairs, and the facts to be learned about Dunces or about editions of Shakespeare and Milton may mean little, may still be interested in the panorama of actual life, not only in Grubstreet but in innumerable other streets as well, that he may piece together from scraps sifted out of the *Journal's* débris—for any newspaper two hundred years old must have in it considerable débris. He may well believe that he is getting back to something like the origins or raw materials of Defoe or Fielding, for certainly it was out of such shreds and patches, and out of such character and spirit as one finds in the *Journal* that they moulded their novels.

Yet that a modern reader, even one with a tolerant mind and a well developed historical perspective and faculty of detachment, should read the *Journal* with complete approval and sympathy is more than can be expected. In its own time one of its enemies called it "vile, dark, and dirty" and his judgment was echoed and re-echoed by many others in language equally plain. There was rarely a time when it was not concerned in warfare of one sort or another, but the only campaign of major importance in which it appears to have been on the side of the angels was the one whose history has just been narrated—the one against Ward.

It is not that it constitutionally chose the wrong side. The various Dunces it attacked—Moore-Smythe, Ralph, Concanen, its rivals the *Bee*, the *Prompter*, the *Hyp-Doctor*, the numerous books and plays it undertook to annihilate— almost none of these deserved encouragement and support. Except for Fielding, Colley Cibber the comedian (apart from Colley Cibber the tragedian and laureate) and Lewis Theobald as an editor of Shakespeare, who was there in its list of victims for whom one should feel it his duty to wax indignant? But its method of attack, its manner of tearing limb from limb the inconsequential objects of its bitterness and malice (as also the more consequential ones)—these savor of the bull fight or the prize ring, indeed, and make

an exciting show, but under the circumstances it is undeniably hard to sympathize with them. In fact the tone of
the *Journal* throughout is not only partisan and prejudiced;
it is hard and sardonic.

As one looks back upon it across two centuries, he finds
this illustrated most sharply in the caustic annotations with
which Russel (and Martyn too, at the beginning) delighted
to adorn the news items he culled from the dailies. As a
record of life these items are most enlightening and entertaining, and Russel's italicized comments are often a delight.
As long as his sarcasms are confined to the sensational and
dishonest collectors of news with their absurd inaccuracies
and exaggerations, one does not mind. But often his clever-
ness, and he could be very clever, is expended on the victims
of misfortune or of the most terrific human brutality. The
most horrible and disgusting crimes of violence he was
capable of treating with a cold blooded and ironical non-
chalance that is little short of appalling. One must remember too that Russel was not an ignorant and uncultivated
man; he was a university graduate and a clergyman of the
Church of England. If such facts did not then connote all
that they are supposed to today, still it is distinctly surprising that they did not guarantee more humanity and refinement of feeling than they did.

All this, however, is judgment of the *Journal* and of
Russel and his colleagues from a modern point of view, from
outside their own age. Their contemporaries may have found
them pretty strong, but certainly not so strong as we do.
Surely the tone and the manners of the *Journal* were not an
innovation. The age was used to Pope and Swift and to innumerable transient satirists who dealt out personalities with
as much gusto and abandon as did the *Journal*. In its quarrels with the other papers, the *Journal*, which never lacked
initiative, did, it is true, "first begin to brawl", but its opponents were not slow to take up the cudgels in their own
behalf and to return blow for blow to the very best of their
ability. Even the *Prompter,* the organ of the comparatively

mild and gentle Aaron Hill, let fly whole avalanches of bil-lingsgate quite equal to anything in the *Journal*. Hill, how-ever, like Pope, denied responsibility and protested that he knew nothing about what was going on. The newspapers of the time were not oracles of dignity and position anyway; they had very little respectability to maintain. The *Journal* and the *Prompter,* as newspapers, could, and did freely, en-gage in squabbles of which people of standing like Pope and Hill preferred to keep clear.

Indeed the *Journal* does not belie the age it lived in. It was a rough, brutal age. On the surface it was elegant; it made great pretenses at classic restraint and refinement, but underneath a very thin crust things were different. Here is merely another illustration of the divergence between litera-ture, at least of the more formal and impressive sort, and the actualities of life. What remains of a belief that an "Augustan" or classic temper shaped and colored the lives of men of this period, when one reads the *Dunciad,* with all its notes and critical paraphernalia, or remembers the realism of Defoe or Fielding, or considers the implications of Rich-ardson's novels, once they are stripped of their sentiment and smug piety? Surely all these illuminate the actual, every-day lives of the various social classes in the early eighteenth century and show us how people thought and acted in practical affairs.

As has just been said, a paper like the *Grub-street Journal* is the raw material for such books. Any newspaper chroni-cles much small beer, but in the sum total of that small beer —in the news items, in the discussions of the thousand and one details that go to make up daily life, in the ideas on medicine and hygiene, on religion, on social manners, on literature and drama, and, what is perhaps more important, in the spirit in which such material is presented, one finds most certainly a chronicle and brief abstract of the time. It would be hard to maintain that the Palladian architecture of both the houses and the formal literature in this period tallied with the spirit and temper reflected in the *Journal* and the other newspapers or in the realistic fiction. Doubtless if one were to drop back two hundred years and pick up the thread of life in London, he would feel that Defoe, Fielding and Hogarth (not to mention the newspapers) had prepared him fairly well for the world he had dropped into—an age of Moll Flanders, Joseph Andrews and Tom Jones, of Beer Alley and Gin Lane and Marriage à la Mode, and of the rough and ready world connoted in the news columns, the editorials and the correspondence of the *Journal* and its rivals.

There is of course nothing to be surprised at in this, unless one has taken too seriously such adjectives as 'classical', 'Augustan' or 'Palladian'. The two currents of life, the actual and ideal (whether 'romantic' or 'classical') always run side by side, their streams sometimes mingling, sometimes diverging sharply. There is always, no matter how civilized and enlightened the age, a plenty of crude brutality. Is there any reason to believe that the brutalities so brazenly recorded in the journalism and the fiction of this period could not be paralleled in our own police records or in the diaries of social workers? Most of us hear fairly often of occurrences which we ordinarily believe can not happen in so advanced an age as ours. But that is not the point. There may be in our age brutality as unredeemed as there was two hundred years ago, but it would never be treated in public print as it was treated in the *Journal*. Sensational crimes are still reported, but horrible details are glossed over, or presented in comparative euphemisms, and where two centuries ago one found utter cynicism and lack of feeling one now finds at the worst an overblown sentimentality and bathos. Morover, fifty years saw a difference. Just as the novels of the later seventeen hundreds, after the rise of humanitarianism and Wesleyanism, are infinitely politer and gentler than their predecessors, so are the newspapers. A reader of the journals of the 1780's notices at once the dissimilarity in tone between them and their forebears of the 1730's. The manners of the *Grub-street Journal* whether in reporting news, or in discussion and controversy would never have been tolerated fifty years later.[47] In its own age it achieved an immediate popularity, a popularity which it lost only when it wore out and became dull. During its prime it was probably regarded by its disinterested readers as rather extreme, somewhat bad-mannered and ill-tempered, but after all as lively and refreshing. It was, one may surmise, only when their own toes or the toes of their friends got trodden on that it became "vile, dark, and dirty".

Indeed, the *Journal* was lively and vivid; it had gusto. Its dominant spirit in its good times was like Hogarth's. Hogarth is often crude and brutal, even terrible, but he is always fascinating. He reveals in astounding detail and with apparently inexhaustible vigor and spirit—satirically and dramatically heightened, of course—the world which the old Daniel Defoe and the young Henry Fielding beheld and reflected in their novels, and which flashes out continually from the pages of the *Journal*. The paper cannot boast that it reflects its age as do these great artists, but on a lower plane, and with an admixture of baser ores and irrelevancies such as must collect in a catch-all like a newspaper, it often reveals the robust and tonic qualities of the age which it shared with them.

[47] In the matter of critical discussion, there were yet to come such famous bludgeonings as those of the *Edinburgh* and the *Quarterly*. Note also "Macpherson on Pinkerton: Literary Amenities of the [later] Eighteenth Century" by W. A. Craigie, *P. M. L. A.*, June, 1927, a good example of later criticism which recalls the early eighteenth century and suggests the tone of the *Grub-street Journal*. (The tone, however, seems to have been amply justified.) But certainly in general the rough and tumble, free-hitting manners of Grubstreet were much ameliorated in later generations.

APPENDIX

APPENDIX

Here are listed all essays, letters, poems, epigrams, etc., which appeared in the first main section of the *Grub-street Journal* and in the *Literary Courier of Grub-street,* and in the column called "From the Pegasus in Grub-street," which ran from number 16 of the *Journal* to the end, number 418. The division between the first section and the Pegasus column is indicated here by a ———. No material from the news items is included. They contain much that is important and interesting, but even the most perfunctory description of selected items seemed to increase the bulk of the appendix out of all proportion, and correspondingly to decrease its usefulness. As it is, it has seemed expedient to try to indicate only in the very briefest way the general import of the items that are listed.

It is hoped that this appendix may be found useful as a key or means of ready reference to the main sections of the *Journal,* and may also furnish anyone who cares to glance through it a sort of bird's-eye view of the paper, and an idea of chronology and proportion which the discussion of general topics in chapter form could hardly give. Incidentally it may reveal the comparative slightness of the Pope material. Matter which concerns Pope has been so described as to indicate that fact, and the only verse headings which have been listed (and verse headings were very frequent) are those from Pope's own poems or from poems concerning him, for instance, Young's *Epistles.* Yet in spite of such emphasis and favoritism the summary fails to make Pope stand out as the *Journal's* dominant interest, especially after its first year.

Pseudonyms, initials, etc., have been noted, since in many cases, though not all of course, they are needed to show the give-and-take of controversy, or the reappearance from time to time of a given correspondent. In cases where correspondents stated or implied that they were submitting the work of someone else, some such phrase as "submitted by" has been used to indicate the fact. It may be pointed out again that after the retirement of Martyn, Bavius and Maevius both meant Russel, and that he also frequently signed himself "J. T." "Poppy," "Conundrum," and "Dactyl," and occasionally "J. B." and "B. B." The "A," "B," and "M" of the *Memoirs* have also been indicated, in parentheses.

The Pegasus column usually included notes to contributors telling them that their papers had been received, could or could not be printed, and so forth. These notes have not been listed except in significant cases, especially such as give some clue to the *Journal's* policy in dealing with its correspondents.

THE GRUB-STREET JOURNAL
1730
January 8

1. Heading from *The Dunciad*. A statement of general policy by Bavius (B) and "Jeffery Quidnunc" (B).

2. Heading from *The Dunciad*. "The Ode for the New Year," with comment by Bavius (M).

3. The decision of the *Journal* to avoid politics, by Bavius (B). The division of poets into Parnassians and Grubeans.

4. Heading from *The Dunciad*. The petition of "Kirleus" to be appointed bookseller to the Society (M).

February

5. Heading from *The Dunciad*. Essay on Miltonic verse (B).

6. An attack on James Miller's *Humours of Oxford,* by Bavius (M). A letter on an epitaph in 5, by Bavius.

7. The attack on the *Humours of Oxford* continued. (M). A note that Thomson is a Parnassian and not a Grubean, by Bavius.

8. An attack on medical writing, by "Ephraim Quibus, M.D." (B). Notice of the death of the *Morning Post* (M).

March

9. An attack on critical emendation of Milton, by "Zoilus" (B).

10. Attack on the legal advantages of the rich, by Bavius (M). "Verses occasioned by a late famous sermon, on Jan. 30," by "Poppy." (*Memoirs:*—"Maevius" [M]).

11. Satirical review of Bradley's *Màteria Medica* (B).

12. Heading from Pope's *Essay on Criticism*. On critical attitudes toward new plays, with special reference to pamphlets concerning Thomson's *Sophonisba* (M). A letter on emendations of Milton, by Bentley, with comment by Bavius.

April

13. Heading from *The Dunciad*. Attack on a deistic pamphlet by Woolston (M). Verses, enclosed in a letter from "Philomusus," with a sarcastic note by Bavius.

14. Satire on the jury system, occasioned by the Abergavenny scandal (B). Two illiterate letters.

15. Account of the election of Gilliver as bookseller to the Society, and the defeat of Curll (M). Lines—"The Character of the Late Lady A—y" [Abergavenny].

16. An attack on Ralph's *Fashionable Lady*, by Bavius (B), with a letter on the same subject by "J. T." (M). A letter on the use of "Esq." in lists of attorneys, and two epitaphs, from the same hand. —— The first appearance of the column "From the Pegasus in Grub-street." A news item concerning Eustace Budgell.

17. Heading from *The Dunciad*. An attack on various Grubean writers as producers of waste paper, by "N. M." A Welsh surgeon's bill. —— Note of the purchase by the King of a house, to be used as a Library, and an attempted robbery of it.

May

18. A burlesque essay toward a new theory of physic (B). Comment on a story of a plant which had made a dumb woman speak (B). Epitaph, and emendations of one published earlier. —— Complaint that Grubeans contribute to the other papers (M). Account of a case in Chancery; the will of the late Admiral Hosier.

19. Heading from *The Dunciad*. An attack on *The Epistle of Calista to Altamont* (in the Abergavenny scandal). The first attack on James Moore-Smythe (A). —— Notice of a charity performance of *The Orphan*.

20. Heading from Young's first *Epistle to Mr. Pope*. A reply to the attack on Pope in the *One Epistle to Mr. A. Pope* (A). Comment on political discussion in other newspapers, and on "Proposals for General Toleration" in the *Craftsman*, by Bavius (M). —— Notice of the death of *The Post-man Remounted*.

21. Heading from Young's first *Epistle to Mr. Pope*. Notice of policy in dealing with contributions (B). A criticism of the *Journal*, in friendly tone, with sarcastic allusions to Ralph, and to other subjects in the *Journal*, with comment, especially on Ralph (by M).

An attack on the author of the *Sessions Paper* (legal), by "N. H.," with comment. Lines on scandalous scribblers, by Bavius (M). —— Further reply to the *One Epistle* (M). Two epigrams on Moore-Smythe (A).

June

22. Heading from *The Dunciad*. An attack on politico-religious writing (M). Verses on Tindal. —— A defence of the Bishop of Rochester against attack in the *One Epistle*. "Verses by Mr. C—l."

23. A letter satirizing physicians, with comment. A ballad, "The true En—sh D—n to be hanged for a R—pe." —— Political news from Northampton. Satire, with a parody, on Fielding's *Tom Thumb,* by Bavius (M). Notice of the whipping of Moore-Smythe (A).

24. Heading from *The Dunciad*. An attack on Woolston by "Philo-Libert." Lines from an "Essay on The Dunciad" (praise of Pope). —— Satire on Curll. Latin verses paraphrased into an epigram on Mun, a piratical bookseller. Epigram on Moore-Smythe (A). Verses on a late sermon. Satirical notice concerning Moore-Smythe's whipping (A).

25. Heading from Young's first *Epistle to Mr. Pope*. Letter from "Philarchaeus" on Bentley's emendation of Milton, with comment. Lines "To Mrs. M. H.," and a ballad, "A king-at-arms disarmed at law." —— A letter on political affairs at Northampton, by "T. H." Comment on verses defending Moore-Smythe. An epitaph intended for Newton. Note concerning a suit of Moore-Smythe against Gilliver, with an epigram (A), and an advertisement of Moore-Smythe as strayed (A).

July

26. A burlesque letter to Moore-Smythe from his "uncle," Wormpowder Moore. Comment on an emendation in Urry's *Chaucer,* with a P.S. ridiculing Bradley, the botanist at Cambridge (B). —— News item of a robbery. Notice concerning a correspondent. An epigram on Moore-Smythe, with annotation. Another epigram on Moore-Smythe (A), and Pope's epitaph on Robert Digby (A).

27. An attack on Woolston, by "N. T." An imitation of Theocritus. —— Verses on Dunces (M). Notice of the *Weekly Medley* as strayed (M).

28. A report on the Cambridge commencement by Maevius. Pope's epitaph on Newton. An epigram of Martial, imitated by "Dactyl" (M). —— Epigram on a print inscribed to Walpole. Satirical remarks on various newspapers, and a scandalous bookseller.

29. The character of the historian Thuanus, by "B. T." A reply of Moore-Smythe to his "uncle," with an epigram on him, and a threat to print the story of his suit against Gilliver. —— A letter from the *Weekly Medley,* with a reply by Bavius (M).

30. A satirical attack on Ralph, as writer of the *Weekly Medley.* Lines on John Short, porter at the Post-office. Account of the absurd action of a jury in Essex. —— A squib on the Anodyne Necklace. A cryptic epigram, with allusion to Col. Chartres.

August

31. On political news writers. —— An attack on Dr. Turner's translation of Ulrich Hutten: *De Morbo Gallico.*

32. "A Dissertation on Anagrams, Chronograms, and Acrostics, by Mr. Poppy." An epigram on Battie's edition of Isocrates. Letter by "Will Slyboots" to Concanen, on his "Speculatist" (A). —— Notice of the publication of a seditious *Statesman's Miscellany.*

33. Proposals for erecting a college for the habitation of Grub-Street authors, by "Giles Blunderbuss, Esq." (B). A political letter on the King of Spain, by "Sortilegus." A letter on political prophecy, with satire on Woolston. A letter from "Philo-Grubaeus," including an epigram in imitation of Dryden's on Milton. —— Notice of a new work by a Grubean on the barometer. A Latin epigram imitated in English by a young gentleman of Eton, contributed by "L. M."

34. An account of Whiston's life of Dr. Samuel Clarke, by Bavius. A correction of the *Journal's* version of Dryden's epigram on Milton, by "D. M.," with a note by Bavius on an allusion to Cibber. Letter and verses by "Philomusus" on the author of verses on the death of Mr. John Philipps, and a reprint of that poem. —— Notice of entertainments at various "theatrical booths."

September

35. Heading from *The Dunciad.* A letter on Concanen's *Speculatist* (A). A burlesque emendation of *Hudibras;* satire on Bentley, by "Zoilus." Notice of an obscure inscription found near Norwich. —— Reprint of six lines, refused by the *Journal,* but printed by the *Universal Spectator,* and explanation that they are plagiarized from verses by Pope.

36. A letter by "A. B." on Whiston's life of Clarke. A letter by "Philophilus" continuing the discussion of Dryden's epitaph on Milton. —— A satirical squib on "Francis Walsingham" (the *Free Briton*).

37. A letter by "B. T." attacking prose translation of classics, with introductory note by Bavius. A letter by "Philomusus," on Whiston's

life of Clarke. Verses—"A Session of the Cambridge Critics" (*Memoirs:*—by Mr. William Pattison of Sidney College). —— A letter on translations of Burnet's *De Statu Mortuorum,* with a note by Bavius. A note by "Jeffery Quid-nunc" on Henley's assurance (M).

38. A burlesque letter from Concanen, with an editorial note (A). An attack by "Faith-and-Troth" on Whiston's logic. Verses by the author of an ode to the Duke of Buckingham. Verses by "Philo-Grubaeus," satire on political writing. Verses, probably "from the same hand," to the artist Bonewitz. —— A statement of policy, with a denial of malicious intent, etc., by Bavius (M).

October

39. A letter on *Hudibras,* by "M. J." A letter ·by "G. P.," telling of the insolence of the deputy-warden of the Fleet. An attack by "Caledonius" on a Cambridge oration on the beheading of Charles I. —— An account by Bavius of a quarrel between the *London Journal* and the *Craftsman* (M). Begins a column of titles of new books and pamphlets.

40. A letter by "Richard Love-Merit" on verses by "James Drake," with allusions to Stephen Duck. Satirical verses on Duck. A second poem on Duck, with a note by Bavius. —— Account of a plot against a merchant of Bristol. An attack on Theobald's method of securing subscribers for his works (A).

41. A letter on *Hudibras,* by "M. J." An attack on a new work on anatomy, with comment by Bavius (B). —— A brief allusion to Stephen Duck, and also to Moore-Smythe, deceased, and his ghost (M).

42. A letter by "J. M." on prose translations of the classics, with a note by Bavius (M). A reply by "Britanno-Scotus" to "Caledonius" in 39, with comment by Bavius. —— Verses on the character of a rural justice. A reprint of verses attacking the *Journal,* and a note signed L. Gilliver.

43. A print of the arms of the city companies, with an account of "the ancient manner" of celebrating the Lord Mayor's day, from Stow's *Survey of London.* —— Verses to Parsons, Mayor of London, by Maevius (M). An account of a case in the Lord Mayor's Court.

November

44. A letter enclosing verses on the Mayor by a "Coffee Boy," with allusions to Theobald and Pope, by "Timothy Tenfoot." "A Ballad, by a Lady." A passage from the *London Journal,* elevated into poetry. An epitaph on Mrs. Ann Jennings. Verses to the

memory of Mrs. Anne Oldfield. An epigram "sent from Newbold-super-Avon." A letter by "S—" on the villainy of booksellers (A). ——Notice of a burlesque commission to choose a laureate. A description of the Lord Mayor's procession.

45. A letter on *Hudibras,* by "M. J." A song, "sent us by an unknown hand." Reprint of lines by "our ingenious brother, Mr. Ward," with a sarcastic introduction. —— Epigram, "On the Candidates for the Laurel" (A).

46. A long discussion of the proper ceremonials for the installation of a laureate (A). An epigram by Bavius on Cibber and Duck as candidates. —— Complimentary allusion to Robert Dyer, on his admission as attorney of the King's Bench. A sarcastic attack on a course on the Solar System given by George Gordon. A reply to an attack on the Queen in the *London Journal.* Verses, with comment by Bavius, in reply to an attack in *Fog's Journal* (cf. allusion to Ward in 45) (M). [The *Memoirs* print an epigram on Walpole, ascribing it to (B), which does not appear in the *Journal,* 46.]

47. A letter by "Philo-Duncius" on political writers. A letter to "Peter—" by "Ruth C—," a Quaker. Verses to the *Free Briton,* by Bavius (M). —— A statement of policy, an answer to criticism, etc. An epigram on Duck. An epigram on Cibber, by Bavius.

December

48. On the character necessary in a good magistrate, by Bishop Atterbury (reprinted), with picture of Parsons, Lord Mayor, and verses in French, English and Latin, all by (M). News item:— Cibber's election as laureate. —— Notice of a meeting of the Society to celebrate Cibber's election.

49. Heading from Pope's *Essay on Criticism.* Editorial statement of policy toward contributors (M). Letter on the earlier quarrel between "Caledonius" and "Britanno-Scotus," with comment. Letter from "Philarchaeus" on transcription of favorite passages in reading, with an allusion to Bentley, and an English version by "Dactyl" of an epigram of Martial (M). Letter from "Simple Simon" attacking Duck's poetry. An epigram on Cibber. Verses: "Apollo's Revenge on Daphne." —— Verses by "Crambo Rimeus" attacking Gilliver. Verses which *Fog's* might use in answer to the *Journal.* Notice of Duck's election to the Society.

50. Heading from Pope's *Essay on Criticism.* A letter on the Cambridge commencement. A defence of Duck, by "L. M." Translation of a Latin passage, requested by certain readers. An epigram on Mrs. Oldfield, by "Philo-Grub." —— A new epitaph in Westminster Abbey, on Henry Withers. Sarcastic comment on verses against Pope in the *St. James Evening Post.* Notice that Duck had modestly declined the honor of election to the society. Notice of the Society's congratulations of Cibber. Two epigrams on Cibber.

51. An article on almanacs (B). —— Paraphrase of an epigram in 50. Three epigrams on Cibber and the laureateship (the second by A; the third by M). Answer to lines in *St. James Evening Post* attacking Pope.

52. An attack by "B. T." on the barbarous Latin of a medical writer. An answer by "Simple Simon" to " L. M." in the discussion of Duck, with various advertisements relative to Duck's poems. A letter by "Courtley Nice," attacking the style of contemporary journalists, with editorial comment. Latin verses. Epigram by Bavius, "Conjugal Sincerity." —— Verse fable in answer to the *Journal's* enemies (M). Verses on the laureateship.

1731

January

53. On empirical experiments on criminals (B). On the original of the character Hudibras. Letter from "Q. S." on almanac advertisements with a reprint of one, and comment by Bavius. —— A reprint of a discussion by Newton concerning the relative value of gold and silver. On the botanical meaning of *laurel* and *bays*. Two epigrams on the laureateship (the first by M). Notice to correspondents.

54. Heading from *The Dunciad*. Cibber's New Year's Ode, with annotations (M). Letter from "Thomas Didymus" enclosing a discussion of epic manners in the *Aeneid*. —— Account of a mistake in *Fog's* of *Beaurimez* for *Bouts-rimez* (M).

55. On primitive poets, Duck, etc. (B). Letter by "O. R." on an error in an almanac. Further annotation of Cibber's Ode. —— Notice of impending election of an assistant surgeon at St. Bartholomew's. Epitaph on William Rollo. A contemptuous attack on "a learned member" (revealed in the *Memoirs* as "Mr. D. Bellamy") (M). Comment on a new *Hymn to the Laureat*. Epigram on a medical quarrel. Epitaph on Mrs. Oldfield. Notice of the failure of Theophilus Cibber's play, *The Lover*.

56. On political disputes, by "Neuter." Verses: *Pandora,* by Bavius. —— Cryptic notice of a duel in Hyde Park. Verses on the apotheosis of "that ever blessed martyr, King Charles."

February

57. On almanac predictions, by Bavius. Letter by "Philomeides I," on church music. —— Reply to a letter in *Fog's,* abusive of Pope and the *Journal*.

58. A long article by Bavius, abridging a *Farewell to French Kicks,* a pamphlet printed in 1715.

59. An account of various obscene Hottentot ceremonials, with implication that they might be applied to the Dunces, by Bavius (B). Verses written from Fleet Prison, with a note on the author, W—ms. —— Comment on a new poem, *Harlequin Horace.*

60. Extended comment by Bavius on *Harlequin Horace.* —— Bentley's epitaph on Newton. An analysis of a new life of Mrs. Oldfield, published by Curll. Various notices, including a repudiation of *The Grub-street Miscellany,* and a promise to publish an authentic selection.

March

61. Another analysis of almanac prediction. —— Notice of the recovery from illness of Henry Ashton, a South-Sea director. A letter from "Belinda" on the Hottentot ceremonials, with comment (M). Verses, "On a beautiful lady who was blind."

62. On impudence, with special reflection on Henley. Verses, *The City Ladies and Country Lass,* "by Mr. Lockman." —— Satire on an open letter to a member of Parliament by "Mr. T. D., Attorney." Verses: "Upon Wit."

63. On *Hudibras,* by "M. J." Reprint of two handbills on the Charitable Corporation. —— Notice of a false news item taken from the *London Evening Post.* Satire on Henley and the *Hyp-Doctor* (M).

64. Further analysis of the Life of Mrs. Oldfield, with special reference to passages on Pope's letters to Cromwell. —— A burlesque of Henley's advertisements.

April

65. Further attack on the almanacs. Letter signed Bavius, with verses by James Moore Smythe. —— Verses: "The Waterman's Reply to the Doctor's Answer, printed in the Craftsman of Saturday last." On jokes in various political writings (M). Doggerel satirizing Henley's advertisements.

66. Further remarks on *Harlequin Horace.* Lines "To Mrs. M. H." Epigram on Moore Smythe's verses in 65 (A). —— Notice of false news items in *London Evening Post* and other papers. Notice to correspondents. Talk of a nurse to a child, with satire on Henley. Other comments on Henley's activities (M).

67. Description of Edinburgh in Scotch dialect, contributed by "G. G." Description of a satirical theatrical print, by "Rogiers Drury." —— Notice of the coming production of a farce by the

actor Hippisley. Verses on Henley, an answer to one of his advertisements attacking Martyn (B), and an epigram on Henley (M).

68. Reprint of the preface to the *Farewell to French Kicks,* an
attack on the deists, Collins and Tindall, with comment (M). Letter
by *Obadiah Anthem,* a parish clerk, attacking the assessment of tithes
by vestrymen. —— A cryptic allusion to a scandal in society. Satire
on Henley's advertisements. Lines: "A dialogue between a vestry-
man and a doctor of divinity."

69. An abridgement of "A. Welstede's" life of Henley, with notes.
Reprint of lines on Henley from *The Dunciad,* with Pope's note.
Predictions for May, by Bickerstaff. Letter from a bankrupt. Lines
from "J. W." on the Warden of the Fleet. —— Notice of the death
of Defoe, with an epigram.

May

70. A letter on Welsh antiquities. Letter to Mr. Ephraim Cham-
bers, by "L. S." calling attention to an error in an article on
Light. Lines to "F. Osborne, Esq." —— Letter by "Salisbury
Steeple" on a new play, *The Contrast.* An attack on the *London
Evening Post* and the *Weekly Register* for plagiarism. This con-
tains two paraphrases of an epigram (M). Satire on Henley.

71. An attack on Henley, with special reference to his grammars.
An epigram on Henley (M). —— On the verses on "Osborne" in
70. A letter enclosing two Latin paraphrases of an epigram by
Allan Ramsay quoted in 70, with alterations by Maevius (M). Lines
on "the contrast between the late Duke of Buckingham and the
author of the *Contrast.*"

72. A reprint of "The Newtonian Creed," with a request that Dr.
Pemberton, a late writer on Newton, explain its meaning. Observa-
tions on an obscure act concerning the Post Office. Another letter
signed "Bankrupt"—satire on the irresponsibility of bankrupts.
More lines from "J. W." in Fleet Prison. —— A letter from "Anti-
Quack" on Henley, and lines on Henley (M).

73. A complaint from a Templar that in spite of all efforts he
does not get on in society; with a contemptuous allusion to Moore-
Smythe. A letter on Welsh antiquities, by "Anglo-Saxonicus." An
attack on Henley, by "M. Marrow-bone." An attack by "Tom
Thunderer" on the author of a political pamphlet, "Narzanes, or the
Injured Statesman," with an answer by "Philo-Narzanes" to advertisements by "Tom Thunderer." Verses to the Deputy Warden of
the Fleet by "J. W." —— Letter asking Bavius to attack "your
laborious brother, *The Last Dying Speech,*" etc. An attack by
"Philo Grubstreet" on *The Contrast.* An epigram on a new picture
of Cibber (M).

June

74. Long attack by Bavius on other journals, especially the *Craftsman* (M). A bill of expenses of the Mayor of Norwich in 1561. —— An attack on the two Cibbers, enclosing lines in Latin and English on them (M).

75. An attack on Tindall, with special reference to his *Christianity as old as the Creation*. Notice of death of Jezreel Jones, naturalist, signed "B. Butterfly," etc., with a letter of his to a sailor in 1711. —— A short leter in Welsh dialect, enclosing verses describing a tavern brawl. Notice of production of *The Grubstreet Opera*, with directions to the Society to attend, by Bavius.

75. Political discussion of the *London Journal* and the *Craftsman*. Jezreel Jones's letter in 75 versified. —— Account of an incident at a funeral. Two epigrams; one on "Danvers, Fog, and Grub," from the *Courant;* the other on the *Courant, London Journal,* and *Free Briton* (M).

77. A defence by "S" of the *Journal's* method. An analysis of passages from Welstede's *Life* of Henley, signed "J. T." —— A letter from "J. W." on the abuses practiced by the Deputy Warden of the Fleet.

July

78. Heading from Pope's *Essay on Criticism*. A letter by "N. M." attacking other newspapers. A letter by William Piers and one by Eustace Budgell, in a quarrel between the two. —— Satiric allusion to the *Craftsman* (M). A letter by "Philo-Grubaeus" on Henley and a rival "Blind Orator." A bill of fare for the wax chandlers' company in 1478. An epigram on Dennis (A).

79. A reprint in parallel columns of a political discussion in *The Craftsman*, a pamphlet, and the *Free Briton*. —— A news item on the prisoners in the Fleet. A reprint of an absurd advertisement of Henley's in the *Daily Journal*, turned into verse (M).

80. A continuation of the political material in 79. —— A burlesque letter from "Philo-Grubaea," revealed as Mrs. Mary Davis, applying for membership in the Society. Lines: "To Mr. Pope, on his being personally abused" (M).

81. Political material continued. —— A second burlesque letter from Mrs. Davis, very illiterate. Another letter from "J. W." on the Fleet Prison. A letter from "W. G.," a Quaker, urging the *Journal* to be kind to Henley. An epigram on Henley.

82. A letter by "S," satire on Bentleian emendation of Milton. An answer to Piers by Budgell. —— A letter from "J. W." on the Fleet. An epigram on Bowman, Vicar of Dewsbury (M).

August

83. Another letter of Budgell to Piers. An illiterate letter enclosing silly verses. A letter from "P. Dulman," containing an emendation of Milton. —— Another letter from "J. W." on the Fleet, with a letter of thanks from the prisoners to the *Journal,* for taking their side. An epigram on newspaper writers (M).

84. Heading from *The Dunciad.* An attack on the *Daily Courant,* by "Elkanah Conundrum" (M). Satirical verses on nonconformists. —— News concerning the prisoners in the Fleet. A letter from "Peter Squib" on customers who read for nothing in book shops. A letter from "the Blind Orator, P. G.,"—satire on Henley. An epigram on Henley.

85. An attack on Bowman's sermon, "The traditions of the clergy destructive of religion." A verse fable (M). —— A petition of the Fleet prisoners, in verse. A paraphrase by Maevius of an epigram translated in the *Universal Spectator.*

86. Heading from *The Dunciad.* Letter to the *Free Briton* attacking ministerial hacks, signed "Elkanah Conundrum." Further attack on Bowman's sermon. Verses attacking "Cheyne's silly books." —— A doggerel description of entertainments at the theatrical booths (M). A sarcastic allusion to Henley's advertisements.

September

87. A continuation of the attack on Bowman. ——A letter from "Philarchaeus" with an emendation of Milton. An allusion to an attack on the *Universal Spectator.* A humorous anecdote versified.

88. Account of Byng's victory over the Spanish fleet in 1718. An epigram on Henley. —— Allusion to Henley.

89. A letter by "Thomas Didymus" on lack of consistency in epic manners in the *Odyssey,*—referred to by Bavius as "an ingenious banter." An emendation of Milton by "Philonous." A verse letter from "Worm-Powder" Moore to Henley. —— Notice of the death of a prebendary of Winchester. An epigram on Bowman (M).

90. An account of a Grub-street colony in Elysium, by "Farewell." A letter from "Thomas Tillage"—satire on country squires. Verses: "A true Tale of a Country Squire." —— On Henley's advertisements. An anecdote about quarrels between chimney-sweeps and millers, and sailors and colliers, with epigrams applying it politically to the newspapers (the second by M).

91. Heading from *The Rape of the Lock.* A humorous letter by "Philo-Grub," on the "Hyp." A letter of suggestions to almanac-writers, by "Philo-Philomath." Verses: "Astropian Gallantry, or the Peach-stone," and an epigram on the same subject. An analysis

of chances in the lottery. —— A versified anecdote. Two speeches made by the new Lord Mayor. A dialogue between Maevius and Bowman (M).

October

92. A satirical attack on Bowman, signed "Aminadab" (in the character of a non-conformist). —— A letter to Bowman by "Scepticus." Verses on the Astrop Peach-stone.

93. Article by "Seeker," with long quotations, on arrest and imprisonment, apropos of the Fleet prisoners. An answer by "Quibus" to an attack on the *Journal* in the *Courant;* also a reference to Henley, with comment by Bavius. —— Discussion of a Latin passage by "Moromastix," with a reply by "Ushero-Mastix," and comment by members of the Society. Verses on Bowman (M).

94. Review of *The Constitutions of the Free Masons,* just published, by "Spondee." Letter to Bowman by "Laicus." —— Several questions and answers in a controversy with "two or three renegado authors." "A candidate's letter to the freeholders of a certain county, versified."

95. A broadside of the arms of the city companies and the Lord Mayor's show, with a prose description. —— Latin verses on the Lord Mayor translated, also verses to the Lord Mayor Elect, by Maevius (M).

November

96. Heading from *The Dunciad.* An allegorical interpretation of the pictures in 95 by T. W—n [Woolston] (M). Verses: "To the R. Hon. The Lord Mayor," by Maevius (M). —— On the affairs of the Fleet prisoners. "A conference between Aaminadab, a Quaker, and William Bowman, Vicar of Dewsbury," with an interpretation by Woolston.

97. The birth-day ode, with notes (M). A letter by "J. B." to the *Free Briton* defending the Mayor and government of London, for action relative to the erection of a statue of King William (M). —— Draught of a bill to prohibit the sale of books by persons "convicted of death," with exceptions in favor of Theobald, Cibber, and Henley. Verses on the controversy over the statue of King William (M).

98. A letter by "A. B." in the controversy over the statue of King William. Verses: "The Modern Poets." —— An emendation of "Chevy Chace," by "Zoilus." Doggerel verses (*Memoirs:*—"occasioned by the folly of persons in hiring horses in the lottery at a most extravagant rate," by M).

99. Long argument in the controversy over King William's statue. —— A letter on a non-conformist clergyman who conformed with hopes of preferment. Lines: "A receipt to make an epigram." Epigram: *Homerus Bentleii ab igne servatus.*

December

100. Continuation of the statue controversy, by Maevius. ——
Letter by "Catholicus" in answer to the letter on conformity in 99.
(Abuse of the *Journal*.) Two epigrams on Bentley's *Milton*.

101. Letter by "A. H." on the dullness of story-tellers. Letter by
"Philo-Bilstone," defending ironically Bilstone of Oxford in a con-
troversy with Thomas Hearne. —— Notes on contributions received.
Humorous news item. Letter from "Wonder," enclosing an epigram
"On Bentley's Homer . . . preserved from fire." Epigram on Wel-
sted and Cooke. A list of Henley advertisements.

102. Fragment of a satire from Swift and Pope's *Miscellanies,*
with a Latin version by a gentleman of Wadham College. Various
accounts in the newspapers of an East India ship attacked by pirates.
—— An attack on Bowman by "Philo-Vermigeneris." Announcement of a pamphlet against Bowman: "Bomanou Kluthi, or, Hark
to Bowman."

103. Letter by a physician discussing medical feuds, with hostile
notes by the editors. An account by "Colunius" of the reception of
Buckingham at the French Court in 1670. Epigram by Bavius, on
a physician being called out of church. —— A letter from a clergyman at Bury, satirical on the plays given by boys at school, with an
epilogue to *Ignoramus.* One of Henley's advertisements, with lines
by (M).

104. Review of the late quarrel over dissenters. A letter from
"Billy Vapour," facetiously praising and criticising the *Journal,* and
describing his own character, with sarcastic notes by the editors.
Verses: "To Mr. Pope"—flattery. —— A letter from "John a
Nokes" complaining that lines he had submitted, burlesquing Cibber's odes, had neither been printed nor returned. The lines printed
herewith.

1732

January

105. Cibber's New Year's Ode, with comment and annotation—
a mock defense of Cibber (M). A "nonsensical" poem in imitation
of Cibber, with a note by Bavius asking that no more be submitted.
—— A letter from "Teague" on the "Anodyne Necklace." Booksellers' notices, with satirical comment, especially in. reference to
Curll and Henley.

106. A letter describing a vision of a visit by Cibber to the
Elysian Fields, by "A. B." A letter enclosing a comment on Horace,
with allusion to Bentley on Milton, and comments by the editors.
Lines by Bavius, "To the King." —— A parody of the last ode.
Notice of false Latin in Welsted's *Dullness and Scandal* (A).

107. Three letters by "The Seeker," "H. P—r," and "W. H." on "Arithmetic, Metaphysics, and Physics," all, according to an editorial introduction, published because of the importunity of their authors. A facetious tale, in verse, by Bavius. —— Reprint of a circular letter to members of Parliament, requesting a reform in processes of law. Notices of false report of the death of a dissenting minister. Letter on punning by "Henry Conundrum," with a punning epitaph on one Theophilus Cave.

108. Heading from *The Dunciad*. A discussion by "J. T." of the introduction to Bentley's *Milton*. A list of the regicides of 1648. An attack by "E. P." on *The Modish Couple*. Lines: "A Recipe to make a modern dramatic Poet. To C— B—, Esq." [Charles Bodens]. —— Comment on a letter in the *Courant*. A patriotic ode to George and Caroline, by "Britannicus."

February

109. A list of the witnesses against Charles I, with doggerel sneering at their social status. A letter from "Philo-Vermigeneris" comparing Cibber with Carpenter, poet laureate of the city of Hereford. Lines by Maevius on the banqueting-house at Whitehall (M). —— A letter from "W. F.," desiring to submit mss. on the last new comedy, and on other dramatic subjects. Humorous advertisement of a shop for razor strops (M).

110. Letter from "Horatianus" attacking Bentley's *Milton*, with editorial comment. "Some account of the state of prisons since the late act." Prologue and epilogue to *The Orphan*, at a public school performance. —— A letter by "Tim Cockade" sneering at Bodens, author of *The Modish Couple*. The testimony of Penkethman, the actor, at a murder trial, as it is said to have been given in blank verse, with introductory note by (M).

111. Three sermons in parallel columns on King Charles the Martyr. —— An epilogue to *Ignoramus*, spoken at a performance at Bury School.

112. An attack on *The Modish Couple*, and managerial methods, by "Dramaticus." A letter by "Conscientious Doubtful" on observance of King Charles' day. Epitaph on a charitable gentleman. —— A letter by "R. D." telling of seeing a barrister throwing dice with an orange girl for oranges. An attack by "T. D." on Henley's advertisements (M). An epigram on sermons on King Charles (M).

March

113. Further attack by "J. T." on Bentley's preface to his *Milton*. An attack by "A. Z." on Bentley's method, with editorial notes. —— Notice of receipt of correspondence on Bentley's *Milton*. A repudiation of a new collection called *Grubiana* (M).

114. A serious moral essay on the "true notion of virtue." A dialogue between two hack writers, indirect praise of the *Journal,* and satire on the booksellers, their hacks, and on Henley (M). —— A detailed analysis of *Grubiana* with a list of errors, and an epigram by Maevius on its publishers (M).

115. A letter on the itch of scribbling, by "Prosaicus"; attacks several persons, especially Cibber. A burlesque letter from C— J— [Charles Johnson] to "Dramaticus," with comment (M). The list of witnesses against King Charles, with bitter comment. A letter from "Philoludicri" retailing another comic anecdote concerning the barrister mentioned in 112. —— A laudatory notice concerning Samuel Sharp, a surgeon. Verses, with satirical comment, on the *Universal Spectator.* Notes to contributors. Notice of approaching publication of *The Select Memoirs of the Society of Grub-street,* with further attack on *Grubiana.* An epigram in reply to one in *The Weekly Register* by Maevius. Notice of a meeting of South Sea stockholders, with allusion to Cibber (M). A letter from "Aly" to Woolston, calling a new pamphlet to his attention, with editorial note.

116. Letter by "A. Z." attacking Bentley's critical method. A note by "A. Z." enclosing a sailor's letter (a narrative) written in 1656. An epigram on Bentley. —— A notice to correspondents. Lines occasioned by a discussion of church and state, and King Charles, in the *London Journal* (M).

117. Attack on *The Modern Husband,* by "Dramaticus." —— An anecdote of the funeral of Col. Chartres. An epigram by Maevius on Henley (M).

April

118. Further attack by Bavius on Bentley (M). Burlesque emendation by "Zoilus" of a passage from *Paradise Lost.* —— Laudatory lines to Walker, the actor, on his approaching benefit, by "M. Dramaticus."

119. Heading from Swift's and Pope's *Miscellanies.* Satirical attack on sensationalism in church services, by "A Free Briton." A letter from "Dramaticus" on the word *theatrical* and managerial methods. Epigram on a young gentleman's presuming to preach in church. —— Lines on Henley, by "Poppy" (M).

120. A satirical attack on a bill to reduce tithes. —— Allusions to an ode in imitation of Horace in the *Courant,* and to Ralph's *Muses Address to the King.*

121. Material cited in reply to a defense of the character of William III in the *London Journal.* A letter from "A. H." on "eastward adoration." Verses spoken at the tripos at Cambridge; satire on a

young curate eager for advancement. —— Note to a correspondent. The epitaph in the Abbey on the late Dr. John Woodward. A letter from "Philo-Dramaticus," contemptuous of *A Lapland Entertainment* at Drury Lane, in which the Cibbers had acted.

May

122. An essay on marriage. Lines: "The Double Contest," a versification of the two anecdotes of the barrister (see *ante*). A satirical allusion to Bentley, by Bavius. —— Lines by Maevius on the character of William III, as presented by the *London Journal* (M).

123. The character of the rich, supercilious young man. An attack by "Downright Honesty" on a new Greek grammar by George Thomson. Laudatory lines on Cheselden. —— Satire in Latin prose and English verse on a lawyer arguing against "robbing the dead" of their bodies for dissection.

124. A continuation of the citations on the character of King William. —— Lines, by "Philo-Grub," "To Caelia."

125. Two letters by "A. Z.," one attacking Bentley's critical method, and the other recalling an earlier quarrel of Bentley with Dr. Colbatch. An epigram on Bentley and Boyle. —— A burlesque letter from "F. Osborne" of the *London Journal*, attacking his opponent "S. T." in the controversy over William III.

June

126. Letter signed "Obadiah"—a defence of the Quakers against a book by Patrick Smith, *A Preservative against Quakerism*. —— An abusive letter from "Claudia Rufina," enclosing verses, also abusive, with an editorial answer, especially to the charge of "stealing Pope's name" (M).

127. A series of letters concerning the fraudulent Charitable Corporation, and the association of the embezzlers with the Pretender at Rome. (This a controversy with the *Free Briton*.) Lines on the same point, by Bavius (M, misprinted W). —— A letter by "Prosaicus," on Fielding's *Covent Garden Tragedy*. Lines by Maevius on scandalous rumors concerning the Pretender's birth (M).

128. On the Charitable Corporation continued. —— An attack by "Dramaticus" on *The Covent Garden Tragedy*. "A Ballad on the Ridotto al Fresco" (A).

129. On the Charitable Corporation concluded (signed Bavius). —— A letter from "Poeticus" to "Dramaticus," insinuating that the latter has recanted, and enclosing "a recantation song," an imitation of an ode by Horace.

130. An attack on Fielding by "Prosaicus." A letter from "A. B." replying to a defence of Fielding by "Wm. Hint, Candle-Snuffer." An attack on Fielding by "Dramaticus." A memorial of J. W., a prisoner in the Fleet. (See *ante.*) —— Two notices of the death of Lady Oglethorpe. A burlesque letter from "Wm. Hint" denying authorship of a letter signed with his name and concerning Fielding's play, with comment on *The Covent Garden Tragedy* (M).

July

131. An examination of some of Bentley's emendations. Comic lines on Bentley (called Zoilus). —— A letter from "De Ripis" enclosing lines on Henley.

132. A reply by "Dramaticus" to a defence of *The Modern Husband* in the *Comedian.* Ridicule of the *Comedian* by Bavius. An attack on Fielding's *Old Debauchees* by "Miso-Clerus" (M). An epigram on Fielding by "D. V." —— Notice concerning the charter of the colony of Georgia. A translation of lines from the *Aeneid.* A letter from "Cluvienus" attacking the *Free Briton.* Epigram on *The Universal Rehearsal,* a paper which had attacked the *Journal* (M).

133. A long attack by "Publicus" on *The Covent Garden Tragedy* and *The Old Debauchees.* Epigram by "F. N." on *The Covent Garden Tragedy.* —— A note concerning the founding of Georgia. A description of a "water-spout" in Pevensey Bay. Lines: "The Retirement," by "Strephon."

134. A discussion of free will. A letter from "Dramaticus" attacking Fielding and the theatre managers. Latin lines ridiculing a pedantic archdeacon. —— Notice to contributors with especial regard to personal lampoons (M). Paraphrase of a passage from Horace.

August

135. A letter from "Theatricus" ascribing the degeneracy of modern youth to the degeneracy of the stage. A reply by "Dramaticus" to "Dramaticus Senior," who had answered him in the *Courant,* with comment by Bavius. —— An answer by "Publicus" to a defence of Fielding in the *Daily Post.* An epigram by Maevius on Fielding's indecency (M).

136. A letter on the discussion of free-will in 134. A review of the controversy over Fielding's plays, by Bavius (M). —— An ironical defence of the *Covent Garden Tragedy,* with a summary of the plot, by "B. B." (M).

137. A letter signed "Eliot" in the discussion of free-will. An analysis of some of Bentley's emendations, by Bavius. A letter by "Philo-Bent" offering an emendation of *Chevy Chace.* —— Com-

ment by Bavius on Fielding's *Prolegomena* to *The Covent Garden Tragedy,* in which he had derided the *Journal.* Lines to Miss Raftor (Kitty Clive).

138. An attack by "Prosaicus" on Fielding as a dramatic writer. A letter concerning divine judgments. —— A letter from "Hobbinol Lubbin" asking admission to the Society, and submitting a translation of the prologue to Persius.

139. Article on "answering" arguments, with special reference to papists and non-conformists, and to Curll, Henley, Bowman, and Tindall. —— Poem in praise of Rich and attacking Cibber, with editorial note disclaiming support.

September

140. Lines "On Divine Poetry" by a school-boy, submitted by "M. B.," who says it puts the degenerate authors of the age to shame. A letter by "The Inspector" on the value of good books of travel. Lines: "The laments of a true lover for the death of a lady," submitted by "Pastor Plorans." Lines: "A begging epistle in rhime from a poor poet," from "Ra. Argill." —— An editorial note on publishing puffs, and notice of difficulty with an advertiser. Lines on Concanen, "On the new Attorney General."

141. The Fielding quarrel resumed by Bavius, with abusive answer to opponents and to attacks on the *Journal* in the *Daily Post.* Epigram by Maevius on Fielding. —— Hit at the *Register* for plagiarism. Lines on the acting of Molière's play under the two titles of *Mock Doctor* and *Forced Physician,* by "Poppy."

142. Heading from Young's first *Epistle to Mr. Pope.* Ironical letter on coffee-house conversation, satirising loose religious and political views, by "D. D." A letter of a clergyman ("Mr. A— F—s") to his curate versified—satire on clerical avarice. —— An obscure epigram, published to please the author. Explanation of changes made in the epigram on Concanen in 140; it had been published in its original form in *Fog's.* Verse fable on poet-asses, with allusions to Pope and Cibber.

143. Continuation of argument against judgments, from 138. A letter from "Prosaicus" attacking a new play, *The Devil of a Duke.* —— Letter from "A. H." attacking two of Theobald's emendations of Shakespeare. Verses attacking "W—" [Welsted], by "P. B."

October

144. Reprint from an introduction to *The State of the Nation,* by "John Gabriel." Two poems on John Gabriel. Letter deploring the death of the actor Wilks, and attacking an actor who had played

Macduff, by "Philo-Dramaticus." An epigram replying to verses on Rich in 139. —— A repudiation of *Grubiana,* republished as *The Grub-Street Miscellany.* Political verses "A Dialogue between P. & W." [Pulteney and Walpole?].

145. A second letter on coffee-house conversation, by "D. D." A letter from "Esther Zealous" a Quaker, attacking Ruth Collins' *The Friendly Writer* (apparently burlesque). Letter from "Philo-Dives," author of the verses on Rich in 139, to the writer of the answer in 144. —— A letter from "A. B.," with comment, on clergy of less than £100 a year acting as justices of the peace. Verses on a quack of great pretences, and honored by royalty.

146. Continuation by Bavius of the examination of Bentley's emendations of Milton. The Curate's answer to the clergyman's letter (see 142), versified. —— An answer in verse of "Philo-Historio" (later "Histrio") to "Philo-Dives." Verses to Henley by a "Mr. Shelton," apparently a criminal, charging him with seducing the author from an honest life.

147. A print, "The Art and Mystery of Printing," as illustration to a dialogue on newspapers and booksellers. (To be cont.) —— "Errata of the Learned":—examples from Mead and Chambers. Epigram by Maevius "On the liberty of the press."

148. "The Grub-Street Journal Extraordinary," October 30, 1732. Reprint of leading article in 147, with a continuation. Also a long "explication" of the picture. A poem to the Lord Mayor. Cuts of the arms of the city companies.

November

149. On the itch of writing, by "H. W." with a note by Bavius. Letter from "Miso Diabolus" on fashionable use of "devil," "devilish," etc. The birthday ode, with notes by Bavius. —— Verses to the Lord Mayor, by Maevius.

150. Heading from Young's first *Epistle.* Further explication by "Bibliopola" of the print in 148. An anecdote of Alexander and a poetaster, Choerilus, by "A. B." A burlesque of Cibber's birthday ode. —— A reply by "Philo Histrio" to "Philo Dives, alias H. W." An epigram by Maevius on Henley.

151. Moral essay on virtue and advancing age. A letter by "Ecclesiasticus" on Henley's history, especially in regard to his leaving the church. —— Burlesque proposals for a work on "Terra Incognita" by "Piraticus." Verses on the Laureate's last ode.

152. A continuation of material from John Gabriel in 144. Lines contributed by "J. B." —— Two odes of Anacreon, translated into Latin and English, by "D. D."

153. A discussion of St. Andrew's Day and the order of St. Andrew, by Bavius. A note by "D. D." on the odes in 152, with other English versions. —— Notices to contributors, with allusions to John Gabriel and Bentley. A note on one of Henley's advertisements, with comment.

December

154. Attack on the artifices of booksellers especially in stealing well-known names, with especial reference to medical works by John Allen and James Alleyne. A prologue addressed to the freemasons. —— The epilogue on the same occasion.

155. The attack on the work of "James Alleyne" continued, by "Isaac de Duobus, N. M." Satire on the theatrical audience. An epigram by Maevius on Henley. —— A discussion of one of Henley's advertisements. The third ode of Anacreon, in Latin and English.

156. An answer to the attack on Alleyne. Signed statement from Nathan Bailey, disclaiming connection with the Alleyne. —— On Henley's boasted connections with great people. Verses on "Sally," a waitress.

157. Letter from "Jeremy Hint," suggesting that money won at cards be given to the poor. Letter from "X" pointing out a chemical error in Alleyne. Letter commending the *Journal* for its attack on booksellers, and telling of the mutilation by a bookseller of Duck's "Hermitage"; an authentic copy of the verses enclosed, with a note by Bavius. —— A further attack on Henley's puffs. Epigrams on Woolston, and on Christmas.

1733

January

158. Passage from Oppian's *Cynegeticks*, in English, submitted by "Graecanicus." Note from "N. J." pointing out errors in Alleyne. A prologue to *Phormio*, at a school performance, contributed by "Philo-Grubaeus." —— A continuation of the attack on Henley. Verses on Henley, by Maevius.

159. On the origin of the Grubstreet Society, by "A. H." The New Year's Ode, with notes. —— Lines: "Good Advice to Sally" (cf. 156).

160. Notes on the New Year's Ode, by Bavius. —— A eulogy of the late Rev. Mr. Smith, master of Tiverton School, by "Philo-Tivertoniae." A ballad on the excise: "The Constitution Clap'd."

161. Continuation of material from John Gabriel (cf. 144 and 152). An Ode, submitted by "A. B." —— Comment by Bavius on Henley's defence of Cibber's reference to the Muses as "Sicilian sisters." Lines: "Sally's Answer."

February

162. Further notes on Cibber's ode, contributed by "Calliopius." Letter from "Medonius," a new student at Cambridge—satire on a snobbish, effeminate fop. Letter and verses attacking shyster lawyers, with an epigram in answer. —— Further comment on Henley's defence of "Sicilian sisters." Doggerel verse on young Cibber.

163. Continuation of the letter on Grubeans in 159, discussing the origin of the Masons. More "Errata of the Learned," contributed by "Calliopius." Verses: "The Town Lady's Answer." —— "An Ode or Ballad," burlesque of Cibber's style, and satire on his "Sicilian sisters."

164. Letter by "Somebody" attacking the Cibbers' re-made plays. Ironical defence by "Will Traffick" of the excise. Epilogue to the *Eunuch,* acted at Westminster School. —— A petition of the ladies of London against the excise. Notice of a benefit performance of *Henry VIII.* Verses to "J. M. Alchymist" by "S. S."

165. An attack on "Betty, or the Country Bumpkins" by "Somebody." Letter from "Calliopius" on various superstitions. Contemptuous reply by "Some-body" to an attack on Gay's *Achilles,* in the *Daily Courant.* —— Comment on this attack, with implication that Ralph was the author. An answer to the epigram on "J. M. Alchymist"—political satire.

March

166. Ironical essay on the present high level of literature and taste, by Bavius. A letter from "Spinosa Taffety," alluding obscurely to some ridiculous person, with a note by Bavius indicating that he does not understand the allusion. Verses in Latin and English, "to Dr. Freind in Westminster School." —— Letter and verses on acting, with allusions to Henley and Ned Ward, by "Philo-Histrio."

167. An attack on *Caelia, or the Perjured Lover,* and on the managers at Drury Lane, by "Some-body." A letter by "D. P." attacking the *Daily Courant* and the *London Journal.* Epigram by Maevius on the lack of gratitude in political leaders. —— A summary of Curl's life of Wilks, the actor. An epigram on Sarah Malcolm, the murderess, by "Dactyl."

168. Article by Bavius against the *Gentleman's* and the *London Magazine,* retailing a feud between them. A letter from "No One," enclosing a list of comic names—"Barrel, a tapster," etc. —— A letter to "Some-body," on certain errors of his concerning Shakespeare. An epigram on the pretended courage of one "Sir Prim," contributed by "Philopatria" (political satire).

169. Letter by "Philoclerus," urging that sequestrated lands be returned to the church—pity for the condition of the poor clergy. Lines: "The Retired Patriot," by "Philo-Grubaeus-Cantab." —— Letter from Hippisley the actor, denying that he has ever libelled or attacked his friends. Verses to "Mr. Orator" [Henley] on his advertisements, by "Conundrum."

170. An attack on a projected new edition of Stephen's *Thesaurus*, by "Calliopius," with a note by Bavius. Continuation of material from John Gabriel. —— A "true copy" of an abusive letter from an M. P. to his constituents. Henley's *Oratory Transactions* versified by Maevius.

April

171. Attack on proposals for a new *General Dictionary*. Answer by Bavius to an attack by the *Gentleman's* on his article in 168. Epigram by "Dactyl" on the courtiers' support of the excise. —— Translation of a fable of Phaedrus by Maevius.

172. Satire on the extension of the excise to Dullness, by "Scriblerus cum Dasho," with allusions to Cibber, Henley, Curl, the newspapers, etc. (to be cont.). A defence of Alleyne's medical work (see *ante*). —— Letter by "B. T." attacking the prospectus of the new edition of Stephens' *Thesaurus*. Note on the subject of piracy, of which the *Journal* and the *Gentleman's* had accused each other. Epigram on the excise, by Maevius.

173. Letter by Maevius replying to an attack in the *Free Briton* on the Council of London for their opposition to the excise. —— An epigram on the *Free Briton*, by "Dactyl."

174. Continuation of article on Dullness in 172, chiefly against Henley ("Pufferus"). Attack on Rich, manager of Covent Garden, by "No-body." A burlesque petition for an appointment as privy councillor, and discussion as to why it was refused. Verses: "The Fortunate Disappointment." —— Satirical comment on a religious conference of women held at Scarborough. "A Song."

May

175. A letter by "Ecclesiasticus" on an error made by Sir Isaac Newton in his "Observations on the prophecies of Daniel." A letter from a young man ("L. R.") in answer to a proposal of marriage made by a young lady. —— Ironical proposals for a chapel of ease at Scarborough, for ladies. An answer to the complaints of the new editors of Stephens' *Thesaurus*, by "Calliopius." Epigram on Charles I, betrayed by the Scotch.

176. A letter from the "Fiddle Faddle Club," satire on Ladies' Clubs. A conclusion of the article on the excise on Dullness (see

172, 174). Lines: "On Good and Ill-Nature—To Mr. Pope." ——
Letter on an English Academy, with discussion of the phrase "never
so much," by "The Censor of Great Britain." Verses by Maevius on
Henley.

177. Declaration of the *Journal's* impartiality, by Bavius. Answer
by "Some-body" to the attack on Rich in 174. A letter suggesting
penalties to prevent unhappy marriages, by "Sancho Panca." Verses
written by Walpole on a window in the Tower, when confined there
in 1712. —— An answer by Maevius to "seven lies" with which
Henley had charged the *Journal,* by Maevius. An epigram on Henley, by "Dactyl."

178. A reply by "A. B." to the complaints of the editors of the
General Dictionary. Letter attacking Theophilus Cibber as manager,
author, and actor. Letter from "J. Ralph" replying to charges made
by "Some-body" in 178. An epigram on the *Hyp-Doctor* and *Free
Briton,* by Maevius. —— Verses on the last *Free Briton* by "Dactyl."

179. A letter in defense, by the "Authors" of the *General Dictionary.* Lines, submitted by "Grubbeanicus," to a gentleman who
had bound up Swift, Pope, and Fielding together. —— A reply by
"Some-body" to Ralph's letter in 178. Further sarcasm on the religious conference at Scarborough. An epigram on "Stonecastle"
(the *Universal Spectator*) as a plagiarist.

June

180. Letter attacking T. Cibber for his methods as manager, and
for stirring up dissension among the actors, by "Musaeus" (apropos
of war between actors and patentees). A letter by "Philo-Dramaticus" supporting the actors. "An Ode," by a young lady. —— A letter
by "Anglus" attacking the political theories of the *Craftsman.* An
epigram on Pope, on his writing Gay's epitaph.

181. Letter on the theatrical quarrel, generally favorable to
actors; suggests various sources from which managers might recruit
their companies. A letter submitting a passage from Vanbrugh's
Aesop relative to the theatrical quarrel. Verses: "Upon the poet
laureate's being expelled the House of Lords." —— Notice of the
death of Pope's mother. Verses: "Plot for Plot," by "Hibernicus."

182. An attack by "Democritus" on news items in the papers. A
burlesque advertisement by "Democritus" of an old woman who "cuts
folks for the simples." A specimen index to Bayle's *Dictionary*
(article on Adam), by "Publicus." Letter from "Sarah Townly"
submitting verses. —— An epigram on the 204 who voted against
the excise, with a note that 204 is a mystical number, the sum of
the squares of numbers from one to eight. "A receipt to cure a love
fit," lines by "Democritus."

183. An essay on curiosity. Narrative of a dream, satire on female honor, by "Oculatus Henroost." "Verses made at sea." —— Verses on "The Flea," a parody of Phillips' lines to Cuzzoni, by "Ironicus."

July

184. Comment on a proposed edition of Chambers' *Dictionary,* by "Publicola." A scheme for establishing the theatre on a new basis, by "Philo-Britannus." Satire on the wonderful work of news writers, by Bavius. Anacreon, Ode III, translated by "D. D." —— Satire on publication of wills, dying speeches, etc., with hits at Curll, by "Scriblerus Incurabilis." Epigram on the *Universal Spectator.*

185. Account of a journey to Paris, in an illiterate letter from a young country squire ("W. Boobykins") "To his papa." A letter from "A. B." enclosing verses on a late marriage. —— The epitaph of Daniel Pulteney in Westminster. Letter from "Scriblerus Incurabilis," desiring a cure for scribbling. Lines by "Epigrammaticus" praising Duley above Gervase and Hogarth.

186. Letter by "Publicola" on the administration of the law and the exploitation of the poor. "Warbletta: A Suburban Eclogue," submitted by "Philo-Histrio." —— A letter from "Democritus" on the importance of punctuation, with a jury list of 1619 in which all the surnames are titles, e.g. "Henry Prince of Godmanchester." Notice to correspondents. Epigram by Maevius on magazine puffs.

187. Attack on T. Cibber's part in the theatrical quarrel by "Musaeus." Continuation by Bavius of his discussion of newspapers in 184. Anacreon, Ode IV, translated by "D. D." —— An account by "Democritus" of extravagant feasts in English history. Epigram by "Dactyl" on a seditious speech said to have been printed for Gilliver —hits at several booksellers.

August

188. Burlesque account by "T. T." of a journey to Wells. A criticism by "B. T." of Bladen's translation of Caesar's account of Briton. —— Anacreon, Ode V, translated by "D. D." Sarcasm on the style of the *London Journal.*

189. A pompous letter in the style of Henley. Two letters on the farce *The Stage Mutineers,* the second by "Philo-Musus." Letter on the vanity of titles, degrees, etc., by "Democritus." —— An obscure epitaph contributed by "Democritus." An epigram on a rapacious lawyer, by "Dullman Clericus."

190. Heading, lines from Pope. Letter on foolish medical fads, especially the use of mercury, by "Democritus." Suggestions for the new Chambers' *Dictionary.* Continuation by Bavius of his remarks

on newspapers (cf. 184, 187). A Latin "imitation" and a Latin "translation" of Anacreon, Ode IV, by "F. C." —— A contemptuous letter by "P. M." to the author of the songs in *The Devil of a Duke*. Verses on Cibber's erecting a booth in Smithfield.

191. Remarks by Bavius on Voltaire's "Letters concerning the English Nation," and a letter exposing Voltaire's inaccuracies regarding the Quakers, by "Ezra." Humorous letter asking Bavius to explain whether a bridle is part of a harness. Lines "To a Young Lady," by R. Savage. —— Note on the bridle letter, above. A letter in Irish dialect, by "Democritus," from an Irishman desiring to be king of Poland. An epigram on a priest and a lawyer, with one in reply by Maevius.

192. A letter by "Old England" on "Tindal's double apostasy." Translation by "Incog." of the obscure epitaph in 189, with a note by Bavius. Burlesque rules of conduct, by "Democritus." Lines: "A Riddle." —— Lines written at a horse-race, submitted by "E. B." An epigram on the lawyer of 189, by "Dullman." Lines: "The Divine of Taste." A further note on harness and bridle.

September

193. An attack on the *Free Briton,* especially for an article on education, by Maevius, with annotations by Bavius. —— Lines "The Valetudinarian," submitted by "Philo-Grubaeus Cantab."

194. Further discussion of newspapers, by Bavius. A letter on gossip, by "Democritus." Anacreon, Ode VI, translated by "D. D." —— A note on a picture of Christ dressed as a Jesuit, with an epigram by a Dominican, translated by Maevius, against Jesuits.

195. A letter by "Witch of Endor," attacking the shifting religious attitude of the *London Journal.* A letter by "Democritus," replying to his letter on gossip in 194. Lines to Mrs. Pritchard, by "R. S." —— A letter and lines satirizing the stupid young country squire, by "Simon Speechless."

196. Further material from John Gabriel (see 170 and *ante*). Another letter on "cutting for the simples," by "Democritus." Verses: "The Modern Goliah"—attack on free thinkers. —— An attack on the *Free Briton* by "P. P—re," for republishing easily accessible material. Letter in pompous language by "Sempronius," satirizing an Oxford preacher of the previous Sunday. Lines ridiculing a lady's literary taste.

October

197. An attack on inoculation by "Democritus," with a history of it, "pretended to be by Voltaire," added by Bavius. Lines: "To Miss, etc." —— Notes and an epigram on Henley. An obscure humorous note.

198. A letter from "Plain Dealer" attacking the *Journal* for its position in the theatrical quarrel. An application from "Matt. Mole" for a job as news writer, with hits at the Cibbers. Verses: "The Puppy-Pupil-Monger," contributed by "Damasippus." —— Notes to contributors. "Ode to Celia," by "R. S."

199. Sarcastic account of Tindall's life, as published by Curll. Another illiterate letter by "Democritus," on "cutting for simples." An epigram of Martial, translated by Maevius. —— Satire on Henley's puffs, by "Nicholas Stentor." An epigram of Martial, translated.

200. A print, "The Art of Trimming," with various interpretations, especially an application to the scandal of Eustace Budgell and Tindall's will, by Bavius. —— An ode to the Lord Mayor, by Maevius.

November

201. A review of Clifton's *State of Physics,* in general unfavorable, by "A. A." Further interpretation, in the form of a dialogue between members of the Society, of the picture in 200, satire on politics, church, South Sea Company, etc. Another interpretation by "H. W."—satire on newspapers, with note that it is erroneous. —— A letter from "Osborne" (the *London Journal*) protesting that he is a man, not a woman. An Ode to the Lord Mayor, by Maevius. A note to correspondents.

202. A letter on the state of the theatre. Cibber's birthday ode for 1733, with notes by Bavius. Laudatory epigram on Dr. Delamaigne, contributed by "Eusebius." —— Letter by "Moll Brazen Face" on a proposal to fill up Fleet-Ditch with old maids. Verses by Voltaire on the king of Poland, translated by Maevius.

203. A reply by "Laertius" to "A. A." on Clifton in 201. Letter on marriage by "I, per se I." The eighteenth idyll of Theocritus, translated by "Pastor Fido." —— A list of conundrums. An "Ode to the Poet Laureate," by Maevius. A note to correspondents.

204. Discussion of the scandal over Tindall's will, with notes by Bavius. —— Verses of Petronius, translated by "Eusebius." A note to correspondents, with a warning to the *Whitehall Evening Post* against piracy.

205. Attack on quacks, by "Aesculapius," with extended comment by Bavius. Epigram on the Budgell-Tindall scandal. —— Letter from "Plain-Dealer" commenting on Budgell's thinness of wit, with an epigram on the same point by "Conundrum." A humorous epitaph on a physician. Note concerning the "Epistle from a Nobleman to a Doctor of Divinity."

December

206. Further discussion of Tindall's will, which is reprinted. Verses: "The Two Thousand Pounds Bond." —— A passage from Jonson's *Poetaster,* as "advice to a Nobleman," the author of the epistle to a doctor of divinity.

207. Satire on church manners, by "Martha Meanwell." Conventional verses, by "Eusebius." A passage from the *Epistle of a Nobleman,* with comment. —— A reprint of the *Bee's* reply to the epigram on Budgell in 205, with resolutions by the Society. Epigram by "Poppy." A note to contributors.

208. The Budgell-Tindall scandal continued. —— An epigram on "Ward," in prison as a dog-poisoner, with a tragic anecdote on the subject. Verses by Maevius in reply to some in the *Daily Courant* on a benefit for Dennis.

209. A letter by "Philo-Clericus" on Christmas pie. Verses to the author of *The Epistle from a Nobleman.* —— The Budgell-Tindall scandal continued. Verses on attacks on the *Journal,* apropos of Budgell, signed ironically "E. B." Note to contributors.

1734

January

210. Attack on the Magazines for theft, with allusion to the Tindall scandal, by "Will Whimsy." A reply to "Miss Meanwell" in 207, by "Theophilus." Comment by Bavius on "Whimsy's" letter. "Epitaph on a Young Lady by Richard Savage, Esq." —— The New Year's Ode, and verses by the bell-man of St. James.

211. Notes by Bavius on Cibber's Ode. Burlesque articles of peace in the theatrical war. An epilogue to the *Adelphi* at Westminster School. —— An acrostic on Mary Hawker, contributed by "E. I." A prologue to the *Eunuch* at Cadington School.

212. Letter by "Townly" on church manners. The Tindall scandal continued. Lines: "The Mistake," by "P. P."—hits at Budgell, Curll, and Henley. —— Letter on the rise in price of French wines, with hits at the Dunces, especially Cibber.

213. Letter by "A. Z." in reply to the letter on Clifton in 201. A petition of the letter "H" for recognition. Lines ridiculing Cibber's Odes, by "I. B." —— A list of old Scotch military terms. Lines on certain medical remedies, by "Philanthropos."

214. Letter by "Jeremiah Gimcrack" on the relation between authors and booksellers, with comment by Bavius. Lines on King Charles' Day, by Maevius. —— Lines by "Dactyl" on verses in the *Bee* "in praise of adoption," apropos of the Tindall scandal.

February

215. An attack by "Atticus" on *The Lady's Revenge*. Lines from the *Odyssey*, translated by "Eusebius," with sarcastic comment and the same passage from Pope's translation, with notes, by Bavius. —— A prologue and epilogue to *The Keepers*, a ballad opera, with a depreciatory note.

216. Letter defending *The Lady's Revenge*, by "Terentianus." Note of a threatened attack on Swift, with a defence of him by his parishioners, libellous verses involved in the affair, and a note by Bavius. —— A list of the effects of "Brother Fannius," deceased (Lord Hervey). Translation of a Greek epigram.

217. Essay on praising people for what they take most pride in. The Tindall scandal continued. Epigram of Anacreon, translated by Maevius. —— Epigram on the Tindall scandal, by "Dactyl."

218. A defence of *The Lady's Revenge* by "Candidus," with reply by Bavius. —— A humorous account of the theatrical war.

March

219. Letter from "Tom Meanwell" asking the *Journal* to discuss questions of trade, and suggesting Fishery. Letter criticising Pope's poetry, with reply by Bavius, boasting of impartiality. Lines "On Florella," by "Eugenius." —— The Tindall scandal continued. Letter signed "L. Gilliver" on Theobald's remarks on "The Epistle on Verbal Criticism." Lines by Maevius on Henley.

220. Attack on a Greek emendation in the preface to Theobald's *Shakespeare*. The Tindall scandal continued. Epigram: "Short, but good, advice to E. B. Esq." [Budgell], by Maevius. —— Further analysis of Tindall's will, by Bavius. Lines by "Dactyl" on Budgell's medals in honor of Tindall.

221. Letter advising stage censorship, with attack on *Chrononhotonthologos* and the taste of the audience. Bavius on the necessity of delay in publishing letters; remarks on *The Lady's Revenge* and Theobald's preface to his *Shakespeare*. Lines: "An Epistle to the Lady Patroness." —— Lines by "Amen," the speech of the City Recorder to the Prince of Orange.

222. On fisheries, by "Tom Meanwell." The character of the University prig, by "Confusus Adeptus." Stanzas, by "Eugenius." —— Lines: "A Receipt to be Happy," political satire.

April

223. On the present state of the law, by "Tom Telltroth." The Tindall scandal continued. Lines: "To a Noble Lord [Hervey] on his late most incomparable Poem," by R. S." —— Lines on Budgell's medal in honor of Tindall, by "Dactyl." Epigram by Maevius.

224. On being quiet in church. Note by Bavius on the quarrel over *The Lady's Revenge,* and an abusive letter by "Baviophilus." Lines "To Mr. Maevius" by "J. W." —— Letter by "Bartholomew Minor" on an ogling clergyman. "The Monkey and Jupiter," a fable in verse by "R. P."

225. On Fisheries, continued by "Tom Meanwell." A prize ode on Tindall, examined. —— Lines to Mrs. Barbier (actress), contributed by "Philo-Histrio." Notice of a benefit for an actor named Rochelle.

226. An attack on "modern infidels"—"Tolands and Tindalls." Attack on electoral abuses. Comment on the Tindall Ode (225) continued. —— Letter from "J. T." and comment, satire on the *London Journal* ("Osborne"). A letter from E. Cooper (actress) begging interest in her benefit performance.

May

227. On the state of the law continued from 223. Description of a penniless poet in a garret by "Omicron." —— Letter of thanks from E. Cooper. Epigram by "Conundrum."

228. On criticising other men's wives, by "Tom Tell-troth." Lines: "The Prospect" by "Q. T." —— Letter signed ironically "Lewis Theobald," asking interest of the Freemasons in his benefit, with a cut. Lines by "Tweedledum Tweedledee" on T. Cibber's marrying Miss Arne.

229. Attack by "N. A." on Theobald's Greek citations in his preface. Further comment by Bavius, declaring Theobald led astray by admiration of Bentley. —— Comment on false Latin in an inscription printed in the *Daily Post,* by "Somebody." Letter on the excise, by "Abracadabra." Epigram by Maevius on Budgell and Tindall.

230. On the tobacco excise, by "Oliver Grub." Attack by "Atticus" on a "Survey of Public Buildings" in the *Register.* —— A vision of the wickedness of England and anger of God. Epigram by Maevius on party quarrels.

231. On gardens. The Tindall scandal continued, by "B. B." —— Epigram by "Dactyl," political satire.

June

232. Letter signed "Lew. Theobald," replying to the attack on his Greek emendations, with answer by Bavius. —— Reply to angry comments in the *Register* concerning the *Journal's* attack on the *Survey of Public Buildings.* Epigram by Maevius on "the Grub-street Architect."

233. Long criticism by Bavius of an installment of the *Critical Survey* in the *Register*. —— Epigram on the same subject, by Maevius.

234. Another letter from Theobald on his Greek emendations, with comment by Bavius. Anacreon, Ode VII, translated by "D. D." ——Reply by "N. A." to Theobald's strictures on his comments on the Greek emendations. Further comment on the *Register's* attack on the *Journal*. Epigram by Maevius on the same point.

235. Essay on assorted subjects, by "Will Whimsey." Further attack by Bavius on the *Critical Survey*. —— Political epigram by "Dactyl."

July

236. A burlesque of the *Critical Survey* by "Vitruvius Grubeanus." Further comment by Bavius. —— Paraphrase of a Latin distich, by "Garbagio de Torvi."

237. "The Critical Review . . . Examined." (To be cont.). —— Attack by Bavius on the *Critical Review*.

238. On the beauty of morning, by "Academicus." Continuation of "The Critical Review . . . Examined," by Mr. Hiram. Anacreon, Ode VIII, translated by "D. D." —— Lines on the marriage of a Mrs. Cash, worth £10,000. Verses by Maevius on *The Critical Survey*.

239. Mr. Hiram continued. Anacreon, Ode IX, translated by "D. D." —— Lines on the Duchess of Marlborough by "A. W."

August

240. A humorous will, moral satire, with remarks on attitudes toward death. Mr. Hiram continued. —— Bavius on the *Critical Survey*. An ode on the marriage of the Duke of Portland.

241. Mr. Hiram continued. Anacreon, Ode X, translated by "D. D." ——Attack on the author of *The Dramatic Sessions,* by "The Laesos." Epigram.

242. Poem "To Mr. Ellis" (the painter), said by the contributor to have been found on waste paper. Mr. Hiram continued. Inscription on a monument to the late Earl of Warwick. —— A reply to "The Laesos" in 241, by "Scriblerus Theatricus," author of *The Dramatic Sessions.* Anacreon, Ode XI, translated by "D. D."

243. Mr. Hiram continued. Lines by "Tom the Water-man," political satire, and allusion to Cibber and Henley. —— Reply by "The Laesos" to "Scriblerus Theatricus." Anacreon, Ode XII, translated by "D. D."

244. Burlesque will of a naturalist, signed "Jonathan Wimble." Mr. Hiram continued. "Verses to a young lady," by "Erronous."

—— Further attack by Bavius on the *Critical Survey.* Epigram on the same point, naming Ralph as the author.

September

245. Mr. Hiram continued. Epigram on Cibber, by Maevius. —— Bavius on the *Critical Survey* continued. Epigram on Ralph.

246. Satire on the bedside manner of an apothecary, by "John-a-Nokes." A burlesque of the confused and cryptic legal style, signed "Oliver Puzzle-Cause," and contributed by "W. R." Mr. Hiram continued. Anacreon, Ode XIII, translated by "D. D." ——Comment on the practice of reprinting material already published and easily accessible. One of Henley's advertisements, and notice of a puppet show, "Punch's Oratory." Epigram by "Dactyl" on pirating booksellers.

247. Letter denouncing the reprinting of standard works, with Rapin's *History* as an example—an attack on it, by "B. T." Mr. Hiram continued. Lines "An Impromptu." —— Bavius on the *Critical Survey,* continued. Lines: "On Wit"—attack on the Dunces.

248. The history of the case of John Goole and Margaret Hudson. Mr. Hiram continued. "An Epitaph, for Miss R. P." —— Reply by "W. H." to the verses "On Wit" in 247. Epigram on Ralph.

October

249. The Goole-Hudson case continued. Mr. Hiram continued. —— Reply to the verses answering those on Wit, in 248.

250. The Goole-Hudson case continued, with a note by Bavius. —— Anacreon, Ode XIV, translated by "D. D." An epigram from the *Daily Post* on Henley with comment.

251. Mr. Hiram continued. "The case of the proprietors of the stock of the York-buildings company." —— Humorous note on a sermon to be let off by a Rev. Mr. Musquet. Anacreon, Ode XV, translated by "D. D." Epigram on Henley, by Maevius.

252. Mr. Hiram continued. The York-buildings case continued. Anacreon, Ode XVI, translated by "D. D." —— Bavius on the *Critical Survey,* continued. Epigram by Maevius on Ralph.

253. Letter praising the actor Stephens at Covent Garden, and comparing him with Cibber and Quin, to their disadvantage, by "Somebody." Mr. Hiram continued. The York-buildings case continued. —— Ode to the Lord Mayor, by Maevius, with allusion to Cibber, and the quarrel with the *Register* over the *Critical Survey.*

November

254. Attack by "Patriophilus" on a French company at the Haymarket. Mr. Hiram continued. The York-buildings case continued.

—— A reply by "Outis" to the attack on Cibber in 253. Anacreon, Ode XVII, translated by "D. D."

255. Mr. Hiram continued. Defense of Stephens, the actor, by "Philo-Stephanus," with comment by Bavius on "Outis's" letter in 254. —— Lines on Gunsmith's Anodyne Pills, with a reply in verse by Maevius.

256. Mr. Hiram continued. A letter by "Laertius" on the treatment of female "vapors." Bavius on the birthday ode. —— Bavius on the Stephens-Outis quarrel. Anacreon, Ode XVIII, translated by "D. D."

257. Long attack on Ward's Pill and Drop, by "Misoquackus." Long prose obituary of Mrs. Grace Butler of Selmeston in Sussex. [Russel had been Rector of Selmeston.] —— Letter on the terms of the deed to a "small clay house"—satire on the legal difficulties of the poor. Note to contributors. Epigram on "Outis Junior," by "Conundrum."

December

258. Mr. Hiram continued. Letter by "Timothy Zeal," analyzing a letter he had found, which he thinks shows evidence of a great conspiracy. A burlesque love letter, contributed by "T. A." Anacreon, Ode XIX, translated by "D. D." —— The Outis controversy presented in doggerel by Maevius.

259. Announcement by Bavius that Ward has not replied to the attack in 257. An attack on Ward, by "Amiculus." Mr. Hiram continued. Lines: "The Gentleman," by Richard Savage. —— Criticism of N. Tindall's translation of Rapin, by "A Subscriber." Reply to "Misoquackus" by "the author of the Purging Sugar Plums." Letter by "Philanthopos" on the death of dogs which had been given Ward's Pills. Comment on a defence of Ward by Henley, with an epigram on the same point by "Conundrum."

260. Summary (with quotation) of an attack on Ward by Dr. Daniel Turner. —— On false notices of death in the dailies.

261. Letter defending Ward and answering "Misoquackus," by "Obadiah Anti-clysterpipus." Letter by "Philagathus" against Ward, but disagreeing with statements of Dr. Turner. Attack on Tindall's *Rapin* on account of omissions, by "Another Subscriber." Mr. Hiram continued. —— Anacreon, Ode XX, translated by "D. D."

1735

January

262. Answer by Joshua Ward to "Misoquackus" with affidavits to refute statements of the latter. —— Letter by "Isaac Bickerstaff,"

satirising Ward's methods of advertising. Epigram, in Latin and English, on Ward, by "U. C."

263. Letter by "Democritus" on several well-known quacks of the last generation. Cibber's New Year's Ode, with annotation by Bavius. —— Letter by "Hannah Housewife," thanking the *Journal* for its exposure of Tindall's *Rapin*.

264. A rebuttal of Ward's letter, with counter-affidavits. —— A letter by "Philanthropos," citing two cases in Ward's favor. Anacreon, Ode XXI, translated by " D. D."

265. Long personal attack on Matthew Tindall, with anecdotes to illustrate his manners and morals. —— Epigram in Latin and English on an expected royal infant, by "U. C."

266. Attack on Bentley's *Horace,* by "Torrentius." Attack on Ward by "Iatrophilus." Verses in Latin and English by "U. C." on the same point as those in 265. —— Letter by "Tom Tarr" urging the *Journal* to further attack on Popery and quackery. Lines by "Dactyl" on various attitudes toward King Charles' Day.

February

267. Letter by "Eugenius Philalethes," detailing a case history against Ward. Proposal for a lottery to get husbands for old maids, by "Democritus." Mr. Hiram continued. Verses by Savage to Walter Harte. —— Examination of some of Ward's evidence, and a case-history against him. Epigram by "Dactyl" on a King Charles' Day anecdote of the Calves Head Club.

268. The character of the city flirt, by "Z. S." —— A horse farrier's bill for attendance on a sick child. A long riddle in verse.

269. Satire on "entertainments," by "Arlequin Chef d'oeuvre." Essay on the endless talker. —— Lines : "A Dream. Inscribed to Mira." Lines "To the author of the Essays on Man," by "T. N."

270. Essay by "Democritus" on the evils of allowing young ladies to associate with servants. Letter from an old maid ("Meager Longchin") who wishes to enter the lottery proposed in 267. Letter attacking the scandalous Fleet parsons, by "Virtuous." Anacreon, Ode XXII, translated by "D. D." —— Notice of a suit by Ward against the *Journal.* Epigram on the celebration of January 30.

March

271. Letter by "Misokuon" demanding the extermination of dogs, because of danger of rabies. Mr. Hiram continued, with an answer to Hiram from the *Daily Journal.* Lines : "To Miss Waller." —— "An epigram on the Calves Head Club" (cf. 267 and 270).

272. Letter deploring the state of the stage and attacking a visit-

ing French company, by "True Briton," with a note by Bavius. Attack by "Orthodoxus" on a proposed translation of Josephus by Whiston, with a note by Bavius. Stanzas on rival French and English Harlequins. —— Letter in support of Hippisley and his daughter, about to make her debut. Note denying a statement by "Misokuon" in 271. Epigram in Latin and English on Walpole.

273. Letter attacking Middleton's "Dissertation" on printing. The bill of a lover's auction. Letter on a bill to regulate printing, especially against piracy and "new" editions, by "Appendix." —— Letter by "Philanthropos" in support of the actor Chapman's benefit. Epigram on Swift's leaving his estate to lunatics.

274. Letter on the value of the periodical essay in improving manners and taste, by "Philaretes." Letter by "Modulus" on legal regulation of the theatre. —— Request by "T. G." for information about a proposed *Geographical Dictionary*.

April

275. An attack on free-thinkers, with citations from an examination of a "Discourse of Free-thinking" of about 1715. —— Letter by "Lynceus Lilliput" on reducing spectacles, to show man his place in the world. Epigram by Maevius, with allusion to the Tindall scandal.

276. Criticism by "A. A." of proposals for a new Turkish history. The comment on the "Discourse of Free-thinking" continued. —— A letter in favor of dogs by "Philaretes," enclosing "Verses sent to a lady with a Lap Dog."

277. Another letter by "Lynceus Lilliput" on reducing spectacles. Letter on regulation of the theatre. Letter on the foulness of London streets. Anacreon, Ode XXIII, translated by "D. D." —— Lines by "Maevius Cornucopia" on famous cuckolds, submitted by "A. Z."

278. On the regulation of quacks. Anacreon, Ode XXIV, translated by "D. D." ——Epigram by Maevius, on Ward.

May

279. On the regulation of quacks, continued, by "Machaon." An attack on two new works of anatomy. On the *Discourse of Free-thinking*, continued. —— Burlesque petition of players against a bill to prohibit acting in places where liquor is sold. Epigram by "Conundrum" on drams and drama.

280. Reprint of a proposal of 1666 to rebuild certain London streets. Stanzas on Handel. —— Anacreon, Ode XXV, translated by "D. D."

281. On the solemnity of oaths. A quotation from Trapp on "Poetic Style," with a Latin paraphrase of Psalm 137. On Scotch schoolmasters by "G. G." On the *Discourse of Free-thinking* continued. —— A reply to "G. G." above.

282. On pretty fellows, by "Powder-Paste Plaister-crown." An ode by a young lady, "The Emulation," contributed by "A. B." (on the trivial education of women). ——Epigram on Ward's suit against the Journal, by "Dactyl."

283. The attack on Ward resumed; some of his claims examined, by "C. J." "A Song by a Young Lady." —— Note on "C. J.'s" letter. Anacreon, Ode XXVI, translated by "D. D."

June

284. A review of the quarrel with Ward, by Bavius. Remarks on *A Discourse of Free-thinking* continued. Lines: "Farinelli." —— Epigram: satire on Ward's suit, by "Conundrum."

285. "A short dissertation upon Puffs." A long list of satirical definitions. Lines: "From Martial." —— Lines: "On Farinelli."

286. On puffs, continued, by "Puffemoffius." "Some Odd Thoughts concerning Matrimony." On the treatment of physicians in China. —— One of the stanzas on Farinelli in 285, as submitted and as revised for publication. Discussion of a point of Latin, by "B. L." "A Song."

287. "Fanny: or Poetry and Paste. Inscribed to Mr. Pope." [On Lord Hervey.] —— Stanzas by B—n defending Harte against Ralph, as the "scribler of an Epistle to the Author of an Essay upon Reason." Satirical note on other newspapers.

July

288. On free-thinking continued. A suggestion to settle war by giving armies Ward's pills, by "Democritus." Stanzas: "Crura Ascititia Anglicé Stilts." ——Verses by Maevius on the death of the *Bee*. Notice of the death of several other papers.

289. Proposal for rebuilding Grub Street, by "Palladio Grubeano," satire on Cibber, Duck, Budgell, Henley, Ralph, etc. ——Ode, "Iris," by "Mr. R—l—s," with sarcastic note.

290. Abridgement of a pamphlet (1719) on the increase of London. —— Anacreon, Ode XXVII, translated by "D. D." Lines: "The Bite," apropos of Curll and Pope's Letters.

291. Attack on a poem "The Vision" published in the *Bee,* and said to equal Addison's in the *Spectator,* and also on another, "Stanislaus," by "Orthodoxus." Lines: "To Mr. T—," by "Amelia." ——

A receipt for composing a love letter. Notice in favor of a Mr. Dunne, whose reputation had been hurt by false arrest. Stanzas: "To the Author of Universal Beauty, a Poem."

292. On familiarity with ancient critics, with much allusion to Pope's "Essay on Criticism." —— Epigram on Curll.

August

293. Satire on medical writing, directed against the oculist Taylor, by "J. T." Letter by "S" praising Pope, but emending a line in the prologue to "Cato." A simile of Addison paraphrased in Latin, by "J. B." An epitaph by "T. W." —— An epilogue by Carey for *The Honest Yorkshireman.* Two epigrams on Curll. An epigram by "B. L."

294. On infidelity and providence. Latin verses to William Thompson, by Maevius. —— Tindall's "Philosopher's Prayer," versified.

295. On happiness, by "R. T." Letter in defense of the Irish, occasioned by the epigram on Thompson in 294, by "Impartial Love-Truth." —— An answer by Maevius to the preceding. Lines: "On a Pipe of Tobacco" by "G. S."

296. On Tindall and his prayer, an attack on the *Bee.* On one of the Latin poems on Tindall in the *Bee,* with notes by "Orthodoxus." —— Lines: "Youths that died to be by poets sung," satire on Budgell's prize poems on Tindall.

September

297. On vanity and flattery, by "R. T." Epigram by "P. W." —— The epitaph of Mrs. Cecil Talbot. Stanzas on anxiety, by "A. B. C."

298. On Tindall's "Philosopher's Prayer," continued. —— "A Fragment of Anacreon," by "Grubaeus Scriblerus."

299. "An Edict or Decree of the Goddess of Dullness"—special allusion to Cibber and Budgell. —— Epigram on seeing a miser at Vauxhall.

300. An attack on deists, with lines "On the Deists' Scheme of Fitness," by "R. T." —— A reply to a defense of "The Philosopher's Prayer" in the *Post-Boy,* by Bavius. Epigram on the same subject, by Maevius.

October

301. On the abuses of installment publication by "Incog," with note by Bavius. Moral essay: a vision of the temples of two goddesses, Pleasure and Health. Verses by "W. B." to a young lady in the country. —— An imitation of Boethius, by "Anicius Severinus Boethius."

302. Another Latin prize poem on Tindall, with comments by Bavius. —— "The Philosopher's Prayer," reprinted exactly, and the *Journal's* rimed version. Letter by "Anti-philos Precat" satirizing Budgell and the "Prayer."

303. On managing a husband, by "Martha Love-Rule," with a passage from *Hudibras*. —— The "Prayer" reprinted again, with notes by Bavius.

304. The third-prize poem on Tindall, with notes by Bavius. —— Letter "To the late authors of the *Bee*," on the "Prayer." Lines by Maevius: "A Dialogue between Prompterus and Pufferus Secundus" [the *Prompter* and the *Bee*].

305. Letter by "F. T." on the persecution of a married man by his mistress. The letter to the *Bee*, continued by Bavius. "Song." —— "An Ode on his Majesty's Birthday," not by the laureate.

November

306. Cibber's Ode, with notes by Bavius. —— A puff of the *Bee* in the *Daily Journal*, with comments, and an epigram on the same point by Bavius.

307. On the "Philosopher's Prayer" (to be cont.). Song: "The Adieu to the Spring Gardens." —— A puff of the *Prompter* "paraphrastically illustrated," and verses on the same subject by Maevius, with a note on the Bee.

308. On the "Philosopher's Prayer" continued. Stanzas on "the happy mean"—allusions to Pope and Cibber. —— A Latin epigram from the *Prompter* attacking Bavius, with attacks on its false Latin by Bavius.

309. A reply by "A. N." to "Martha Love-Rule" in 303. —— A remedy for bed-bugs, by "X." A political epigram by "A. B."

December

310. On wig-boxes, by "Oxoniensis," general satire. Attack on the oculist, Dr. Taylor, by "Peter Queer." —— Letter by "Philo-Grubeus" on Henley and the "Prayer." Epigram by "Philo-Martial" on the *Bee* and the *Prompter*, Budgell and Hill. Note by Bavius on the first essay.

311. Two more Latin poems on Tindall, with comment and reply by Bavius to attacks in the *Prompter*. —— Letter complaining about the space given up to the quarrel with the *Bee*, by "Jack Nab." A defense of Taylor by "Tim Justice" with a note by "J. H." [Huggonson]. Epigram on biblical commentators.

312. Attack on Henley for his defense of the "Prayer," by "Philo-Grubaeus." Attack on foreign actors and singers by "Staunch

Old Briton." An ode on "Tobacco" by "Gabriel John," burlesque of Cibber. —— Further reply by Bavius to hostile epigrams in the *Prompter*.

313. "A Rhapsody in Praise of Garrets," by "Oxoniensis." Two more prize poems on Tindall, with notes by Bavius, also a Latin epigram on the same subject with comment by Bavius. A letter from "H. R.," deriding the Tindall contest, and enclosing satirical lines. Puff by "W. L." of new Latin school texts by "Mr. Stirling." —— Remarks on the *Prompter's* epigrams, continued, by Bavius. A note to contributors.

1736

January

314. On the difficulties of writing essays, with a list of useless subjects. "To a gentleman on his refusing a visit from some young ladies," by "D. C." —— Ode to the Mayor, by Maevius. On the *Prompter's* Latin, continued, by Bavius. A verse advertisement of a lost dog. Note of Bavius' resignation.

315. An attack on Curll's edition of Pope's Letters, by "D. L." Attack on a French dancer, by "Cato." Cibber's New Year's Ode, with notes. Satirical letter on the quality of theatrical entertainments and public taste. —— Comment by Bavius on false Latin, and abuse of him, in the *Prompter*.

316. Taylor's preface to his treatise on the eye, with a letter by "Peter Queer" attacking Taylor. "An excellent new Ballad," by "Simon." —— Bavius' speech of resignation. Contemptuous letter from "D. D." on Curll. Epigram on the *Prompter* and *Daily Journal* by "Dactyl."

317. Satire on the newspapers, by "Histrio-Aspis." Reply by J. Taylor to "Peter Queer." "An Epitaph on Jacob Tonson." —— Bavius' reply to the attacks of the *Prompter*. An epigram on the *Prompter's* false Latin, by "Philosophus."

318. "A Preface upon Prefaces," by "Oxoniensis." Verses to the memory of Mrs. Eliz. Frankland. —— Bavius in quarrel with the *Prompter*, continued.

February

319. Essay upon Conversation, by "J. T." Political epigram, by "Cluvienus." —— Bavius on the quarrel with the *Prompter*, continued.

320. A list of errors in the translation of Rapin, by "Philalethes." Letter to the *Prompter*, by "Candidus" (submitted by Bavius) on various old quarrels of the *Journal*. —— Further attack on the "Prayer" and the *Prompter's* defense of it, by Bavius.

321. On the pronunciation of *Cleomenes,* etc., by "Philellen." A passage of Horace, paraphrased by "Palaeophilus." Explanation by "Outis Junior" of the meaning of "Outis," with an editorial note. "To Mrs. Cibber, An Ode," by "Theatricus." —— The quarrel with the *Prompter,* continued by Bavius.

322. On the decay of learning, and pedantry. —— On the quarrel over two rival plays, Miller's *Man of Taste* and Popple's *Double Deceit,* by "Neither-side."

March

323. On marrying helpless insane patients to members of the family of the doctor who has charge of them, by "Farewell." On the Popple-Miller quarrel, by "Neither-side." Lines by "Endymion," "An Astronomical Paradox." —— Bavius' quarrel with the *Prompter,* continued. Defence of *The Man of Taste* against the *Prompter.*

324. Account by "Puff" of attempts to write a poem, with a prose poem on "Merlin." "The Physical Cause of a Lunar Eclipse," by "Philo-Mathematicus." Reasons against the repeal of laws on witchcraft, by "T. B.". —— Bavius *vs.* the *Prompter,* continued. Note by J. H. [Huggonson] on the Popple-Miller quarrel. Humorous paraphrase of *Integer vitae.*

325. On errors in Rapin, by "Philalethes." A dissenting "Call renewed from the City to the Country" for the repeal of the Test Act. Request by "Common Sense" that the *Journal* drop the quarrels over the "Prayer" and *The Double Deceit,* with editorial reply. —— Note by Huggonson to Popple. Letter by "A. B." praising new prints by Rysbrack. An advertisement by Hippisley of his benefit.

326. Attack on amateur actors on the public stage (apropos of an experiment by Aaron Hill), submitted by "Meanwell." Note by "J. H." on Popple's conduct and manners. —— Bavius *vs. Prompter,* continued. A receipt to make "neat Port," to supply the place of gin, by "B. I."

April

327. Proposals to tax theatre tickets and use the income to free Christian slaves. "An epistle from a young gentleman at Bath." —— Note by J. H. on the manners of Popple and of C. H. (Charles Hill). Letter by J. English on the acting of Charles Hill in *Zara.* An epigram on Cibber, in answer to one in the *Daily Journal.*

328. Proposals, etc., continued from 327. On the appropriation of church property by the state, by "T. B." —— Notice of the theft by the *Post Boy* of verses from the *Journal.* Lines by "Common Sense" on seeing Pope at Pasquin.

329. Attack by "B. T." on Bentley's emendation of the classics. Letter on leaving estates to charity. —— Satirical letter by "Pow-

der-Paste Plaister-Crown," enclosing a model love letter. Note that Pope had not attended *Pasquin*. "To the East Wind," by "B. B."

330. Pasquin examined. On Quaker's tithes, by "T. B." "To Arethusa," by "Endymion." —— Reprint of a history of plots against royalty, of 1571.

331. Reply to attacks on Rapin. Advertisement by the actor Stoppelaer of his benefit. Notice of successful operations on the eye by Dr. Taylor. —— Mock advertisement of an auction of silly poems. Note to contributors.

May

332. Pasquin examined (continued from 330), by "Marforio." Latin and English lines to the Princess Augusta, by "A. Q." and "L. C." —— Remarks on Rapin concluded, by "Caledon" ("A Vindication of the Antiquity of the Scottish Nation").

333. On Greek accent, by "Prosodiophilus." On confinement of the sane in mad houses to get money from them, by "Phileleutherus." Lines on "The Astronomical Paradox" by "Endymion" (cf. 323). —— The Popple-Miller quarrel reviewed.

334. On errors in Rapin, by "Philalethes." On authorized editions of the Bible, by "A. B.". Lines: "An Epistle to Mr. Pope" and "A Rhapsody." —— The Popple-Miller quarrel continued. A burlesque petition from wives of shoemakers, apropos of "cobbling" plays.

335. "Hibernus" on false patriotism, apropos of Rapin and Scotch antiquity. On burlesque pedantic quarrels among Oxford students, by "Flat-Cap-Copper-Nose." Lines by "T. C." on a new bust of Dryden. —— The Popple quarrel continued. A Ballad on Quakers' tithes.

June

336. "Hibernus" continued from 335. Letter from "Gratus" on the successful use of a remedy published in 309. —— The Popple quarrel continued. Stanzas "On Marriage."

337. A children's petition to Parliament (1669) for relief from severity of school discipline, abridged. Verses: "To the Prince," submitted by "Puff." —— On the Fleet parsons, by "T. S."

338. "The Mad Doctor, A New Ballad," in Latin and English, by "S. B." Remarks by "J. H." [Huggonson] on the ballad on Quakers' tithes in 335. —— On the attractions of Vauxhall, by "Freedom."

339. The children's petition, continued. —— An account of some of Ward's "cures." Lines, "Seven Wonderful Cures." Note from "Freedom" promising another contribution.

July

340. "Philalethes" on Rapin. A letter on Vauxhall, by "Freedom." Attack on charges of admission at the theatres, by "Haberdasherus." —— An attack on *Fog's* and the *Daily Post,* which had attacked two clergymen.

341. On legal and religious oaths. —— Answer by Joseph Clutton, apothecary, to a defence of Ward by his brother, William Ward.

342. On matrimony, by "Eusebius," illustrated by a Turkish tale. —— Clutton's answer to Ward, reprinted complete, including the section in 341.

343. On Scotch antiquities, continued, by a new correspondent, taking the side of "Caledonius" against "Hibernus." Account of the successes of the oculist Taylor. Notice of a suit for damages against Taylor, won by the plaintiff. —— A Ward case history (numbered LI), by "M-Q." Stanzas on the marriage of the Prince of Wales. Notice to correspondents.

344. On Scotch antiquities, concluded, by "John of Lochaber," (this discussion having grown out of criticisms of Rapin). —— Joseph Clutton to John Smith, on subject of Ward. Notice to correspondents.

August

345. Criticism by "Thomas Didymus" of Whiston's *Primitive Eucharist Reviv'd.* On Vauxhall manners, by "Anticonstabularius." Stanzas on Senesino. —— A case from Clutton's pamphlet against Ward. A Ward case (LII).

346. On Rapin and Scotch antiquities (to be cont.). Attack on Dr. Taylor by "Fair-play." A note on Horace, by "T. W." —— Ward case (LIII). Reply by Clutton to an attack in the *Advertiser.* Note to correspondents.

347. Oration on Dullness by "Sir John Thickskull." —— Reply by Clutton to a second letter by William Ward (to be concl.).

348. The discussion of Scotch antiquities continued. Epistle to Chesterfield by Carey, (reprinted, being out of print; contains praise of Pope). —— Clutton's letter in 347 concluded.

September

349. On Scotch antiquities, continued from 348. On cheating and gambling, by "Philo-Innocentiae." —— Ward case (LV), contributed by "A. J."

350. On the death of the *Prompter,* with a review of the quarrel with it. —— Ward case LVI. A notice by Thomas Barber attacking Mrs. Mapp, bonesetter. Lines on Semiramis, by the author of "Friendship in Death."

351. Review of Clutton's campaign against Ward, with a list of burlesque case-histories, ridiculing Ward's claims (to be cont.). "Epigram Extempore" and "Verses on Second Thoughts," on the "E—l of B[urlingto]n, by [Hervey]." —— On Scotch antiquities, concluded, by "Philalethes."

352. Satirical letter on obscenity in the theatre. Ward case LVII, by M. Rymes. A note to distillers, by "Ephemeristes." Letter to Clutton concerning one of his case histories. Two Odes in imitation of Horace. —— Lines "Of the Praise of Tobacco," (parody of Aaron Hill). Threatening letter to Huggonson by "G. F.," apropos of attacks on Ward, with reply by Huggonson. Two epigrams on Hervey, addressed to Burlington.

353. Satirical letter on curing madmen by matrimony, an attack on the abuse of the insane, by "Arcularius Buckthorne." Answer to "Ephemeristes" in 352, by "Peter Open-law." Horace I, 5, paraphrased, by "A Trueblue, Esq." —— A note and couplet in reply to verses on Hervey in 352. A verse fable on Hervey.

October

354. "Hibernus" on Scotch antiquities. Verses on punch, by "L. Love-punch." —— Ward case LVIII, by "Didymus." Attack by "A. B. C." on a proposed *History of China,* to be published by Watts, in opposition to one by Cave. Note on the quarrel with the *Prompter.*

355. Attack by "A. B." on Ward's pretensions. On an act concerning the relations between attorney and client, by "B. A." Stanzas, "Punch's Dying Speech." —— "Philo-Charity," proposing a benefit for victims of an accident at the Covent Garden Theatre. An epigram, "To — Esq., F. R. S."

356. John Colson, describing the plagiarism of a book of his by a Dr. Philip Nichols. Stanzas by "X. X.": "The Looking Glass." —— Letter by "A. B." on the acting of a play at the request of Mrs. Mapp. Ward case LX.

357. Reply by "C. D." to the letter on Mrs. Mapp in 356. On a mill to grind out syllogisms, by "Sawney the Scot." Stanzas: "A Dream," by "M. G." —— A note on Latin scansion, by "Phil-Iambus." Ward case LXI.

November

358. Cibber's Birthday Ode, with notes. —— Ward case LXII. Lines on a new book, *The Antiquities of Surrey.* Notice of receipt of orders to stop advertisements of two punch-houses.

359. "A. B." in reply to "C. D." in 357, on Mrs. Mapp. Stanzas

by "A. B." on a distiller's having to give up his trade and go into wine. —— Detailed account of the history of a Ward case already published.

360. Letter congratulating the *Journal* for repressing a poem on punch (the cause of punch advertisements being cancelled), and citing passages from Cheyne on the evils of punch drinking. —— An extract from Fuller's *Pharmacopœia,* opposed to quotations from Cheyne.

361. Letter praising Mrs. Cibber and comparing her with her rival, Mrs. Clive, by "Reader of Speculations." The evils of libertinism, by "J. D." A passage of Juvenal, translated by "A. Q." —— Epigram on Mapp, Taylor, and Ward.

December

362. "Hibernus" on antiquities. —— Letter by "R. S." congratulating the *Journal* for its attacks on quacks, with editorial note.

363. Letter from Theophilus Cibber, defending his wife against the charge of over-ambition. Attack on Watts' *History of China,* by "P. L." —— Defence of Taylor by "S. S.," with editorial note. Note to contributors.

364. "Pharmacopola Rusticus" on the fad for specifics. Passages from the new *History of China.* —— "Mediator" on the Cibber-Clive quarrel. Stanzas: "Advice to Mrs. Clive," by "Humphrey Oddwit."

365. Attack by "P. L." on Watts' *China* continued. On the rapacity of men-midwives, by "Philopauperis." —— Letter from John Watts defending his *China,* and attacking Cave's methods of advertising.

366. "Haberdasherus," citing examples of actors who had surrendered favorite parts for the good of the theatre. Horace, IV, 5, imitated. —— Examination of a new life by Curll of the Rev. Mr. George Kelly. Lines on a quarrel between the *Craftsman* and the *Gazetteer.*

1737

January

367. "P. L." on Watts' *China,* continued. "Haberdasherus," replying to an attack in the *Daily Journal* on his letter in 366. —— On oaths, by "A. Z." Punning distich in Latin, by "Simon Lovewit."

368. Reply by "Amicus" to attack in the *Daily Journal* on Giffard, actor-manager, apropos of the Cibber-Clive quarrel. The New Year's Ode, with notes. —— On false Latin in the dedication of a new edition of Eutropius. Editorial support of "Haberdasherus," in quarrel with the *Daily Journal.* Burial statistics from Edinburgh.

369. Notice of the plagiarizing by "G. Smith" of an astronomical essay by Thomas Wright. On coffee house conversations, by "P. M." On a society of Puffers, with hits at Henley, Ward, etc., by "Pufferus." —— Further reply by "Haberdasherus" in quarrel with the "Occasional Prompter" in the *Daily Journal,* with editorial note. Satirical epigram on Cibber, by "E. S."

370. On the evils of spirit-drinking, by "A. B." —— Note apropos of the new edition of Eutropius. The quarrel with the *Daily Journal* continued.

February

371. In defense of Punch, replying to the *Journal,* 360. In defense of certain oaths, by "Philorchus." "Philo-Patriae," attacking treatment of condemned prisoners in Newgate. —— Reply by George Smith to attack in 369.

372. Attack by "Villiomarus" on the methods of Stirling's school edition of Persius. A note on tax legislation under Charles II, by "U. B." Ballad: "A Tale of a Tub." —— Quarrel with the *Daily Journal* continued. Stanzas: "On Colley Cibber's printed Case."

373. "A Modern Polite Conversation," by "J. B." —— Answer by Thomas Wright to George Smith. The quarrel with the *Daily Journal* continued.

374. On Latin emendations, by "A. Z." The "Conversation" in 373 reprinted. —— Attack on the *Journal* for its malice, by "Honestus," with editorial reply. Latin lines on the death of D. Talbot, by "Vice Cotis." Epigram: "A Dialogue at Court." Latin distich.

March

375. "Empirico-Mastix," in censure of Stirling. Attack by "Legion" on the publishers of Rapin. Attack on harlequinades, by "Shakespeare, Jonson, etc." On the Wright-Smith quarrel, by "Philo-Filch." An epilogue to *King John,* as amended by Cibber. —— The quarrel with the *Daily Journal* continued.

376. Defence of "Lun" (Rich) from attack in the *Daily Journal,* by "A. B." Horace, I, 24, imitated by "N. Y." Lines: "To Mr. Pope." —— On Henley's defence of the *Daily Journal.* Reply by "Phil Aret." to "Phil Filch," in 375. "Ode on Miss A——," and verses to the same person.

377. On Oldmixon's *Lives of the English Bishops,* by "A. B." Attack on Dr. Taylor. Story of a young man who thought he was marrying money. —— On theatre manners, by "Hat Off." Reply by Smith to Wright. Further remarks on the *Hyp Doctor's* defence of the *Daily Journal.*

378. Attack on Stirling, by "Empirico-Mastix." Reply to "Phil Aret." by "Phil Filch." Reply by "Haberdasherus" to the defence of Rich in 376. Stanzas on Pope's imitation of Horace, IV, 1, by "Philo Moravius." —— The reply to the *Hyp Doctor* continued. Lines: "A Farewell to Friendship," by "Philo-Grubeus." Notice that "Fatal Curiosity," a new play, is in reality an old one.

379. On diet, especially the evil effect of tea, by "South Briton." —— On annuities, by "The Afflicted Widow." On the Wright-Smith quarrel, by "Tom Tell-troth."

April

380. Letter in praise of the clergy, by "Eusebius Old-fashion." On a bill against rogues and vagabonds. —— Psalm 38, in heroic couplets.

381. "Part of the Preface to the Memoirs of the Society of Grub-street, which will be published next week." —— "Mercator Londinensis" on the South Sea Annuities. Latin lines on Philip Hardwick, by "U. C."

382. On marriage and love, by "Philo-Math." Continuation of discussion of a pending bill (see 380) by "E. O." Horace III, 13, paraphrased. —— A note on deciphering manuscripts. On the death of the *Daily Journal*.

383. Attack on the "Mad Doctor," who undertook to cure all insanity, by "Jack the Giant-Killer." A passage from Claudian, translated by "A. Q." —— On a flagrant puff of Ward's cures.

May

384. A suggestion by "Scenicus" to improve pantomime, suggested by a passage from Apuleius, here reprinted. Violent reply to "Jack the Giant-Killer," by "The Advertiser," with editorial note. —— Two epitaphs on Gay, one of them Pope's. A puff of Ward, with comment.

385. On interest on annuities, by "J. T." A cure for mad dog bite by "R. M." and "On the Bite of a Mad Dog," by "P. L." On inconsistencies in Whiston's proposed *Josephus,* by "A: Z." —— A satirical dialogue on the story of Jack the Giant-Killer.

386. On Quaker's tithes, by "E. O." On annuities, by "A. A." On pastorals, by "R. S." —— Notes to contributors.

387. A discourse on the best method of teaching Latin, by James Pearce, submitted by "E. M." Reply by "The Letter Writer" (Jack the Giant Killer) to "The Advertiser" in 384. —— On the quarrel with the "Mad Doctor," (The Advertiser).

June

388. Reply by "B. J." to "E. O." on Quakers in 386. On Pearce's Latin method, by "M. E." —— Lines: "Calista to Sempronia" (apparently apropos of the Abergavenny scandal of 1730; Lady Abergavenny was "Calista").

389. On bad manners and morals of servants by "E. O." On a puff of a new book on "Dialling," by "Sciographicus." Arguments used by Quakers against tithes. —— A defence of his Latin method, by James Pearce. Stanzas on the previous Sunday, submitted by "J. L."

390. "E. O." on Quaker's tithes. —— Continuation of discourse on manuscripts in 382.

391. A whimsical letter by "And per se And" in comment on a late attempted suicide, on the latest quarrels of the *Journal,* and enclosing a "Song." An obituary of "the Lady Geneva" [gin]—satire on the excise. —— An obscure letter from "Ladies" of various London parishes to their friends at New Tunbridge Wells.

392. Verse epistle from a naval officer at Jamaica, submitted by "C. F." The letter of "And per se And" in 391, continued by "Et Caetera." —— A ballad by a mantua maker, submitted by "A. B."

July

393. Attack on Quakers and Papists, by "A. Z." Arbuthnot's epitaph on Col. Chartres, done into Latin by a boy of Charleston, S. C. On surveying, by "A. B." —— Extempore verses by Stephen Duck, "Agar's Wish," submitted by "Y. Z." Notes to contributors.

394. Reply to "A. B." in 393 by "C. D." The whim of "And per se And" in 391, continued by "Cipher o." On puffs of various surgeons, by "Anti-pufferus." A humorous letter of proposal signed "A Cock," submitted by "Peregrine Viator." —— A whimsical letter on "Dialling," by "Gnomonicus."

395. On deciphering manuscripts. Reply to "A. Z." in 393, by "C. V." On methods of instruction in Latin, by "E. English." A song in "The Orphan," translated into Latin. —— Reply to "Sciographicus" in 389, by "John Eager." Notes to contributors.

396. On the drug, manna, by "P. L." A passage from *Pastor Fido* translated. —— A note on the reply to "Sciographicus," by "Sam Sharp." Note on false Latin in the *Gazetteer.* Notes to contributors.

August

397. On the current lottery, by "N. P." "The Attorney's Clerk, An Eclogue." —— Letter by "J. T." on the phrase "Grape Street, otherwise Grub Street." Reply to "Sam Sharp," by "John Eager."

398. On the liberties of Gentlemen Commoners at Oxford, by "Occidit." On Quaker's tithes, by "E. O." —— Illiterate footman's letter, by "B. G." Lines on an interview with a young lady, and upon saluting a young lady.

399. Lines, submitted by "E. G.," with editorial comment. A scheme for disposing of a list of old maids in the Lottery, by "The Proprietors." A Latin epigram, submitted by "Eumenides." Pastoral stanzas. —— A reply to "J. T." in 397 by "W. P."

400. On alterations in the prayer book, by "J. F." (this letter a year old). Verses in Latin and English by "U. C." on controversies between Catholics and Distenters. A ballad of the time of Charles I, "London's Ordinary." —— "Verses wrote at Crambo" (i.e. the rimes given and the lines filled in).

September

401. Letter from "Patience Puzzle-head" on interpretations of the phrase "figure cypher." Attack by "R. T." on "Eumenes," who had contributed Latin epigrams in translation to the papers. An Ode by a "Sea Chaplain." —— Epigram on Ward and Henley, by "G. S."

402. On Marriage. Ode on the text: "I believe in one God." —— "A Panegyric on a Louse, in the Style of Milton."

403. The biography of an upstart, by "I Knowman." "Janus. An Ode," on the birth of the Princess Augusta. "The Comet. A New Song," and an epigram on the death of the Lord Chancellor, both submitted by "Eusebius Redivivus." —— Epitaph on a fawn named Fanny, with editorial note.

404. Reply to the article on Gentleman Commoners in 398, by "T." On the lottery, by "D. M." On methods of teaching Latin, by "E. M." —— Conclusion to a ballad in 316, by "Simonides."

405. "Remarks on the Bridge Lottery," by "M." Reply to "E. M." in 404, by "M. E." Letter by "J. B.," author of the epitaph in 403, enclosing stanzas "To Miss H—." —— Letter by "A Bankrupt" against publicity given bankrupts. Lines on the piracy of the magazines.

October

406. Attack on Dr. Morgan's *Moral Philosopher* [free-thinking], by "Poplicola." On Latin teaching methods, by "E. M." and also a reply by him to "M. E." —— Lines on Mr. Ba—t's erecting almshouses to atone for his vices. Note to contributors.

407. On the excise, by "J. G." with a note by "T. O." Another whimsical love letter, contributed by "Peregrine Viator." A song, "Celia in Love" by "Eusebius." —— Further attack on magazine piracies.

408. Correspondence of Tillotson and William Penn, contributed by "B. J." —— A series of Henley's puffs. Stanzas on "The Burlesque Orator," contributed by "A. O. Anonymous." Note to contributors.

409. A dialogue of six characters, Misses Tattle, Clack, etc., by "H. B." —— Argument by "D. D." that the Penn-Tillotson letters did not show that Quakers were not apt to turn Catholics.

November

410. Continuation by "T. O." of his note in 407 (attack on managers of the *Evening Post*). Cibber's birthday ode, with notes. —— Note to contributors.

411. On a new edition of Dale's *Pharmacologia* (to be cont.) Stanzas: "The Insipid Triumviri"—attack on Cibber, submitted by "A. O." —— A list of Henley puffs.

412. On Dale, continued. "An Answer to Caleb D'Anvers' Court Ballad," communicated by "A. O. Anonymous." —— A defence of "A. O. Anonymous" against attacks by Henley in the *Daily Post*.

413. A long poem describing an entertainment in Yorkshire, in honor of the king's birthday. —— Notice of a death due to Ward's medicines. A list of Henley puffs.

December

414. On proposals for Garland's *Geographical Dictionary*, by "L. P." "Lines to Miss H—ll," ("written by a deceased author, and communicated by Mr. A. O.") —— More Henley puffs. Satirical letter on Henley by "The Man in the Moon."

415. Answer by Garland to the article in 414. Continuation of the life of an upstart (see 403) by "Know-man." —— An account "of some late comical transactions at the Oratory [Henley's]." A note to contributors.

416. "Occidit" on Gentleman Commoners (see 404). Illiterate letter "Wittness Rob. Browne" apropos of the account of Henley's Oratory in 415. Comic lines, an invitation to a birthday. —— Further account of the Oratory. Stanzas: "Monsieur D—'s Address . . . [at] Stationers Hall, on his appearing in full Court Mourning."

417. Middle section of the Preface to *The Memoirs of Grubstreet* (see 381). —— A list of Henley puffs. Lines in Latin and English on having neither supper nor credit, by "A. B." "and my chum."

418. The Preface to the *Memoirs* concluded, and signed Bavius. —— Announcement of the *Literary Courier of Grub-street*, and directions to contributors.

1738

January 5

1. Remarks on the cessation of the *Journal*, with reasons for its decline, and a detailed account of the new policy of the *Courier*, by "Eph. Quibus." An attack by John Huddleston on a Spanish grammar. A New Year's Ode in imitation of the Laureate. Verses by "A. B.", "The Lady's Lap-dog."

2. Tacitus' account of Nero's burning Rome, in Gordon's translation, with discussion of causes of great fires and notes of errors by Gordon. "The Elbow Chair. An Ode," by "Indolens." Lines on the death of the Queen. On Henley's selling bound files of the *Hyp-Doctor*.

3. A section of the statement of policy in 1, reprinted with a flattering letter from "R. C." comparing the *Courier* with other papers. Reply to "Occidit" in the *Journal* on Gentleman Commoners, by "Kin-janges Mn-yatts." Letter to "T. B." by "R. R." on Gordon's *Tacitus*. Latin lines *In obitum Reginae*, by "E. J." Stanzas deriding Cibber as laureate, by "W. C."

4. On the character of a prime minister, translated from the Spanish. Letter "To Mr. R. R." on Gordon's *Tacitus*. More Latin lines on the death of the Queen.

February

5. On the faults of boarding schools, by "E. M." Reply by "Rob. Browne," an associate of Henley, to an attack on lines in the *Journal*, in an illiterate letter and verses. On giving tips ("veals") to servants, by "A. B." Verses, by "A. O. Anonymous" on Mrs. C—P—s (apparently a prostitute) turning Catholic.

6. An attack on some of Bentley's emendations of Horace, by "T. B." A reply "To Mr. T. B." by "R. R." on the subject of Tacitus.

7. A note by old Oxford contributors on the difficulty of getting the *Courier* at Oxford, with a note by "Eph. Quibus" on "foul play from booksellers." Another letter on Gentleman Commoners, by "H." Attack by "R. C." on a note on the *Aeneid,* in the *Craftsman.* Stanzas: "The Lawrel, written by an Oxford Hand, 1730, To Dean S—t in Dublin. Communicated by A. O. Anonymous." Note to contributors, by "Eph. Quibus."

8. Criticism of one of the Latin epitaphs on the Queen, by "Philocalus." On a plan to improve the linen trade, by "W. H." Lines on "The Worm Powder Operator," communicated by "A. O. Anonymous," with a couplet from *The Dunciad*, and addressed to Pope.

March

9. A reply to Garland's defence of his *Geographical Dictionary* (see the *Journal*), by "L. P."

10. Letter by "Bossamius" asking for copies of the *Courier* at Oxford. Letter on incivility to strangers in church, by "Paul Crape." Attack on a new method of short-hand, by "Abathes." Lines "To the Memory of Ann Rose. . . . Communicated by A. O. Anonymous." A reply by Bavius to "R. C.," who had attacked the *Journal* and also the social manners of scholars. Epigram on a new comedy, *The Nest of Plays*.

11. "Publicola" on proposals for a second volume of Miller's *Gardener's Dictionary*. "R. C.," in reply to Bavius. Letter by "P. P." on a false news item in the *Advertiser*.

12. An attack by "Baruglosse" on a new type of schools called academies, for boys of the lower classes. Reply by Bavius to "R. C." Attack on Solomon Lowe's *Latin Grammar* by "Alexander Doughty."

13. A list of terms of measure used in trade, by Solomon Lowe, as a specimen passage in a supplement to his *Mnemonicks*. A reply by "P. P." (see 11) to a defense in the *Advertiser*.

April

14. An admonition of Pope for "profaneness, which has lately crept into his works," by "Septuagenarius." Lines "To a very old bachelor, intending to marry a very young maid," by "Anonymous." Notice to contributors (who will have to pay to get their letters published).

15. Letter by "C. E." on mad dog bites (see *Journal* 385).

16. Poem from Congreve's *Love for Love* (not so credited), with a Latin translation. Letter from "Nonsense" defending nonsense, signed "N." Attack by "R. H." on a letter in *Weekly Common Sense*, libelling "a young nobleman." Editorial note on Solomon Lowe, who had complained in the *Advertiser* of his treatment in the *Courier*.

17. Attack on a sculpture on a new building in the Inner Temple. "Prologue designed for the sixth night of Mr. Thompson's play" [*Agamemnon*], submitted by "A. Z."

May

18. A series of letters on Puffing. Lines "To a Young Lady," by "K."

19. Letter criticising the *Courier* for its lack of political correspondence, by "Cha. Friendly." A dedication to a treatise, "Reasons against a War." Lines "Upon Handel's Statue being placed in Vauxhall.

20. Story of the siege of a house whose occupant refused to allow foreclosure of a mortgage, in military terms.

21. On a treaty between France and Spain, by "Z. Z." A French political epigram translated by a young boy, submitted by his father "Nat. Doubt," with editorial comment.

June

22. "Mr. Pope's Journey to Oxford. In an epistle to . . . the E. of B—n, versified." Lines "To the Rev. Mr. Foster" (contains praise of Pope).

23. Letter by "Pusillanimus" asking for advice as to proper action, since he has been abused in character and person by an acquaintance.

24. Mock attack on the *Courier* by "Z. Z." with a *Eulogy,* in imitation of Voiture, submitted as a specimen of his own abilities.

25. "Z. Z.'s" *Eulogy* continued. (This is apparently an attack on Walpole.)

26. An attack on Heidegger, who had advertised a season of Italian opera, and crude satire on opera itself, by "Philo F—t."

July

27. A letter from a true wife to her husband, urging him to give up his doubtful ways and his false political ambitions, by Mary C—.

28. Letter from "Tony Goodfellow," a sorcerer. (Apparently political satire; French and Spanish allusions, and attack on Catholic influence; obscure and indirect. Concludes with lines: "The Best in Christendom.")

29. Attack on *A Collection of French Letters translated by Mr. Reresby,* by "Publicola." Letter and verses by "P. A." on British degeneracy, inspired by a visit to Vauxhall. Letter by "Publicola," suggesting the value of published summaries of new books.

30. "Crispinus," defending an apothecary who had refused to use a certain specific remedy, and whose patient had died. Letter from "P. A." submitting an improved version of the last stanza of his poem in 29. The 93rd Psalm paraphrased. "On seeing Mr. Handel's statue in Vauxhall Gardens," by "K." Doggerel mixture of Latin and English, addressed to indigent garretteers.

INDEX

33288